T0257665

IET COMPUTING SERIES 60

Intelligent Multimedia Technologies for Financial Risk Management

Other volumes in this series:

Intelligent Multimedia Technologies for Financial Risk Management

Trends, tools and applications

Edited by
Simon Grima, Kiran Sood, Bharat Rawal,
Balamurugan Balusamy, Ercan Özen and
Gerald Goh Guan Gan

The Institution of Engineering and Technology

Published by The Institution of Engineering and Technology, London, United Kingdom

The Institution of Engineering and Technology is registered as a Charity in England & Wales (no. 211014) and Scotland (no. SC038698).

The Institution of Engineering and Technology
Futures Place
Kings Way, Stevenage
Hertfordshire SG1 2UA, United Kingdom

www.theiet.org

British Library Cataloguing in Publication Data
A catalogue record for this product is available from the British Library

ISBN 978-1-83953-661-8 (hardback)
ISBN 978-1-83953-662-5 (PDF)

Typeset in India by MPS Limited

Cover Image: Thana Prasongsin / Moment Thailand via Getty Images

Contents

8   Natural language processing and multimedia applications in finance   **161**

Jagjit Singh Dhatterwal, Kuldeep Singh Kaswan, Kiran Sood and Simon Grima

9   Digital disruption and multimedia technological innovations in the banking world   **183**

Enid Masih, Shanti Swaroop Chauhan, Vartika Singh, Balamurugan Balusamy and Simon Grima

Call for Authors – The IET International Book Series on Multimedia Information Processing and Security

Multimedia data (and more generally multimodal data) stands as one of the most demanding and exciting aspects of the information era. The processing of multimedia has been an active research area with applications in secure multimedia contents on social networks, digital forensic, digital cinema, education, secured e-voting systems, smart healthcare, automotive applications, the military, insurance and more. The advent of the internet of things (IoT), big data, cyber-physical systems (CPSs), robotics as well as personal and wearable devices now provide many opportunities for the multimedia community to reach out and develop synergies.

This book series comprehensively defines the current trends and technological aspects of multimedia research with a particular emphasis on interdisciplinary approaches. The authors will review a broad scope to identify challenges, solutions and new directions The published books can be used as references by practicing engineers, scientists, researchers, practitioners and technology professionals from academia, government and Industry working on state-of-the-art multimedia processing, analysis, search, mining, management and security solutions for practical applications. It will also be useful to senior undergraduate and graduate students.

Proposals for coherently integrated International co-authored or multi-authored edited research monographs will be considered for this book series. Each proposal will be reviewed by the book series editors with additional peer reviews from independent reviewers. Please contact:

- Dr. Amit Kumar Singh, Department of Computer Science & Engineering, National Institute of Technology, Patna, India; Emails: amit_245singh@yahoo.com; amit.singh@nitp.ac.in
- Prof. Stefano Berretti, Media Integration and Communication Center (MICC) & Department of Information Engineering (DINFO), University of Florence, Italy; E-mail: stefano.berretti@unifi.it

About the editors

Simon Grima is the head of the Insurance Department and deputy dean of the Faculty of Economics, Management and Accountancy, and associate professor at the University of Malta. He has served as the president of the Malta Association of Risk Management (MARM) and president of the Malta Association of Compliance Officers (MACO). He is among the first Certified Risk Management Professional (FERMA) on the board of and chairman of the Scientific Education Committee of both the Federation of European Risk Managers (FERMA) and the Public Risk Management Organisation (PRIMO), and he is also a member of the curriculum development team of PRIMA. He acts as an independent director for financial services firms, sits on several risk, compliance, procurement, investment and audit committees, and carries out duties as a compliance officer, internal auditor and risk manager. His research and consultancy focus on governance, regulations and internal controls.

Kiran Sood is a professor at Chitkara Business School, Chitkara University, Punjab, India. She is also an affiliate professor at the University of Malta. She received her undergraduate and postgraduate degrees in commerce from Panjab University, respectively, in 2002 and 2004. She earned her Master of Philosophy degree in 2008 and Doctor of Philosophy in Commerce with a concentration on Product Portfolio Performance of General Insurance Companies in 2017 from Panjabi University, Patiala, India. Before joining Chitkara University in July 2019, Kiran had served four organisations with a total experience of 19 years. She has published various articles in various journals and presented papers at various international conferences. She serves as an Editor of the refereed journal, particularly the *IJBST International Journal of BioSciences and Technology*, *the International Journal of Research Culture Society* and *The Journal of Corporate Governance, Insurance, and Risk Management (JCGIRM)*, 2021. Her research mainly focuses on regulations, marketing and finance in insurance, insurance management, economics and management of innovation in insurance. She has edited more than ten books with various international publishers such as Emerald, CRC, Taylors & Francis, AAP, WILEY scrivener, IET, Rivers Publishers, and IEEE.

Bharat Rawal is a professor in cybersecurity at Benedict College, USA. His research focuses on network security, cloud computing and security, blockchain, AI/ML, quantum computing, and the development of next-generation cyber defense and operation technologies. He is a member of IET, IEEE, ACM, and AMA. He has published two books, hundreds of research articles in conference and journal publications, and holds two US patents. He received his PhD degree in information technology on "split protocols" from Towson University, MD, USA. He has served in various leadership roles in academia and industries including CEO and President.

Balamurugan Balusamy is an associate dean of student engagement at Shiv Nadar University, Delhi-NCR, India. His research s focuses on Blockchain and data sciences and engineering education. He has published over 200 plus high impact factor papers and contributed to 80 edited and authored books. He has given over 195 talks at international events and symposium. He serves in the advisory committee for several start-ups and forums and does consultancy work for industry on Industrial IOT.

Ercan Özen is an associate professor of finance and banking in the School of Applied Sciences, University of Uşak, Turkey. He is chair of the International Applied Social Sciences Congress. He is also a certificated accountant, member of the Agean Finance Association and member of TEMA (Turkey Combating Soil Erosion, for Reforestation and the Protection of Natural Resources Foundation).

Gerald Goh Guan Gan is an associate professor in the Faculty of Business, Director of Strategy & Quality Assurance and a member of the Centre of e-Services, Entrepreneurship and Marketing in the Faculty of Business at Multimedia University, Malaysia. His research interests cover the fields of knowledge management, information systems, environmental sustainability, business management, and mass communication. He is a fellow of the Chartered Management Institute (UK) and the Malaysian Institute of Management.

Foreword – Prof. Ramona Rupeika-Apoga

Intelligent multimedia technologies for financial risk management are technology applications that combine AI elements such as machine learning, predictive analytics, and natural language processing to analyze, identify, and manage risks in the financial sector. These technologies can help you make better decisions about investment risks, customer segmentation, creditworthiness assessment, market analysis, fraud detection and prevention, and other topics. Deep learning for predictive analytics, AI for pattern recognition and data mining to identify risks, and natural language processing to identify relevant principles and regulations are new trends in intelligent multimedia technologies for financial risk management. Furthermore, big data analytics, cloud-based solutions, and blockchain technology are increasingly being used to improve risk analysis accuracy and create a secure financial environment.

Automated market analysis, predictive analytics, asset and portfolio optimization, customer segmentation and scoring, enterprise risk management, machine learning algorithms, regulatory compliance monitoring, and fraud detection and prevention are some tools companies can use to implement intelligent multimedia technologies for financial risk management. Data scientists and risk analysts can also analyze and predict risk using various software and modelling techniques, such as Monte Carlo simulations.

This book can provide valuable insight into the most recent financial industry trends. It can help you understand how AI and other elements, such as predictive analytics, natural language processing, and cloud-based solutions, are used to assess and mitigate risk. This book can also assist in identifying best practices and strategies for implementing and managing these technologies.

I hope readers enjoy this fascinating journey of knowledge and stay aware of the mazes of Intelligent Multimedia Technologies!

Yours sincerely,
Dr. Prof. Ramona Rupeika-Apoga
University of Latvia

Foreword – Series editors Singh and Berretti

Multimedia (and more generally multimodal data) stands as one of the most demanding and exciting aspects of the information era. The processing of multimedia has been an active research area with applications in secure multimedia contents on social networks, digital forensic, digital cinema, education, secured e-voting systems, smart healthcare, automotive applications, the military, finance, insurance and more. The advent of the Internet of Things (IoT), cyber-physical systems (CPSs), robotics as well as personal and wearable devices now provide many opportunities for the multimedia community to reach out and develop synergies.

Our book series comprehensively defines the current trends and technological aspects of multimedia research with a particular emphasis on interdisciplinary approaches. The authors will review a broad scope to identify challenges, solutions and new directions The published books can be used as references by practicing engineers, scientists, researchers, practitioners and technology professionals from academia, government and Industry working on state-of-the-art multimedia processing, analysis, search, mining, management and security solutions for practical applications. It will also be useful to senior undergraduate and graduate students as well as PhD students and Postdoc researchers.

This book entitled *"Intelligent Multimedia Technologies for Financial Risk Management: Trends, Tools and Applications"* focuses on the financial analysis and risk management of multimedia data. The unique contribution of this volume is to bring together researchers from distinct domains that seldom interact to identify theoretical, technological, and practical issues related to the management of financial records, information, data, and security. The book is intended to enhance the understanding of opportunities and challenges in multimedia analytics and finance applications at the global level. We hope the readers will find this book of great value in its visionary words.

Dr. Amit Kumar Singh, Book Series Editor
Department of Computer Science and Engineering
National Institute of Technology, Patna 800005, India

Prof. Stefano Berretti, Book Series Editor
Department of Information Engineering
University of Florence, Florence 50139, Italy

Chapter 1

Applications of multimedia in diverse fields: an overview

Kuldeep Singh Kaswan[1], Sandeep Lal[2], Jagjit Singh Dhatterwal[3], Kiran Sood[4] and Simon Grima[5,6]

Abstract

In this chapter, we discuss the preliminary concepts of multimedia and how this evolution of the Internet of Things (IoTs) has drastically driven a change in demand and needs. In a world where everything is connected, performance is reaching new heights; science fiction is becoming science fact. Self-driving cars and computers that can learn and think, a reality of today, were thought of as fiction not so long ago. The way we work and live today will never be the same. The skills we need are dramatically different. The exponential growth of multimedia technologies and applications has presented the computerised society with opportunities and challenges that, in many cases, are unprecedented. It is becoming more and more popular because of the effectiveness of its applications in all aspects of human life. The world is undergoing major upheaval, reorganisation, and a shift toward a disruptive new framework. This transformation is exponential. Everything that used to be dumb and disconnected is now wired or wireless, and smart – cars, cities, homes, ports, farms, even bodies. These amplify each other to create a perfect storm of change and disruption. Like everything else, we will need to wait and see; time will tell. This chapter will focus on the general applications of multimedia in various fields, such as art and science, the financial sector, education, healthcare, engineering, business, and scientific research.

Keywords: Internet of Things; Multimedia; Financial sector; Education; Healthcare; Engineering

[1]School of Computing Science & Engineering, Galgotias University, India
[2]Faculty of Law, PDM University, India
[3]Department of Artificial Intelligence & Data Science, Koneru Lakshmaiah Education Foundation, India
[4]Chitkara Business School, Chitkara University, Punjab, India
[5]The University of Malta, Malta
[6]Faculty of Business, Management and Economics, University of Latvia, Latvia

1.1   Introduction

Intelligent multimedia data analytics (IMDA) and financial risk management is a rapidly growing field combining advanced analytics with multimedia data to improve financial risk management. This field is driven by the increasing availability of multimedia data, such as video, audio, and image, and the need for more sophisticated methods to extract insights from this data. This essay will explore the trends, tools, and applications of this field and how it is used to improve financial risk management.

One of the key trends in IMDA and financial risk management is the increasing use of machine learning (ML) and artificial intelligence (AI) techniques. These technologies are being used to automatically analyse multimedia data and extract insights that can be used to identify financial risks. For example, ML algorithms can analyse financial transactions' video footage to detect fraudulent activity. In contrast, AI-based systems can analyse social media data to identify potential financial risks (Grima *et al.*, 2016a, 2017a, 2016b).

Another trend in this field is using big data technologies to handle the vast amounts of multimedia data generated. These technologies enable organisations to store, process and analyse large amounts of data, which is essential for extracting insights from multimedia data. For example, organisations can use big data platforms such as Hadoop and Spark to store and process multimedia data. At the same time, ML and AI techniques can extract insights from this data.

In terms of tools, there is a wide range of tools available for IMDA and financial risk management. These include ML libraries such as TensorFlow and scikit-learn, big data platforms such as Hadoop and Spark, and specialised multimedia analytics tools such as OpenCV and FFmpeg. Additionally, several commercial solutions provide end-to-end multimedia data analytics and financial risk management solutions (Grima *et al.*, 2017b).

One of the most important applications of IMDA and financial risk management is financial risk management. Using multimedia data, organisations can identify potential financial risks and take proactive measures to mitigate them. For example, banks can use video footage of financial transactions to detect fraudulent activity, while insurance companies can use social media data to identify potential risks. This field is also used in other industries, such as healthcare, retail, and transportation, to improve risk management.

In summary, IMDA and financial risk management is a rapidly growing field driven by the increasing availability of multimedia data and the need for more sophisticated methods to extract insights from this data. Using ML, AI, and big data technologies is helping organisations to analyse multimedia data and identify potential financial risks (Grima *et al.*, 2018; Gauci and Grima, 2020). The field offers a wide range of tools and applications, and it is likely to continue to grow in importance as organisations increasingly rely on multimedia data to improve risk management.

One can remember when our math teacher in school told us we needed to be good at calculating because, without that knowledge, we would be unable to work anywhere or be considered illiterate. Later, mechanical calculators became the new toy, which still meant that one had to be good at calculations since these were not affordable or too bulky to carry. As battery-operated calculators entered the market and became more compact and the pace of digitalisation took over our lives, has calculation and what it takes our brain remained useful?

The world of intelligent multimedia has disrupted and is disrupting the norm for the older generations. Still, maybe it is the norm for the millenniums who expect to have faster and more efficient intelligent robots thinking and making decisions for them. Trends, tools, applications, the way we think, the taxonomy we use, the needs, jobs, etc., are changing so fast that it is easy to become overwhelmed and hooked on artificial recreation. Is the world turning into robots? Or is intelligent multimedia helping us discover and live better?

One is outsourcing our functions and memory to mobile phones, laptops, and robots in the hope that AI can help address simple tasks. The Internet, LAN and wireless networks have made global multimedia accessible and possible. Is this a good thing? Does this come with a catch? Does using a memory tool make your physical memory worse over time? We can wait to see the effect it might have at a later stage. Still, at this point, AI using cookies, etc., can, for example, save you time making lists of web pages you have visited or want to visit, which often requires the user to put in a lot of input to record their interests. Moreover, assistant apps such as 'Google Assistant' and 'Alexa' can help scans nearly everything that you consume or want to consume on that web browser, including but not limited to 'documents, messages, files, newsletters, notes, presentations, spreadsheets, [and] tweets', according to its website.

Intelligent multimedia offers unlimited possibilities for services in all areas and all needs, be they financial, environmental or social. Be it in medicine, religion, politics, banking, investment, infrastructure, music, entertainment simulations, etc., and the sky is the limit!

Can we define AI multimedia as a 'Superhuman'? Should we be warned of any danger, this can bring to the table? You indeed need humans to build and train robots, and robots are a reflection of who builds them. But should we consider that not all humans are 'Angels' and that not all machines are built with good intentions? On the other hand, can there comes a time when these 'Superhumans' will be so fast and intelligent that they will take the lead or their human masters? (Newcomb, 2023).

Although we know there will always be bad intentions, it is important to have global standards and regulations that are correctly steered away from bad intentions and focus on doing good to protect humans. We need to craft regulation that targets the dangerous designs of AI while leaving extraordinary economic value on the table through safer algorithms. Because if not, we might end up in a situation where these 'Superhumans' become a problem from which we cannot turn back (Newcomb, 2023). What if your life depended on a game played against a 'SuperHuman' – would you be happy about that?

However, intelligent multimedia is here to stay and has become a part of everyday life, a necessity at the top of the hierarchy list of nearly every human being.

1.1.1.   Trends in intelligent multimedia data analytics

One of the key trends in IMDA is the increasing use of deep learning techniques. Deep learning algorithms, such as convolutional neural networks (CNNs) and recurrent neural networks (RNNs), have been highly successful in tasks such as image and video classification, object detection, and scene understanding. These techniques are particularly useful for tasks such as image and video analysis, which require learning complex patterns and representations from large amounts of data.

Another trend in IMDA is the integration of multimodal data. Multimodal data comes from multiple sources, such as text, images, and audio. Integrating multimodal data allows for more comprehensive and accurate analysis, enabling multiple sources of information to make predictions or extract insights. For example, in video analysis, the integration of audio and text can provide additional information about the context of the video, such as the spoken language or the names of people or objects in the video.

Another important trend is the use of edge computing for multimedia data analysis. Edge computing refers to the ability to perform data processing and analysis at the source of the data, such as on a smartphone or IoT device, rather than in a centralised data centre. It allows for real-time processing and analysis, which is critical for surveillance and autonomous systems tasks.

Finally, there is a growing emphasis on using explainable AI (XAI) in multimedia data analysis. XAI refers to the ability to understand and explain the decisions made by AI systems, particularly important in fields such as healthcare, finance, and legal, where the decisions made by AI systems can have significant consequences (Gauci and Grima, 2020; Grima *et al.*, 2021a).

In summary, IMDA is a rapidly growing field that is seeing significant advancements in deep learning, integration of multimodal data, edge computing, and XAI. These trends are driving the development of new and powerful tools for extracting insights from multimedia data and are likely to continue to shape the field in the future.

1.2   Tools used in IMDA

IMDA is a field that involves the use of various tools to extract useful information from multimedia data such as images, videos, and audio recordings. These tools help analysts and researchers process, analyse, and understand the data to make better decisions and gain insights.

ML is one of the most important tools in IMDA. ML algorithms are used to analyse multimedia data and extract features that can be used to classify, cluster or identify patterns in the data. For example, CNNs are commonly used in image recognition and object detection tasks, while RNNs are used in speech recognition and natural language processing (NLP).

Another important tool in IMDA is computer vision. Computer vision algorithms analyse images and videos and extract information such as object recognition, scene understanding, and facial recognition. These algorithms can identify objects and people in images and videos, track movement and behaviour, and even generate 3D models of objects and scenes (Grima *et al.*, 2016a, 2017a, 2016b).

Data mining and visualisation are also important tools in IMDA. Data mining algorithms extract useful information from large datasets, while data visualisation techniques present the information in a clear and easy-to-understand format. These tools are used to identify patterns and trends in the data and make communicating the findings easier to others.

In addition to these tools, several other technologies are used in IMDA, such as NLP, deep learning, and cloud computing. These technologies are used to process and analyse large amounts of data and to make it possible to run complex algorithms and models on powerful machines (Grima *et al.*, 2017a, 2016b).

Overall, IMDA is a field that relies heavily on a wide range of tools and technologies to extract useful information from multimedia data. ML, computer vision, data mining, and data visualisation are a few tools used in this field to help analysts and researchers make better decisions and gain insights.

1.3 Application software used in IMDA

IMDA is a field that involves the use of various software applications to analyse and extract meaningful insights from multimedia data such as images, audio, and video. These software applications are designed to automate the data analysis process and make it more efficient and accurate (Grima *et al.*, 2017b, 2018).

Computer vision is one of the most widely used software applications in IMDA. Computer vision is a subfield of AI that analyses and understands images and videos. Computer vision algorithms recognise objects, faces, and other features in images and videos. This can be useful in various applications such as image search, image recognition, and video surveillance.

Another important software application in IMDA is speech recognition. Speech recognition is a technology that enables computers to understand and transcribe human speech. This technology is used in various applications, such as voice-controlled assistants, home appliances, and voice-controlled vehicles.

Another application of IMDA is in the field of NLP. This field deals with the interaction between computers and human languages. NLP algorithms are used to analyse and understand text and speech. This can be useful in various applications such as sentiment analysis, text summarisation, and language translation.

Finally, ML is also a critical software application in IMDA. ML is a subfield of AI that enables computers to learn from data. ML algorithms are used to analyse multimedia data and extract meaningful insights. This can be useful in various applications such as image classification, speech recognition, and NLP.

All in all, IMDA is a field that involves the use of various software applications to analyse and extract meaningful insights from multimedia data. These software applications include computer vision, speech recognition, NLP, and ML. These software applications are designed to automate the data analysis process and make it more efficient and accurate.

1.4 Write an essay on using IMDA in risk management and internal controls

This technology can enhance risk management and internal controls in various industries. One of the main advantages of using IMDA in risk management is the ability to automatically identify and alert potential risks. For example, in the financial industry, IMDA can monitor video surveillance footage in real-time to detect suspicious behaviour and potential fraud. Similarly, IMDA can be used in the healthcare industry to analyse medical images, such as X-rays and CT scans, to detect potential health risks.

Another advantage of using IMDA in risk management is the real-time analysis of large amounts of data. This can be particularly useful in industries such as transportation, where vehicles, sensors, and cameras generate vast amounts of data. By analysing this data in real-time, IMDA can identify potential risks and alert the appropriate personnel to take action.

In addition to risk management, IMDA can also be used to enhance internal controls. For example, IMDA in manufacturing can monitor the production process, detect deviations from standard operating procedures, and ensure that the manufacturing process complies with regulations and that the products produced are of the highest quality (Gauci and Grima, 2020; Grima *et al.*, 2021a).

IMDA is a powerful technology that can enhance risk management and internal controls in various industries. This technology can help organisations become more efficient and effective in managing risks and ensuring compliance by automatically identifying and alerting potential risks and analysing large amounts of data in real time.

1.5   The metaverse

One of the key applications of IMDA is in computer vision, which involves using algorithms to analyse and understand visual data. For example, IMDA can detect and identify objects in images and videos automatically or track the movement of objects in real time. This has many practical applications, such as self-driving cars, surveillance, and robotics.

Another important application of IMDA is in NLP, which involves using algorithms to analyse and understand text data. For example, IMDA can automatically extract information from text documents or generate natural-sounding responses to text-based queries. This has many practical applications, including search engines, chatbots, and virtual assistants.

The metaverse is a virtual world where people can interact with each other and with virtual objects in a shared space. The metaverse is becoming increasingly relevant as new technologies, such as virtual (VR) and augmented reality (AR), are developed. IMDA can play an important role in the metaverse by allowing virtual objects and characters to respond to real-world inputs, such as speech and gesture recognition.

IMDA is a rapidly growing field that has the potential to revolutionise the way we interact with multimedia data and the metaverse. Using advanced algorithms and technologies to extract valuable insights and information from multimedia data, IMDA can help individuals and organisations make better decisions, automate tasks, and create new and innovative experiences. As the amount of multimedia data generated continues to grow and the metaverse becomes more relevant, the field of IMDA will become increasingly important.

The metaverse and AI are two of the most well-known twenty-first-century technologies. Each can improve a variety of sectors, better various aspects of people's lives, and boost various business operations' effectiveness. Healthcare, gaming, administration, marketing, education, and other sectors can benefit from AI and the metaverse application. Typically, these technologies are viewed independently without considering their interaction and potential for cooperation.

To be more precise, the term 'metaverse' refers to a future iteration of the Internet that users with VR headsets, AR, and more widely used gadgets, such as smartphones and desktop or laptop computers, would be able to access. Between this idea and the current web2, there is a huge difference. The idea of the metaverse is very dissimilar to even the possible decentralised web3, where communication still occurs through social media messengers and services like Zoom, Microsoft Teams, or Discord and content is still accessed through websites and applications. The term 'metaverse' refers to an immersive virtual environment where users can access information using VR, AR, and other technologies while represented by personalised avatars.

Some of its components do, even if the metaverse has yet to arrive. A few businesses, like Epic, began referring to certain of their goods as metaverses. For instance, the battle royale game Fortnite is sometimes referred to as a metaverse since it allows people to interact using virtual avatars and uses VR technology to display various events.

The idea of the metaverse is predicated on some capabilities or promises that this technology will have. In the decentralised world, identity verification, smart contracts, and exchange-traded products (ETPs) are some of these important promises. Let us outline each goal to understand how AI can support and improve the metaverse.

The metaverse depicts a decentralised universe, which is the first promise. Like web3, it gives people ownership over their data, digital assets, and identities that are safe and impenetrable because they are recorded on a distributed ledger. This objective will empower all users interacting with the Internet, which will be the reverse of the current web2, where a small number of centralised tech businesses control the greatest influence.

The next goal is to confirm identities. The metaverse uses blockchain technology to authenticate users' identities and guarantee that only users who completed the authorisation can access data. Some of the top figures in the tech sector think that self-sovereign identities (SSI), which are digital identities connected to real-world verification and authorisation data (such as biometrics), should be implemented in the metaverse.

Smart contracts are another promise associated with the metaverse notion. Transactions are automated and protected using these contracts. Smart contracts are computer programs or transaction protocols that can automatically record, control, or carry out actions based on a signed agreement's parameters to describe this technology further. The metaverse is therefore anticipated to have this capability to guarantee that diverse acts, such as trading, are carried out by the established agreements.

And last but not least, the metaverse technology is anticipated to include ETPs. This objective is straightforward to comprehend: the original cryptocurrency of the metaverse will be utilised for buying–selling transactions, and rewarding AI apps for completing tasks.

We can now move on with the partnership between AI and the metaverse because we are well aware of the objectives the metaverse must meet. Let us now discuss how AI can advance humankind's efforts to create it.

One of the best uses of AI that streamlines many company processes and helps users find solutions to their problems much more quickly is chatbots. This method of communication will be used in the metaverse as well. Chatbots can help users in the metaverse by giving them instructions and information about various goods and services, answering their questions, carrying out transactions on users' behalf, taking orders, etc., in addition to their current roles in customer service, marketing, sales, and other areas. For instance, if a user is having trouble finding a particular item, the chatbot can quickly fix the issue by pointing the user in the right direction within the metaverse.

Learn more about chatbots here: virtual idiot, you! The #ChatbotRescue mission and why chatbots fail device to the customer and saving them 2.0: Chatbots and robotic process automation (RPA) are growing. You may also find out more about the top chatbots here: best chatbots powered by AI.

In addition, AI can be used to design inclusive user interfaces that will facilitate everyone's trips through the system, including those of persons with impairments. AI can therefore contribute to the metaverse being a user-friendly and simple-to-use platform. Users can communicate with the metaverse in their local language and through photos and videos thanks to technologies like NLP, speech recognition, computer vision, translation, and AR, which will improve user-metaverse interactions.

Another way AI can work with the metaverse is through digital avatars. For instance, AI can use NLP, VR, and computer vision to help build environments, speech, and images for users to interact with as lifelike avatars.

AI can engage with the metaverse in various ways, including through digital avatars, chatbots, interfaces, and more. AI may advance even farther, though, until the arrival of the metaverse, which will open up new prospects for collaboration among various technologies.

1.6 Medical devices

One of the most significant applications of IMDA in medicine is in the area of medical imaging. AI algorithms can be trained to analyse medical images, such as X-rays, CT scans, and MRI images, and extract information that can aid in diagnosis and treatment planning. For example, AI algorithms can identify and classify tumours in medical images, which can help radiologists make more accurate and efficient diagnoses. Similarly, AI algorithms can be used to analyse videos of patients, such as videos of patients walking, to help identify and diagnose movement disorders.

Another area where IMDA is being used in medicine is in the analysis of electronic health records (EHRs). AI algorithms can be trained to extract information from EHRs, such as lab results and vital signs, and identify patterns and trends that can aid in diagnosis and treatment planning. For example, AI algorithms can identify patients at risk of developing certain conditions, such as diabetes or heart disease, so that preventative measures can be taken.

IMDA is also being used to improve the efficiency and effectiveness of clinical processes. For example, AI algorithms can automate the scheduling of appointments and the routing of lab results, which can help reduce wait times and improve patient satisfaction. Additionally, AI algorithms can identify patients most in need of follow-up care, which can help ensure that patients receive the care they need in a timely manner.

IMDA is a powerful tool used in the medical field to improve patient outcomes, streamline clinical processes, and reduce healthcare costs. As the field of IMDA continues to evolve, it is expected to play an increasingly important role in future healthcare delivery.

Medical device firms are creating three primary AI medical devices as technology develops:

1. Management of chronic illness artificially intelligent medical gadgets could monitor patients and administer care or medication as necessary. Patients with diabetes may, for instance, wear sensors to track their blood sugar levels and deliver insulin to control them.
2. Diagnostic imaging: To conduct medical imaging with greater image quality and clarity, businesses are creating medical devices using AI. Additionally, these tools would lessen a patient's radiation exposure.
3. The IoT for medical devices: A wireless, interconnected, and connected digital device used by healthcare professionals to manage data, inform patients, cut costs, monitor patients, and perform more effectively and efficiently.

1.7 Entertainment

One of the main ways IMDA is being used in entertainment is through analysing social media data. By analysing the conversations and interactions on platforms like Twitter, Facebook, and Instagram, IMDA can provide valuable insights into what content resonates with audiences and what types of content are likely to succeed in the future. This information can be used to inform the development of new content and to target advertising more effectively.

Another area where IMDA is being used in entertainment is video and audio content analysis. IMDA can analyse a piece of content's visual and auditory elements, such as colour, sound, and movement. This information can be used to understand how different elements of a piece of content impact audience engagement and to make adjustments to the content to optimise its impact.

IMDA is also being used in the field of gaming. By analysing player behaviour and preferences, IMDA can be used to create more engaging and personalised gaming experiences. This can include creating custom levels and challenges based on a player's skill level or providing more accurate recommendations for games and content based on a player's preferences.

In summary, IMDA is a powerful tool for analysing multimedia data in the entertainment industry. By providing insights into audience behaviour and preferences, IMDA is helping to inform the development of new content and to create more personalised and engaging experiences for audiences. With the continued growth of multimedia data, IMDA will become an increasingly important tool for the entertainment industry.

1.8   Security

One of the key ways these devices are being used is in the field of surveillance. With advanced cameras and other sensors, IMDA can detect and track individuals, vehicles, and other objects in real-time and allows security personnel to quickly identify and respond to potential threats and gather valuable intelligence on the movements and activities of individuals in a given area.

Another important application of IMDA and security devices is in the field of data analysis. These devices can be used to analyse large amounts of data from various sources, such as social media, video feeds, and other types of multimedia. This can help organisations to gain insights into customer behaviour, market trends, and other important information that can be used to make more informed decisions.

Additionally, IMDA and security devices can also be used to improve the efficiency and effectiveness of security systems. For example, these devices can be used to automatically identify and track individuals who are authorised to enter a given area while denying access to unauthorised individuals. This can reduce the need for human intervention and improve the overall security of a facility.

Despite the many benefits of IMDA and security devices, some potential concerns and challenges are associated with their use. For example, using these devices can raise privacy and civil liberties concerns, as individuals may be monitored and tracked without their knowledge or consent. Additionally, the use of these devices can also raise concerns about bias and discrimination, as the algorithms used to analyse data may be based on certain assumptions and stereotypes that can lead to unfair treatment of certain groups.

IMDA and security devices are powerful tools that can enhance security and improve data analysis. However, organisations must also be aware of the potential concerns and challenges associated with their use and take steps to mitigate these risks. It can include implementing strict privacy and security protocols and regularly reviewing and updating the algorithms used to analyse data to ensure that they are fair and unbiased.

1.9   Health

One key application of IMDA is in the field of healthcare. With the increasing availability of medical imaging technology, healthcare providers can now collect vast amounts of data in images, videos, and other multimedia. By using advanced algorithms and techniques, doctors and researchers can analyse this data to identify patterns and insights that can aid in diagnosing and treating diseases. For example, medical imaging can be used to identify early signs of cancer, monitor the progression of a disease, or even detect the presence of a disease before symptoms appear.

Another important application of IMDA is in the field of entertainment. With the increasing popularity of video and audio streaming platforms, media companies can now collect vast amounts of consumer preferences and behaviour data. By using advanced algorithms and techniques, these companies can analyse this data to identify patterns and insights that can aid in creating and distributing content. For example, by analysing consumer preferences and behaviour data, media companies can identify which types of content are most popular and create new content that is likely to be well-received by viewers.

Finally, IMDA also has potential uses in the field of security. Security personnel can detect and respond to potential threats by analysing data from cameras and other sensors in real-time. For example, by analysing data from security cameras, security personnel can identify patterns of suspicious behaviour and respond quickly to potential threats.

IMDA is a powerful technology that has the potential to revolutionise many industries and fields. This technology can help healthcare providers improve patient outcomes, media companies create more engaging content, and security personnel respond more effectively to potential threats by extracting valuable insights and information from a wide variety of multimedia data. As technology evolves, we will likely see even more innovative uses for this technology.

1.10   Financial services

One of the most promising applications of IMDA in the financial services industry is customer service. By analysing customer interactions, such as phone calls and video chats, IMDA can identify patterns and trends in customer behaviour, which can be used to improve the overall customer experience. For example, IMDA can be used to analyse customer sentiment and identify areas of frustration, which can be used to improve the training of customer service representatives. Additionally, IMDA can be used to analyse customer interactions to identify areas of confusion, which can be used to improve the design of online self-service portals.

Another important application of IMDA in the financial services industry is fraud detection. By analysing multimedia data, such as video footage of ATM transactions, IMDA can identify patterns and trends indicative of fraudulent behaviour. For example, IMDA can be used to analyse video footage to identify movement patterns that indicate someone is trying to hide their face, which can be used to flag potentially fraudulent transactions. Additionally, IMDA can be used to analyse audio recordings to identify patterns of speech that indicate someone is trying to conceal their identity, which can be used to flag potentially fraudulent phone calls.

In addition to customer service and fraud detection, IMDA can improve overall financial services operations. For example, IMDA can be used to analyse bank branches' video footage to identify customer behaviour patterns, which can be used to optimise the layout and design of bank branches. Additionally, IMDA can be used to analyse customer interactions with online self-service portals to identify areas of confusion, which can be used to improve the design of these portals.

IMDA has the potential to revolutionise the financial services industry by providing valuable insights that can be used to improve customer service, detect fraud, and improve overall operations. As technology evolves and improves, IMDA will likely become an increasingly important tool in the financial services industry.

1.11 Insurance

The use of disruptive technologies in the insurance industry is going to see an immense amount of growth in the coming times. New technology is transforming traditional operations in the insurance sector. The convergence of technologies plays an important role in reducing the operation expenditure of insurance companies. Many insurers are using predictive analytics to collect to understand and forecast customer behaviour. Calculating the risk factors, such as fraudulent claims, is another tedious task for actuaries where multimedia can help. AI is another domain usage to which insurance companies can transfer the underwriting process. It also enables insurance advisers to design solutions to meet the unique demand of their clients. During COVID-19 times, when there was a lock-up, it was difficult to meet and interact with the customers, especially since selling health insurance was the most difficult thing, and one of the subject matters of a health insurance contract is the medical report. This has developed the need to use chatbots where customers can interact with them and help them solve various problems. These chatbots can complete the entire process starting from policy application to filing claims and many other things. Drones are another transformative move in the insurance world, where drones can be used in risk assessment and calculation, surveying factories, farms, and places difficult to reach by humans. Drones are saving a lot of money for insurers associated with assessing and underwriting risk. Hence, the latest technological developments can help insurance providers increase revenue and profitability.

Information technology (IT) plays a crucial role in the insurance industry by enabling companies to automate processes, improve operational efficiency, and enhance the customer experience. Some specific ways that IT is used in insurance include:

1. Policy administration: IT systems manage and automate the policy issuance, renewal, and underwriting processes.
2. Claims processing: IT systems are used to manage the claims process, from initial filing to final settlement, helping to reduce processing time and improve accuracy.
3. Customer relationship management: IT systems manage customer interactions, such as policy enquiries and claims, and provide real-time customer service.

4. Data analysis: IT systems are used to analyse large amounts of data, such as claims data, to identify trends and make informed business decisions.
5. Cybersecurity: IT systems protect sensitive information, such as policyholder data, from cyber threats, including hacking and data breaches.
6. Overall, IT has greatly impacted the insurance industry by enabling companies to operate more efficiently and serve customers better.

1.12 People's needs and retail shops

The IT and retail industries are intertwined as technology have become a crucial aspect of the retail sector. It has enabled retailers to provide a better customer experience and streamline operations.

Examples of IT solutions used in the retail industry include:

1. E-commerce platforms for online shopping
2. Point-of-sale (POS) systems for in-store transactions
3. Inventory management systems to track stock levels
4. Customer relationship management (CRM) software to manage customer interactions
5. Data analytics to gain insights into customer behaviour and sales trends.

Moreover, integrating new technologies such as AI, AR, and the IoT further transforms the retail industry, providing retailers with new opportunities to optimise their operations and engage with customers in innovative ways.

1.13 Banking services

One of the main uses of AI is in the financial world. Here, the term 'Online Financial institutions', 'Web Banking', 'E-mail', or 'Internet' have become household names offered by recognised firms or their delegates using technologies controlled either immediately by the bank's administration or through another source (Abdullah and Shamsuddin, 2009). Finally, e-banking is an encompassing term for the phase by which a client can achieve commercial bank correspondence in electronic medium without altering its structure, as well as the methods and techniques that digital marketplace of banks, private citizens, or relationships to access financial records, execute transactions, or acquire knowledge on money-related items and administrations via a powerful system. In addition to the respective channels, banking, money orders, digital payments, and web-based processing are the terms used to describe the many types of e-banking. Telebanking and digitised or interactive transactions payment options and debit card transactions are also part of e-banking (ATMs). E-banking is an interaction wherein records can be accessed and controlled to perform exchanges using the web by utilising PCs, cell phones, and other online applications. Using these financial aids, bank clients deal with their exchanges online without being truly present in the financial lobby or premises (Abdullah *et al.*, 2013).

Web-based banking administrations are 24 h connected to a record data with perspective on the entirety of the client's financial exchanges that empowers them to get insights about current savings, overdraft accounts, advance specifics, letters of credit, cheque book status, swapping scale worth of unfamiliar monetary forms, and numerous other pertinent subtleties.

Notwithstanding, by utilising web-based banking services, clients can make national and international settlements. These administrations additionally empower them to access and print a bank articulation with fewer costs without visiting the bank. Data innovation stretches out an enormous advantage to banks and monetary establishments to offer these types of assistance by taking advantage of a broad public organisation foundation (Abell and Lim, 1996).

1.13.1 Benefits of e-banking

(A)   Bank customers can do non-conditional errands via web-based transactions by (Abernathy and Clark, 1985):
   • Finance viewing.
   • Reviewing previous interactions.
   • Obtaining bank financing.
   • Viewing images of paid cheques.
   • Asynchronous record explanations are downloaded.
   • Downloading programs for flexible banking, digital payment, and other services.

(B)   Bank clients can use Internet banking to complete payment information by:
   • Transferring assets between a client's affiliated institution, regional converters, and global marketplaces.
   • Continuing to buy companies.
   • Lending institutions and exchanges, such as participation remuneration, are examples of this.
   • Credit/debit exchanges (credit or debit).
   • Utility bill registration and payment.

(C)   Aside from the aforementioned financial contract, a bank member can also undertake additional errands, such as
   • A financial institution corporation.
   • Supervisors from diverse clients with varying levels of authority.

1.13.2 Electronic banking protocols

The following are the primary goals of the 'E-Banking Rules' (Adham and Ahmad, 2005):

• The fundamental purpose of e-banking legislation is to motivate institutions to incorporate screening procedures in their e-banking products, administration, and realistic risk administration.

- The e-banking requirements are meant to encourage banks to progress and experiment.
- It ensures client assistance.

1.13.3 Services

'E-Banking' provides a variety of solutions and services, the very well of which are as follows:

- Transactions operations include commodity exchanges, bill portioning, advanced application, and other transactions.
- There will be no self-confidence techniques such as demanding check book halt or making sections, online vocalisation or energising a client's relevant information (Ahuja and Lampert, 2001).

Advantages of net banking

The advantages stated below are based on the business's client's perspective. A consumer may save time and resources by using e-banking services. Such organisations, moreover, get good client relationships with the board (CRM) (Alam *et al.*, 2007).

- **Services**: Development has made it unbelievably simple for the banking and the individual to get there effectively merely by registering on the bank's website e-organizations. Consolidate immense organisations like money-related orchestrating capacities, practical preparation and expecting contraptions, credit number crunchers, adventure examination gadgets and worth trading stages. Close by this, most banks also give the workplace of online duty records and cost arranging (Al-Gahtani *et al.*, 2007).
- **Convenience:** This is undeniably one of the primary advantages that outweigh any shortcomings of Internet banking services. Negotiating a deal and parts at the press of a finger from the comforts of one's own house or workplace without having to leave is an office that nobody would pass up. When compared to visiting the banking for everything nearly the same, seeing information on the web is significantly faster and more profitable. Without question, even non-esteem-based companies, for example, take a gander at items available, revitalise records, ask about charge expenditures of individual investment items, and so on (Al-Qirim, 2007).
- **Reasonable price:** This implies that a portion of the bank's hold funds may be distributed to clients by giving them increased costs on shops and demanding reduced costs on promotions. Numerous bankers provide fewer store locations to encourage consumers to use e-banking and impose lower fees for additional liquid funds. This type of financing generates fewer real initiatives and bigger profits. The demand for larger work areas and more people to communicate with customers is essentially reduced, providing it economically beneficial to banks (Ajzen and Fishbein, 1980).
- **Moving ability:** E-banking has exceeded anyone's expectations over the last 2 or 3 years as convenient web banking, which concurs boundless

transportability to the client, who can now manage financial trades even while moving (Akulava, 2015).

- **Increased convenience and time savings:** E-banking transactions may be completed 24 h a day, 7 days a week, without the need for true interaction with the company.
- **Frequent and immediate provision of information:** Groups and individuals have far more immediate access to knowledge since they can search for numerous documents at a simple tap.
- **Adequate cash managing:** As a large collection of cash, Estonian banks' major mechanisms are available on the World Wide Web regions; e-banking workstations accelerate the liquidity position and increase the appropriateness of organisational procedures.
- **Velocity:** Because the reaction time of this portion of trading is quite quick, customers may wait until the last second before shifting the commodities (Assink, 2006).
- **Managing money:** Before influencing any transaction on the web, individuals can retrieve their transaction history of distinct recordings and do an 'actually imagine a circumstance in which' evaluation in independence. This results in stronger support for the authorities. Closely related to the advantages discussed above, E-banking also assists with studying and printing balance inquiries, seeing trade information, moving components, a fraction of online helping bills, online ordering, and so on. Clients may also use E-banking to qualify for numerous types of vehicles, contracts, houses, estimating, children, or individual advancements (Atherton and Hannon, 2000).
- **Controlling E-funds:** Other than giving enormous benefits to its clients to the extent that the straightforwardness of cost trades, E-banking furthermore have explicit issues in controlling, overseeing, arranging, and completing the macroeconomic methodologies by making issues for bank the board, regulatory and managerial subject matter experts. They start for potential or cross-line trades as well concerning local trades, which rely upon advancement applications which cause various security-related issues (Baker and Sinkula, 2002).
- **Financial affairs:** Online transactions harm the perception of the monetary supporter that the normal appointment to the main branch used to excite. Personalised relationships with bank employees assist a customer with speedier additional assistance or any unusual services that may not be offered to the general public. Similarly, a representation would provide basic monetary advice to the customer via individual communication (Baiyere and Salmela, 2013).
- **No easy for cash withdrawal:** Certain organisations, such as registration and bank imprinting, cannot be completed over the Internet. Handling specific concerns and grievances necessitates an actual visit to the institution, which cannot be accomplished through the web (Blili and Raymond, 1993).
- **Secure web banking:** This is the most dangerous trap of the web-based business strategy, which the average client should be prepared for. Even though a plethora of complex cryptography writing operating systems is

anticipated to secure your record, there is generally a degree of cracking by intelligent portions in the sophisticated globe. On the Internet, development assaults, espionage, virus, and other unauthorised programming are common.

• **The capability to apply transnational innovation to local needs:** Before agricultural nations may embrace advancement for their immediate needs, a significant degree of infrastructure and qualitative cutoff strengthening is required. Capability to increase community opinion for E-finance: most e-finance drives in non-modern countries have been the eventual outcome of pleasing undertakings between the private and public regions (Boden and Nucci, 2000).

1.14 Machine learning

ML is a subfield of AI that focuses on developing algorithms and statistical models that enable computers to perform tasks that normally require human intelligence, such as perception, reasoning, and decision-making. It involves training algorithms on large amounts of data to enable them to make predictions, recognise patterns, and perform various tasks.

There are several types of ML algorithms, including:

1. Supervised learning: Algorithms are trained on labelled data and then used to predict new, unseen data.
2. Unsupervised learning: Algorithms are trained on unlabelled data to discover hidden patterns or relationships in the data.
3. Reinforcement learning: Algorithms learn by interacting with an environment and receiving feedback through rewards or penalties.

ML is being applied in a wide range of industries, including finance, healthcare, retail, and transportation. For example, in the financial industry, ML algorithms are used for credit scoring, fraud detection, and algorithmic trading. In the healthcare industry, ML is used for medical diagnosis, drug discovery, and personalised medicine. Overall, ML plays a significant role in the development of AI and is driving breakthroughs and advancements in various fields (Chang *et al.*, 2015).

1.15 Deep learning

The idea behind deep learning is to absorb complicated inputs and provide results depending on them. Additionally, because it is created to be effective enough to function without human assistance, it may be able to repair itself. As a result, once a data point is acquired, this system learns from its triumphs and mistakes (Chau and Turner, 2002).

There are several significant areas in the financial industry where AI, or to be more exact, deep learning, may be utilised. So, let us go through some of the key applications of deep learning:

- Market prediction for stocks
- Automating the process of trading strategy analysis
- Economic stability
- Evaluation of robo-advisory loan applications
- Customer credit card research

Deep learning is a subfield of ML concerned with artificial neural networks (ANNs) that have multiple layers. It is based on the idea that a neural network can learn a hierarchical representation of data, where lower layers learn simple features, and higher layers learn more complex representations.

Deep learning algorithms are designed to handle large amounts of complex and unstructured data, such as images, speech, and text. They can be used for various tasks, including image classification, speech recognition, NLP, and game playing.

Some of the key advantages of deep learning include:

- Improved accuracy: Deep learning algorithms can achieve high accuracy on complex tasks, especially compared to traditional ML algorithms.
- Automated feature extraction: Deep learning algorithms can automatically extract features from raw data, reducing the need for manual feature engineering.
- Robustness: Deep learning algorithms can handle noisy and incomplete data, making them suitable for real-world applications.

Deep learning has been making significant progress in various fields, including computer vision, speech recognition, and NLP. It is also being applied in healthcare, finance, and retail industries, where it is used for medical diagnosis, fraud detection, and customer behaviour analysis.

1.16   Natural language processing

Data now drive finance, and the most important data may be found written down in papers, texts, websites, forums, and other places. Finance experts read financial news, analyst reports, and other sources extensively. Automatic text processing can speed up transactions and greatly reduce the amount of routine manual labour (Chell and Baines, 1998).

The raw textual data from many financial fields is converted into useful insights with NLP techniques and algorithms. NLP and ML have emerged as the go-to technology for traders, portfolio managers, analysts, banks, and other financial institutions as they work to enhance their financial analyses. The financial sector uses NLP, from retail banking to hedge fund investment. Working with unstructured financial data requires using NLP techniques such as sentiment analysis, chatbot question–answering, document categorisation, and topic clustering.

NLP is a subfield of AI and computational linguistics that deals with the interaction between computers and human (natural) languages. It involves the development of algorithms and models to process and analyse human language, including text and speech.

NLP is used in a wide range of applications, including:

- Text classification: Algorithms can be trained to categorise texts into different classes, such as spam vs. non-spam, positive vs. negative sentiment, and news categories.
- Sentiment analysis: NLP algorithms can analyse the sentiment of text, determining if it is positive, negative, or neutral.
- Named entity recognition: NLP algorithms can identify named entities such as people, places, and organisations in text.
- Part-of-speech tagging: NLP algorithms can identify and categorise the words in a sentence, such as nouns, verbs, and adjectives.
- Machine translation: NLP algorithms can translate text from one language to another, making communication between people who speak different languages easier.
- Chatbots: NLP algorithms can be used to develop chatbots, computer programs that can converse with human users in natural language.

NLP is a rapidly growing field with significant potential to improve human–computer interaction and revolutionise how computers process and understand human language.

1.17 Blockchain technology

Blockchain is a decentralised and distributed digital ledger technology that enables secure and transparent record-keeping of transactions. It was originally developed as the underlying technology for the digital currency, Bitcoin, but it has since been adopted for many other uses.

Some key characteristics of blockchain technology include:

- Decentralisation: The ledger of transactions is maintained by a network of computers rather than by a single central authority, making it highly resistant to tampering or censorship.
- Immutable: Once data is recorded on the blockchain, it cannot be altered, ensuring the integrity and security of the records.
- Transparency: Transactions on the blockchain are visible to all participants, creating a transparent and verifiable record-keeping system.
- Cryptography: Blockchain uses cryptography to secure transactions, ensuring they are tamper-proof and private.

Blockchain has potential applications in many industries, including finance, healthcare, supply chain management, and voting systems. For example, in finance, blockchain can create decentralised exchanges, streamline the clearing and settlement of trades, and reduce the risk of fraud. In healthcare, blockchain can securely store and share patient data, improving care coordination.

Overall, blockchain has the potential to transform the way we store and share information, making systems more secure, transparent, and efficient.

The banking and financial sectors will profit greatly from this. Here are some examples of how companies are using blockchain technology (Kaswan *et al.*, 2022a):

- **Transfers of funds**

For customers and financial organisations, sending money abroad offers a variety of issues and difficulties. People send billions of dollars abroad yearly, yet the transaction is frequently expensive, time-consuming, and error-prone (Agarwal *et al.*, 2021; Kaur and Bansal, 2021).

All of that might change with blockchain. Several large institutions have used blockchain technology for international payments, saving both time and money. Customers may bypass the time-consuming practice of travelling to a money transfer facility, waiting in line, and paying transaction fees by using blockchain money transfers to perform electronic transactions with mobile devices.

Affordable, direct payments: Most money is transferred through financial entities like banks or credit card processing facilities. Each of these stages adds another complication and can incur costly expenses. For retailers, blockchain-based transactions have several advantages.

Lessening of fees: When clients pay with a credit card, retailers must pay processing costs that reduce their profit. Blockchain payments streamline the transfer procedure, which lowers or eliminates costs.

Eliminated inadequate funds: Consumers occasionally use bad checks to pay for products or services, which results in a loss for businesses and additional costs, as well as the potential for a legal nuisance to recover. Blockchain-based payments can give business owners the peace of mind that the transaction will go through successfully in seconds or minutes.

1.18   Robotic automatic process

Robotics is a branch of engineering and computer science that deals with the design, construction, and operation of robots and the development of algorithms for their control, perception, and decision-making. Robotics involves a range of disciplines, including mechanical engineering, electrical engineering, and computer science.

There are many different types of robots, ranging from industrial robots used in manufacturing to autonomous robots used in exploration, search and rescue, and service. Some of the key applications of robotics include:

- Manufacturing: Robotics is widely used to automate repetitive and dangerous tasks, increase production efficiency, and improve product quality.
- Healthcare: Robotics is being used in healthcare for tasks such as surgical procedures, rehabilitation, and telemedicine.
- Service: Robotics is used to provide services in hospitality, retail, and entertainment.
- Exploration: Robotics is being used in space and underwater exploration and in hazardous environments on Earth.

- Defence: Robotics is being used in defence for tasks such as surveillance, reconnaissance, and demining.

Overall, robotics is playing an increasingly important role in many industries and driving new breakthroughs and advancements in various fields.

Here are a few main advantages of implementing RPA in finance and accounting.

- Digitize and automate processes: smart bots can accurately enter and re-enter financial data, automating repetitive operations. Avoid processing mistakes: rule-based procedures prevalent in the insurance and mortgage industries are well suited for automation. RPA bots can complete all the findings and comparison without making expensive errors.
- Automate documentation and standardisation: RPA simplifies the finance and accounting sector by allowing the standardisation of official documents and the upkeep of vital data and client records. Improve efficiency and profits: process transformation results from increased automation in the financial sector. Additionally, advantages result from effective corporate operations and processes (Varma and Nijjer, 2022; Mittal *et al.*, 2020).

1.19   Distributed computing technology

Distributed computing is a model for empowering omnipresent, advantageous, on-request network admittance to a common pool of configurable processing assets (e.g., networks, servers, capacity, applications, and administrations) that can be quickly provisioned and delivered with negligible administration exertion or specialist organisation interaction. With distributed computing, various clients share similar actual assets, safely isolated at the legitimate level, supporting heterogeneous client stages like cell phones and workstations. Since the send-off of Amazon EC2 in 2006, the accessibility of high-limit organisations, minimal expense PCs, stockpiling gadgets, and boundless reception of administration-situated engineering and autonomic processing has driven, generally speaking, development in the distributed computing market.

As a general rule, FIs characterise their 'cloud system', which will rely upon their capacities and size. Those techniques are made by joining the cloud sending and administration models accessibility.

A cloud organisation model is principally recognised by proprietorship, size, and access. The most well-known sending models are private, public, and mixture mists, while the European Banking Authority (EBA) perceives local area mists as a sub-type. While the EBA4 definitions of the various models are exceptionally compact, they are additionally steady with those given by other public and private establishments. The private cloud uses a company's current PC servers or, at times, can be facilitated by a CSP (otherwise called virtual private cloud).

Notwithstanding, if the private cloud is on-premises or off-premises (facilitated by a CSP), the framework is accessible for the select use of a solitary organisation. Conversely, a public cloud is presented by a CSP to clients who share a similar cloud foundation simultaneously. Contrasting degrees of isolation are given depending on the cloud assets.

A cross-breed cloud is made out of at least two unmistakable cloud foundations. The two veils of mist work as one-of-a-kind substances yet are bound together by normalised innovation that empowers information and application transportability (e.g., cloud blasting for load adjusting between mists). In a mixture cloud, information and applications can move between private and public stages for more prominent adaptability.

At last, the local area cloud alludes to a foundation accessible for the restrictive use by a particular local area of organisations, including a few establishments of solitary gathering. Concerning the assistance models, the primary ones are Infrastructure as a Service (IaaS), Platform as a Service (PaaS), and Software as a Service (SaaS). IaaS gives handling, stockpiling, and organisation administrations in a virtual climate.

PaaS permits clients to create and oversee applications without building or keeping up with any framework and gives an application advancement and sending climate in the cloud by offering the capacity of using PC programming dialects and devices accessible from the specialist organisation. At long last, SaaS offers direct support to people or undertakings.

Size, innovative intricacy and guidelines, and security concerns set the reception speed of the cloud in various ventures. Computerised local organisations were brought into the world in the cloud; they were in the principal wave and are the most exceptional concerning reception. They made their innovation without preparation and needed inheritance frameworks to coordinate; however, this is not average across enterprises. The reception progress in retail or media and promoting is higher than in the monetary business (banking and protection). In finance, the intricacy of innovation is raised, value-based center banking is exceptionally coordinated with heritage advancements, and guidelines inside the administration are stricter around rethinking and information protection.

1.20   Administrative consistence intricacies

Administrative consistency intricacies refer to the complex and intricate details that arise in administrating an organisation's policies, procedures, and systems. This often involves ensuring consistency in decision-making, maintaining standardisation in processes and procedures, and ensuring that the rules and regulations are applied evenly across the organisation (Sood *et al.*, 2022b; Garg *et al.*, 2023; Grima *et al.*, 2021b). It requires careful attention to detail and a thorough understanding of the regulations and policies in question to avoid errors or inconsistencies that can impact the organisation's overall effectiveness.

1.21   Future technology in finance

The future of technology and multimedia is rapidly evolving and expanding, driven by advancements in AI, VR, and AR and the increasing popularity of mobile and wearable devices. These developments are transforming how we interact with technology and each other, leading to new and innovative forms of entertainment, communication, and education (Sood *et al.*, 2021, 2022a, 2022b).

One of the key trends in the future of technology and multimedia is the further integration of AI and ML into a wide range of applications and devices. This will result in more personalised and intuitive experiences for users and the automation of many tasks that humans currently perform.

Virtual and AR will also play a major role in the future of technology and multimedia, creating immersive and interactive experiences that blur the lines between the physical and digital worlds. Additionally, the rise of 5G networks and the IoT will facilitate the development of new connected and intelligent devices, creating a more connected and intelligent world.

Overall, the future of technology and multimedia is highly exciting and full of possibilities. The innovations and advancements in these fields will continue to shape how we live, work, and interact with the world.

1.22 Conclusion

Although we know that manufacturers, regulations, and politics impact digital innovation, end-users must be at the heart of every innovation. Suppliers should emphasise the socioeconomic benefits of digital technology, particularly their revolutionary powers. Future studies and innovation should investigate digital technology adoption across a large and diversified sample of the economy.

IT has undergone significant changes over the years, leading to changing user expectations and demands. Some of the major changes in the expectations with IT development include:

- Increased usability: users expect IT systems to be intuitive and user-friendly, with clear and concise interfaces.
- Increased mobility: users expect to be able to access information and applications from anywhere, at any time, using a range of devices, including smartphones, laptops, and tablets.
- Increased speed: users expect IT systems to be fast, with quick response times and the ability to handle large amounts of data.
- Increased security: users expect IT systems to protect their personal and sensitive information from cyber threats.
- Increased integration: users expect IT systems to be integrated, allowing for a seamless exchange of information between different applications and platforms.
- Increased automation: users expect IT systems to be able to automate tasks, reducing the need for manual input and increasing efficiency.
- Increased personalisation: users expect IT systems to provide a personalised experience tailored to their specific needs and preferences.

As technology continues to evolve, these expectations will likely change. IT companies and organisations must continuously adapt and innovate to meet the changing expectations of their users (Muddumadappa *et al.*, 2022; Chen and Su, 2022).

References

Abdullah, N.H. and Shamsuddin, A. (2009). 'Technology adoption among SMEs in Malaysia: development of an assessment process'. In: *PICMET '09 – 2009 Portland International Conference on Management of Engineering & Technology*, Portland, pp. 2644–2648.

Abdullah, N.H., Wahab, E., and Shamsuddin, A. (2013). 'Exploring the common technology adoption enablers among Malaysian SMEs: qualitative findings'. *Journal of Management and Sustainability*, vol. 3, no. 4, pp. 78–91, ISSN: 1925-4725, E-ISSN: 1925-4733, Published by Canadian Center of Science and Education.

Abell, W. and Lim, W. (1996). 'Business use of the Internet in New Zealand: an exploratory study, 1996', In: *Second Australian World-Wide Web Conference*, Southern Cross University Press, Lismore, NSW, Australia, pp. 33–39.

Abernathy, W.J. and Clark, K.B. (1985). 'Innovation: mapping the winds of creative destruction'. *Research Policy*, vol. 14, no. 1, pp. 3–22.

Adham, K.A. and Ahmad, M. (2005). 'Adoption of web site and e-commerce technology among Malaysian public companies'. *Industrial Management & Data Systems*, vol. 105, no. 9, pp. 1172–1187.

Agarwal, A.K., Tiwari, R.G., Kaushal, R.K., and Kumar, N. (2021). 'A systematic analysis of applications of blockchain in healthcare'. In: *2021 6th International Conference on Signal Processing, Computing and Control (ISPCC)*. IEEE, pp. 413–417.

Ahuja, G. and Lampert, C.M. (2001). 'Entrepreneurship in the large corporation: a longitudinal study of how established firms create breakthrough inventions', *Strategic Management Journal*, vol. 22, nos. 6/7, pp. 521–543, Special Issue: Strategic Entrepreneurship: Entrepreneurial Strategies for Wealth Creation.

Ajzen, I. and Fishbein, M. (1980). *Understanding Attitudes and Predicting Social Behavior*, Prentice-Hall, Englewood Cliffs, NJ.

Akulava, M. (2015). 'Gender and Innovativeness of the Enterprise: The case of transition countries, BEROC working paper series No. 31', Belarusian Economic Research and Outreach Center (BEROC).

Alam, S., Khatibi, A., Ahmad, M., and Ismail, H. (2007). 'Factors affecting e-commerce adoption in the electronic manufacturing companies in Malaysia'. *International Journal of Commerce and Management*, vol. 17, no. 12, pp. 125–139.

Al-Gahtani, S.S., Hubona, G., and Wany, J. (2007). 'Information technology (IT) in Saudi Arabia: culture and the acceptance and use of IT'. *Information & Management,* vol. 44, no. 8, pp. 681–691.

Al-Qirim, N. (2007). 'The adoption of ecommerce communications and applications technologies in small businesses in New Zealand'. *Electronic Commerce Research and Applications*, vol. 6, no. 4, pp. 462–473.

Assink, M. (2006). 'Inhibitors of disruptive innovation capability: a conceptual model'. *European Journal of Innovation Management*, vol. 9, no. 2, pp. 215–233.

Atherton, A. and Hannon, P.D. (2000). 'Innovation processes and the small business: a conceptual analysis'. *International Journal of Business Performance Management*, vol. 2, no. 4, pp. 276–292.

Baiyere, A. and Salmela, H. (2013). 'Review: disruptive innovation & information technology charting a path'. In: Deng, H. and Standing, C. (Ed.), *ACIS 2013: Information Systems: Transforming the Future: In Proceedings of the 24th Australasian Conference on Information Systems*, Melbourne, Australia, 4–6 December, pp. 1–11.

Baker, W.E. and Sinkula, J.M. (2002). 'Market orientation, learning orientation and product innovation: delving into the organisation's black box'. *Journal of Market Focused Management*, vol. 5, no. 1, pp. 5–23.

Blili, S. and Raymond, L. (1993). 'Information technology: threats and opportunities for small and medium-sized enterprises'. *International Journal of Information Management*, vol. 13, no. 6, pp. 439–448.

Boden Jr., R.J. and Nucci, A. (2000). 'On the survival prospects of men's and women's new business ventures'. *Journal of Business Venturing*, vol. 15, no. 4, pp. 347–362.

Boeck, H., Bendavid, Y., and Lefebvre, E. (2009). 'Evolving B2B e-commerce adaptation for SME suppliers'. *Journal of Business and Industrial Marketing*, vol. 24, no. 8, pp. 561–574.

Brown, K. (2000). *The Interactive Marketplace: Business-to-Business Strategies for Delivering Justin-Time, Mass-Customized Products*. McGraw-Hill, Martinsburg, WV.

Chandy, R. and Tellis, G. (1998). 'Organising for radical product innovation: the overlooked role of willingness to cannibalise'. *Journal of Marketing Research*, November, vol. 35, no. 4, pp. 474–488.

Chang, Y., Kim, H., Wong, S.F., and Park, M-C. (2015). 'A comparison of the digital divide across three countries with different development indices'. *Journal of Global Information Management (JGIM)*, vol. 23, no. 4, pp. 55–76.

Chau, S.B. and Turner, P. (2002). 'A framework for analysing factors influencing small to medium-sized enterprises (SMEs) ability to derive benefit from the conduct of web based electronic commerce (EC)-34 Australian case studies'. In: *Proceedings of the 10th European Conference on Information Systems*, Gdansk, Poland, pp. 625–639.

Chell, E. and Baines, S. (1998). 'Does gender affect business performance? A study of microbusinesses in the business services in the United Kingdom'. *Entrepreneurship and Regional Development*, vol. 10, no. 2, pp. 117–135.

Chen, L. and Su, S. (2022). 'Optimization of the trust propagation on supply chain network based on blockchain plus'. *Journal of Intelligent Management Decision*, vol. 1, no. 1, pp. 17–27.

Christensen, C.M. (2006). 'The ongoing process of building a theory of disruption'. *The Journal of Product Innovation Management*, vol. 23, no. 4, pp. 39–55.

Christensen, C.M. and Raynor, M.E. (2003). *The Innovator's Solution: Creating and Sustaining Successful Growth*. Harvard Business School Press, Boston, MA.

Chwelos, P., Benbasat, I., and Dexter, A.S. (2001). 'Research report: empirical test of an EDI adoption model'. *Information Systems Research*, vol. 12, no. 3, pp. 304–321.

Cloete, E., Courtney, S., and Fintz, J. (2002). 'Small business acceptance and adoption of e-commerce in the Western-Cape Province of South Africa'. *EJISDC*, vol. 10, no. 4, pp. 1–13.

Cruz-Jesus, F., Oliveira, T., and Bacao, F. (2018). 'The global digital divide: evidence and drivers'. *Journal of Global Information Management*, vol. 26, no. 2, pp. 1–26.

Danneels, E. (2004). 'Disruptive technology re-considered: a critique and research agenda'. *Journal of Product Innovation Management*, vol. 21, no. 4, pp. 246–258.

Dhatterwal, J.S., Kaswan, K.S., and Balusamy, B. (2022). 'Emerging technologies in the insurance market'. In: *Big Data Analytics in the Insurance Market*. Emerald Publishing Limited, Bingley, pp. 275–286.

Garg, M., Singhal, S., Sood, K., Rupeika-Apoga, R., and Grima, S. (2023). 'Price discovery mechanism and volatility spillover between national agriculture market and national commodity and derivatives exchange: the study of the Indian agricultural commodity market'. *Journal of Risk and Financial Management*, vol. 16, no. 2, p. 62.

Gauci, G. and Grima, S. (2020). 'The impact of regulatory pressures on governance on the performance of public banks' with a European Mediterranean region connection'. *European Research Studies Journal,* vol. XXIII, no. 2, 2020. pp. 360–387.

Grima, S., Grima, A., Thalassinos, E., Seychell, S., and Spiteri, J.V. (2017). 'Theoretical models for sport participation: literature review'. *International Journal of Economics and Business Administration*, vol. V, no. 3, 2017 pp. 94–116.

Grima, S., Grima, A., Thalassinos, E., Seychell, S., and Spiteri, J.,V. (2018). 'A study of the determinants of sports participants by Maltese Nationals'. *European Research Studies Journal*, vol. XXI, no. 2, 2018, pp. 110–133.

Grima, S., Hamarat, B., Özen, E., Girlando, A., and Dalli-Gonzi, R. (2021). 'The relationship between risk perception and risk definition and risk-addressing behaviour during the early COVID-19 stages'. *Journal of Risk and Financial Management*, vol. 14, p. 272. https://doi.org/10.3390/jrfm14060272

Grima, S., Kizilkaya, M., Sood, K., and Erdem Delice, M. (2021). 'The perceived effectiveness of blockchain for digital operational risk resilience in the European Union insurance market sector'. *Journal of Risk and Financial Management*, vol. 14, no. 8, p. 363.

Grima, S., Romanova, I., Bezzina, F., and Chetcuti Dimech, F. (2016). 'Alternative investment fund managers directive and its impact on Malta's financial service industry'. *International Journal in Economics and Business Administration*, vol. IV, no. 1, 2016, pp. 70–85. Earlier Version at the

International Conference University of Latvia 2014 – New Challenges of Economic and Business Development 2014, Page 51.

Grima, S., Seychell, S., and Bezzina, F. (2017). 'Investigating factors predicting derivative mishandling: a sociological perspective'. *European Research Studies Journal*, vol. XX, no. 4A, 2017, pp. 3–17.

Kaswan, K.S., Dhatterwal, J.S., and Balyan, A. (2022). 'Intelligent agents-based integration of machine learning and case base reasoning system'. In: *2022 2nd International Conference on Advance Computing and Innovative Technologies in Engineering (ICACITE)*, IEEE, pp. 1477–1481.

Kaswan, K.S., Dhatterwal, J.S., Sood, K., and Balusamy, B. (2022). *Role of Blockchain Technology in the Modern Era*. Wiley Online Library.

Kaur, B., and Bansal, R. (2021). 'Examining behavioral intentions of practitioners to use forensic accounting technique as fraud detection and prevention mechanism'. *SPAST Abstracts*, vol. 1, no. 01, 3080.

Mittal, A., Aggarwal, A., and Mittal, R. (2020). 'Predicting university students' adoption of mobile news applications: the role of perceived hedonic value and news motivation'. *International Journal of E-Services and Mobile Applications (IJESMA)*, vol. 12, no. 4, pp. 42–59.

Muddumadappa, P.M.B., Anjanappa, S.D.K. and Srikantaswamy, M. (2022). 'An efficient reconfigurable cryptographic model for dynamic and secure unstructured data sharing in multi-cloud storage server'. *Journal of Intelligent Systems and Control*, vol. 1, no. 1, pp. 68–78.

Newcomb. T. (2023). 'Superhuman Algorithms Could 'Kill Everyone' in Due Time', Researchers Warn. Published January 26, 2023. New technology. Security. Popular Mechanics. www.popularmechanics.com/technology/security/a42675408/superhuman-algorithms-could-kill-everyone/

Sood, K., Seth, N., Jindal, M., and Sadawarti, H. (2021). 'Big data: a boon for food and servicepreneurship'. In: *Entrepreneurship and Big Data*. CRC Press, London, pp. 55–69.

Sood, K., Seth, N., and Grima, S. (2022). 'Portfolio performance of public sector general insurance companies in India: a comparative analysis'. In: *Managing Risk and Decision Making in Times of Economic Distress, Part B*. Emerald Publishing Limited, Bingley.

Sood, K., Balamurugan, B., Grima, S., and Marano, P. (eds.). (2022). *Big Data Analytics in the Insurance Market*. Emerald Group Publishing, Bingley.

Varma, P. and Nijjer, S. (2022). 'Examining the role of fintech in the future of retail banking'. *ECS Transactions*, vol. 107, no. 1, p. 9855.

Chapter 2

Evolution of multimedia banking and technology acceptance theories

Luan Vardari[1] and Samra Jusufi[2]

Abstract

This research aims to investigate and expand knowledge on the development of multimedia banking acceptance theories and technologies. This research looks at the evolution of multimedia in the banking sector, the stages of multimedia technology, the models of the technology acceptance model (TAM), and the theory of reasoned action (TRA). We relied on secondary data to carry out this research. We attempted to gather information from both new and old studies and compare them. The findings of this study reveal that banks are now very close to their customers due to technological advancements; on the other hand, customers can access and use many services (almost all) online, which connects them more with the bank.

The rapid advancement of information and communication technology is regarded as one of the most significant breakthroughs, particularly since the end of the twentieth century. Computers, the Internet, video games, mobile phones, electronic banking, and digital satellite systems are devices established due to the innovation of information and communication technology. In interactive transactions, such as telebanking and tele-shopping, the transaction is transferred to the relevant center in written and voice form, regardless of the person's language. NFC technology, social media networks, and mobile devices are all being used by financial institutions to improve efficiency and effectiveness. At the same time, the rise of new media increases consumer purchasing power and paves the path for non-banks and other financial organizations to compete more effectively. Even though multimedia banking is widely available in the market, many banks need help attracting visitors to their websites. Many of these phenomena have been attributed to traditional brick-and-mortar banking, which can assist bankers in attracting more consumers to the new wave. As a result, banks must also design a framework that combines the most modern technology components of multimedia banking.

Keywords: Banking sector; Multimedia banking; Digital banking; New media

[1]Faculty of Economy, University of Prizren 'UKSHIN HOTI', Republic of Kosova
[2]Department of Business and Administration, University of Prizren 'UKSHIN HOTI', Faculty of Economy, Republic of Kosova

2.1   Introduction

Banking has always been a very information-intensive sector to acquire, analyze, and transmit relevant information to all consumers while highlighting the differences between their products and services (Kardaras and Papathanassiou, 2001). Every day of the week, consumers may use computers to access essential bank goods and services 24 h a day. Moreover, most consumers can now accomplish their banking tasks and activities using the Internet anytime and from any location (Tarhini *et al.*, 2016). Because of the following factors, e-banking is far superior to traditional banking systems: transaction processing costs are drastically reduced; payment efficiency is increased; financial services are provided; and the banker–customer link is strengthened (Al Kailani, 2016).

The telephone and automated teller machine (ATM) were at the forefront of the first wave of multimedia technology. These advancements paved the way for remote sales and the shift from branch transactions to ATMs and off-site telephones (Vijayan *et al.*, 1970). The second wave of technological developments focused on using personal computers (PCs) for financial management and information reporting via online network services. Due to the struggle for control of the customer connection between content producers, delivery providers, and gateway providers, numerous variants of multimedia banking have developed, each of which has quite distinct strategic repercussions for the players in the sector (Vijayan *et al.*, 1970). Finally, the third wave was dominated by the introduction of digital currencies kept on smart cards. E-cash has developed in two distinct ways. The first was the advancement of encryption technology, which allowed for the secure transmission of funds over the Internet. The second was the development and widespread use of 'electronic wallets', which made it possible to transfer small sums of money using smart cards for everyday purchases (Vijayan *et al.*, 1970).

The TAM is a well-known paradigm for studying how well information systems are accepted (TAM). The use of the system is determined by peoples' attitudes toward service, which is linked to their goals and conduct. The reasoned action (TRA) theory is a well-established social psychology paradigm focusing on intentionally planned behavior (Fishbein and Ajzen, 1975). According to Fishbein and Ajzen (1975), concerning theoretical explanations of human actions, the TRA can do so in a logical, efficient, and observant way.

2.2   Evolution of multimedia in the banking sector

Information Technology (IT) is the primary means by which banks gather, analyze, and distribute relevant data to all applicable customers while ensuring that their products or services are distinct from those of their competitors. This is done to maintain a competitive advantage in the marketplace (Kardaras and Papathanassiou, 2001). Nowadays, a bank customer can remotely access information about his accounts, manage his statements, and perform other financial procedures. Any type of remote banking system is advantageous to a bank because it raises the institution's performance indicators, lowers costs without lowering product quality, and, most importantly, increases the bank's customer base, which is essential for banks to thrive in a market that is saturated with competition (Tskhadadze, 2019). Corporate executives in the banking sector have used various strategies to entice clients to buy their products. E-banking is one example. Banks provide these technology services intending to provide clients with quick and cost-effective services (Affran, 2020).

Banks have a good understanding of their client's expectations and needs. As a result, client happiness and bank service delivery are not separated (Altobishi *et al.*, 2018). The development of Internet banking has contributed to the most significant supply of banking services and higher, quicker, and more affordable products. Essential bank products and services are available to customers around the clock, 7 days a week, when they utilize their laptops. Most customers can now use Internet financial to carry out their financial operations and transactions at any time and location (Tarhini *et al.*, 2016).

Customers today expect new degrees of ease and flexibility not met by traditional means, in addition to critical and valuable services (Alsamydai *et al.*, 2012). As a result, incorporating e-services is becoming increasingly important to deliver quality and engaging client service (Bultum, 2014).

Because of this, organizations are moving their focus to e-services to support their entire company processes, both before and after the phases in which transactions occur. These findings show how critical it is to understand the variables that affect how customers use online banking services. To attain favorable results in the market, it is necessary to research such factors (Gilaninia *et al.*, 2011). The use of information systems that are already well established and have reached their maturity level in the banking industry has a substantial impact on the development of more efficient financial services. In addition, the Internet provides a quick distribution route for client banking services, making them more convenient and cost-effective (Salem *et al.*, 2019).

E-banking has improved dramatically over traditional banking systems for the following reasons: significantly lowering transaction processing costs; improving the effectiveness of payments, financial services, and the interaction between bankers and customers (AlKailani, 2016).

The Internet is one of the most promising and quickly increasing financial service mediums. Various payment and transfer options are now available to customers thanks to the development of different information technologies. They are created using a client's personal computer or mobile phone with Internet connectivity (Tskhadadze, 2019).

2.3 ATMs and telephones

The initial swell of multimedia technology – the telephone, an invention that dates back more than a century, and the automated teller machine were the primary focuses of the first wave (an invention just over 30 years old). Because of these advancements, businesses began moving their transactions away from bank branches and toward ATMs and off-site telephones. The ATM enabled US banks to circumvent the interstate banking prohibitions embodied in the McFadden Act of 1927 (Vijayan *et al.*, 1970). The first form of communication was telephony. The means of communication through it are fairly common. Customers could contact the bank to obtain information about their accounts and product guidance. Even though the Internet is more widely utilized and costs less, this technique is still in use. Banks had many call center employees and offered telephone services, but they did not accept the commission, which drove up the cost of their operations. Another method of delivering remote banking services is through ATMs and payment enquiry devices. When this form of remote banking service was first developed, the bank had to make a significant expenditure. This included producing and purchasing specialized equipment, building a technical foundation, and developing the infrastructure and logistics. Despite this, ATMs are widely available, and modern large banks have vast networks of these devices for the convenience of their clients. The number of services offered is expanding, safety is improving, and remote banking services' key benefit is that ATMs supply cash (Tskhadadze, 2019). The banking industry's rapid technological advancements made the ability to switch to a swift, flexible, and practical model possible. The development of automated teller machines (also known as ATMs) is one example of a technological advancement that has led to a decrease in the frequency of face-to-face interactions with bank employees or even its elimination. These machines have also had a definite and unfavourable impact on how an account is maintained through workouts and exchanges (Onyesolu *et al.*, 2012). Through the spread of new technical innovations, members of society judge a new technology's success and continuation. However, due to the exclusion, they obtained from the inconveniences of bank transactions, paper-based validation, and a long line, ATM technology has taken over and spread worldwide. Bank personnel and clients are more at ease. Cash withdrawals, cash deposits, balance inquiries, mini statements, last few transaction information, and other subsidiary transactions like paying phone and utility bills are just a few of the main transactions a consumer can perform using an ATM. Additionally, an ATM is referred to by various titles, including money point, computerized managing accounting machine, and money machine (Das *et al.*, 2011; Wan *et al.*, 2005). The rise in ATM fraud has almost overtaken the rapid rise in the number of ATMs used. Even while the personal identification number (PIN) or secret password is one critical part of the security of ATM transactions, many other types of security are essential, including the security of the ATM, the security of the user, and the safety measures of the card. New confirmation systems are created when ATM fraud increases (De Luca *et al.*, 2010). The purpose of layered security in the current corporate environment is to give ATMs a higher level of security. This multilayer security includes client validation, transaction, physical machine, and client security. To keep the current customers and to increase their confidence in the security of automated banking systems or ATM account management frameworks, it is necessary to develop unique, sophisticated systems to protect against unauthorized access to customer accounts and, in addition, to ensure the client's security. With the use of automated teller machines, the demand for quick access to banking transactions has increased due to the development of electronic transactions and banking systems

(ATMs). The increase in ATM fraud has been strongly related to the rapid growth in ATM transactions. The two major obstacles to the broad adoption of ATM transactions are security issues and fraudulent transactions. A password, prior computer system, or ATM expertise is insufficient for ATM security. Security is crucial in ATMs in several areas, including the physical machines, the transactions, the user authentication and integrity, and ultimately the user security itself. Therefore, fraud prevention and security have become crucial components to expanding ATM usage and boosting customer confidence and trust in ATMs (Prasad, 2018). Although it has a long history as a mass communication tool, up until recently, the telephone had a minimal impact on the electronic media landscape. Early broadcast telephone services provided information and entertainment programs in an audio text accessible in Great Britain, Hungary, and the United States via subscription. In the 1980s, long-distance operators started offering interactive 900 services after adding a variety of features in the ensuing decades. With touch-tone phones, users may retrieve information, carry out transactions, or respond to inquiries, making them the first widely utilized interactive medium. A \$500 million yearly revenue from audio text has been made possible by recent technological and policy advancements, and this money is predicted to triple by the middle of the 1990s. Comparatively, consumer videotext services only make up around half of that amount (LaRose *et al.*, 1992).

2.3.1 Telecommunication – vitalization through ATM

ATM is a switching technology that applies small, fixed-size cells to a quick, packet-oriented transfer method for asynchronously multiplexed heterogeneous traffic. The transport technique (or 'mode') for B-ISDN services was designated as ATM by the CCITT in 1988. ATM 'has the potential to replace the multiple competing technologies that are today required to be integrated into a coherent whole.' (Martin *et al.*, 1997). The objective of an ATM is to transmit all traffic (including voice, video, and data) through a single switching fabric based on cells. The cell streams are multiplexed and distributed across a single bearer line or carrier facility by ATM. Utilizing cell addresses for multiplexing is possible. In other words, each link has a different cell address issued to each user or function. ATM also shows a single communication method that can function over short and long distances using standard LAN and WAN technologies. In a nutshell, ATM is a development in wireline network technology that can offer interchangeable support for different services and is being incorporated into wireless networks. The severity of the distinction between isochronous (voice and video) and asynchronous (data) services in the planned transport system has also been lessened as a result of B-success ISDNs through ATMs (Neelakanta, 2018).

2.4 PCs and online services

The second wave of technical innovations was the most significant when using PCs to manage funds and report data via online network services was introduced. The majority of these jobs were completed via internet network services.

Many multimedia banking models have emerged due to a battle between content, delivery, and gateway providers for customer relationship control. Each model has various strategic repercussions for industry participants (Vijayan *et al.*, 1970). One of the most critical areas of banking development in modern times is the development of remote banking systems. The bank reaches a new level of customer service by creating and developing conditions for remote service delivery.

On the one hand, the swift expansion of the retail industry necessitates the development of inexpensive and efficient customer–bank communication channels. High-quality services, however, give a distinct advantage in the fiercely competitive bank market. Bank customers use a 'remote banking' system to perform various procedures remotely. It is optional to go to the bank branch; using a computer or a phone would suffice. The primary premise underlying all remote banking service delivery systems is the two-way transmission of various information between the customer and the bank over a distance.

Because a bank client can now access information about his accounts, manage them, and complete various activities from a remote location, the bank simultaneously ensures sufficient security and secrecy of such communication. This is because a bank customer can now complete a variety of activities. Therefore, even when they are not physically present, the customer has access to their accounts, payments, transfers, opening deposits, and a wealth of data (such as the current exchange rates for various currencies or the locations of local ATMs) (Tskhadadze, 2019).

A customer's degree of satisfaction is commonly used in product and service development, supervision, and evaluation, according to Anderson *et al.* (1994). Furthermore, many studies have been undertaken in the banking industry to evaluate customer satisfaction and service quality (Cronin and Taylor, 1992; Fornell, 1992; Goode and Moutinho, 1995; Johnston, 1997; Levesque and McDougall, 1996).

People who have a deep-seated aversion to IT applications (PCs, the Internet) could find it challenging to switch from traditional banking to online banking. It is more likely that a customer's prior views will be compatible with Internet banking if they have some previous Internet experience and basic computer ability (Giovanis *et al.*, 2012). Customers can now carry out a wide range of banking, bill payment, and money management activities without leaving the comfort of their homes, thanks to the proliferation of home banking programs based on PCs. These services are also available outside the regular business hours maintained by the branches, and their prices are typically lower than those of alternative options. Banks can reduce their distribution costs through electronic home banking (Mols, 1998). According to Tilden (1996) and Kalakota and Frei (1997), the cost of processing an electronic transaction is approximately six times lower than the cost of processing a check. As an illustration, Tilden (1996) noted that PC banking would enable banks to reduce expenses significantly, and Kalakota and Frei (1997) cited estimates that support this claim. According to Evans and Wurster (1997), electronic home banking may decrease switching barriers, complicate cross-selling, make it more difficult to collect client information, and force banks to compete on a product-by-product basis.

2.5   E-cash and interactive video

The third wave dealt with digital currency stored on smart cards. Two distinct paths led to the development of e-cash. The first was the creation of a technology known as encryption, which made it feasible to send money over the Internet securely. The second innovation was the development and widespread use of 'electronic wallets', which simplified the process of exchanging minute sums of money through smart cards for routine purchases. Digital signature-enabled smart card devices can be linked to any multimedia device, such as a computer, personal digital assistant (PDA), mobile phone, or interactive television, to allow customers to make deposits and withdrawals without having to visit a bank. Moreover, customers do not have to go to banks or ATMs to transfer money since they may use smart card devices to accomplish it (Vijayan *et al.*, 1970).

What exactly is meant by 'e-cash'? To begin, let us take a moment to discuss what electronic cash is. Many cryptographers have recently been interested in these new technologies, notably offline untraceable electronic currency (CFN90, FY93, Oka95, CP93b, CP93a, CP93c, PW92, Bra93, FY94, BGK95, DC94, EO94, OO92, FTY96, CMS96, Pai93, CFMT96, Sim96, Tsi97, etc.). In its fundamental structure, an electronic cash system comprises three participants (a bank B, a user U, and a shop S) and four key activities (account establishment, withdrawal, payment, and deposit). User U will initially open an account with bank B during the account establishment protocol phase of a coin's life cycle. Coins are withdrawn from B, and cash is spent at merchant S as a part of a payment and withdrawal process. S participates in a deposit procedure with bank B to deposit a currency. If bank B, in conjunction with store S, cannot establish a connection between the coin and the user, the electronic currency system is considered anonymous. The system is offline if shop S does not interact with bank B while processing the payment. If a coin is spent twice in an offline system, the user's identity will probably be exposed to protect the bank's confidentiality. One should be aware that an offline system can be utilized online, and the bank will check for double-spending at the time of purchase if there is a possibility of that happening (the cost is, of course, the involvement of the bank). Formal security models of off-line models for e-cash are given in [FY93, Tsi97] and online e-cash systems are presented in [Sim96]. Currently, most of our attention is focused on online systems; however, the concepts being discussed apply to a broader setting (Frankel *et al.*, 1997). Electronic cash and other cryptographic payment systems allow some degree of user anonymity while the transaction is taking place. This is done to imitate the characteristics of the exchange of physical currency electronically. It has been brought to everyone's attention that there are circumstances in which the anonymity of notes is undesirable for crime prevention. There can also be regulatory and legal limits that preclude anonymous financial transfers. Therefore, the complete anonymity of users might not be suitable in some situations and might act as a roadblock to the growth of online commerce. The fundamental contribution of this paper is the idea that anonymity should be considered a control parameter to permit flexibility in the degree of privacy that noteholders have. It is based on the hypothesis that in light of the legal, social, technical, and efficiency restraints already in place (which are decided by the dynamic conditions and constraints), it is impossible to achieve the desired results (Davida *et al.*, 1997). When a user purchases electronic cash, the user remains anonymous to the bank and the retailer. This simulates a sense of anonymity associated with traditional cash transactions. Both proponents and opponents of unknown payment systems present several compelling points. Arguments in support of the anonymity of electronic cash are often presented in the form of protecting the users' right to privacy and preventing the acquisition of users' personal information.

On the other hand, anonymous e-cash may encourage fraud and criminal behaviors such as money laundering, anonymous blackmailing (perfect), and illegal purchasing. Given the actual legal and social constraints and the additional technological constraints (of bandwidth, computational, and storage efficiencies) that electronic implementations may impose, we propose treating anonymity as a control parameter that can be changed by allowing flexibility in the level of user anonymity as conditions demand. This approach is justified because electronic implementations may impose it due to legal and societal limits and extra technology constraints (bandwidth, computational, and storage efficiency). When the option to regulate anonymity is selected, revocation of anonymity is enabled. Using discriminators, this functionality should only be enabled on a case-by-by-case basis. One can use them to identify which digital currencies are to be unlocked and which are to be kept secret. Potential differentiation is based on the transaction's time and the retail establishment where the purchase was made. For the e-cash system's ability to revoke users' right to anonymity to be of any use, further discriminators may need to be implemented (Davida *et al.*, 1997).

There are now two separate models that make up state-of-the-art regarding the levels of anonymity that can be revoked (Davida *et al.*, 1997): (1) coin tracing, which involves identifying a coin after it has been withdrawn from a bank; and (2) owner tracing involves identifying the person who owns a coin.

The anonymity level regulating factor A procedure known as 'owner tracing' is used by trustees to identify the coin's owner after payment has been made. Regarding big monetary transfers, traceability after purchase is essential to meet legal and regulatory obligations. In-store branches have evolved into a testing ground for new technology and serve as a venue for fine-tuning sales methods. The shortage of bank tellers at physical locations has led to the rise of interactive video banking as a potential workaround. Video banking presents a possible opportunity for the Bank of Oklahoma, Tulsa, to expand its branch network to locations where a traditional branch is not legally permissible or environmentally sustainable. This expansion could occur in areas where the bank would otherwise be unable to open an attachment. At the beginning of this year, the financial institution conducted a pilot test of the idea in the lobby of its primary office and 1 of its 14 in-store branches. ISDN telephone lines provide the connection between the call center at the bank and the two-way video unit, which functions as an extension of the call center. Most of the dealings in a conventional branch, such as filling out an application for a loan, are handled by service experts displayed on a screen. In addition to this, the machines can scan documents and print out temporary checks. In the future, the financial institution plans to equip the device with the capacity to print out prepaid debit cards at the ATM. Vane Lucas, Senior Vice President at Bank of Oklahoma, says that the bank is more focused on complementing traditional delivery channels and using its contact center for the time being. Interactive video banking has the potential to open doors to new markets, but Lucas says that the bank is more concerned with expanding existing markets. Implementing interactive video technology is a component of the in-store transaction diversion strategy utilized by Bank One. The devices can initiate account openings, submit loan applications, retrieve account information, and schedule appointments with bank employees (Monahan, 1997).

2.6 TAM

This well-known concept is known as the TAM. Perceived usefulness (PU) and perceived ease of use (PEOU), both of which are linked to a mindset toward usage that, in turn, is related to intention and conduct, influence system use (actual activity), according to this paradigm. The TAM identifies these two ideas as crucial to the computer acceptance process. PU is an abbreviation for 'performance uplift', which refers to the chance that a prospective user would increase their performance. Tests on various samples under various conditions have shown that the TAM is a realistic and accurate model for understanding the acceptance of information systems.

Furthermore, many expansions to the original TAM model have been offered. The TAM2 model, recently presented by Venkatesh and Davis (2000), is an extension of the original TAM. Objective criteria and cognitive instrumental processes impact the perceived usefulness and aim.

An academic research tradition has grown around the TAM, which has been used in several settings to study various aspects of IT. The vast majority of TAM studies have consisted of empirical investigations, and the survey method has shown to be relatively successful in these investigations. The TAM is an advanced model successfully applied in various settings (Lai *et al.*, 2005). Lai (2005) concluded that the TAM construct was stable regardless of the gender, age, or IT skill level of the subgroups included in their sample. According to these studies, people of different genders, ages, levels of technical expertise, and educational backgrounds all conceived of the TAM concept in very similar ways. Due to these findings, they understood the validity of TAMs in technological adoption studies (Lai *et al.*, 2005). There has been much analysis of the acceptability of IT in the last two decades. On both the human and organizational levels, there have lately been several theoretical breakthroughs that offer new insights into acceptance and usage. Among these several theories, the TAM (or technology acceptance model) has gotten the greatest attention (Plouffe *et al.*, 2001). Information systems are implemented in businesses for various reasons, including reducing expenses, increasing production without an accompanying rise in costs, and improving the quality of the service or product. It has been noted that the users' dispositions toward a new information system and their level of acceptance of the system substantially impact the information system's ability to be successfully adopted (Pikkarainen *et al.*, 2004). The TAM has been the subject of substantial research, and the findings of that research have revealed that the TAM is superior to other models (TRA and TPB) in terms of its capacity to explain an attitude toward making use of information systems (Mathieson, 1991). TAM can dependably explain a significant amount (typically about 40%) of the variation that may be seen in usage intentions and behavior. Several studies have defined the 'use' of an information system as 'user acceptance' of the information system in question. Furthermore, the time an information system is employed might indicate how widely it is adopted (Pikkarainen *et al.*, 2004).

2.7 TRA

Fishbein and Ajzen's (1975) TRA is an accepted paradigm in social psychology, which deals with the variables that influence conscious action. The TRA is a theoretical framework that is intuitive, economical, and wise in describing human behavior.

Figure 2.1 depicts the behavioral intention considered the immediate antecedent of an individual's conduct by the TRA. According to Ajzen and Fishbein (1980), most activities with social consequences can be controlled voluntarily, and, as a result, their intentions can be anticipated. As outlined in theory, two elements determine whether or not behavior and intention are linked. These are (a) a measure of intention must match the behavioral criterion in action, target, context and time, and (b) an intention must not alter before it is noticed (Ajzen and Fishbein, 1980). According to the TRA, a person's behavioral intention is determined by a personal aspect known as attitude toward behavior and a person's sense of societal pressures, known as the subjective norm. Attitude toward a behavior is a private variable. Subjective criteria are established based on a collection of views known as normative beliefs. The term 'the likelihood that relevant referent persons or groups would accept or disapprove of conducting the activity' is how Ajzen and Madden

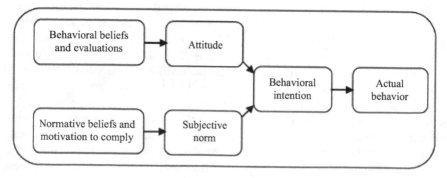

Figure 2.1   TRA (Fishbein and Ajzen, 1975)

(1986) define normative views. To approximate a subjective norm, the TRA multiplies each person's normative belief by incentivizing them to comply with the referent. Then it adds up the cross-product for all relevant referents. This provides an estimate of the subjective norm.

Because the TRA is such a general model, it does not describe the beliefs responsible for a particular behavior (Davis *et al.*, 1989). As a consequence, researchers who employ the TRA are required to initially ascertain the significant concepts that the participants have concerning the behavior being investigated. In addition, the TRA is more concerned with predicting behavior than predicting results (Foxall, 1997). Because TRA is based on behavioral intentions, the model's predictability is restricted to situations in which choice and action are significantly connected. We notice the strongest correlations when there is little time between articulating a purpose and its subsequent behavior. Assessing someone's choices and actions simultaneously is not a foolproof way to determine whether or not a model is accurate in its capacity to forecast the future. Let us take the most extreme example possible. At its best, it only substantiates the underlying attitudes that underpin modern behavior. The actual conduct should be assessed objectively and unobtrusively to evaluate TRA. There should be no indication that this measurement is related to the intention assessment phase that preceded it (Davies *et al.*, 2002). Another one of the conditions of the TRA is that there must be consistency in behavior.

The Theory of Rationally Acting Customers, or TRA, is based on the premise that customers will rationally collect and evaluate all pertinent information in an organized manner. In addition, TRA thinks that individuals think about the probable outcomes of their actions and base their choice to act or not on this line of thinking (Pikkarainen *et al.*, 2004).

2.8 Conclusion

This study's objective was to trace the development of multimedia banking throughout its duration. As a result, researchers could classify actions into three primary categories: the personal computer category, the automated teller machine category, and the electronic money category. These successive evolutionary waves have resulted in a great banking revolution. However, these innovations have introduced new dangers that have the potential to alter traditional market shares by introducing new participants into the financial sector. This, in turn, has harmed those institutions unwilling to embrace change or adopt wireless.

Businesses are moving their focus to e-services to support their entire company's activities before and after the transactional stages. As a result, the Internet is one of the most promising and rapidly expanding financial service mediums. Traditional banking systems have greatly outperformed online banking for several reasons, including significantly cheaper transaction processing costs, improved payment efficiency, excellent financial services, and the banker–customer link.

References

Affran, S. (2020). "Electronic banking: an object of fallacy or system of functionality." *European Journal of Business and Management Research*, 5(4), 1–6.

Ajzen, I. and Fishbein, M. (1980). *Understanding Attitudes and Predicting Social Behavior*. Englewood Cliffs, NJ: Prentice-Hall.

Ajzen, I. and Madden, J. (1986). "Prediction of goal-directed behaviour: attitudes, intentions, and perceived behavioural control." *Journal of Experimental Social Psychology*, 22, 453–474.

AlKailani, M. (2016). "Factors affecting the adoption of internet banking in Jordan: an extended TAM model." *Journal of Marketing Development and Competitiveness*, 10(1), 39–52.

Alsamydai, M., Yousif, R., and Al Khasawneh, M. (2012). "The factors influencing consumers' satisfaction and continuity to deal with E-banking services in Jordan." *Global Journal of Management and Business Research*, 12(14), 129–142.

Altobishi, T., Erboz, G., and Podruzsik, S. (2018). "E-Banking effects on customer satisfaction: the survey on clients in Jordan Banking Sector." *International Journal of Marketing Studies*, 10(2), 151–161.

Anderson, E. W., Fomell, C., and Lehman, D. R. (1994), "Customer satisfaction, market share, and profitability: findings from Sweden." *Journal of Marketing*, 58(3), 53–66.

Bultum, A. (2014). "Factors affecting adoption of the electronic banking system in the Ethiopian banking industry." *Journal of Management Information System and E-commerce*, 1(1), 1–17.

Cronin, J. J. and Taylor, S. A. (1992). "Measuring service quality: a reexamination and extension." *Journal of Marketing*, 56(3), 55–68.

Das, S. and Debbarma, J. (2011). "Designing a biometric strategy (fingerprint) measure for enhancing ATM security in the Indian e-banking system." *International Journal of Information and Communication Technology Research*, 1(5), 197–203.

Davida, G., Frankel, Y., Tsiounis, Y., and Yung, M. (1997, February). "Anonymity control in e-cash systems." In *International Conference on Financial Cryptography* (pp. 1–16). Springer, Berlin, Heidelberg.

Davies, J., Foxall, G., and Pallister, J. (2002). "Beyond the intention–behaviour mythology: an integrated model of recycling." *Marketing Theory*, 2, 29–113.

Davis, F., Bagozzi, R., and Warshaw, P. (1989). "User acceptance of computer technology: a comparison of two theoretical models." *Management Science*, 35, 982–1003.

De Luca, A., Langheinrich, M., and Hussmann, H. (2010). "Towards understanding ATM security: a field study of real-world ATM use." In *Proceedings of the Sixth Symposium on Usable Privacy and Security* (p. 16). London: ACM.

Evans, P. B. and Wurster, T. S. (1997), "Strategy and the new economics of information." *Harvard Business Review*, September–October, 71–82.

Fishbein, M. and Ajzen, I. (1975). *Belief, Attitude, Intention, and Behaviour: An Introduction to Theory and Research*. Reading, MA: Addison-Wesley.

Fornell, C. (1992). "A national customer satisfaction barometer: the Swedish experience." *Journal of Marketing*, 56, 6–21.

Foxall, G. (1997). *Marketing Psychology: The Paradigm in the Wings*. London: Macmillan.

Frankel, Y., Davida, G., Tsiounis, Y., and Yung, M. (1997). "Anonymity control in E-cash systems." In: Hirschfeld, R. (eds), *Financial Cryptography. FC 1997*. Lecture Notes in Computer Science, vol. 1318. Springer, Berlin, Heidelberg.

Gilaninia, S., Fattahi, A., and Mousavian, S. (2011). "Behavioral factors tend to use the internet banking services case study: system (SABA), the Melli Bank, Iran." Ardabil. *International Journal of Business Administration*, 2(3), 173–179.

Giovanis, A. N., Binioris, S., and Polychronopoulos, G. (2012). "An extension of the TAM model with IDT and security/privacy risk in the adoption of Internet banking services in Greece." *EuroMed Journal of Business*, 7(1), 24–53.

Goode, M. and Moutinho, L. (1995). "The effects of free banking on overall satisfaction: the use of automated teller machines." *International Journal of Bank Marketing*, 13(4), 33–40.

Johnston, R. (1997). "Identifying the critical determinants of service quality in retail banking: importance and effect." *International Journal of Bank Marketing*, 15(4), 111–116.

Kalakota, R. and Frei, F. (1997). "Frontiers of online financial services." In Cronin, M. J. (ed.), *Banking and Finance on the Internet* (pp. 19–74). New York, NY: Van Norstrand Reinhold.

Kardaras, D., and Papathanassiou, E. (2001). "Electronic commerce opportunities for improving corporate customer support in banking in Greece." *International Journal of Bank Marketing*, 19(7), 292–298.

Krishna Prasad, K. "A study on multi-phase security solutions to ATM banking systems." *International Journal of Applied Engineering and Management Letters (IJAEML)*, 2(2), 116–126.

Lai, V. S. and Li, H. (2005). "Technology acceptance model for internet banking: an invariance analysis." *Information & Management*, 42(2), 373–386.

LaRose, R. and Atkin, D. (1992). "Audiotext and the re-invention of the telephone as a mass medium." *Journalism Quarterly*, 69(2), 413–421.

Levesque, T. and McDougall, G. H. G. (1996). "Determinants of customer satisfaction in retail banking." *International Journal of Bank Marketing*, 14(7), 12–20.

Martin, J., Chapman, K. K., and Leben, J. (1997). *Asynchronous Transfer Mode: ATM. Architecture and Implementation*. Upper Saddle River, NJ: Prentice Hall PTR.

Mathieson, K. (1991). "Predicting user intentions: comparing the technology acceptance model with the theory of planned behaviour." *Information Systems Research*, 2(3), 173–191.

Mols, N. P. (1998). "The behavioural consequences of PC banking." *International Journal of Bank Marketing*, 16(5), 195–201.

Monahan, J. (1997). "Video banking and beyond. American Bankers Association." *ABA Banking Journal*, S13.

Neelakanta, P. S. (2018). *ATM Telecommunications: Principles and Implementation.* London: CRC Press.

Onyesolu, M. O. and Ezeani, I. M. (2012). "ATM security using fingerprint bio-metric identifier: an investigative study." *International Journal of Advanced Computer Science and Applications*, 3(4), 68–72.

Pikkarainen, T., Pikkarainen, K., Karjaluoto, H., and Pahnila, S. (2004). "Consumer acceptance of online banking: an extension of the technology acceptance model." *Internet Research*, 14, 224–235.

Plouffe, C., Hulland, J., and Vanderbosch, M. (2001). "Richness versus parsimony in modelling technology adoption decision—understanding merchant adop-tion of a smart card-based payment." *Information Systems Research*, 12(2), 208–222.

Salem, M. Z., Baidoun, S., and Walsh, G. (2019). "Factors affecting Palestinian customers' use of online banking services." *International Journal of Bank Marketing*, 37(2), 426–451.

Tarhini, A., El-Masri, M., Ali, M., and Serrano, A. (2016). "Extending the UTAUT model to understand the customers' acceptance and use of internet banking in Lebanon: a structural equation modeling approach." *Information Technology & People*, 29(4), 830–849.

Tilden, M. (1996). "Channel vision." *Retail Banker International*, 28, 12–15.

Tskhadadze, N. (2019). "Use of remote banking technology." In *International Conference Communicative Strategies of Information Society (CSIS, 2018)* (pp. 108–111). Atlantis Press.

Venkatesh, V., and Davis, F. D. (2000). "A theoretical extension of the technology acceptance model: four longitudinal field studies." *Management Science*, 46(2), 186–204.

Vijayan, V. P., Perumal, V., and Shanmugam, B. (1970). "Waves of multimedia banking development." *The Journal of Internet Banking and Commerce*, 9(3), 1970.

Wan, W. W., Luk, C. L., and Chow, C. W. (2005). "Customers' adoption of banking channels in Hong Kong." *International Journal of Bank Marketing*, 23(3), 255–272.

Chapter 3

Banking, Fintech, BigTech: emerging challenges for multimedia adoption

*Mukul[1], Sanjay Taneja[1], Ercan Özen[2], Rakesh Plaha[1]
and Mark Laurence Zammit[3]*

Abstract

There is no denying that technological advancements are transforming the financial services business. Many of the enormous technology companies we associate with 'BigTech' operate in various sectors, but the most prominent are those centred on social media, telecom, Internet search and online retail. In this study, trends and patterns of BigTech entry into emerging markets and developing economies (EMDEs) were analyzed. Also this study depicts the case study of digital payment trends in India and further, presents the driver of BigTech activity in EMDE's, Pros and cons of BigTech firms entering the financial services, opportunities & risks for BigTech firms in EMDE's and the impact of COVID-19 on BigTech firms' activities. After all of us have received our vaccines, we will look back on 2022 as a turning point in our understanding of these goods and their influence on our society. We should be able to raise better questions about corporate policies and practices in the future, even if the economy has irrevocably altered. Some of us may even hurl our phones into a deep ravine and focus our attention and energy on something other than screens, such as attending real-life parties and concerts.

Keywords: Opportunity; Challenges; Banking; Fintech; BigTech; COVID-19

3.1 Introduction

BigTech organisations, which are enormous corporations with well-established technological platforms, are more critical in the financial system and have started to offer financial services (Bassens and Hendrikse, 2022; Gibney, 2022). Growing faster than many of the world's major financial institutions in the last decade, a few BigTech companies now rival or surpass those very same institutions. BigTech companies gain

[1]University School of Business, Chandigarh University, India
[2]Faculty of Applied Sciences, University of Uşak, Turkey
[3]Department of Insurance and Risk Management, University of Malta, Malta

from having large client bases and from analysing their customers' data, which they may use to improve their services. They may leverage this to expand across various industries, including financial services, swiftly. Financial resources are also an advantage since they can frequently obtain cash and finance at cheaper costs than some of the larger financial institutions (Prado and Bauer, 2022; Robertson, 2022).

There is no denying that technological advancements are transforming the financial services business. Many of the enormous technology companies we associate with 'BigTech' operate in various sectors, but the most prominent are those centred on social media, telecom, Internet search and online retail. On every continent, they may be found, as can the majority, if not all, of our member countries (Hind *et al.*, 2022). Three aspects make up the business model of BigTech: (i) the data they already have on consumers, (ii) the sophisticated analytics they employ to understand the demands of their customers further, and (iii) the dependence on powerful network effects, which come from an enormous client-based BigTech companies possess. As network effects drive engagement, user activity, and the collection of even more data, their spread into financial services may happen very fast. In contrast to other Fintech start-ups, BigTech's foray into financial services has taken a different path. To 'reverse' the unbundling, BigTech is using the same new technology that enabled Fintech start-ups to provide partial financial services, such as aggregation and consumer interface services (Usman, 2022). They benefit from cross-subsidization and economies of scale from their size and breadth due to their worldwide customer based on non-financial goods. That puts them in a solid position to take a large chunk of the financial services industry when they begin offering them. This 'bundling' has the potential to be beneficial in several ways. BigTech's may utilise their knowledge of consumer preferences, such as consumer purchasing patterns and credit worthiness, to provide financial services to clients that conventional credit providers may neglect (Norris, 2022; Verdegem, 2022). Financial depth can benefit both a personal and a societal level.

As a result, why should financial authorities be worried about BigTech? If BigTech's non-financial services are to have a broader impact, the cloud services provided by BigTech are a practical case study. Many companies in the financial sector rely on virtualized computing services provided by the cloud to keep their operations running smoothly. From the most important financial institutions to the newest start-ups, all of them are represented here. However, there is considerable dependence on a few critical suppliers. Bank of England estimates that over 70% and 80% of banks and insurers use only two cloud providers for Infrastructure as a Service 'IaaS'. More than two-thirds of cloud-based services worldwide are offered by only two BigTech companies, while four BigTech companies provide the other half. It is easy to see how heavily dependent the financial industry are on BigTech's products and services to function. The collapse of any of these companies, or the failure of a service, might have a considerable effect on markets, customers, and financial stability (Văduva *et al.*, 2022). BigTech may already be 'too-critical-to-fail' in certain areas because of the significance of these services. The financial services market share in most countries has yet to be materialised by Fintech businesses. Consequently, they are not yet systemically important. Regulators face new problems with BigTech. The Financial Stability Board ('FSB'), in its publications on BigTech's possible financial stability concerns, mentioned the following: the activities of these companies, even if they are not systemic in themselves, could still pose a significant financial risk, significantly because they can be rapidly scaled up, and their interconnections with regulated financial entities, such as partnerships to originate and distribute financial products, could magnify these risks (Birch and Bronson, 2022; Bronson and Sengers, 2022; Desai, 2022; Wörsdörfer, 2022). Albeit, as discussed in their paper (Bains *et al.*, 2022), 'BigTech are applying new approaches to existing financial services products and services such as underwriting using big data and are also applying machine learning for their key business decisions, such as pricing and risk management across multiple financial sectors. Incumbent financial firms have also increased their reliance on BigTech firms to host core IT systems (for example, cloud-based services, which have the potential to improve efficiency and security). This rapid and significant expansion of BigTechs in financial services and their interconnectedness with financial service firms are potentially creating new channels of systemic risks' (Bhatnagar, *et al.*, 2022a; Bhatnagar, *et al.*, 2022b, 2023; Dangwal, *et al.*, 2022a, 2022b; Jangir *et al.*, 2023; Özen *et al.*, 2022; Özen and Sanjay, 2022; Singh *et al.*, 2021; Taneja *et al.*, 2022, 2023).

There are unique hurdles for regulators due to these qualities. On top of that, regulators' reaction depends on their country's BigTech industry and the structure and missions of their own institutions and agencies. Regarding the previously stated non-financial service, certain jurisdictions are attempting to reduce the excessive concentration of cloud service providers by placing obligations on their regulated organizations (Hellman, 2022). However, enforcing current outsourcing and third-party provider laws in foreign countries might be challenging. Lock-in risk and vulnerabilities linked to data control and access are highlighted in the FSB's research on cloud services' financial stability implications (Phan *et al.*, 2022).

Additionally, current regulatory frameworks that would typically apply to BigTech concentrate on BigTech's financial operations and aim to govern them directly or via regulated organizations. As sensible as it may appear, tackling the possible stability consequences of BigTech with the idea of 'same activity, same risk, same laws' may prove insufficient. There may be specific activity-based rules imposed on BigTech's financial services, but BigTechs themselves are not usually subject to comprehensive group regulations or monitoring. This might provide BigTechs with a competitive edge – not via innovation and better goods, but rather through the advantages they obtain from a less thorough regulatory environment (Medeiros, 2022). Using the 'same activity, same risk' strategy, incumbent financial institutions may find themselves at a disadvantage, opening the door to arbitrage. Unintended effects may result from several current regulatory frameworks (such as Open Banking), which are meant to encourage competition in the market. As a result, BigTechs can take a more considerable portion of the market. They also flout international regulations that apply to data governance, operational resilience and group-wide hazards but are fragmented by the BigTechs. Regulatory arbitrage, policy loopholes, and a build-up of financial stability concerns across borders are all possibilities in this environment. Regulators have a difficult task in responding to BigTech's financial services development. Regulation in different countries is based on different institutional frameworks and the role of BigTech. BigTech's potential advantages need regulatory safeguards and risk reduction on the part of the international community. BigTech's influence on financial services is still a mystery to most of us (Fuchs *et al.*, 2022).

3.2   Trends and patterns of BigTech entry into emerging markets and developing economies (EMDEs)

Emerging markets and developing economies (EMDEs) have seen a more significant and widespread development of BigTech corporations into financial services than advanced economies ('AEs'). BigTech companies in EMDEs also provide a greater variety of financial services than in AEs. EMDEs' lower financial inclusion levels generate a market for BigTech businesses' services, especially among low-income and rural populations underserved by conventional financial institutions. BigTech firms may fill this market gap. Financial services supplied by BigTech companies may also attract customers in low-income nations. People in EMDEs may also embrace BigTech's use of cutting-edge technology or would have an increased need for services like remittances from outside. BigTech enterprises in EMDEs have been able to provide financial services because of the widespread use of mobile phones and the Internet within these markets. BigTech companies now have the ability to provide financial services to previously underserved clients, for example, owing to a lack of credit history, thanks to this technology and the data it creates. BigTech companies also use consumer data from their primary technology operations to make loan choices (Mest, 2016). Figure 3.1 highlighted the trend of the digital payment in the India from 2015–2019.

The entry into financial services of BigTech in emerging markets has been faster and more far-reaching than in developed countries. Lower levels of financial inclusion, especially among low-income people, are partly to blame for this disparity in financial EMDEs' systems. BigTech enterprises have the opportunity to reach previously

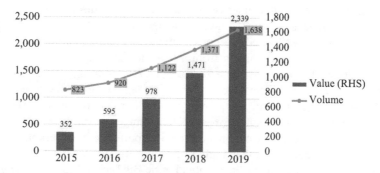

Figure 3.1   Digital payments trend in India: digital payments volume (in crore) and value (in ₹ lakh crore). Source: *RBI Annual Report 2022*

underserved communities as a result of these trends. There has been a dramatic increase in the number of people using mobile payment systems, particularly those linked to social networks, across various nations. Additionally, BigTech enterprises in EMDEs frequently provide more financial services than those in AEs. Several BigTechs in Asia provide lending, insurance, and investment goods through their platforms and established financial institutions. This is especially true in various Asian nations.

3.2.1   A case study of digital payment trends in India

While it is impossible to assess cash payments in each nation effectively, the growth of other digital payments may be reliably tracked. All in all, digital payments in the nation have grown at a compound annual growth rate ('CAGR') of 61% over the previous 5 years in terms of volume and value; this shows that digital payments are becoming more commonplace. Direct debits (ECS, NACH) and credit transfers (NEFT, quick payments (IMPS and UPI) have seen explosive development in digital payments, with CAGRs of 65% and 42%, respectively. Volume and value growth rates for prepaid and stored value wallets and cards were 96% and 78% throughout the study period.

The universal payments interface ('UPI') and card payments are driving digital payment development in India, with banks like HDFC Bank taking the lead. Retail digital payments grew by 70% year-on-year in the fiscal year 2019–2020 despite a near halt during the COVID-19-led lockdown, reaching $520 billion. According to a survey by Morgan Stanley, the percentage of such payments has increased from 5% of GDP 3 years ago to over 20% of GDP today. According to the survey, UPI and card payments are driving this exponential development in digital payment patterns. UPI's share of retail digital payments now stands at roughly 55%, with the survey predicts a further increase in use after WhatsApp launches a global version.

The retail industry is regaining footing as COVID-19 recedes and the economy begins to open up once again. Digital payments have been a significant factor in this recovery. Consumers and businesses alike could continue their business despite the impending lockdown in 2020 because of the convenience of digital payment methods. In 2020–2021, digital transactions accounted for 98.5% of all non-cash retail payments, according to statistics from the Reserve Bank of India ('RBI'). Figure 3.2 depicts the trend of the retail digital payments from 2015–2019 in India.

RBI conducted a pilot study in 2018–2019 to better understand the retail payment behaviours of individuals in six cities: Delhi, Kolkata, Bengaluru, Mumbai, Chennai, and Guwahati. The results showed that convenience was the overwhelming reason for people to switch to digital payments. Aside from making a transaction without waiting in line, convenience has been the main driver for digital payment acceptance.

UPI has been at the forefront of this payments revolution significantly. Even though it only makes up 10% of all retail payments today, this percentage will likely rise several times over in the next few years. The federal government has also begun to promote digital payments due to realising this transition. This year's budget maintained its focus on digital payments, as it did last year. In last year's budget, Rs. 1,500 crore was allotted to promote and develop digital transactions and payment methods in rural and neglected sections of the nation (Chakraborty *et al.*, 2022).

Figure 3.2   Retail digital payments. Source: *RBI Annual Report 2022*

The central bank recently lifted the maximum on e-Rupi vouchers issued by the government to 1 lakh per voucher from 10,000 and permitted one voucher to be used numerous times till it was redeemed entirely. Direct benefit transfers without a bank account are likely to be facilitated.

3.3   Drivers of BigTech activity in EMDEs

Policymakers should closely monitor new markets and educate themselves on the hazards and possibilities they provide. Officials in numerous countries are further regulating Fintech credit systems. There is a never-ending discussion over how to regulate the world's largest digital enterprises, as seen by recent legislative measures in China, the EU, and the United States (McNeill, 2021). As a result, maintaining financial stability and market integrity will need a new trade-off: protecting customer data. Regulatory interventions relating to essential regulatory responsibilities such as client onboarding and improved authorisation procedures have also been emphasised by Fintech businesses. Most Fintech companies have been unable to enhance their primary regulators or supervisory relationship's assistance despite industry calls for more decisive regulatory help. International studies and peer-to-peer learning may teach authorities a lot (Rikap and Lundvall, 2020).

According to market capitalisation, BigTech businesses already exceeded global systemically important financial institutions ('G-SIFIs'). BigTech's financial services have proliferated in numerous countries, notably payments and lending to small- and medium-sized enterprises ('SMEs'). While most BigTech firms begin with payments, often as a support for their 'main' company (e-commerce, advertising, etc.), the sequence of business sectors and the way payments are handled extensively, BigTech activity in finance is driven by:

(a) **Fintechs that are already in place**. Businesses of all types seek new income streams as APIs make it easy to incorporate banking services into any product.
(b) **Scalability**. In order to enhance the use of their financial services offerings, digital companies may already leverage their large user bases.

(c) **Increase in investor interest**. Record-breaking $22.8 billion in financing was obtained by financial technology businesses in Q1 this year, an increase of 98% over the same period in 2014.

(d) **The impact of a data network**. Tech companies have enormous quantities of personal data on their customers. Custom financial products may be created with the use of this technology.

BigTech businesses are disrupting conventional financial institutions by expanding into new markets. There are, however, a variety of other ways to communicate. BigTech companies provide some of the essential third-party services provided by banks (Tran *et al.*, 2022). Amazon Web Services ('AWS') is the largest cloud computing company in the world, serving a broad range of financial institutions with its services. Ali Cloud, a subsidiary of the Ali Group, dominates the Asian cloud service industry, while Microsoft and Google are also significant players. Artificial intelligence and machine learning are now being offered by a slew of BigTech firms to businesses, including financial institutions (Standaert and Muylle, 2022).

One should consider the following for demand side factors:

(a) Demands from customers.
(b) Customers' tastes and preferences.
(c) Demographics.
(d) Put your faith in modern technologies.
(e) Customer satisfaction is our number one priority.

Changing demographics, consumer value, and preferences are all examples of demand-side forces. According to several research and polls, younger generations are more likely to use Fintech and BigTech than older generations. More than half of the people surveyed by EY in 2017 were between the ages of 25 and 34 and between the ages of 35 and 44, respectively, when it came to using Fintech products (41%). It is expected that Fintech acceptance will rise when younger generations join the market since their tastes and expectations are quite different from those of prior generations (Kowalewski *et al.*, 2022).

Speed, convenience, and better user-friendliness are sought-after attributes in all transactions, including financial ones, for today's customers. Millennials have much confidence in technology and IT companies. According to studies, the data misuse incidents may be weakening public confidence in technology as a whole (Kolade *et al.*, 2022). Finally, ethical concerns in their purchasing decisions seem to drive today's customers. Financial technology (e.g., P2P lending) is seen as more socially responsible and beneficial than conventional banking by customers, according to some studies (EY 2017).

The following elements are critical in terms of supply:

(a)   Access to the data.
(b)   The advantage of technology.
(c)   Funding.
(d)   There is a lack of rules.
(e)   Absence of rivals.

Regulation is a crucial supply-side factor influencing Fintech and BigTech market positions. Fintech and BigTech adoption may be helped or hindered by rules, according to growing studies. According to the Cambridge Centre for Alternative Finance (CCAF 2019), countries with less stringent (or more appropriate) banking rules have more significant quantities of various Fintech services or investments. According to the research results, there is little evidence to support the commonly held idea that regulatory arbitrage encourages Fintech adoption. According to researches, countries with superior regulation, the rule of law, anti-corruption, ease of entrance, and profitability of current intermediaries have more alternative financing options available to businesses.

3.4 Pros and cons of BigTech firms entering the financial services

Various modes of engagement exist between BigTech corporations and financial institutions. One such model is partnerships where BigTech firms offer financial institutions technological infrastructure. There are several industries in which BigTech companies compete directly with established financial institutions (Panjwani and De, 2020). Depending on the institution and the market, incumbent financial institutions' reactions to the entrance of BigTech businesses into the financial services industry and the impact on their business models will likely differ (LeBaron *et al.*, 2020).

3.4.1 *Benefits to the financial services industry from BigTech activities*

(a) Convenience is one of the benefits of BigTech to enter into financial services. By integrating financial services into their platforms, such as Uber, Internet businesses want to make their customers' lives simpler. Food delivery and suggestions, car monitoring, and other modes of transportation have all been added to the popular ride-hailing app's repertoire of services and features. As a result of the financial integration, the app would become one of the most comprehensive 'super-apps' on the market (Strelets and Chebanov, 2020).
(b) The supply of financial services has the potential to be made more innovative, diverse, and efficient as a result of these factors.
(c) Partnerships between financial institutions and BigTech businesses are becoming more common. Google's bank accounts will be available via Citibank. This package will also include a credit union from California. Goldman Sachs helped establish Apple's credit card. If Amazon chooses to provide checking accounts in the future, it is allegedly investigating a partnership with J.P. Morgan Chase. As part of a strategy to avoid becoming a bank, these agreements also benefit users since the financial organisations know how to supply these services adequately. Consumers may be more inclined to put their money in the hands of technological companies if they see familiar bank brands affiliated with them (Venkata Appala Naidu and Vedavathi, 2019).

(d) EMDEs, where BigTech enterprises can enhance access to financial services for previously unbanked people, may also benefit from financial inclusion efforts.
(e) BigTech enterprises may also improve financial inclusion and access to previously unexplored areas (Frank, 2020).
(f) With BigTech companies' third-party services, consumers may access previously unattainable technology like artificial intelligence and data analytics.
(g) Adults who do not have bank accounts are referred to as 'unbanked' people. The absence of close financial facilities and the desire to save costs are two common justifications for not having a bank account. When it comes to banking convenience, unbanked people are at a disadvantage (Freeman and Sykes, 2020). For example, people may have to pay their utility bills in cash. Digital accounts like those supplied by BigTech, according to the Milken Institute Review, may aid the unbanked by:
   (I) Providing financial services without the need to go to a physical place.
   (II) Lowering the costs of banking
   (III) As a result of competing with conventional banks, they are more likely to provide relevant services.

For instance, the 'Amazon Cash programme enables customers to purchase on Amazon after depositing cash at partner businesses and kiosks', as noted in the article.

3.4.2 Risks associated with the BigTech firms to enter financial services

(a) Financial stability may be jeopardised due to the actions of comprehensive technology businesses.
(b) There is a risk that the competition from BigTech businesses would weaken financial institutions' capacity to weather financial storms.
(c) Hazards arise from operational risks such as those caused by lapses in governance, risk, and process controls, as well as from mismatches in maturity and liquidity levels.
(d) Financial services may in the future be dominated by a few BigTech corporations rather than a wide range of providers. The collapse of these companies might have a significant impact on the economy.

3.5 Technological growth: opportunities & risks for BigTech firms in EMDEs

It is still early days for 'big technologies' in financial services, but given their scale and client base, these businesses have the potential to impact the industry significantly. This edited speech offers a preliminary evaluation of the advantages and disadvantages and a list of issues that need more investigation.

The Bank for International Settlement's annual general assembly in Basel, Switzerland, recently discussed the giant digital companies. The conversation focused on their ability to enter the financial services industry even though each of their companies had previously built solid foundations (Alpert, 2020).

The risk–benefit equation introduces new risks and rewards by introducing large internet companies into banking. Financial stability and consumer protection in new contexts may be handled by modifying or extending current regulations. However, there are several noteworthy additions. The financial statute, competition policy, and data privacy regulation must be integrated into public policy regarding big technology in the financial sector (Fraser, 2020).

3.5.1   It is the 'DNA' of big tech's business strategy

Direct user-to-user interactions are a vital part of the business strategy of huge digital companies. The collection and storage of user data is a critical by-product of their operation. The information is then used to provide various services that utilize natural network effects, resulting in further user engagement. Data generated by increased user engagement is then sent back into the system – the so-called 'DNA' (data, network, and activities) loop.

Self-reinforcing DNA loops are standard. The more data there is, the greater the network effects, generating even more data. Major IT companies with well-established platforms have an advantage in the financial services industry (Eleodor, 2019).

The nature of their current platform dictates the nature of their competitive advantage. Data from e-commerce platforms may be combined with financial and consumer habits information to provide a wealth of knowledge on the habits of merchants and purchasers. SMEs and consumers' credit scores may benefit from including these data points in credit scoring algorithms. There is a wealth of information on people and their interests, as well as their social media networks, at the disposal of enormous tech companies. Google and other search engines have a large user base, so they may deduce their preferences based on what people look for online. If you are looking for a financial product, you may utilize social media and search engines like Google and Bing as a marketplace for third-party financial services, such as insurance (Cohen and Mello, 2019; Popkin, 2019; Smyth, 2019).

3.5.2   Access to financial services and big data

It is possible to open financial services to those previously excluded because of these benefits. Let us look at the case of borrowing. Lenders spend a lot of time and money screening applicants for creditworthiness. Audited financial statements are rare among SMEs in emerging markets. A significant portion of the population lives in areas where banks do not have a physical presence. Hence, they are unable to access official financial services. In this type of environment, great technologies are at their best. They do not have to worry about a lack of knowledge since they can get it from their already-existing platforms (Mayer-Schönberger and Ramge, 2018).

The expense of monitoring and enforcing loans is another barrier to lending. To mitigate the risk of default, banks often ask borrowers to put up collateral. Big IT companies have a unique ability to handle the challenges of surveillance and enforcement. Deducting sales income payments from a large IT company's payment account may be relatively simple. Furthermore, if a significant tech company holds sway, the mere prospect of being demoted or excluded from its network will be enough to punish a borrower.

Unlike banks, major tech companies' supply of corporate loans does not seem to correspond with asset values as much. This might be a contributing factor. On the other hand, the availability of credit from large technology lenders is significantly less susceptible to the housing market than the credit choices of banks (Piore, 2018; Tréguer, 2018).

3.5.3 Regulating the financial sector

BigTech has numerous advantages. Costs, on the other hand, are an issue. In some instances, the costs are related to re-emerging previous regulatory difficulties in new contexts. In this scenario, the solution necessitates a revision of the rules to reflect the new context. A rethink of the rules will be essential if such adaption quickly outruns the present text of the requirements. The risk-based approach should be followed, and the regulatory toolset should be appropriately adjusted (Bassens and Hendrikse, 2022).

In relation to payments, large technologies may already be systemically significant entities. As payment businesses, prominent digital companies in China have a similar function in money market fund (MMF) products, where consumers save their payment balances. These MMF's, in turn, invest primarily in unsecured bank deposits. Bank deposits and interbank loans with a maturity of fewer than 30 days make up around half of the assets, introducing systemically crucial links between BigTech and the banking system. Deposit withdrawals might be a conduit for a substantial redemption shock to reach the banking system. The Chinese government has responded to these concerns by enacting additional regulations, including a limit on quick redemptions and requiring all payment companies to clear on a single, public platform (Kapsis, 2020; Singleton and Reveley, 2020).

3.5.4 Power in the market and rivalry

In addition to conventional financial regulations, BigTech brings in additional factors. The DNA loop, which explains the advantages of BigTech, also carries the price of market dominance and data privacy. A confined ecosystem limits rivals' ability to construct competing platforms and challenge the incumbents. Major platforms may strengthen their positions by increasing entry hurdles or framing their platforms as 'bottlenecks' for various services, which might favour their goods at the expense of other suppliers. Cross-subsidization and product bundling are two different strategies that might restrict competition even further. For financial regulators, these are challenges more recognisable to competition authorities and economists who study industrial organisations (Katz, 2021).

Data is a second, equally vital dimension. The decentralised (or Coasian) method, which gives consumers ownership of their data, is one solution to the issue. A customer might then choose which data-sharing and selling service providers they want to work with (Srivastava, 2021). The DNA feedback loop, on the other hand, makes it challenging to implement the decentralized Coasian technique smoothly. In addition to their financial services, BigTech companies may gather extra data from their ecosystems in social networking, search engines, and e-commerce. Big IT companies will be able to use more data better due to the increased returns that data has as it grows in breadth and size. As a result, well-designed restrictions on the use of data may help level the playing field for competitors. Additional privacy laws, while providing limited access to specific data, might improve effective competition by reducing the DNA loop. Open banking policies throughout the globe and the European Union's General Data Protection Regulation ('GDPR') are two examples of this. Through open banking, licenced third-party financial service providers may access client data directly. These organisations, in everyday practice, also establish technical standards for application programming interfaces. Both policies might be considered measures to encourage increased effective market competition since they include the transfer of data ownership from giant tech companies to users (Cohen and Mello, 2019; Eleodor, 2019; Smyth, 2019).

But some of the new rules also restrict what may be shared about you. Open banking rules limit the data that may be transmitted selectively. Access to the information is likewise prohibited. Customers must also provide permission to use their personal data under the GDPR. Both regulations have hampered large IT firms' attempts to enter the financial sector (Andrews, 2019; Popkin, 2019). Not only does GDPR regulate the use of personal data but also regulates the original acquisition and transmission of personal data by companies and to third-parties. Regulatory fines due to breach of GDPR regulations are exorbitantly high up to 4% of a company's annual turnover. Amazon Europe was in 2021 fined an exorbitant €746 million by Luxembourg's National Commission for Data Protection (CNPD), the largest fine to date, via a complaint by French regulators alleging that Amazon (among other BigTech companies such as Apple, Facebook, etc.) had manipulated customers for commercial means by choosing what advertising and information they would receive (statista.com)

3.5.5 Coordination of policy and the need for education

The public policy approach must be unified in light of the many new problems. First and foremost, there is a pressing need for improved coordination among national agencies, particularly those in charge of competition, financial regulation, and data protection. Currently, their missions and methods are not always aligned.

There is also a need for international collaboration on norms and standards as the digital economy spreads across boundaries. In light of Facebook's recent plan to develop a digital currency called Libra, international cooperation is becoming more critical.

Innovation is here to stay, and a lot of it will positively impact our lives and economies. With those advantages firmly in mind, some degree of financial system upheaval and structural change should not just be allowed but desired. On the other hand, we should be extra cautious regarding disruption for the sake of trouble. Clear thinking is more important than ever to maximise the advantages of financial inclusion and efficiency while minimising the hazards.

3.6 Venture capital from EMDEs in facilitating BigTech firms

3.6.1 *Meaning of venture capital*

When financiers contribute money to start-ups and small-scale firms that they sense have the capability for long-term realization, they are called as venture capitalists ('VCs'). Investors, investment banks, and other financial organisations often provide venture capital (Esposito *et al.*, 2022; Prado and Bauer, 2022; Shachmurove, 2021). Although money is one way to communicate it, managerial or technical know-how may also be donated. Venture capitalists are often interested in companies that have the potential for rapid development or that have already seen rapid expansion and are poised for further growth. The possibility of above-average profits is an appealing pay-out, despite the risk for investors who put money into the venture. Venture capital is becoming an increasingly popular and, in some cases, a mandatory source of funding for start-ups with little to no operational experience (under 2 years), particularly for those without access to capital markets, bank loans, or other debt instruments. Another disadvantage is that investors often have a voice in how the firm is run since they get stock in the company due to their investment (Amona *et al.*, 2018; Corsi and Prencipe, 2019; Lins, 2019).

3.6.2 *Venture capitalists' impact on BigTech management*

Some of the most successful high-tech businesses, such as Digital Equipment, Apple, Intel, and Lotus Development, have been funded by venture capitalists since the late 1970s. A one-hundred-fold rise in only 8 years has seen the venture capital invested in high-tech companies soar from $39 million in 1977 to over $4.1 billion in 1985. In the financial world, venture capitalists focus on high-risk equity investments. Many venture capitalists focus on rising high-tech enterprises that cannot start or continue growth due to limited financial resources. These businesses, unable to acquire money from traditional sources like commercial banks or the public market due to a lack of collateral or adequate cash flow, turn to venture capital as an alternative funding source (Hain and Jurowetzki, 2018).

Investment banks, like venture capitalists, act as a link between potential investors and enterprises needing funding. However, a venture capitalist is generally far more engaged in the firm than a standard commercial banker, both in terms of time and money. Over half of the stock in a venture capital firm may be retained by the investors, who then become equal partners in the company with the founders. Consequently, venture capitalists may significantly impact the company's management in addition to their position as financial intermediaries (Richstein and Lins, 2018a, 2018b). Venture capitalists, for example, may provide marketing, business strategy, and CEO recruiting assistance and suggestions to high-tech start-ups. Venture capitalists may also attend board meetings and significant events to carefully monitor management choices relating to bank loans, receivables financing, R&D and resource allocations (Bertoni *et al.*, 2015; Colombo and Shafi, 2016).

Regarding financing, venture capitalists are gatekeepers who frequently select whether companies will obtain financial support; if the financing is granted, they may become significant players in managing the future investment initiative ('FII'). Eight hypotheses are derived from this study's theoretical framework on the link between venture capitalists and high-tech company management. We also offer results from exploratory qualitative field research to test the validity of these claims (Colombo *et al.*, 2014; Primack, 2014).

3.6.3 The BigTech firm and the dependency perspective

Entrepreneurs in the high-tech industry have a concept that has the potential to be commercially viable. Most of the time, they have the requisite technological know–how to carry out the research and development required to make the concept a reality. In addition to funding, venture capitalists may provide their experience and contacts in the financial and marketing sectors, as well as access to their personal networks. Venture capitalists are prepared to risk their money and their experience in order to make risky investments with the expectation of a large return. Even while most BigTech companies that started out with venture capital fail in the marketplace, those who succeed often boost the value of the investment by 800% when they go public (Grilli and Murtinu, 2014; Jing, 2014).

While the high-tech entrepreneur accepts the venture capitalist's financial assistance and management advice, they must give up a significant portion of the company's equity, and the company's top management may also have obligations to respond positively to the venture capitalist's cues. Having a stake in a large IT company offers venture capitalists a lot of power and the ability to influence management. The fact that just one-third of one percent of all high-tech company concepts are ever accepted and obtain money from venture capitalists provides venture capitalists enormous influence since other sources of finance are difficult to come by. Because of the way venture capitalists spend their money, they may have a tremendous impact. Investors do not put down the whole amount of money all at once and instead spread it out over time (Bertoni *et al.*, 2013; Wang *et al.*, 2013). This is a risk management tactic to effectively manage their investment portfolios. Even if the business survives the first few years and goes public, a venture capitalist's stock position may not be fully liquidated until 6 months to a year after the company's IPO, potentially longer. Taking on advisory responsibilities for the investee firm might help venture capitalists preserve their investment. Otherwise, they will have to bear the costs of other people's labour and risk their whole investment if the venture capitalists do not assist to manage the BigTech business (Ozmel *et al.*, 2013; Zhou, 2012).

3.7 Impact of COVID-19 on BigTech firms' activities

Not all sectors were affected equally by the epidemic. Large IT businesses were ahead of the curve when governments started using emergency lockdowns as a mitigating factor to the pandemic. Employees were given the green light to work from home weeks before most other firms. For many in the IT industry, it was not a big deal: because they pioneered the use of videoconferencing and digital collaboration technologies, their employees were well-versed in their usage (Norris, 2022; Zeng *et al.*, 2020).

New and well-established platforms may now be used more widely and quickly thanks to COVID-19, which has ushered in a new era of digital advancement. BigTech (the leading information technology corporations) and digital enterprises generally fared better in the short and medium term in this unprecedented crisis than the rest of the economies, despite substantial disparities. As a result of their efforts, many of these companies have helped to speed up the pace of digital transformation by ensuring that products and services are available to most people. The problem is that not all platforms and digital companies have responded similarly; some are on the verge of bankruptcy (Kshetri, 2020; Storeng and de Bengy Puyvallée, 2021).

For the rest of us, our routines had to change. Social networking, Amazon.com, and DoorDash were formerly seen as conveniences or occasional luxuries, but they quickly became essential. We relied on Amazon to purchase things we could not obtain in a shop since it was the only option. For a long time, the only method to get food from a restaurant was to order food delivery. In order to view individuals who were not in our closed social circle, we relied on Facebook Inc. and Instagram. Zoom Video Communications Inc. has supplanted the conference room at work and other places where people congregate (such as bars and living rooms) (Aamir and Atsan, 2020; Stamolampros and Korfiatis, 2018; Tuma *et al.*, 2020).

An inflationary risk on goods is being created by COVID-19's influence on the IT industry. An increase in remote working and more attention on the value chain has resulted from the disruptive nature of the market. The possible decrease in carbon emissions may also lead to a renewed interest in sustainable practises (Banga *et al.*, 2022).

The shift was much more pronounced for those in charge of a company. It is not enough for stores to depend on foot traffic, take just cash, or refuse to provide updates online. New customers and payments rapidly became the sole means of attracting new consumers and being paid by them over the Internet (Davari *et al.*, 2022).

Technology CEOs have long aspired to build a future like this for us, and their profit reports demonstrate this. There has been a 42% increase in the S&P 500 over the past year, but several technology businesses have done much better. Twitter Inc. (increased 10% in the last year) and Snap Inc. (up 409% in the previous year) have seen their user engagement surge. The Christmas season was a huge success for Amazon (up 68%). An increase of 68% in revenue for Google's parent Alphabet Inc. Zoom (up 205%) saw its revenue more than treble in the most recent quarter.

Additionally, tech businesses could grow during this period because they were unwilling to sit back and collect their money. Facebook took advantage of the year to make a foray into the e-commerce sector, a move that has never been successful on the platform. As a result of increasing demand, Instacart Inc. changed its business strategy and quadrupled its value in only five months. It is currently considering going public this year, which would be great for the company. Amazon became one of the world's biggest employers, taking on tens of thousands of new employees.

However, the IT industry was placed under the spotlight at this time. Even though IT businesses have become lifelines for many, they are often unreliable and unable to tackle all of the issues that arise due to their size. Amazon and their employees contracting COVID-19 in their warehouses, Google was charged with institutional racism, and Zoom had to deal with security difficulties due to the proliferation of health misinformation on Facebook. Amazon, Apple, Facebook, and Google were the focus of a 16-month congressional probe that concluded in October. The Federal Trade Commission (FTC) has filed a lawsuit against Facebook, alleging it has monopolistic power. The Department of Justice also sued Google for doing the same thing.

After all of us have received our vaccines, we will look back on 2022 as a turning point in our understanding of these goods and their influence on our society. We should be able to raise better questions about corporate policies and practices in the future, even if the economy has irrevocably altered. Some of us may even hurl our phones into a deep ravine and focus our attention and energy on something other than screens, such as attending real-life parties and concerts.

References

Aamir, S., and Atsan, N. (2020). The trend of multisided platforms (MSPs) in the travel industry: reintermediation of travel agencies (TAs) and global distribution systems (GDSs). *Journal of Tourism Futures*, 6(3), 271–279. https://doi.org/10.1108/JTF-10-2019-0121

Alpert, D. (2020). Beyond request-and-respond: why data access will be insufficient to tame big tech. *Columbia Law Review*, 120(5), 1215–1254. https://www.scopus.com/inward/record.uri?eid=2-s2.0-85088558377&partnerID=40&md5=6178fc88eef3dc03ca352eb49b2d9657

Amona, D., Gyoshev, S., and Islam, N. (2018). Exit performance of venture capital backed high-tech start-ups. In *2018 IEEE Technology and Engineering Management Conference, TEMSCON 2018*. https://doi.org/10.1109/TEMSCON.2018.8488455

Andrews, L. (2019). Facebook, the media and democracy: BigTech, small state? In *Facebook, the Media and Democracy: Big Tech, Small State?* Taylor and Francis. https://doi.org/10.4324/9780429466410

Bains P, Sugimoto N, and Wilson C. (2022). *BigTech in Financial Services: Regulatory Approaches and Architecture. International Monetary Fund*, https://www.elibrary.imf.org/view/journals/063/2022/002/063.2022. issue-002-en.xml

Banga, I., Paul, A., and France, K. (2022). E.Co.Tech-electrochemical handheld breathalyzer COVID sensing technology. *Scientific Reports*, 12(1), 4370. https://doi.org/10.1038/s41598-022-08321-x

Bassens, D. and Hendrikse, R. (2022). Asserting Europe's technological sovereignty amid American platform finance: countering financial sector dependence on Big Tech? *Political Geography*, 97, 102648. https://doi.org/10.1016/j.polgeo.2022.102648

Bertoni, F., Croce, A., and Guerini, M. (2013). The effectiveness of public venture capital in supporting the investments of European young high-tech companies. In *Entrepreneurial Business and Society: Frontiers in European Entrepreneurship Research*. Edward Elgar Publishing Ltd. https://www.scopus.com/inward/record.uri?eid=2-s2.0-85089640131&partnerID=40&md5=ce4b17ba7bb9042c703532f96bc522e7

Bertoni, F., Croce, A., and Guerini, M. (2015). Venture capital and the investment curve of young high-tech companies. *Journal of Corporate Finance, 35*, 159–176. https://doi.org/10.1016/j.jcorpfin.2015.08.012

Bhatnagar, M., Özen, E., Taneja, S., Grima, S., and Rupeika-Apoga, R. (2022a). The dynamic connectedness between risk and return in the fintech market of India: evidence using the GARCH-M approach. *Risks, 10*(11), 209. https://doi.org/10.3390/risks10110209

Bhatnagar, M., Taneja, S., and Özen, E. (2022b). A wave of green start-ups in India— The study of green finance as a support system for sustainable entrepreneurship. *Green Finance, 4*(2), 253–273. https://doi.org/10.3934/gf.2022012

Bhatnagar, M., Taneja, S., Kumar, P., and Özen, E. (2023). Does financial education act as a catalyst for SME competitiveness. *International Journal of Education Economics and Development, 1*(1), 1. https://doi.org/10.1504/ijeed.2023.10053629

Bhatnagar, M., Taneja, S., and Rupeika-Apoga, R. (2023). Demystifying the effect of the news (shocks) on crypto market volatility. *Journal of Risk and Financial Management, 16*(2), 136. https://doi.org/10.3390/jrfm16020136

Birch, K. and Bronson, K. (2022). Big Tech. *Science as Culture, 31*, 1–14. https://doi.org/10.1080/09505431.2022.2036118

Bronson, K., and Sengers, P. (2022). Big Tech meets big ag: Diversifying epistemologies of data and power. *Science as Culture, 31*(1), 15–28. https://doi.org/10.1080/09505431.2021.1986692

Chakraborty, B., Chatterjee, M., and Bhattacharjee, T. (2022). Impact of analyst report on the behavior of retail investors: a study during COVID-19 in India. *Journal of Financial Reporting and Accounting*. Ahead-of Print. https://doi.org/10.1108/JFRA-10-2021-0310

Cohen, I. G. and Mello, M. M. (2019). Big Data, Big Tech, and protecting patient privacy. *JAMA – Journal of the American Medical Association, 322*(12), 1141–1142. https://doi.org/10.1001/jama.2019.11365

Colombo, M. G., Piva, E., and Rossi-Lamastra, C. (2014). The sensitivity of high-tech entrepreneurial ventures' employment to a sales contraction in a negative growth scenario: the moderating role of venture capital financing. *Managerial and Decision Economics, 35*(2), 73–87. https://doi.org/10.1002/mde.2645

Colombo, M. G. and Shafi, K. (2016). The impact of patenting on the size of high-tech firms: the role of venture capital and product market regulation. *Economia e Politica Industriale, 43*(1), 85–103. https://doi.org/10.1007/s40812-015-0023-4

Corsi, C. and Prencipe, A. (2019). High-tech entrepreneurial firms' innovation in different institutional settings. Do venture capital and private equity have complementary or substitute effects? *Industry and Innovation, 26*(9), 1023–1074. https://doi.org/10.1080/13662716.2018.1561358

Dangwal, A., Kaur, S., Taneja, S., and Özen, E. (2022a). A bibliometric analysis of green tourism based on the Scopus platform. In J. Kaur, P. Jindal, and A. Singh (Eds.) (eds.) , *Developing Relationships, Personalization, and Data Herald in Marketing 5.0* (pp. 242–255). Hershey, PA: IGI Global. https://doi.org/10.4018/978-1-6684-4496-2.ch015

Dangwal, A., Taneja, S., Özen, E., Todorovic, I., and Grima, S. (2022b). Abridgement of renewables: it's potential and contribution to India's GDP. *International Journal of Sustainable Development and Planning, 17*(8), 2357–2363. https://doi.org/doi.org/10.18280/ijsdp.170802

Davari, D., Vayghan, S., Jang, S. S., and Erdem, M. (2022). Hotel experiences during the COVID-19 pandemic: high-touch versus high-tech. *International Journal of Contemporary Hospitality Management, 34*(4), 1312–1330. https://doi.org/10.1108/IJCHM-07-2021-0919

Desai, K. (2022). Facebook / GIPHY Merger – the end of Big Tech's spending spree? *European Competition and Regulatory Law Review, 6*(1), 85–91. https://doi.org/10.21552/core/2022/1/13

Eleodor, D. (2019). Big tech, big competition problem? *Quality – Access to Success, 20*, 49–57. https://www.scopus.com/inward/record.uri?eid=2-s2.0-85073394515&partnerID=40&md5=be79ed1e98bab48e5ed4af7d656da072

Esposito, C., Gortan, M., Testa, L., *et al.* (2022). Can you always reap what you sow? Network and functional data analysis of venture capital investments in health-tech companies. *Studies in Computational Intelligence, 1015*, 744–755. https://doi.org/10.1007/978-3-030-93409-5_61

Frank, L. (2020). Boundedly rational users and the fable of break-ups: why breaking-up big tech companies probably will not promote competition from behavioural economics perspective. *World Competition, 43*(3), 1–12. https://www.scopus.com/inward/record.uri?eid=2-s2.0-85095678614&partnerID=40&md5=41978d40449ce28e53fc9bf3bd3da48c

Fraser, M. (2020). Big trouble for Big Tech. *New Labor Forum, 29*(1), 98–100. https://doi.org/10.1177/1095796019891155

Freeman, W. C. and Sykes, J. B. (2020). Antitrust and "big tech." In *Key Congressional Reports for September 2019: Part VII.* Nova Science Publishers, Inc. https://www.scopus.com/inward/record.uri?eid=2-s2.0-85089334934&partnerID=40&md5=75e715eb446d87c70eb80a93a21cae14

Fuchs, M., Dannenberg, P., and Wiedemann, C. (2022). Big Tech and labour resistance at amazon. *Science as Culture, 31*(1), 29–43. https://doi.org/10.1080/09505431.2021.1937095

Gibney, E. (2022). Open-source language AI challenges big tech's models. *Nature, 606*(7916), 850–851. https://doi.org/10.1038/d41586-022-01705-z

Grilli, L. and Murtinu, S. (2014). Government, venture capital and the growth of European high-tech entrepreneurial firms. *Research Policy, 43*(9), 1523–1543. https://doi.org/10.1016/j.respol.2014.04.002

Hain, D. S. and Jurowetzki, R. (2018). Local competence building and international venture capital in low-income countries: exploring foreign high-tech investments in Kenya's Silicon Savanna. *Journal of Small Business and Enterprise Development, 25*(3), 447–482. https://doi.org/10.1108/JSBED-03-2017-0092

Hellman, J. (2022). Big Tech's 'Voracious Appetite,' or entrepreneurs who dream of acquisition? Regulation and the interpenetration of corporate scales. *Science as Culture, 31*(1), 149–161. https://doi.org/10.1080/09505431.2021.2000597

Hind, S., Kanderske, M., and van der Vlist, F. (2022). Making the car "Platform Ready": How Big Tech is driving the platformization of automobility. *Social Media and Society, 8*(2), 1–13. https://doi.org/10.1177/20563051221098697

Jangir, K., Sharma, V., Taneja, S., and Rupeika-Apoga, R. (2023). The moderating effect of perceived risk on users' continuance intention for FinTech services. *Journal of Risk and Financial Management, 16*(1), 21. https://doi.org/10.3390/jrfm16010021

Jing, H. (2014). Dynamic relevance of high-tech industry and venture capital of China. *Information Technology Journal, 13*(3), 566–571. https://doi.org/10.3923/itj.2014566.571

Kapsis, I. (2020). A truly future-oriented legal framework for fintech in the EU. *European Business Law Review, 31*(3), 475–514. https://www.scopus.com/inward/record.uri?eid=2-s2.0-85100652004&partnerID=40&md5=b50404735f1d025c106af24f447aebc2

Katz, M. L. (2021). Big Tech mergers: innovation, competition for the market, and the acquisition of emerging competitors. *Information Economics and Policy, 54*, 100883. https://doi.org/10.1016/j.infoecopol.2020.100883

Kolade, O., Adepoju, D., and Adegbile, A. (2022). Blockchains and the disruption of the sharing economy value chains. *Strategic Change, 31*(1), 137–145. https://doi.org/10.1002/jsc.2483

Kowalewski, O., Pisany, P., and Ślązak, E. (2022). Digitalization and data, institutional quality and culture as drivers of technology-based credit providers. *Journal of Economics and Business.* https://doi.org/10.1016/j.jeconbus.2022.106069

Kshetri, N. (2020). COVID-19 meets Big Tech. *Computer, 53*(8), 10–13. https://doi.org/10.1109/MC.2020.2996698

LeBaron, G., Mügge, D., Best, J., and Hay, C. (2020). Blind spots in IPE: marginalized perspectives and neglected trends in contemporary capitalism. *Review of International Political Economy, 28*(2), 283–294. https://doi.org/10.1080/09692290.2020.1830835

Lins, E. (2019). When do subsidies facilitate high-tech firms' access to venture capital? An examination of cross-national and national grants. *International Journal of Globalisation and Small Business, 10*(3), 191–209. https://doi.org/10.1504/IJGSB.2019.100119

Mayer-Schönberger, V. and Ramge, T. (2018). A big choice for big tech: share data or suaer the consequences. *Foreign Affairs, 97*(5), 48–54. https://www.scopus.com/inward/record.uri?eid=2-s2.0-85055448754&partnerID=40&md5=78380aaf1e9410fd5e7f418b9b977d3d

McNeill, D. (2021). Urban geography 1: 'Big tech' and the reshaping of urban space. *Progress in Human Geography, 45*(5), 1311–1319. https://doi.org/10.1177/03091325211021945

Medeiros, B. (2022). "There's no way Abraham Lincoln could work at Google": Fox News and the Politics of Breaking Up Big Tech. *Journal of Communication Inquiry, 46*(1), 39–59. https://doi.org/10.1177/01968599211039211

Mest, C. E. (2016). Conference covers hospitality's four biggest tech trends. *Hotel Management, 231*(11), 39. https://www.scopus.com/inward/record.uri?eid=2-s2.0-84999048201&partnerID=40&md5=31ed9724f3bdf79a196ad54c56c7faad

Mukul, Özen, E., and Taneja, S. (2022). Critical evaluation of management of NPA/NPL in emerging and advanced economies: a study in context of India. *Yalova Sosyal Bilimler Dergisi, 12*(2), 99–111. https://dergipark.org.tr/en/pub/yalovasosbil/issue/72655/1143214

Norris, T. (2022). Educational futures after COVID-19: Big tech and pandemic profiteering versus education for democracy. *Policy Futures in Education.* https://doi.org/10.1177/14782103221080265

Özen, E. and Sanjay, T. (2022). Empirical analysis of the effect of foreign trade in computer and communication services on economic growth in India. *Journal of Economics and Business Issues, 2*(2), 24–34. https://doi.org/https://jebi-academic.org/index.php/jebi/article/view/41

Ozmel, U., Robinson, D. T., and Stuart, T. E. (2013). Strategic alliances, venture capital, and exit decisions in early stage high-tech firms. *Journal of Financial Economics, 107*(3), 655–670. https://doi.org/10.1016/j.jfineco.2012.09.009

Panjwani, M., and De, S. (2020). Study of cloud security in hyper-scalers. In *Proceedings of the 7th International Conference on Computing for Sustainable Global Development, INDIACom 2020,* pp. 29–34. https://doi.org/10.23919/INDIACom49435.2020.9083727

Phan, T., Goldenfein, J., Mann, M., and Kuch, D. (2022). Economies of virtue: the circulation of 'Ethics' in Big Tech. *Science as Culture, 31*(1), 121–135. https://doi.org/10.1080/09505431.2021.1990875

Piore, A. (2018). No, big tech didn't make us. *Technology Review, 121*(5), 18–21. https://www.scopus.com/inward/record.uri?eid=2-s2.0-85052871965&partnerID=40&md5=688a19b2fe00b6d2bf796fa0722e49de

Popkin, G. (2019). How scientists can team up with big tech. *Nature, 565*(7741), 665–667. https://doi.org/10.1038/d41586-019-00290-y

Prado, T. S. and Bauer, J. M. (2022). Big Tech platform acquisitions of start-ups and venture capital funding for innovation. *Information Economics and Policy, 59,* 100973. https://doi.org/10.1016/j.infoecopol.2022.100973

Primack, D. (2014). Venture capital will thrive even if tech IPOs don't. *Fortune, 169*(1), 20. https://www.scopus.com/inward/record.uri?eid=2-s2.0-84892635387&partnerID=40&md5=80c82dec141f2920ddb866a9b06f03e3

Richstein, R. and Lins, E. (2018a). Venture capital for German high-tech new ventures: disentangling the role of human capital for funding success. *International Journal of Entrepreneurship and Small Business, 33*(1), 88–111. https://doi.org/10.1504/IJESB.2018.088682

Richstein, R. and Lins, E. (2018b). Venture capital for German high-tech new ventures: disentangling the role of human capital for funding success. *International Journal of Entrepreneurship and Small Business, 33*(1), 88–111. https://doi.org/10.1504/IJESB.2018.10009490

Rikap, C. and Lundvall, B.-Å. (2020). Big tech, knowledge predation and the implications for development. *Innovation and Development*, *12*, 389–416. https://doi.org/10.1080/2157930X.2020.1855825

Robertson, V. H. S. E. (2022). Antitrust, Big Tech, and democracy: a research agenda. *Antitrust Bulletin*, *67*(2), 259–279. https://doi.org/10.1177/0003603X221082749

Shachmurove, Y. (2021). Clean-tech venture capital investment in the United States, 1995–2020 [Inversión de capital riesgo en tecnología limpia en Estados Unidos, 1995–2020]. *Estudios de Economia Aplicada*, *39*(3), 5574. https://doi.org/10.25115/EEA.V39I3.5574

Singh, V., Taneja, S., Singh, V., Singh, A., and Paul, H. L. (2021). Online advertising strategies in Indian and Australian e-commerce companies: a comparative study. In A. Singh (ed.), *Big Data Analytics for Improved Accuracy, Efficiency, and Decision Making in Digital Marketing* (pp. 124–138). Hershey, PA: IGI Global. https://doi.org/10.4018/978-1-7998-7231-3.ch009

Singleton, J. and Reveley, J. (2020). How exceptional is Australian financial sector misconduct? The Hayne Royal Commission revisited. *Law and Financial Markets Review*, *14*(2), 77–83. https://doi.org/10.1080/17521440.2020.1759219

Smyth, S. M. (2019). The Facebook conundrum: Is it time to usher in a new era of regulation for big tech? *International Journal of Cyber Criminology*, *13*(2), 578–595. https://doi.org/10.5281/zenodo.3718955

Srivastava, S. (2021). Algorithmic governance and the international politics of Big Tech. In *Perspectives on Politics*. Cambridge University Press. https://doi.org/10.1017/S1537592721003145

Stamolampros, P. and Korfiatis, N. (2018). Exploring the behavioral drivers of review valence: the direct and indirect effects of multiple psychological distances. *International Journal of Contemporary Hospitality Management*, *30*(10), 3083–3099. https://doi.org/10.1108/IJCHM-04-2017-0239

Standaert, W. and Muylle, S. (2022). Framework for open insurance strategy: insights from a European study. *Geneva Papers on Risk and Insurance: Issues and Practice*, *47*(3), 643–668. https://doi.org/10.1057/s41288-022-00264-8

Storeng, K. T. and de Bengy Puyvallée, A. (2021). The Smartphone pandemic: how Big Tech and public health authorities partner in the digital response to Covid-19. *Global Public Health*, *16*(8–9), 1482–1498. https://doi.org/10.1080/17441692.2021.1882530

Strelets, I. A. and Chebanov, S. V. (2020). Digitalization of world trade: scope, forms, implications. *World Economy and International Relations*, *64*(1), 15–25. https://doi.org/10.20542/0131-2227-2020-64-1-15-25

Taneja, S., Bhatnagar, M., Kumar, P., and Rupeika-Apoga, R. (2023). India's Total Natural Resource Rents (NRR) and GDP: an augmented Autoregressive Distributed Lag (ARDL) bound test. *Journal of Risk and Financial Management*, *16*(2), 91. https://doi.org/doi.org/10.3390/jrfm16020091

Taneja, S., Jaggi, P., Jewandah, S., and Özen, E. (2022). Role of social inclusion in sustainable urban developments: an analyse by PRISMA technique. *International Journal of Design and Nature and Ecodynamics*, *17*(6), 937–942. https://doi.org/10.18280/ijdne.170615

Taneja, S., Kaur, S., and Özen, E. (2022). Using green finance to promote global growth in a sustainable way. *International Journal of Green Economics, 16* (3), 246–257. https://doi.org/10.1504/ijge.2022.10052887

Taneja, S. and Özen, E. (2023). To analyze the relationship between bank's green financing and environmental performance. *International Journal of Electronic Finance, 1*(1), 1. https://doi.org/10.1504/ijef.2023.10050554

Tran, L. Q. T., Phan, D. T., Herdon, M., and Kovacs, L. (2022). Assessing the digital transformation in two banks: case study in Hungary. *Agris On-Line Papers in Economics and Informatics, 14*(2), 121–134. https://doi.org/ 10.7160/aol.2022.140210

Tréguer, F. (2018). Seeing like big tech: security assemblages, technology, and the future of state bureaucracy. *In Data Politics: Worlds, Subjects, Rights.* Taylor and Francis. https://www.scopus.com/inward/record.uri?eid=2-s2.0-8510356 2329&partnerID=40&md5=7dc52d28b9d46e91f640469b3f877baa

Tuma, L. A., Stanley, C., and Stansbie, P. (2020). Teaching innovation grant COVID-19 online social distance teaching project and virtual event. *Journal of Teaching in Travel and Tourism, 20*(4), 395–401. https://doi.org/10.1080/ 15313220.2020.1793259

Usman, M. (2022). Breaking up Big Tech: lessons from AT&T. *University of Pennsylvania Law Review, 170*(2), 523–548. https://www.scopus.com/ inward/record.uri?eid=2-s2.0-85128692667&partnerID=40&md5=5aa413f3547 3edbcb3a59e3ed4c730bb

Văduva, S., Burtic, D., Văduva, L., and Hisrich, R. (2022). Towards a Romanian entrepreneurial and ecological university: learning talent management from "Big-Tech." In F. I. S. Fotea and S. L. Vaduva (Ed.), *Springer Proceedings in Business and Economics* (pp. 207–224). Springer Science and Business Media B.V. https://doi.org/10.1007/978-3-030-82751-9_12

Venkata Appala Naidu, C. H. and Vedavathi, K. (2019). A study on existing material on big data technology and related solutions. *Journal of Computational and Theoretical Nanoscience, 16*(5–6), 2495–2501. https:// doi.org/10.1166/jctn.2019.7921

Verdegem, P. (2022). Dismantling AI capitalism: the commons as an alternative to the power concentration of Big Tech. *AI and Society.* https://doi.org/10.1007/ s00146-022-01437-8

Wang, L., Wang, S., and Zhang, J. (2013). Venture capital backing and over-valuation: evidence from the high-tech bubble. *Financial Review, 48*(2), 283–310. https://doi.org/10.1111/fire.12004

Wörsdörfer, M. (2022). What happened to 'Big Tech' and antitrust? And how to fix them! *Philosophy of Management, 21,* 345–369. https://doi.org/10.1007/s40926-022-00193-5

Zeng, Z., Chen, P.-J., and Lew, A. A. (2020). From high-touch to high-tech: COVID-19 drives robotics adoption. *Tourism Geographies, 22*(3), 724–734. https://doi.org/10.1080/14616688.2020.1762118

Zhou, J. (2012). Research on appraisal model of venture capital investing project based on high-tech outcome transformation with uncertain linguistic information. *Advances in Information Sciences and Service Sciences, 4*(1), 224–229. https://doi. org/10.4156/AISS.vol4.issue1.29

Chapter 4

Multimedia technologies in the financial market

Luan Vardari[1], Edisa Koro[2] and Ercan Özen[3]

Abstract

Over the course of the past decade, most businesses have been affected by the introduction of new technologies and innovations, which have caused varying degrees of disruption (with relation to technologies, goods and services already on the market, as well as existing modes of conducting business) and altered the competitive landscape. For instance, within the realm of financial services, there has been a growth in the number of retail banking propositions that are digital or available solely online. On the one hand, this has enabled existing businesses to enhance their efficiency and cut their overhead costs. On the other hand, it has also promoted new entrants into these businesses.

Banks must use new technology to handle long-term industry concerns such as shifting regulations, low interest rates, and pressure on returns. This is in order for banks to address long-term industry challenges such as these. In addition, banks struggle to meet the ever-evolving demands of their clients and to make effective use of emerging technologies in order to effectively develop innovative new products and services. This is a challenge for the banking industry. This chapter presents the results of an analysis of the significant technological and innovative trends affecting investment banking that are anticipated to have an effect on the industry. It also presents a vision for the investment bank of the future and highlights the ramifications for the industry as well as for future policy. Additionally, it provides a vision for the future investment bank.

This chapter analyzes the most important technological and innovative changes that will affect investment banks serving the capital markets, along with the opportunities and repercussions that these trends bring.

Keywords: Multimedia technology; Financial markets; Banks; Mobile banking; Interactive banking

[1]University 'UKSHIN HOTI' Prizren, Faculty of Economy, Kosovo
[2]Department of Business and Administration, University 'UKSHIN HOTI' Prizren, Faculty of Economy, Kosovo
[3]University of Uşak, Faculty of Applied Sciences, Turkey

4.1   Introduction

The idea of "software as a service" has been lauded as a novel approach to the distribution of software services due to the fact that it enables the more rapid implementation of software modifications (Bennet *et al.*, 2001). A fee must be paid by the customer before they may make use of the software, either permanently or for an extended length of time (Janssen and Joha, 2011). Customers are able to conduct service transactions on their own, without the assistance of a company's service staff, when they use technology that enables self-service (Galdolage, 2020). In the case of client communication, retail banks in particular make use of a variety of service channels, each of which plays a vital function (Gunawardana and Perera, 2015). There is little doubt that the quality of service provided by retail banking institutions all around the world has increased during the past few years (Ndubisi *et al.*, 2007). Despite its sensitivity to criminal conduct, the surveillance system (automated teller machine) ATM has not been adequately integrated with an image processing tool to detect illegal actions. This is despite the fact that ATM was designed to monitor criminal behavior (Sikandar *et al.*, 2019). The high cost of transactions is a fundamental obstacle that must be overcome before basic financial institutions can be developed and utilized.

A wide range of digital financial services can reduce transaction costs, including ATMs, debit cards, mobile money and digital credits. In spite of this, the existing body of research hardly never investigates indirect transaction costs (Bachas *et al.*, 2018). Within the realm of financial services, there has also been a rise in the number of retail banking ideas that are digital or are made available exclusively online. This technological breakthrough has been powered, in large part, by a significant rise in the amount of processing power that is commercially accessible as well as a general trend toward cheaper cost (Broderick and Vachirapornpuk, 2002). When it comes to the provision of financial services, we could use a chatbot in a variety of capacities, including as an HR assistant, a market information assistant, a workflow assistant, a social media assistant, an assistant to financial analysts, a scheduling assistant, and a general brand ambassador. These are some of the many areas of a firm that could undergo radical transformation as a consequence of the implementation of a chatbot. They contribute to the reduction of time and personnel costs, as well as an increase in efficiency, which ultimately results in a gain in company value (Ravi and Kamaruddin, 2017). Kiosks typically operate around the clock, seven days a week, providing customers with improved and more individualized service at a cost that is substantially lower for the financial institution. The early response of management to the changing demands of retail customers and the subsequent actions to provide relevant and customized services through new distribution channels can help the bank maintain its position as the market leader and make it easier for customers to locate the institution (Prahalad and Hamel 1994). Customers' perspectives and loyalty intentions toward Mobile banking (MB) are crucial for banks and app developers, and raising an understanding of the major factors that impact loyalty intentions when using MB would assist them to gain a competitive advantage (Mohammadi, 2015). This contemporary branchless service is currently delivered via downloadable banking applications (Farah *et al.*, 2018). This cutting-edge system also allows safe financial transactions such as paying bills and money transfers to take place in real-time (Tamilmani *et al.*, 2021).

4.2   Cloud-based software-as-a-service (SaaS)

SaaS is a new way to deliver software services since it allows faster software deployment (Bennet *et al.*, 2001) and reduces the need for in-house installation, control, and maintenance (Gonçalves and Ballon, 2011). One of the most important reasons to utilize software as a service is because it allows software administration and control to be transferred to the SaaS provider. It is commonly argued that SaaS would alter the connection between buyers and sellers (Olsen, 2006), as well as that SaaS has consequences for both business and management (Sääksjärvi *et al.*, 2005).

In the model of software distribution known as SaaS, programs are first developed, then deployed and maintained on the servers of the SaaS provider, and only then are they made available to end users through the Internet. The consumer is responsible for paying a price in order to use the program or to use it for a predetermined amount of time. The second scenario is analogous to a subscription, which can be easily canceled because it does not necessitate a significant financial commitment. Although it is not required, the software's ownership typically remains with the SaaS provider of the product even though it is not required. The license and development expenses associated with traditional models are somewhat substantial, but variable distribution costs are significantly lower than those associated with hardware (Janssen and Joha, 2011). In the past few years, there have been several technology advancements that have made it viable to advertise computing not as a product but rather as a service:

- ✓ *Cloud computing.* Cloud computing offers low-cost software scaling and the supply of low-cost software services to a broad user community.
- ✓ *Bandwidth.* The availability of bandwidth allows you to connect virtually anywhere, anytime.
- ✓ *Modular software.* A modular service architecture that allows users to decouple functionality, configuration, and service composition (Janssen and Joha, 2011).

A SaaS model is a type of business model in which the software is not directly owned and maintained by the company. SaaS focuses on providing services rather than transferring ownership of the software to the customer. Advantages include greater IT control, no installation or development costs, and access to applications that might not otherwise be available. Disadvantages and threats are associated with continuity, performance, privacy, ensuring IT functional control, and impacting future innovation and development directions. Some dangers arise from the fact that both the software and the information exist on the SaaS provider's systems, although ownership of the information remains with the user (Janssen and Joha, 2011).

4.3   Self-service multimedia banking kiosks

The first interactive self-service kiosk, established at the College of Illinois in 1977, was designed to provide information about the school and attracted over 30,000 visitors in its first six weeks of operation (Berry *et al.*, 2002). This was followed by the first Internet-connected kiosk, which was set up at a computer trade show in 1991 with the primary goal of finding missing children (Frantz and Durlak, 1992). A kiosk terminal (or simply a kiosk) is a computer designed for the use of a limited number of tools or for performing specific activities at a specific location. Kiosks come in different designs and sizes, and with different accessories (keyboards, speakers, scanners, barcode readers, printers, etc.). A connection to the Internet is now a mandatory part of any kiosk, as kiosks are designed for quick and easy access to information, whether it is publicly available or limited (Dzhurov and Atanasova, 2021).

These devices are used in a variety of fields:

In trade and tourism: kiosks are placed in larger stores or shopping malls to allow customers to easily and quickly learn about a product or service without the need for a salesperson to be present. Short commercials can also be placed to inform consumers about new offers and items available in the store.

Banks and financial institutions: establish information kiosks to familiarize patrons with the operations available at the institution as well as the process of a financial transaction. The kiosk can also play short educational films introducing potential users to new and interesting services provided by the institution—a simple marketing campaign (Dzhurov and Atanasova, 2021).

Customers are able to execute service transactions on their own using self-service technologies, which eliminates the need for interaction with an organization's service experts (Galdolage, 2020). Due to rapid technological improvements, low hardware prices, and rising labor costs, SSTs have become increasingly popular in the service industry (Hagen and Sandnes, 2010). They allow consumers to manufacture their services using SSTs (Kim *et al.*, 2012), resulting in cost savings and increased efficiency (Kim and Yang, 2018). A kiosk must now have an Internet connection since kiosks are meant for rapid and simple access to information, whether it is publicly available or restricted (Dzhurov and Atanasova, 2021).

4.3.1   SSTs in banking sector: global and local contexts

Retail bank customers can get in touch with the banks in a number of ways, such as through ATMs, automated telephone banking (ATB), web banking, and text message banking. In particular, retail banks use a number of service channels, each of which is important for keeping in touch with customers (Gunawardana *et al.*, 2015). Banks have jumped on the SST bandwagon to improve customer service, increase the number of transactions, keep up with technology, and give customers more ways to bank, such as ATM, mobile, and online banking. This has helped all of these metrics get better for the banks. There is no doubt that the quality of service offered by retail banks around the world has gotten much better over the past few years (Ndubisi *et al.*, 2007). This change in technology started when ATMs and debit cards were introduced. Core banking soon followed (the customer becomes a customer of the entire bank rather than the branch, with branches interconnected).

Internet banking is available, which is another SST option. Its original function was to provide information on the bank's products and services around the clock and 7 days a week, but it today also facilitates financial transactions (Galdolage and Rasanjalee, 2022). MB is one another SST that banks are putting a lot of effort into promoting (Kumar and Bose, 2013). Self-service banking is gaining popularity as more customers choose to complete their day-to-day financial transactions independently, rather than relying on the assistance of bank workers (Galdolage and Rasanjalee, 2022).

4.4 Image-enabled ATMs

Putting image processing into video surveillance systems is a hard problem that has been the focus of research and development for many years. The surveillance system for ATMs has not been properly connected to an image processing tool that can spot illegal activity, even though ATMs can be used for crimes. On the other hand, the modern image enhancement techniques that are usually used to find hidden or obscured faces, people doing things that are not normal, and illegal objects may not work for ATMs because of the different environments they work in (e.g., lighting and camera view), as well as strange movements and illegal devices (Sikandar *et al.*, 2019).

Around the world, media often report on a variety of criminal acts that take place at ATMs, such as robberies. Robberies at ATMs pose a risk not only to less developed countries but also to more developed countries. According to recent reports, criminals do not appear to be deterred by the contemporary video surveillance technology because the recorded films are utilized for forensic examination of the effects of the theft rather than for the prevention of ATM crimes. As a result, the timely detection of criminal activity at ATMs with the use of surveillance cameras has developed into a significant concern for ensuring the security of the ATM environment. Because of the quick pace of development in today's technology, video surveillance cameras, when combined with various image processing methods, can be utilized in ATMs to detect fraudulent behavior and set off an alarm (Sikandar *et al.*, 2019).

4.5 Digital account opening

The widespread adoption and use of basic financial institutions is significantly hampered by transaction fees. ATMs, debit cards, mobile money, and digital credit are a few examples of digital financial services that could reduce transaction costs. Contrarily, indirect transaction costs are rarely considered in current research (Bachas *et al.*, 2018). Government and nonprofit organizations' procedures for transferring funds are being digitalized, and rewards are now automatically and digitally put into bank accounts that are connected to card payments or mobile money accounts. These technologies offer the ability to connect with the millions of participants in money transfer schemes around the world (Bachas *et al.*, 2018).

Payments are the lifeline of the financial system. They connect buyers and suppliers, enable governments to conduct business with their citizens, and link friends and family in networks of financial support. Similarly, payments are the foundation of financial services (Radcliffe and Voorhies, 2012). According to a recent World Bank Gallup survey of 148 countries, only 24% of people in sub-Saharan Africa and 33% of adults in South Asia have a formal account at a financial institution. In high-income countries, 89% of people work. This growing "cash-digital divide" creates two mutually reinforcing inequalities in the financial lives of impoverished people. First, it makes basic financial transactions that you and I take for granted more expensive and risky for them. These two inequities are addressed below:

✓ The poor's dependence on real currency causes significant friction in their financial lives.
✓ The poor's dependence on physical money perpetuates their exclusion from the formal economy (Radcliffe and Voorhies, 2012).

4.5.1   What does digital financial inclusion look like?

So how can we bridge the gap between cash and digital media? Basically, we need to build low-cost "on-ramps" that allow poor people to convert physical currency into digital money, and we need to connect these on-ramps to formal institutions so that poor people can meet their financial needs in digital form. Digital financial inclusion is not achieved until poor customers can transact (at a reasonable cost) with peers, banks, governments, and utilities (Radcliffe and Voorhies, 2012).

1. Access to a network, such as a telecommunications network, allows consumers to connect to the provider's transaction approval system via a cell phone or other digital interface.
2. Cash-in/cash-out networks enable low-income customers to exchange physical cash for digital money (and vice versa).
3. A system for capturing and validating consumer identities.
4. A virtual account that can be used to make digital payments.
5. A payment platform (or a network of interconnected platforms) that allows consumers to interact with contractors independently of the payment provider (Radcliffe and Voorhies, 2012).

4.6   Interactive banking portals

With the rise of e-commerce, retail banks have had to change the way they build and keep relationships with their customers in a big way. When it comes to banking, which has traditionally been a business with a lot of customer contact, the lack of direct human interaction in online channels means that every part of service must be used as a chance to improve or reinforce customer views of quality (Broderick and Vachirapornpuk, 2002).

Service quality is one of the most important ways to set yourself apart from other service providers and gain a competitive edge because it is so easy to compare options online (Groos *et al.*, 2000; Santos, 2003). Because of these improvements, service quality is an important part of online banking. Content, context, communication, and business are the "four Cs" of the Internet. Portals are hybrid or integrative business models that do not strictly follow content, context, communication, or commerce. These "four Cs" are combined into a corporate plan (Afuah and Tucci, 2001; Bauer and Hammerschmidt, 2002). Because portals are better than regular websites in a number of ways, online customers should be happier and more loyal if they use them. In an ideal world, these benefits will lead to a portal that is not only the starting point of a Web surfer's journey but also the only source of information that a Web surfer will ever need.

Because the portal provides solutions for everything, the user no longer has to browse numerous different specialist websites, which eliminates the transaction costs associated with doing so (such as fees, time, risk, and stress). The fact that the user does not have to navigate away from the gateway website offers a substantial time savings advantage (Bauer *et al.*, 2005).

4.7 Person-to-person (P2P) payments

P2P payments, sometimes referred to as customer-to-customer payments or peer-to-peer payments, are monetary transactions that take place between individuals. P2P payments were originally restricted to in-person interactions only because users were required to physically trade money with one another. Users were able to send money to one another using their online bank or a third party such as PayPal throughout the 1990s and 2000s, when peer-to-peer (P2P) payments over the Internet saw a considerable surge in popularity. Consumers are now able to pay each other via mobile applications thanks to the expansion of P2P payment systems to the mobile channel (Kleivene, 2018). P2P payments can be made by individuals to their friends and family members, as well as to others, for the purchase of goods and services. This final category is what people sometimes mean when they talk about "micro-merchants." People who sell products through classified advertisements or online auction sites like eBay fall into this category. Examples include gardeners, babysitters, independent tradesmen, and people who sell things through online auction sites (Bradford and Keeton, 2012).

4.7.1 Nonbank-centric P2P payment methods

In nonbank-centric P2P protocols, payments are started, approved, and checked in the same way. Most of the time, the payer needs to have an account with the intermediary before the payment can be made. Most of the time, the person who is getting paid must also have an account or open one in order to get the money. Most of the time, when you sign up for an account, you have to make a user ID and a password, as well as give your home address, e-mail address, and phone number. Another important criterion is to choose a way to pay for the intermediary account and payments. A bank account or a payment card are the two most common ways to do this (Bradford and Keeton, 2012).

4.7.2 Bank-centric P2P payment methods

If the P2P service is run by a bank, the person who sends the money can get it in any bank account. The bank that runs the service tells the person who is getting the money and asks for his or her account information via e-mail or SMS. On the other hand, strategies that focus on banks are different from methods that do not focus on banks in two important ways. First, the payment is made when the payer talks directly with his or her bank instead of going through a third party that is not a bank. Second, the money used to make the payment is not in the buyer's or the payee's account, even if it is only for a short time. The money is always sent directly from the payee's bank account to the payee's bank account, even if it does not have to happen all at once (Bradford and Keeton, 2012).

4.8   Chatbots/virtual personal banker

The term "chatbot" is an acronym made up of the words "chat" and "robot." Chatbots use artificial intelligence (AI) to mimic the way people talk or the way interactive chat apps behave. The United States of America is credited with developing the very first chatbot in the year 1966. Chatbots, on the other hand, were not applicable at that time since there were not enough powerful devices and a widespread network infrastructure to support them. It is recommended that chatbots not be utilized in regular life as they are only useful in a research setting. In recent years, a great number of chatbots that are capable of being incorporated into people's everyday lives have been developed. E-commerce (EC) services, such as customer care centers, the Internet, financial counseling, and other similar services, are where chatbots are most widely utilized (Lai *et al.*, 2018).

A service or piece of technology known as a chatbot is one that facilitates communication with a computer program through the use of text messages. The chatbot understands what you are saying and either answers with a message that is comprehensible and pertinent or completes the task that you have requested on your behalf. A variety of different services can be provided by a chatbot. It can, among other things, check the weather forecast, transmit important messages related to one's health, and even buy a new pair of shoes. You can communicate with the chatbot via a number of other channels, including SMS, Siri, WeChat, Telegram, Slack, Facebook Messenger, and Skype, in addition to the ones listed above (Ravi and Kamaruddin, 2017).

There are many different business settings suitable for the implementation of chatbots. They are helpful in decreasing the amount of time and personnel costs as well as enhancing efficiency, which ultimately results in a higher value for the organization. In the field of financial services, we can use a chatbot to assist with human resources (HR), market information (market information assistant), workflow assistance (workflow assistance), social media assistance, financial analyst assistance (financial analyst helper), scheduling assistance, and general brand ambassador duties. According to Ravi and Kamaruddin (2017), the following are the many facets of a company where the implementation of a chatbot could result in a paradigm change.

4.8.1 Banking chatbot business

The following tasks need to be carried out and managed by a general banker or other financial professional:

✓ Give information about possible investments, such as stocks, bonds, market conditions, investment opportunities, and your financial situation.
✓ Educate yourself on the current state of the markets for stocks, bonds, currencies, and any other relevant financial instruments.
✓ Guidance to customers regarding the terms of contracts, stock and bond loans, as well as other strategies for capital-raising.
✓ Place orders for securities, stocks, bonds, currency exchange, and other types of financial products, and then send those orders.
✓ Searching for potential new customers.
✓ Preserving a cordial relationship with one's clientele.
✓ Carry out the customer's required transactions in a timely manner.

Due to the fact that these specialized and time-consuming jobs can only serve one customer at a time and require some time to deliver a service, many customers are forced to choose between convenience and quality of the product or service they receive. In addition, the topic of financial services encompasses the realms of finance, data on customers, and personal privacy (Lai *et al.*, 2018; Table 4.1).

Table 4.1 Advantages and disadvantages of banking chatbot

Professional and chatbot-related capabilities	Financial professional	Chatbot for use in banking
Reliability	High	–
Security	High	–
Training cost	High	Low
Service hours	Limited	Unlimited
Service power	Limited	Unlimited
Adjustability	Low	High

Source: Lai *et al.* (2018).

4.9   Video banking services

Video banking is an interactive type of communication that uses a kiosk device. They are usually placed in high-traffic areas (Hakimovich, 2021). A video banking kiosk is a self-contained device that allows retail customers in remote areas to connect with personal banking stations or servers in contact centers via two-way video conferencing and multimedia capabilities. Kiosks often remain open 24 h a day, 7 days a week. As a result, they are able to offer improved and more individualized service to consumers at a far reduced cost to the bank.

The proactive response of management to the ever-changing needs of retail customers, as well as subsequent actions to provide relevant and specialized services through new distribution channels, can help the bank maintain its position as market leader and make it easier for customers to find the bank (Prahalad and Hamel 1994). Using a computer touch screen at the kiosk, consumers may pick the cashless banking service that best meets their needs (Paradin and Ghazarian-Rock, 1998). As can be seen in Figure 4.1, bank staff respond to consumers via their PC-based workstations; this interaction, which is referred to as a session, takes place during the transaction. In situations where information is required, either the server or the customer might take control of the kiosk's activities.

The workstation has one or two computer screens mounted on a desk, a keyboard and mouse for entering and retrieving data, and a video camera on or near the computer screens to take a picture of the server and show it to the customer. The customer can then interact with the image on the computer screens.

A feedback monitor has been placed in close proximity to the computer screens so that the servers may check their appearance when the video is being transmitted. A telephone is placed on the table, and it is used to facilitate spoken communication

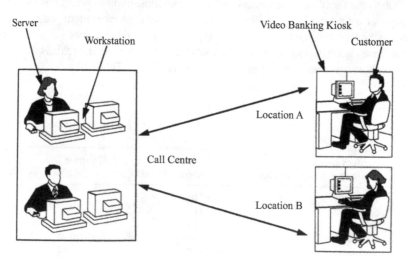

Figure 4.1   Video banking kiosk configuration. Source: *Paradin and Ghazarian-Rock (1998).*

between the customer who is located in the kiosk and the waiter. The server looks to be using a headset with a microphone that is attached to it in order to facilitate hands-free contact with the customer (Paradin and Ghazarian-Rock, 1998).

4.10 Mobile and TV-based banking

MB allows users to perform financial services through portable devices such as cell phones to connect to a server, make payments and transactions, or use other services (Oliveira *et al.*, 2014). Customers' views and loyalty intentions towards MB are critical for banks and application providers, and improving awareness of the key elements that influence loyalty intentions when using MB would help them gain a competitive advantage (Mohammadi, 2015).

Traditional customer chores can be considerably improved by MB, which can save time, money, and customer care time while freeing up resources to protect the quality of mobile networks, according to Malaquias and Hwang (2016). This can result in a significant improvement of traditional customer duties. In addition to this, the position of MB within mobile ecosystems, and particularly mobile devices, offers the potential to lower financial expenses in comparison to other traditional banking channels (Baabdullah *et al.*, 2019). Customers of banks are the primary users of m-banking since it allows them to communicate with the bank while they are on the move and in real time using mobile devices like cell phones, phones, or tablets (Baptista and Oliveira, 2015). In the early 2000s, MB first appeared in the form of text or short message service (SMS) messages (Yu, 2012). This cutting-edge branchless banking service is currently provided through the use of downloadable banking apps (Farah *et al.*, 2018). Customers are able to access a broad variety of information through the use of the M-banking features, including checking statements, checking account balances, and the location of ATMs. This cutting-edge technology also makes it possible to engage in financially safe actions in real time, such as paying bills and transferring money (Tamilmani *et al.*, 2021). When referring to the same kind of banking technology, the phrases multimedia banking, Internet banking, e-banking, and online banking are frequently used synonymously in the research that has been done on the topic (Vijayan *et al.*, 1970). Pastore (2001) and Williamson (2001) explored the usage of interactive Web TV as a gateway and multimedia delivery channel. The number of homes with a television is bigger than the number with a personal computer, and many people like watching television. This channel can be used by viewers for a variety of purposes, including online shopping and banking, education, and entertainment. This channel is utilized by vendors in an effort to strengthen their audience's brand loyalty and presence in the market. Customers place a high level of value on websites that are not only dynamic and interesting but also provide site visitors with a positive experience while they are there. This encourages repeat visits from site users.

4.11 Safe deposit boxes with iris-scanning biometrics

Theft of one's identity is rapidly becoming the most prevalent form of fraud committed in the United States. Despite this, we continue to send orders and other sensitive information by e-mail in the ASCII language, which is the language with the lowest common denominator for electronic text. This happens across unsecured telephone lines. We make use of passwords, cards, personal identification numbers, and keys in order to obtain access to information that is restricted or to files that are top secret. On the other hand, various forms of identification are susceptible to being lost, stolen, falsified, misplaced, or given away. In addition, these tools are typically employed in the process of person identification. They are unable to independently confirm or authenticate the individual's assertion that they are who they say they are. The verification of users' IP addresses is used by many systems to limit access to only those users who have a particular domain name or Internet address. This method, in its most basic form, assigns a person's identity to the computer system that they are employing. Anyone who has access to a certain computer has the ability to mimic the machine's legitimate owner.

The use of biometric hardware to ensure one's safety is becoming an increasingly practical option. The term "biometrics" comes from the Latin phrase "life measurement," and the concept behind it is that every individual possesses a distinct set of physiological traits that, in theory, a computer might identify (Desmarais, 2000). The use of biometric tools in the future holds a lot of potential. A number of potential applications have been proposed for them, including ATMs, access control, computer security, and time clocks. Optimists anticipate a wide range of additional uses, including but not limited to the following: passports, driver's licenses, applications for mortgage loans, health records, safe deposit boxes, credit card transactions, electronic commerce, drug dispensing, lottery tickets, and jails.

In general, biometric technologies are inexpensive. They require little to no additional hardware and merely routine movement patterns to function properly. Because of this, they are appealing, particularly in situations in which consumers in faraway locations need to be serviced. The ideal characteristic for a biometric system would be one that was simple, quick, unobtrusive, applicable, and widely accepted in society. The majority of biometric technologies need a significant amount of computer power, and some users consider biometrics to be an infringement of their privacy. Approaches based on biometrics need to strike a compromise between a number of different factors, including cost, user acceptance, ease of use, and precision. Even while security professionals may be concerned about the use of passwords, the expenses associated with potential security breaches are typically less than the cost of biometrics when one takes into account the purchase price, the costs associated with setup, and the discomfort factor (Desmarais, 2000).

4.11.1   Physiological biometrics

Finger/hand: Because fingerprint technology has been used in law enforcement for over a century, it is the most commonly used biometric. On the other hand, the majority of those who work in prisons and law enforcement agencies are white males between the ages of 18 and 36 who have relatively decent fingerprints. It may be more challenging to obtain the fingerprints of certain people. Around 2% of fingerprints taken from the general population cause confusion in computer systems. If it is sufficient to match only a few prints that have been locally stored, fingerprint scanners could be beneficial in the context of private security applications (Desmarais, 2000).

Face/eye: Additionally, face recognition satisfies the majority of the criteria necessary for an ideal biometric solution. With the exception of camera phones, it is simple, quick, quite useful, and does not intrude in any way. According to Desmarais (2000), the technology behind video cameras is now quite affordable, and some monitor makers even build camera lenses into their products to enable users to participate in video conferences.

4.12 Conclusion

Banks are institutions that always function with the utmost care and security. Technological advancements require banks, like other organizations, to stay up to date with time and technological progress. They carry out their activities using cutting-edge technology and sophisticated software. The deployment of sophisticated technology allows the bank to function more powerfully and attain market competitiveness. Customers always choose to employ the services of a bank that provides trust and customer care around the clock. The utilization of sophisticated technology allows the bank to complete duties more conveniently and quickly. Although the bank's initial expenditure on supplying new technology is greater, the future expenses of carrying out the operations may be lower. As a consequence of this, we were able to demonstrate in this study the significance of technology in the banking industry, the trust it instills in clients, and the competitive power of the market.

References

Afuah A., and Tucci, C.L. (2012) Crowdsourcing As a Solution to Distant Search. *AMR*, 37, 355–375, https://doi.org/10.5465/amr.2010.0146

Baabdullah, A. M., Alalwan, A. A., Rana, N. P., Patil, P., and Dwivedi, Y. K. (2019). An integrated model for m-banking adoption in Saudi Arabia. *International Journal of Bank Marketing*, 32, 452–478.

Bachas, P., Gertler, P., Higgins, S., and Seira, E. (2018, May). Digital financial services go a long way: Transaction costs and financial inclusion. In *AEA Papers and Proceedings* (vol. 108, pp. 444–448).

Baptista, G., and Oliveira, T. (2015). Understanding mobile banking: The unified theory of acceptance and use of technology combined with cultural moderators. *Computers in Human Behavior*, 50, 418–430.

Bauer, H.H., Hammerschmidt, M. and Falk, T. (2005), "Measuring the quality of e-banking portals", *International Journal of Bank Marketing*, Vol. 23 No. 2, pp. 153–175. https://doi.org/10.1108/02652320510584395

Berry, L. L., Seiders, K., and Grewal, D. (2002). Understanding service convenience. *Journal of Marketing, 66*(3), 1–17.

Bradford, T., and Keeton, W. R. (2012). New person-to-person payment methods: have checks met their match? *Economic Review-Federal Reserve Bank of Kansas City, 41*, Q III.

Broderick, A. J., and Vachirapornpuk, S. (2002). Service quality in Internet banking: the importance of customer role. *Marketing Intelligence and Planning, 20*(6), 327–335.

Desmarais, N. (2000). Body language, security and e-commerce. *Library Hi Tech, 18*(1), 61–74. https://doi.org/10.1108/07378830010314483

Dzhurov-Student, M. S., and Atanasova, G. (2021). Applications and benefits of using kiosks and integrated kiosk software in education sphere. In *60th Annual Scientific Conference - University of Ruse and Union of Scientists*, Bulgaria, pp. 266–271. https://conf.uni-ruse.bg/bg/docs/cp21/bp/bp-39.pdf

Farah, M. F., Hasni, M. J. S., and Abbas, A. K. (2018). Mobile-banking adoption: empirical evidence from the banking sector in Pakistan. *International Journal of Bank Marketing, 36*(7), pp. 1386–1413.

Frantz, S. C., and Durlak, R. M. (1992). Interactive computer kiosks for vertebrate Ipm—status report. In *Proceedings of the Fifteenth Vertebrate Pest Conference*, p. 29.

Galdolage, S. (2020). Customer choice of self-service kiosks in service transactions. *South Asian Journal of Marketing, 1*(2), 98–137. Retweeted from http://repo.lib.sab.ac.lk:8080/xmlui/bitstream/handle/123456789/1711/5.pdf?sequence=1&isAllowed=y

Galdolage, B., and Rasanjalee, R. M. K. (2022). Why do people move towards self-service technologies? Insights from banking sector in Sri Lanka. *Journal of Business and Technology, 6*(1), 19–41.

Gonçalves, V., and Ballon, P. (2011). Adding value to the network: Mobile operators' experiments with Software-as-a-Service and Platform-as-a-Service models. *Telematics and Informatics, 28*(1), 12–21.

Gunawardana, H. M. R. S. S., and Perera, W. L. M. V. (2015). Impact of self service technology quality on customer satisfaction: A case of retail banks in Western Province in Sri Lanka. *Gadjah Mada International Journal of Business, 17*(1), 1–24.

Hakimovich, B. A. (2021). Measures to increase the popularity of banking services. *International Journal of Modern Agriculture, 10*(2), 3943–3949.

Janssen, M., and Joha, A. (2011). Challenges for adopting cloud-based software as a service (SaaS) in the public sector. In *ECIS 2011*.

Kleivene, L. E. (2018). P2P mobile payments: Investigating the factors of adoption among students in Germany. In *Omnichannel Branding* (pp. 45–67). Springer Gabler, Wiesbaden.

Kumar, V. V., and Bose, S. K. (2013). Adoption of Self Service Technologies (SST) – A study on the intention of management students to use Internet Banking Services. *Journal of Contemporary Research in Management, 8*(1), 47–58.

Lai, S. T., Leu, F. Y., and Lin, J. W. (2018, October). A banking chatbot security control procedure for protecting user data security and privacy. In *International Conference on Broadband and Wireless Computing, Communication and Applications* (pp. 561–571). Springer, Cham.

Malaquias, R. F., and Hwang, Y. (2016). An empirical study on trust in mobile banking: A developing country perspective. *Computers in Human Behavior*, *54*, 453–461.

Mohammadi, H. (2015). A study of mobile banking loyalty in Iran. *Computers in Human Behavior*, *44*, 35–47.

Ndubisi, N. O., Wah, C. K., and Ndubisi, G. C. (2007). Supplier-customer relationship management and customer loyalty: The banking industry perspective. *Journal of Enterprise Information Management*, *20*, 222–236.

Oliveira, T., Faria, M., Thomas, M. A., and Popovič, A. (2014). Extending the understanding of mobile banking adoption: When UTAUT meets TTF and ITM. *International Journal of Information Management*, *34*(5), 689–703.

Olsen, E. R. (2006, June). Transitioning to software as a service: Realigning software engineering practices with the new business model. In *2006 IEEE International Conference on Service Operations and Logistics, and Informatics* (pp. 266–271). IEEE.

Paradi, J. C., and Ghazarian-Rock, A. (1998). A framework to evaluate video banking kiosks. *Omega*, *26*(4), 523–539.

Pastore, M. (2001). Web traffic in July: That's entertainment. *Cyberatlas*. http://www.cyberatlas.internet.com/big_picture/print/0,,5931_863201,00.html.

Prahalad, C. K., and Hamel, G. (1994). *Competing for the Future* (vol. 25). Boston, MA: Harvard Business School Press.

Radcliffe, D., and Voorhies, R. (2012). A digital pathway to financial inclusion. *Available at SSRN 2186926*.

Ravi, V., and Kamaruddin, S. (2017, December). Big data analytics enabled smart financial services: opportunities and challenges. *In International Conference on Big Data Analytics* (pp. 15–39). Cham: Springer.

Sääksjärvi, M., Lassila, A., and Nordström, H. (2005, June). Evaluating the software as a service business model: From CPU time-sharing to online innovation sharing. In *IADIS International Conference E-Society* (pp. 177–186). Qawra, Malta.

Santos, J. (2003). E-service quality: A model of virtual service quality dimensions. *Managing Service Quality: An International Journal*, *13*, 233–246.

Sikandar, T., Ghazali, K. H., and Rabbi, M. F. (2019). ATM crime detection using image processing integrated video surveillance: A systematic review. *Multimedia Systems*, *25*(3), 229–251.

Tamilmani, K., Rana, N. P., Wamba, S. F., and Dwivedi, R. (2021). The extended Unified Theory of Acceptance and Use of Technology (UTAUT2): A systematic literature review and theory evaluation. *International Journal of Information Management*, 57, 102269. https://doi.org/10.1016/j.ijinfomgt.2020.102269

Vijayan, V. P., Perumal, V., and Shanmugam, B. (1970). Waves of multimedia banking development. *The Journal of Internet Banking and Commerce*, *9*(3), 1970.

Williamson, K., Wright, S., Schauder, D., and Bow, A. (2001). The Internet for the Blind and Visually Impaired. *Journal of Computer-Mediated Communication*, 7(1). 0–0. JCMC712, https://doi.org/10.1111/j.1083-6101.2001.tb00135.x

Yu, C. S. (2012). Factors affecting individuals to adopt mobile banking: Empirical evidence from the UTAUT model. *Journal of Electronic Commerce Research*, *13*(2), 104.

Chapter 5

Data analytics in finance

Jagjit Singh Dhatterwal[1], Kuldeep Singh Kaswan[2], Meenakshi Dahiya[3] and Priya Jindal[4]

Abstract

The financial advisory business is rapidly transitioning from a conventional worldview to an advanced technological approach to engaging with customers. Both the monetary network operator and the client are experiencing digital transformations. For instance, the banking sector has progressed from a notebook and ledger entry model to data and analytics-driven financial transactions encompassing physical and digital consumer activity. This chapter explores numerous banking, finance, and insurance (BFSI) scenarios where big data analytics is becoming increasingly important. Our observations have significant consequences for audit committees and the apparent unwillingness to adopt useful big data approaches for fear of becoming too far advanced for the technologies that corporations ultimately use. Future study possibilities are also identified in scientific finance, real-time operational and financial intelligence, collaboration technologies, and peer-to-peer markets.

Keywords: Big data analytics; Autoregression function; Moving average; Regression analysis; Cognitive networks

5.1 Forecasting economic variables through linear and nonlinear time series analysis

The conventional direct relapse trend analysis and exploring the determinants often begin with a framework. In a Manual to Multiple regression (1985), Peter Kennedy makes the following five assumptions about the model: (1) the reliant variable can be transmitted as horizontal capabilities of a special configuration of independent

[1]Department of Artificial Intelligence & Data Science, Koneru Lakshmaiah Education Foundation, India
[2]School of Computing Science and Engineering, Galgotias University, India
[3]Faculty of Law, PDM University, India
[4]Chitkara Business School, Chitkara University, Punjab, India

variables alongside a disquieting involvement term (error in judgement); (2) the normal valuation of the mental stress parameter is zero; (3) the perplexing progressions fluctuate over time and are sensitive to outliers; and (4) viewpoints on the unlimited dependent variable can be expressed.

While relapse can serve as a preliminary step for both data series and regression analyses, it is the researchers' responsibility to provide the graphs and data that will indicate if expectations are being met in a certain setting (Abbasi *et al.*, 2012).

A periodical series prediction is a device that forecasts the prospective positive aspects of succession by analyzing the link among the qualities exhibited in succession and the hourly rate of their occurrences. Several time sequence evaluation methods can be applied to develop a prediction system.

Suppose there has been any uniformity and also infrequent fluctuation in the data represented in the past. In that case, model-based approaches may identify this variation and use this data to suit the actual data as closely as possible as might reasonably be expected, contributing to future gauging correctness (Kaswan and Dhatterwal, 2020).

There are various standard approaches used in time series analysis. Among them are a few examples:

- Emotional Smoothing
- Direct Time Series Regression and Curve fit
- Autoregression Function
- ARIMA
- Intervention Analysis

Since aggregation is uncommon in this assumption, we will concentrate our investigation on regression analysis. Until the eighteenth century, time series analysis was characterized by the idea of a simulated universe. Yule (1927) was responsible for removing the potential of deterministic communicating in time series analysis by arguing that each generalized linear may be viewed as an affirmation of a combinatorial cycle. A three-stage iterative process for time series in the 1970s distinguished confirmation, appraising, and reinforcement (AICPA, 1998). These creators were responsible for a significant portion of the ideas included in ARIMA models, so ARIMA exhibiting is now commonly known as Box–Jenkins demonstrating ARIMA stands for Exponential Smoothing Averaging. The idea behind these techniques is that the collection handled in the response differently may be divided into three parts:

- Autoregressive (AR)
- Composed (I) or difference
- Moving average (MA)

At both the constant variance and periodical levels, an ARIMA model can include any component or combination of parts. ARIMA models are classified into several types, the most common of which being ARIMA(p, d, q)(P,D,Q), where p denotes the request for constant variance autoregressive collaboration synchronized into the optimization method

- P the solicitation for a periodic autoregressive cycle.
- Suggests the solicitation for nonseasonal blend or differencing (and D the solicitation for an intermittent joining or differencing).
- q implies the solicitation for the nonseasonal moving ordinary cooperation united in the model (and Q the solicitation for a periodic moving normal cycle) (AICPA, 2011).

An ARIMA (2,1,1), for example, is a nonstationary ARIMA model in which the procurement for the vector autoregression element is 1, the authorization for the blending or independent component analysis is 1, and the procurement for the run-of-the-mill movable part is also 1. Numerical methods do not have to have all three components. An ARIMA(1,0,0), for example, has a vector autoregression piece of requirement 1 but no qualifying or movement typical portion. Furthermore, an ARIMA(0,0,2) just received a conventional traveling component of solicitations.

5.1.1 Autoregressive dependent framework

To spiral downward, numerical methods employ different factors to forecast an outcome variable (the series variable). The word autoregressive implies that previous series numbers are used to predict the continuing time series analysis. As a result, the integrated moving average ARIMA component of an ARIMA model seeks the aggregate variable's unconstrained prospective gains, or, at the very least, values from prior time periods, as indicators of the series variable's continuing worth. For example, the reality could ultimately show that a fair mark of current month-to-month bargains is the arrangements from the prior month.

The request for multiple linear regression indicates a temporal separation between the different findings and the loosening sequence variable used as an indicator. According to an AR(1) component of the optimization method, the value of the other results in the preceding cycle $(t-1)$ is a good predictor and indication of what the sequence will be right currently (at time period t). This concept applies to higher-order processes (Alanyali *et al.*, 2013).

A fundamental integrated moving average (Arima Model (AR(1)) precondition representation is as follows:

$$y(t) = \Phi 1 y(t-1) + e(t) + a \tag{5.1}$$

As a result, the sequential consideration at the uninterrupted time point $(y(t))$ is equal to the sum of (1) the preceding series regard $(y(t-1))$ multiplied by a weight coefficient (1); (2) a dependable a (paying more attention to the sequence mean); and (3) a misstep portion at the continuing time point $[e(t)]$.

5.1.2 Models based on moving averages

As indicated, an ARIMA model's vector autoregression ingredient aims to relax the possible benefits of the findings state. In contrast, the normal movable component of the simulation utilizes various future benefits of the modelling blunder as indicators.

A handful of experts investigate conventional moving parts as other occurrences or computer stresses. That is, an unexpected shift in the surroundings happens, influencing the series' continuing worth along with potential significant properties. In this way, the error portion over the time series data span is afterwards associated with the series' features (Alles, 2015).

The request for the simple moving component implies the distance between the mistake and the continuous variables. For example, if the model's blunder loosens the series parameter (1) interval, this is a regular shifting course of frequency (1) and is commonly termed an MA(1) process, which may be expressed as:

$$y(t) = \Phi 1 * e(t-1) + e(t) + a \tag{5.2}$$

The series respect at the uninterrupted time point $(y(t))$ is now equal to the sum of three parts: (1) the specified time point's modelling mix-up $(e(t-1))$ multiplied by a weight parameter (here 1); (2) a steady parameter (getting accustomed to the sequence mean); and (3) a muddled component at the continuously time point $(e(t))$.

The integrating (or independent component analysis) component of an ARIMA model provides a method of answering to float inside a time series model. To analyze the availability element of the strategy, a lagged dependent variable series includes reducing the possible benefits of adjacent series values. Once again, the example slain by differencing is included in the numbers by incorporation (exchanging the differencing action). Differentiation can be used at the nonstationary or occasional level, and modest independent component analysis, but mostly impressive, can be used. A differentiating sequence (nonseasonal) would be:

$$x(t) = y(t) - y(t-1) \tag{5.3}$$

where the lagged dependent variable series values $(x(t))$ are analogous to the uninterrupted series consideration $(y(t))$ minus the prior series consideration $(y(t-1)$.

The concept assumption of normality is commonly used in regression analysis to describe how a certain group of variables varies over time. The assumption of normality is divided into three components. In any instance, the series has a constant average, which means that there is no trend for the average' mean to increase or decrease with time (Alston et al., 2012). Second, the sequence modification is recognized consistently after a certain time. Consequently, any aggregation setup remains constant throughout the sequence. For example, if the series has an AR (2) plan, being available throughout the series is usual. Any violation of the order of integration causes the ARIMA model assessment concerns when the regression model is not constant. It is hard to determine the recognized variants. This is because the series' means changes over time, and linkages and relationships between the variables in the ARIMA model will be deformed or malformed. Will clinically insane relationships and interconnections be acknowledged if the median of the explanatory variables is fixed?

The ARIMA integration is frequently connected with a particular case from the sequence, which would disregard the dependable mean piece of homogeneity of variance. In time series analysis, it is frequently the case that the means of a parameter augments or decreases with time.

To create a series with an application of formal elements, we can create another series that is the specialization of the major series. A first solicitations differential motivates the original series, which is the qualifications between the varieties in the continuous period, especially less the succession regarded in the preceding span of time. The lagged-dependent variable series will occasionally have a valid mean. In the event that the nonstationary series lacks a correct mean, it may be necessary to take the lagged-dependent variable series' first difference. This modification is referred to as second solicitations interpolation since the primary sequence has now differed twice. The solicitations for participating is the period at which a series should be varied. Interpolation can be done at a periodical (rhythmic movements time less the frequency from the preceding time span) or non-incidental (force timeframe less the information from the previously span of time) level (Amoore, 2011).

5.1.3 Artificial neural networks in finance

Understanding instances and patterns in accounting transactions is of enormous relevance to the corporate sector to aid the particular cycle. One other era of processes, incorporating cerebral hemisphere affiliations, data-based constructions and hereditary estimates, has stood out for evaluating instances and predictions.

Cognitive networks, particularly, are being employed broadly for monetary management with regard to protective exchanges, different exchange dealing, item expected growth and surveillance dividends. The use of brain networks in time series analysis is based on the ability of mind memories to construct nonlinear bounds. In all sincerity, mind powers granted a clever strategy that does not require a pre-assurance throughout the exhibiting architecture because they unquestionably learn the association inborn in the circumstances. Taking the lagged-dependent variable series' first difference may be necessary. This modification is referred to as second solicitations interpolation since the primary sequence has now been differed twice. The solicitations for participating are the period at which a series should be varied. Interpolation can be done at a periodical (rhythmic movements time period less the frequency from the preceding time span) or non-incidental (force timeframe less the information from the previously span of time) level (Appelbaum *et al.*, 2016).

The word cerebral hemisphere network refers to a basically linked collection of models, portrayed by a huge limit area and adaptable plan, decreasing from focal points, for example, the assessment of the psyche work. Mind nets saw two significant advancements in menstrual cycles: the mid-1960s and the mid-1980s. They were a critical step forward in the field of artificial intelligence (AI). Natural revelations engaging with the approaches to operating of the psyche as an interconnection of components interconnected neurons prompted Imitation Ensemble

Techniques. The neural network is estimated to have roughly 10 billion networks, each of which is associated with 10,000 different neurons. Each neuron assists messages via connections, which govern the consequences of the information on the neuronal. These neural pathways are recognized. To accept an important role in the psyche's technique of acting, communicating a signal from one neuronal to the next via synapses is a perplexing complex cycle in which unambiguous neuro-transmitter chemicals are freed from the transmitting side of the confluence. The result is to increase or decrease the electrochemical gradient within the receiving cell's body (Bell and Carcello, 2000).

It created handling devices intended to reproduce the formation of a regular practical architecture capable of performing reasoning boundaries through learning. The cerebrum organization can be a computer program or a machine designed to know and understand in a circumstance similar to the human brain. Mind enroll-ment is a choice rather than tailored management, a working equation that natural models influence. These systems are composed of several fake neurons and their interactions.

A natural neuron is known as a perceptron in a numerical method. While in clinically insane synapses, the dendrite receives electrical signals from multi-ple synapses' axons, in the training algorithm, these control pulses are referred to as nominal attributes. Control pulses are modified in numerous totals at the brain connections between dendrites and axons. This is demonstrated effec-tively in the perceptron by multiplying each data point by a number known as the weight.

In any event, the significance of a cerebrum relationship has differed in the field in which they are utilized. As a result of this fact, we shall explore Haykin's (1998) representation of a brain network as a massively equivalent scattering pro-cessing. That has a hallmark predisposition for caring for experiencing data and making it available for usage, like the human brain, in two fundamental ways: an associate obtains the information through an educational interaction (Benoit and Van den Poel, 2012).

The data is stored using synaptic loads, which are ventral tegmental area association properties.

- An organization obtains information through an instructional interaction.

The data is stored using synaptic loads, which are interneuron association properties.

Using this formulation, we may feel that the offer high-quality backslide modelling can collect data through the least-squares system and save that data in the simple regression parameters to separate a cerebrum connection from normal measurable techniques. It is a mental relationship in this meaning. You may argue that a straight downhill slide is an excellent illustration of explicit cerebral hemi-sphere linkages. On the other hand, a straight downward slide has a definite model construction and a sequence of limited constraints before obtaining the data. Alternatively, the above framework makes irrelevant implications about strong performance management and ideas. As a result, cerebrum involvement can generate a large range of modelling techniques without requiring you to assess a clear relationship between dependent variables and free early elements. Given everything, the type was not resolved permanently during the classroom learning environment. If a direct correlation between the explanatory and relationship between variables is valid, the results of the reasoning association should eagerly vague those of the immediate backslide model. Accepting a nonlinear relationship is more reasonable. The cerebrum association will subsequently vague the "right" model development. Cerebrum networks offer the flexibility of different designing sorts, learning algorithms, and endorsement frameworks (Bhattacharya *et al.*, 2011).

5.2 Big data analytics tools for financial forecasting

In general, a large portion of the information on which associations relied fell within the transmission of money work. For bookkeeping and control reasons, finance developed into a characteristic overseer of data on the association's activities, incorporating collaborations with outside partners and controllers. Despite its significant role, the money work would generally be viewed as an expense community rather than a value generator; however, this appears to be changing. According to the Association of International Certified Professional Accountants, new developments are shifting the focus to a greater emphasis on esteem creation.

In another report, the AICPA discovered that a majority of money pioneers universally accept that the skills of their groups must "change fundamentally" throughout the following years, based on findings from an investigation of more than 5,500 money experts across 2,000 associations in 150 nations.

Given the money capacity's focal job as caretaker of monetary data, it is not unexpected that when associations choose whom to place accountable for acquiring and examining pertinent "Large Data" for key purposes, finance is often the primary port of call. Test groups face difficult questions for assessing and presenting new outside information sources. Inner information issues must additionally be tended to. Normally, groups have significant inside information assets available to them, yet this is often scattered across different frameworks, which might be skewed and depend on obsolete inheritance advances (Brown-Liburd *et al.*, 2015).

5.2.1 *How could back groups conquer the difficulties of working with enormous amounts of information?*

The principal change we needed to make was simply to improve our information. We have a ton of information, and once in a while, we simply were not utilizing that information and were not giving as much consideration to its quality as we currently needed. The subsequent region is working with our kin and verifying that we are incorporating a few parts of our business. We are concentrating our abilities, and we are democratizing its utilization. I think the other viewpoint is that we perceive collectively and as an organization that we do not have adequate abilities when all is said and done, and we require cooperation across a wide range of substances beyond American Express.

Many money and depository groups will perceive the difficulties that Gupta depicts. One specialized approach that can offer a simple, practical arrangement while dividing information among frameworks is Application Programming Interfaces (API). APIs permit subsets of information to be partaken in a normalized manner, quickly and safely between various frameworks. Regular advantages incorporate wiping out human blunders while smoothing out and accelerating information moves and supplanting cluster handling with continuous data (Busta and Weinberg, 1998).

5.2.2   How does robotization help enormous information examination?

The robotization of conventional errands like planning, estimating and execution checking, joined with further developed admittance to inside information and the capacity to use information taken care of from outside sources, is liberating money and depository groups to zero in on more essential, esteem-adding exercises, for example, recognizing new business valuable open doors, focusing on regions for speculation and improving gamble the executives.

At a common sense level, when fittingly carried out, the capacity of robotized cycles to quickly recognize deviations from ordinary examples, like uncommon instalments, or to see information from various sources (e.g., bookkeeping, depository, deals, authentic exchanges, estimates) through a solitary focal point, upgrades the abilities of money and depository groups, in monetary control as well as generally across the association.

5.2.3   How can arising advances enable huge information?

Mechanical advances, for example, computerized reasoning and AI, which merge and dissect huge volumes of information continuously, upgrade the ability to rapidly examine dubious movement and work on the exactness of conclusions. Include applicable Big Data, for example, financial conjectures, news sources or virtual entertainment movements, and the bits of knowledge that can be uncovered go significantly further – for instance, catching business sector signals or featuring data that can be utilized to advance income, illuminate money choices, upgrade situation arranging and further develop risk the executives (Cao *et al.*, 2015).

5.2.4   How can huge information change finance?

With developing attention to information's capability to add esteem, new jobs are being done in finance groups for engineers and information experts whose obligations range from making information models and calculations to recognizing patterns and creating diagrams and visual introductions. These new positions help to connect the business investigation abilities hole and improve the money and depository work. Specialized abilities for these jobs incorporate information mining and extraction, measurable displaying and information investigation with different instruments sent to aid these undertakings (e.g., SQL, Python, R, and information perception instruments).

Deloitte focuses on the case of a $1 billion food maker whose money group drove a spend-examination drive that increased production network proficiency and decreased costs by working on inventory network acquiring administration (Gepp *et al.*, 2010). Finance expanded its capacity by utilizing an investigation solution to assess obtaining and providing and then conveying the information to purchasers consistently by individual product.

5.2.5   What's next for huge information in finance?

The past model opens doors in planning, making it possible for finance groups to progress to more essential jobs. According to the AICPA's new research, this shift is already taking place as money groups change to become more esteem-adding colleagues.

5.2.6   About cash analytics

As a committed income-gauging programming supplier, cash analytics assists our clients with utilizing all wellsprings of inner and outside information to develop their money-further estimating processes.

By utilizing APIs to concentrate information from all sources right away, and information representation apparatuses to show that information, cash analytics empowers our clients to perform a high-esteem examination on all of their interior and outside cash-determining information.

Assuming you might want to see an exhibit of our product while we go through the subtleties of how the mechanical interaction functions practically (Gray and Debreceny, 2014).

5.3   Financial time series analysis

Market perceptions and precise investigations have revealed that monetary time series, such as market records and resource costs, are frequently determined by multiscale factors, ranging from long-term financial cycles to short-term fluctuations. This proposes that monetary time series are possibly installed with various timescales. Customarily, Fourier analysis has been an amazing asset in tracking down a ghastly portrayal of time series. Nonetheless, the Fourier bases are, by supposition, fixed and direct. Then again, nonstationary and nonlinear elements are often seen in monetary time series. These attributes can barely be captured by straight models and require a versatile and nonlinear methodology for investigation. For a really long time, strategies in view of a brief time frame, Fourier change, and wavelets have been created and applied to nonstationary time series; however, there are still difficulties in catching nonlinear elements, and the frequently recommended suspicions make the techniques not completely versatile

(Sood *et al.*, 2021, 2022). This necessitates the use of a versatile and nonlinear examination methodology (Green and Choi, 1997).

One elective methodology in versatile time series examination is the Hilbert-Huang change (HHT). The HHT strategy can deteriorate any time series into swaying parts with nonstationary amplitudes and frequencies utilizing experimental mode decay (EMD). This completely versatile strategy gives a multiscale decay to the first time series, which gives more extravagant data about the time series. The Hilbert change is later used to extract each part's prompt recurrence and quick sufficiency. The decay onto various timescales likewise considers remaking up to various goals, giving a smoothing and sifting instrument that is great for boisterous monetary time series. The strategy for HHT and its varieties has been applied in various fields, from design to geophysics. There have been a few examinations of the varieties and options in contrast to EMD, including enhancement-based strategies and commotion-aided approaches. We apply the integral gathering observational mode decay for monetary time series with an elevated degree of natural commotion (CEEMD). Like EMD, CEEMD deteriorates any time series, fixed or not, into various inherent mode capacities that address the nearby qualities of the time series at various timescales; however, the timescale partition is improved by settling mode blending in EMD. The clamour-aided approach is also more vigorous than natural information commotion. In past investigations, CEEMD has helped anticipate and handle signals. Later utilization of EMD and the clamour helped varieties incorporate. It used EMD and HHT to fund date back to work by Huang and co-creators on displaying contract rate information.

In past examinations, EMD has been utilized for monetary time series gauging and looking at the relationship between monetary time series. The investigations that took on the full HHT methodology for AI showed up in the electrical design field. Nonetheless, in the greater part of the past investigations involving EMD or HHT as determining highlights, the deterioration was pre-executed in a general time frame, including preparing and testing information, which is not pragmatic while doing continuous gauging. Furthermore, both EMD and HHT loan data from the past and the future to register ongoing qualities, which can result in data spillage in the anticipating system. However, because the forecast depends on the end impact of EMD, the decay error becomes very large near the end of the period. Previous research has left it unclear how to pass the end impact test (Griffin and Wright, 2015).

In this section, utilizing CEEMD and Hilbert ghostly examination, we infer the immediate energy-recurrence range related to monetary time series to inspect the properties of different timescales implanted in the first time series. Significant interpretable multiscale yields from the HHT strategy are perceived as another arrangement of elements, called HHT highlights. At the end of the day, our technique radically grows the list of capabilities accessible to AI. Unlike previous studies; our primary goal is to find a novel way to incorporate HHT features with end impact adjustment into AI techniques for extrapolating forecasts on monetary time series. We likewise concentrated on the element determination issue when involving HHT for AI.

5.4 Web analytics, visual analytics, service analytics, multimedia analytics, textual data analytics

Mixed-media examination has zeroed in on pictures, video, and somewhat sound and gained ground in single channels. The interactive media investigation has not zeroed in on text examination. The visual examination, like its predecessor, data perception, has focused on the client's communication with information during the insightful cycle in addition to the essential science. By and large, we utilize the expression "investigation" to refer to the examination of human evaluation. The overarching issue we cover in this instructive engagement is the solidification of sight and sound investigation and visual evaluation to supervise media knowledge collected from various sources with various purposes or ambitions and incorporating all media varieties and mixes used in the same way (Guerard *et al.*, 2013). To start the instructional exercise, we give the historical backdrop of the two particular fields – mixed media investigation and visual examination – noticing their critical advancement as the years progressed. We then provide a review of every one of these fields. We discuss the significance of combining interactive media examination and visual investigation for managing the computerized information that is currently available. Then, present the joining of media examination and visual investigation into the field of sight and sound examination. We depict an illustration.

Regarding the Infomedia project at Carnegie Mellon University's potential in this sector, because of the linear time nature of sound and video narratives, particularly during their immediate, simple tape transfer, the academics discovered that extracting proof and backup resources from massive video collections can be time-consuming. Thanks to synced information and sorting, access to the resources worked on increased when these accounts were automated. The researchers also combined data visualization, library science, and discourse recognition with their video analysis to create compelling user interfaces for investigating the mixed video and sound media. Their plans were the consequence of logical investigations into the manners in which people examine mixed media and, accordingly, represent sight and sound examination (Preety *et al.*, 2021).

5.4.1 Interactive media analysis

Present-day interactive media data recovery (MIR>) research has been conducted in the traditional fields of PC vision, improved image management, and example acknowledgement studies, which began in the last part of the 1970s to the mid-1980s. Over the next 30 years, new developments in the interactive media innovative work (R&D) people group emerged. During the 1980s, when computerized photos were not widely available, the audit was occasionally about boundary discovery, cutoff and curvature revelations, region creation, form I.D., semantic segmentation, and so on, of separate images or structural parts of images. During the 1990s, when both computerized processes and photos were becoming increasingly important in our everyday lives, information photograph recovery (CBIR) and information video cut rehabilitation (CBVR) were two of the most significant R&D achievements of the decade. Forceful shot limits for differentiating proof and informative collecting researchers to determine were two of the most successful investigating concentrates inside investigators and modern-day assessments laboratories.

The emergence of the World Wide Web (WWW) further characterized the 1990s, bringing much media material to our personal computers and energizing the rapid advancement of sight, hearing, and news organizations. In 1993, the crucial ACM Multimedia (MM) global social meeting, which included MIR as a vital rallying point, was organized. Even during the 1990s, the MIR sociological class's primary R&D goal was to nurture PC-driven advancements for specialized usage essentially (Hastie *et al.*, 2009). Interestingly, the essential objective of the 2000s is to create human-driven advancements that overcome any barrier between broad clients and the innovations that convey sight and sound data to the clients. We truly do see more endeavors to recover video or picture data as well as sound data.

Notwithstanding, we have not seen fruitful instances of media data combination in scholastic writing or patent applications. By and large, sound data recovery does not assume a significant role in advancing mixed media data recovery studies. Text-based computer forensics research is much less important. There have been a few studies on archives comprising images and text or other mixed-media frameworks. The introduction of portable mobile phones and the widespread availability of interactive media message services prompted the industry to produce better organizing innovations to organize visual and audio data and improved skimming and summary innovations to access the data. The decade of the 2000s also marked the debut of the primary ACM International Conference on Multimedia Feature Extraction in 2008. MIR has developed its own identity and is no longer merely an R&D tracking section of the more traditional media immediate area (Hoerl and Kennard, 1970). Finally, it is a widely held belief that there are no addressed issues within the MIR people group, which incorporates the more conventional picture and video recuperation local area. "Occasionally, an overall issue is reduced to a more minor specialty issue where high exactness and accuracy can be quantitatively demonstrated, yet the overall issue remains to a great extent perplexing."

5.4.2   *Visual analytics*

Visual investigation research and development has resulted in a somewhat new set of advancements. Visual investigation anticipates providing logical thinking innovation supported by human collaborations via powerful and dynamic visual connection points for all media types as scale-autonomous examination approaches. Visual investigation has a long history in computer graphics and perception, and it has outgrown data representation. Visual investigation acquires essential math for representation and the change of data into calculable structures. It also acquires information sciences to deal with complex data. In visual examination, a high-dimensional scientific space is created to empower the recognition of the normal and disclosure of the startling during logical reasoning. Visual investigation analysts imagine an exceptionally captivating instinctive visual connection point that depends on mental standards and empowers a manner of thinking for dissecting mixed media data across numerous applications. This vision arose from the normal evolution of PC designs and representation (Hogan *et al.*, 2008). PC illustrations began during the 1970s with an emphasis on activity, acknowledgment, and computer-aided planning and designing for car and airplane ventures. There was likewise a wide interest in creating and applying PC design advances to logical areas.

A center distribution setting in an R&D plan prodded interest in the likely effect of logical PC designs. Therefore, numerous major exploration programs in logical perception and the IEEE visualization gathering were sent off in the mid-1980s. While non-logical utilizations of representation were additionally of interest, a reasonable spotlight on logical areas arose, animating exploration and subsidizing perception in science, stargazing, barometrical sciences, and numerous other fields, essentially expanding their capacities. A conference of US government bodies that took place in the mid-1990s requested a few researchers in research habitats to consider perception from unstructured text reports. At that point, numerous analysts were envisioning natural arrangements for drug revelation; nonetheless, creating representations for message examination appeared to be extremely challenging and had minimal numerical establishment.

In handling text representation, scientists zeroed in on imagining 200–2,000 archives in a generally basic configuration. This was completed as a prototype in mid-1994 and was displayed on the front of the instructions for the first IEEE Scientific Conference on Knowledge Discovery. As many noticed the great hold entryways had on data comprehension in the late 1990s, this sector of concentration swiftly grew. The Spatiotemporal Framework for Information Retrieval and Exploration (SPIRE) breakthrough served as the foundation for most of this work. This current situation prompted the United States Department of Homeland Intelligence to establish the National Visualization and Analytics Center (NVAC) at the Lawrence Livermore National Laboratory (Huang *et al.*, 2014).

The 2001 fear-based, oppressed minority assault on the United States sparked a rethinking of technologies to reduce the risk of future attacks through scientific investigation of all architectural and data kinds. Similarly, professionals were perplexed by the growing volume and variety of data. (PNNL) in 2004 to consider alternative representational approaches. The PNNL-developed INSPIRETM improvements demonstrated the feasibility of novel representation methodologies. In 2005, a group of 40 professionals from business, academia, administration, and public labs collaborated on a visual inquiry plan published in the book *Illumination of the Path: The Technology Development Framework for Dynamic Optimization*. This research and development strategy was the foundation for visual inquiry and established fresh thinking for multi-modular visual observation. Full mixed media examination has been delayed to this point, so we are endeavoring to focus on the basic new setup of advances expected to break down picture, text, video, geospatial, sound, designs, tables, and different types of data. Sight and sound investigation are a basic requirement for a wide scope of applications, including but not limited to clinical, financial, online entertainment, and security applications.

5.4.3   Multimedia analysis

Data recovery in mixed media encompasses topics such as client collaboration, information examination, AI, extraction, data representation, and so on. Multimedia information retrieval (MIR) people group does not characterize text or archive data as interactive media information. Furthermore, picture media addresses most of what the MIR people group creates. Video media is frequently contemplated; however, sound media only appears in a modest number of utilizations. A more troublesome issue is managing mixed-media data accumulated from various sources with various objectives or targets. The accompanying overview of studies presents short portrayals of companion audited review papers on different media themes: it addresses picture and video data recovery. The paper covers customary (1) video investigation subjects from variety, surface, shape, and spatial similitudes; (2) video parsing points, for example, worldly division, object movement examination, outlining, and scene examination; and (3) video deliberation themes like skimming, key-outline extraction, content-based recovery of clasps, ordering, and commenting. It depicts a pretty full methodological framework for early-generation image data recovery technologies. The discussion focuses on (1) highlighting aspects of solvent extraction such as tone, surfaces, structure, variation format, and divisions; (2) describing image ordering strategies such as multilayered reduction and multi-faceted reordering; and (3) describing picture recovery structures developed in the 1990s. Many of the processes mentioned in this published study are already standard technology for the vast majority of visual and audio foundations and apps (Huang *et al.*, 2014). It excels at image processing, design analysis, and artificial intelligence. The study opens with a discussion of essential features such as tone and appearance. It then moves on to the more sophisticated notion of "highlight reels." It may be extracted from a photograph and used to organize an order of global elements, eye-catching elements, signals, patterns, and an article highlighting. The study also addresses AI topics like proximity coordination and semantically translating, as well as improving organizational performance points like picture arranging, accumulating, and questioning. It addresses content-based information retrieval (CBIR). The paper includes genuine solid areas for a mining flavor that covers all aspects of data disclosure for informational image collections. Despite specific focuses like imprint extraction, clustering, request, portrayal, and equivalence planning, the paper also inspects non-particular issues like feel, security, web, and describing. Two incredibly late papers are radiant for summing up the bleeding edge in multimedia analysis as the beginning peruser endeavors to answer the request "Visual Concept Search Solved?" in their paper in *IEEE Computer*. In ACM Communications, Grauman's article "Gainfully Searching for Similar Images" reviews new computations that enable energetic yet flexible image search. Subscription rates for massive social affairs of examinations focus on the sphere of visual evaluation. The Crucial Technology Development

Strategy was published. After 5 years, an extraordinary issue of the *Journal of Data Interpretation* focused on the heritage and the future of images obtained. Furthermore, the lead piece in that great issue addressed five examples of overcoming hardship, demonstrating the importance of significant new developments. The Emergence of Multimodal Analytics: Combining Multimedia Analyses with Obtained From the statistical Human communication is understood to be nonlinear and non-static. Phonetic analyses of communications through movements in the late 1970s and early 1980s concluded that visual imagery is essentially as rule-based and inventive as speech. Nonetheless, researchers discovered that unmistakable indications in language convey enormous grammatical and phonological knowledge. Even in our technologically connected environment, we find it more enjoyable to communicate openly and honestly. It is difficult to judge another person over the internet or even a shadow or darkness between them. The perception of sensory perception is nearly identical. Different media types designed for various purposes are constantly familiar to us for comprehension. To complete our investigation swiftly, we feel the PC should have the option to access this information to meet our immediate needs, exploiting the different deep relationships among the entertainment kinds people have set up for educational objectives. A record may contain numbers, graphics, and even audio cuts that reconfigure the narrative, and the manner in which such elements are used to create the overall message is unknown. Visual evaluation has served as a guide for managing massive amounts of data. Sight-and-sound evaluation has made enormous breakthroughs in dissecting all forms of media. Supercomputing pronunciation has also made significant progress in extracting importance from massive databases of messages and discourse. We recognize that these fields complement each other really well. As part of their collaboration, we depict the task for Infomedia to complete (Humpherys *et al.*, 2011). The Infomedia Research Company at Cornell University used speech recognition, image processing, and language advancements to collect synchronized information for improved navigation into and among video groups. Benchmarking talks, such as the National Institute of Standards and Technology (NIST) Text Retrieval Conference (TREC) video track (TRECVID) assessment collection, charted progress over time. Infomedia's effort concentrated on automated metadata development and connection and associated foci using such information to bring meaningful, successful recovery from mixed media corpora. Rather than dictating how a client should read a massive text collection, the Informedia software includes a variety of perspectives that are addressed in greater depth. Talk confirmation can provide an open recording to use for resources containing a sound story track, such as narratives or news reporting. Informedia researchers Alex Hauptmann and Michael Witbrock initially examined the precision of recordings created by customizable talk affirmation (ASR) for video recovery, demonstrating how the knowledge rehabilitation possibility may be enough despite ASR record blunders. The problem was further explored by the NIST TREC Spoken Documentation Information Extraction (SDR) program from 1997 to 2000, which concluded in 2000 that the recovery of records from news programs, integrating ASR for recordings, allowed modestly interesting information reconstitution, even with sentence botch velocities of 30%, in cases when specific records are accessible. A significant amount of Infomedia Research has focused on using the various modalities of text, image, and speech to compensate for needs that cannot be fully automated. Interface work gets the client too involved in issues in mechanized dealing with, for instance, a completed plan of trees being misrecognized collectively or the adage "Sax" being misrecognized as a person in named substance marking. Through such work and benchmarking practices like TRECVID, the client will undoubtedly have more tools at his disposal with which to oversee more important volumes of information. Dynamic learning allows the client to check for errors so the system can learn from them when building future classifiers. Notwithstanding, electronic communication structures can be utilized to enhance esteem. ASR engines can offer a tight word-time defensive strategy that maintains the precise trajectory of important bits within a larger sound or video. Another direction has been to utilize operationally costly processes that can pass on extended confirmation to the annoyance of properly managing time. MoSIFT, for example, is a method for rapidly detecting techniques in the perceptive video that employs consistent material that is not completely set in stone from the optical stream and is built with specified appearance properties. The worth of these video recovery procedures is measured by continuous participation in global comparing discussions, for example, NIST TRECVID, which graphs the development of video evaluation undertakings (IAASB, 2016).

5.4.4   Interactive media analysis

NIST TRECVID, led by Alan Smeaton, Wessel Kraaij, and Paul Throughout (Baliyan *et al.*, 2022) has detailed the progression of numerous video rehabilitation tasks over the years, including shot identification, conceptual sequencing, and scheduled and intelligence-recovery implementation. Shot categorization degrades a video arrangement into part shootings with more diverse levelled handling to organize shots with espouses and to allow a visual chapter-by-chapter guide within the film to be built using thumbnail picture depictions for shots. A screenplay of shot thumbnails serves the same purpose as ASR sound ordering: it provides a tool to evaluate and study a direct video display. Conceptual sequencing, the programming duty of assigning semantic labels to video sequences (such as shots), might be a critical advancement for filtering, arranging, scrutinizing, searching, and other visual exploitation. As time passed, NIST TRECVID test results revealed how some graphical ideas, such as the presence of countenances or text, could eventually be brilliantly tagged to video, while others, such as extension, transport, or bloom, remained testing. Given the fluctuating exactness of programmed characterization for various semantic labels, the Informed Bunch created interfaces with the client in mind to determine whether more noteworthy accuracy for a specific undertaking and tagging merits a less conspicuous review (getting fewer applications with predicted better accuracy) or a more obvious review (doing more ranging from three all with each other and not missing something of significance) that should be imitated. Allowing the passenger control algorithm on storyboard interactions into shots, which labelling to attach as pathways, and the majority of it has consistently resulted in improved implementation on video recuperation tasks over time. In other words, NIST TRECVID studies have confirmed the value of a human expert for shot-based restoration tasks, where a human administrator as part of the visual investigative activity outperforms completely computerized looking. Surprisingly, in TRECVID 2009, the best mechanization search frameworks defeated the best intuitive seek accommodations 3 times out of 24. As certain visual organizing plans, for example, face positioning, have been devised, those operations that may most benefit from such plans will also exhibit remarkable improvements (like finding hordes of individuals or individuals at work areas, two of the three points that worked so well for the mechanized hunt). NIST TRECVID reports progress for key sets of workouts that aid in graphical inquiry.

5.4.5   Visual analytics

Another work in assessment began in 2005 when the field of visual examination was defined. The most common issue heard by analysts in perception was a lack of infor-mation. Hence, another task was begun at NVAC to make manufactured informational indexes extremely close to genuine information without issues of order or actually recognizable data. This undertaking currently makes the informational collections for the yearly IEEE Visual Analytics Science and Technology (VAST) Challenges (http://hcil.cs.umd.edu/localphp/hcil/vast10/index.php). The engineered informational index project was initially expected to last around ten years, beginning with generally simple dissecting information that would eventually turn out to be more intricate information. Today, these informational indexes are openly accessible and are being utilized in classes, industry, and government-financed research programs. Every informational collection is a "ground truth" situation that approximates genuine circumstances but is open for investigation. What's more, another program was laid out to go beyond con-venience assessment to utility assessment. This is a significant change. We need to have the option to assess advancements to show the adequacy of the connection point as well as the scientific improvement that was the objective of the point of interaction. The objective is to foster assessment processes that empower analysts to demonstrate the expanded logical worth of new advancements experimentally. Late advancement in the field of visual investigation has been evident in the introductions given in huge gath-erings of US government examiners. It has become established in intelligence that perception for information revelation and representation for delineation of proof have essentially various qualities. Visual investigation has advanced so far that experts can now search for additional information rather than bemoaning the issue of too much information (James *et al.*, 2013).

5.5   Predictive, prescriptive, descriptive analytics

5.5.1   What is descriptive analytics?

Typically, the first stage of business insight is elucidating investigation. It utilizes information conglomeration and information mining to gather and coordinate ver-ifiable information, creating representations such as line diagrams, bar outlines, and pie graphs. The enlightening investigation, like measurable demonstrations, presents a reasonable image of what has occurred previously, but it stops there – it does not do translations or suggest future activities.

5.5.2 What does the spellbinding investigation show?

The engaging examination is useful to distinguish replies to straightforward inquiries concerning what happened before. While you are doing this kind of investigation, you will regularly begin by recognizing KPIs as benchmarks for execution in a given business region (deals, finance, activities, etc.). Then, you will figure out what informational indexes will illuminate the investigation and where to source them from, and then, at that point, gather, and set them up. You will utilize different techniques to see examples and measure execution, for example, design following, grouping, synopsis insights, and relapse investigation. Finally, you will form opinions to make the information more quickly and effectively reasonable. On account of instruments like Sigma, even non-specialized chiefs can do this kind of examination without SQL or other coding abilities.

5.5.3 Instances of expressive examination

Chiefs from every office in an organization, from finance to operations, can benefit from the expressive examination. The following are a couple of models:

- The outreach group can realize which client portions created the most note-worthy dollar sum in deals a year ago.
- The showcasing group can reveal which web-based entertainment stages generated the best profit from promoting speculation last quarter.
- The money group can follow month-over-month and year-over-year income development or decline.
- Activities can follow stock keeping unit (SKU) interest across geographic areas over the last year.

5.5.4 What is diagnostic analytics?

You will need to know why it worked out when you realize what occurred. That is where symptomatic investigation comes in. Understanding why a pattern is created or an issue happens will make your business knowledge significant. It keeps your group from making off-base speculations, especially connected with confounding relationships and causality.

5.5.5 What does symptomatic examination show?

Normally, there is more than one contributing element to some random pattern or occasion. Demonstrative examination can uncover the full range of causes, guaranteeing you see the total picture. You can likewise see which variables are most effective and focus on them. You will use some of the same methods for illustrative investigation, but you will go further with drill-down and relationships. You may also need to obtain additional datasets to illuminate your investigation fully. Sigma makes this simple, particularly when associated with Snowflake's strong abilities.

5.5.6 Instances of demonstrative examination

Each group in an organization can benefit from the demonstrative investigation. See these models:

- The outreach group can recognize shared qualities and ways of behaving among productive client sections that might explain why they are spending more.
- The promoting group can examine the distinguishing characteristics of high-performing web-based entertainment promotions in comparison to all the more ineffectively performing ones to comprehend the reasons for performance disparities.
- The money group can contrast the planning of key drives with month-over-month and year-over-year income development or decline to assist with deciding connections.
- Activities can take a gander at territorial atmospheric conditions to check whether they are adding to interest for specific SKUs across geographic areas.

5.5.7 What is predictive analytics?

At the point when you realize what occurred previously and comprehend the reason why it worked out, you can then start to anticipate what is probably going to happen later on in light of that data. The prescient examination takes the examination a stride further, utilizing measurements, computational demonstrating, and AI to decide the likelihood of different results.

5.5.8 What does the prescient investigation show?

Through prescient examination, the pair estimates possible future results and recognizes the probability of those occasions occurring. It assists associations with better preparation and reasonable objective setting, as well as keeping away from pointless gambling. It also enables organizations to more precisely anticipate future execution in light of past execution and the factors currently influencing it. Perhaps the most significant type of prescient investigation is imagining a scenario where examination includes changing different qualities to perceive what those changes will mean for the result. When business groups can conduct rapid, iterative analysis to evaluate options, they are motivated to pursue better opportunities more quickly. Sigma was planned with this ability.

5.5.9 Instances of prescient investigation

Prescient examination is particularly strong for groups since it permits chiefs to be more certain about what's in store. The following are a couple of models:

- The outreach group can get familiar with the income capability of a specific client portion.
- The advertising group can anticipate how much income they are probably going to produce with a forthcoming effort.

- The money group can make more precise projections for the following financial year.
- The tasks group can all the more likely anticipate interest for different items in various districts at explicit times in the forthcoming year.

5.5.10   What is prescriptive analytics?

Prescriptive examination is where the activity is. This type of examination advises groups on what they should do based on the expectations set. It is the most intricate sort, which is why only about 3% of organizations use it in their business. While involving AI in prescriptive investigation is presently standing out as truly news-worthy, the truth is that this innovation has quite a way to go in its capacity to produce significant, noteworthy experiences. Exploiting AI at scale requires running many queries looking for measurable abnormalities. However, arbitrarily recognized inconsistencies do not necessarily point straightaway to businesses opening doors. Until AI innovation progresses, uncovering genuinely significant business bits of knowledge requires human association – dissecting information regarding business processes, market patterns, and company objectives, and deciphering it.

5.5.11   What does the prescriptive investigation show?

Prescriptive investigation guesses what, when, and why an occasion or pattern could occur. It lets you know which activities have the highest potential for the best result. It permits groups to fix issues, further develop execution, and take advantage of significant chances. While the amount of information required for prescriptive analysis suggests that it will not be suitable for everyday use, it has a wide range of applications. For instance, how the outreach group can further develop the deal interaction for each target vertical:

- Assisting the showcase with joining and figuring out what item to advance in the next quarter.
- Methods for the money group to reduce risk across the board;
- Assist the tasks with joining and deciding how to improve warehousing.

5.6   Expert methods for financial regression and classification problems

A decision tree that recursively gains parts from higher to lower hubs is typically built by a series of nearby decisions and frequently includes the issue of clamour overfit chime. To address this, various recommendations have been made to upgrade all components using transformative calculation. Regardless, numerous previous studies attempted to find the best tree by applying the parts of a highly valued tree to another tree. On account of complicated information, i.e., informa-tion that contains a great deal of commotion and uncommon qualities, the split with a high wellness esteem at one hub is curious to the information test at that hub; the wellness esteem does not work regardless of whether this is applied to another information test. A technique for looking through all parts of one tree without trading branches has also been proposed. However, due to a large number of combinations of highlights and their dividing focuses, or edge values, such a technique is impractical for complex data. Bilevel GA, which performs highlight determination and looks for the request and selection of chosen highlights by independent transformative calculation, has been proposed as of late as a productive strategy for, by and large, improving the general construction of a tree. This technique, in particular, has demonstrated high assessment precision while requiring only a small amount of scale information. However, the tree's evaluation capacity becomes irregular when an element used for the split of the upper hub changes, as indicated by the concurrent hunt of the component request and the edge esteem. Hence, utilizing an absurd inquiry strategy assumes coherence. To address this, the pursuit technique is a GA that rehashes individual choice, hybridity, and change because it improves parts that become non-deterministic polynomial time (NP) – hard when complex information is used. Likewise, while utilizing such a GA, a split that is powerful for an area locale separated by unambiguous upper hubs can be applied to a district isolated by other upper hubs. As a result, the tree's wellness value does not always improve with age, and the best tree is unlikely to be considered.

5.7 Factor models for big data in options stochastic modelling and pricing

Single-factor stochastic unpredictability models cannot explain the relationship between the instability level and the incline of the grin, regardless of whether they are useful in producing grins and sneers. We have found that the model further develops the single-consideration model's term structure aspect as well as the moneyness aspect. They have shown that the two-factor model considers greater adaptability in demonstrating restrictive skewness and kurtosis for given degrees of contingent difference, which is reliable with the finding that the incline of the slope generally develops autonomously from the level of unpredictability:

$$dS = \mu SDt + \sqrt{v_1}SdZ_1 + \sqrt{v_2}SdZ_2,$$
$$dv_1 = \kappa_1(\theta_1 - v_1)dt + \sigma_1\sqrt{v_1}dZ_3,$$
$$dv_2 = \kappa_2(\theta_2 - v_2)dt + \sigma_2\sqrt{v_2}dZ_4,$$

where μ is the prompt return per unit season of the basic resource, θ_1 and θ_2 are separately the long-run methods for v_1 and v_2, κ_1 and κ_2 are the paces of mean-inversion, while σ_1 and σ_2 are the instantaneous volatilities of v_1 and v_2 per unit time individually.

5.7.1 Bachelier design

The higher the perceived cost, the higher the cost share prices, assuming that the reimbursement rate is negative and the inventory cost parts satisfy the preceding SDE:

$$dS(t) = S(0)\sigma dB(t) \tag{5.4}$$

where $S(t)$ is the spot price of the basic security at time t; $B(t)$ denotes the average Brownian movements and represents the stock price volatility. When contemplating an over-European call option, its selection is fulfilled at the outset. Osborne improved the Bachelier approach in 1959 by demonstrating the stock cost process using the statistical mechanics of mass diffusion. He supported this practice in conceptual terms in light of the Weber–Fechner rule, which states that people perceive the strength of improvements on a linear scale rather than a straight scale.

5.7.2   Scholes–Merton (BS) model in the dark

In 1973, Black and Scholes developed the Black–Scholes formula, which was revolutionary throughout the history of choice valuation hypotheses. The remarkable component of this model is presenting the gamble as a nonpartisan measure and asserting that the limited worth of subordinate security under this action is, to be sure, a martingale.

5.7.3   Demand model

MJD Model Demand Process is defined as a never-ending time stochastic cycle $X=X(t)$: $t0$ with the properties of autonomous augmentations, fixed increases, and stochastic progression. Aside from the Markovian and fixed circulation properties presumption on stock value, it is also critical to demonstrate what happens when $S(t)$ has the properties that huge leaps for outrageous market developments and little leaps and dispersion for prompt exchanging.

5.8   Financial mathematical and statistical tools

5.8.1   Insertion and extrapolation

The introduction is a factual method that, through an investigation of the time series of known figures of the populace, say from 1921 to 1991, one can include the populace figure for 1985. At the same time, extrapolation permits us to gauge or expect an incentive for a few future pieces of information. In financial analysis, addition is frequently used to ensure the internal rate of return of a task, to figure out the respect development (YTM) of a security or debenture, and in other situations where the time value of money is considered and an introduction must be made utilizing the present and future worth tables. In a monetary investigation, extrapolation is used to anticipate future deals, costs, benefits, long-term capital requirements, and the creation of budget reports for monetary establishments, banks, etc.

5.8.2   Decision theory

The Bayesian methodology is based on Bayes' well-known research paper, "An Essay towards tackling an issue in the Doctrine of Chance" (1763) (Smeaton *et al.*, 2009). The Bayesian idea depended on the choice hypothesis.

Bayesian analysis is a modern method used by experts to decide whether to conduct an investigation study. This sort of investigation will be reliant upon different options in contrast to the specific issue, the accessibility of new or extra data, and the hypothesis of likelihood. In the choice hypothesis, there are certain arrangements of rules and certain arrangements of options. We need to choose those standards and choices to obtain an ideal outcome. The term "ideal" means benefit expansion or cost minimization.

5.8.3   Decision-making under states of assurance

A venture expert should arrive at a conclusion about putting resources into one of the three speculation portfolio bundles. Every venture portfolio contains various extents of normal stock, modern bonds, and land. The table beneath gives the increases of putting resources into these portfolios under various conditions of nature (S1, S2, and S3) in light of the projection of changes in stock costs, yields on security, and appreciation in land values. Under certain conditions, we must choose the option that provides the greatest benefit. In this manner, in the province of nature, S1, the examiner decides to put resources into portfolios C and S2, in portfolios B and S3, in portfolio A because that elective gives the investigator the greatest advantage in that specific state.

5.8.4   Decision-making under states of vulnerability

When making decisions under vulnerability, the leader is aware of various potential natural conditions but lacks the data to assign any probabilities of event to them (hopeful or sceptical). Assuming the leader is hopeful, he trusts that, given the determination of any methodology, "nature" will act in a way that gives the best prize. Subsequently, the leader recognizes the greatest benefit associated with the determination of every other option, and the limit of these is picked as the choice. This model is known as the Maximax Criterion. Going on with a similar model, we can compute the limit of every option as displayed in the above table, and the limit of these will give us the choice to be picked. Accordingly, in the above model, the most extreme advantage is gotten from the elective C. The investigator accepts that nature will act according to state S1. Assuming the chief is cynical, he accepts that nature neutralizes him and is persuaded that whatever system is chosen, nature will answer to have the least conceivable benefit. In this manner, the chief first recognizes the most reduced benefit compared to another option and then selects that elective, which is the limit of the above-mentioned least benefits. Along these lines, this rule is called the Maximin Criterion. Along these lines, in the above model, the chief decides to put resources into portfolio A. Note that this approach ensures the base benefit. Yet, on the off chance that, the leader in the middle between these extremes (neither hopeful nor totally critical) yet indicates his degree of confidence by a record of optimism, which is allotted a worth somewhere in the range of 0 and 1, both 0 and 1, inclusive, decision is made in view of weighted benefits. The elective which gives limit of the weighted benefits is the choice picked by the leader. This approach is known as Hurwitz Criterion.

Laplace rule – When the chief has no unequivocal data about the likelihood of events of the different conditions of nature, he simplifies suspicion that each is similarly possible.

Lament criterion – Loss of chance is a typical peculiarity in the business world. This measure considers the disappointment related not to having gotten the best that would have been conceivable if the condition of nature to happen were known ahead of time.

5.8.5   Correlation analysis

Business chiefs can likewise utilize this sort of investigation to respond to questions, including examining quantitative information on two factors. They include information from bivariate populaces.

Connection investigation is helpful to give data to the promoting chief regarding the connections among different items and administrations with the same highlights and to have a similar dissemination region or area. For instance, the top managerial staff of Bata Company is confronted with the issue of assessing the yearly deals in a shop to be opened in X spot where Bata has not opened previously. They need this data to design the size of the shop, how much stock to be placed on the feature, and the quantity of representatives to be employed. A response to this issue might be found genuinely by laying out the overall relationship in the urban areas where the organization is currently working, say between the extent of a city-utilized workforce or working populace and deals in its Bata shops. From the size of "X" utilized workforce, an assessment of the yearly deals in that new shop can be assessed, and the top managerial staff ought to have the option to put together its choices with respect to this gauge.

5.8.6   Cost volume benefit (CVP) or break-even
investigation

It is a graphical and arithmetical portrayal of the connections among the volume of results, expenses, and incomes. It is perhaps the best apparatus used for determining an area. Since every single area will have an alternate expense for construction and deal volume, CVP assists the chief in recognizing where the benefits are high.

5.8.7   Tests in ventures

There are many principles that determine how the previous information on offer costs can be utilized to get a hint with respect to what's in store for offer costs. Such principles would be useful to a financial backer because they could be used to predict when offer prices would likely rise. The financial backer could purchase the offers and sell them in the future at a more exorbitant cost, thereby procuring a benefit. Factual tests have been applied to analyze whether such guidelines can convey what they guarantee. Could financial backers who follow these guidelines benefit more than those who do not follow these guidelines? Do these principles truly provide information about what to expect in terms of costs or offers? Are momentary offer cost changes not arbitrary in nature? The following are the consequences of two tests applied to past offer information to discover whether such information has any data applicable to future offer cost gauges.

5.8.8 Serial relationship tests

The sequential relationship has been utilized to track down the connection coefficient between current changes in a share's cost and past changes in the equivalent share's cost. It was observed that the relationship coefficient was extremely close to zero. In the event that the ongoing offer cost changes are uncorrelated with past offer cost changes, how could the principles in light of an investigation of past offer costs have any predictive worth?

5.8.9 Run tests

The relationship coefficient is unduly affected by outrageous perceptions. It was contended that a couple of outrageous and unrepresentative perceptions might have contorted the consequences of the above sequential connection tests. As a result, run tests were devised. Here, just the headings of offer cost changes were thought of. The exorbitant impact of outrageous perceptions was removed because the extent of cost changes was overlooked. In commonplace run tests, the progressions in share costs may be denoted by +, which means an increase, and −, which means a decrease. A run is said to keep going as long as the cost shifts do not take a different path. For instance, given an offer's accompanying day-to-day value changes, we can recognize three runs. Run tests reveal that the number of runs is nearly equal to the number of runs that would be expected if offer price changes were arbitrary. As a result, it appears to help that offer price changes are irregular.

5.8.10 Simulation

Recreation is a procedure in which decisions must be made while in a vulnerable state. Reproduction as a quantitative technique requires the setting up of a numerical model that would address the interrelationships between the factors associated with the genuine circumstance where a choice is to be made. For instance, all auto-producing organizations have a test track on which the vehicles are first determined. The test track has every one of the curves, inclines, potholes, and so on that can be found on the streets on which the vehicles would be thusly determined. The test track is, consequently, a reenacted rendition of the genuine states of the different streets. Since improvements and suppositions are, for the most part, expected in scientific methodologies, they are not needed for recreation. Recreation has found application in the space of business navigation. Models include speculation evaluation under vulnerability, investigation of portfolio execution, holding line issues, corporate monetary models, corporate preparation, and stock choices.

5.8.11 Decision tree analysis

The outcome network created for specific circumstances cannot demonstrate the legitimate interrelationship between the various steps of a muddled circumstance.

Presenting time relationships in a matrix is additionally troublesome. These viewpoints can frequently be best shown in an organizational structure called the choice tree. Successive choices are frequently expected to tackle complex issues. The previous choices affect the later ones. A choice network is a wasteful device for addressing consecutive choices. The choice tree is a method for addressing the sequential, multi-stage rationale of a choice issue. The choice tree is a branch of the likelihood tree. It uses two images: a crate to address a choice hub and a circle to address an opportunity node. It guides a director to choose a methodical way. For instance, the money supervisors of the soap-fabricating organization finding success in the initial 2 years of the company tasks are thinking about setting up one more plant to fulfill the developing need for the item. Assuming the interest is extremely high, the new venture is supposed to acquire Rs 2 million per annum. The likelihood that the interest is extremely high is 0.55. The firm can set up either a huge plant costing Rs 10 million or a little plant costing Rs 5 million. Either plant will require one year to fabricate, and as such, no benefits are procured in year 1. Both the plants have an expected existence of 4 years, after which their worth is viewed as immaterial. If the plant proves popular, the company can expand in year 2 at Rs 6 million. On the other hand, if there should be an occurrence of low interest, the firm can lessen the enormous plant in year 2 and recuperate Rs 3 million. The development or reduction of plant size will take an entire year, so that no benefits will be obtained in 1 year. The money manager can depict the entire choice interaction in a realistic modular known as a "choice tree." The choice tree is viewed as a numerical modular for the selection situation. Choice focuses, or hubs, and conditional nature focus or hubs, are present in all choice trees.

The images that address these are:

- A choice hub from which one of a few options might be picked.
- A condition of nature hub out of which one condition of nature will happen.

5.8.12   Sampling technique

Assuming the populace is endless, a finished specification is beyond the realm of possibilities. Additionally, assuming the units are annihilated throughout review, 100c/o examinations, however conceivable, are not the slightest bit alluring. However, regardless of whether the population is limited or the review is not horrendous, examinations are not taken as a plan of action 100% of the time for a variety of reasons, for example, authoritative and monetary ramifications, the time factor, and so on, and we rely on inspecting. Testing methods assist the promoter in determining the input regarding their deals, interactions, items, administrations, costs, etc. For example, one method for determining the normal existence of his plant's pencil-cell batteries is to work each cell until its life is completed and record the existence length so that the normal existence can be processed. In any case, assuming that each cell is spent along these lines, the production would not have any cells for clients. In such a case, examining is the method for determining normal cell life. Inspecting methods like simple arbitrary examination (SAE), systematic testing, stratified irregular examination (SIE), and group inspection have wide applications in the space of showcasing research.

5.8.13 Standard deviation

A venture should be assessed on two aspects: return and hazard. A financial backer cannot partake in an exceptional yield with next to no openness to risk. The higher the return, the higher the gamble in question, and the lower the openness to risk, the lower the return. Risk is characterized as the opportunity for injury, harm, or misfortune. The risk in ventures is the possibility of the recognized genuine returns being significantly lower than the normal returns. The gamble in a speculation is regularly estimated by the difference, or SD, in the profits from the mean or anticipated return. The thought is that the higher the scattering value, the higher the gamble. Frameworks, Applications, and Products in Data Processing (SAP) Business Analytics SAP now has subsidiaries in over 50 countries worldwide and is one of the world's largest programming organizations (the third-largest income autonomous programming supplier), employing over 27,000 people and serving more than 17,500 clients, which include the majority of the Fortune 500. It has in excess of 44,000 establishments, in excess of 120 nations, and in excess of 10 million individuals profiting from SAP ECC. It chiefly centers around six significant ventures: purchasing, processing, economics, discrete enterprises, welfare systems, and the service industry are all examples of industries. It is supported by robust areas for a Develop Network (SDN) social class, exchanging data using Internet-based diaries, chats, planning documents, and collections, and has professional helpers in powerful partnerships such as Adobe, Artificially Created, HP, IDS Scheer, Open Text, and Smart Ops.

SAP claims to generate revenue by providing excellent plans, in contrast to vast amounts of its unquestionable competition, for example, Oracle, which spends massive sums of money acquiring competition in the market. When Xerox opted to exit the PC market, it anticipated retaining IBM development in its systems integration. As part of the moving costs, IBM bought SDS/SAPE functionality, which was then provided to the laying out personnel from SAP for roughly 8% of the organization's laying out stack. On April 1, 1972, the organization established its command center in Weinheim and an office in Manheim, Germany, and registered as a private partnership under the normal German code "System analyse und Programmentwicklung." However, most of the time was spent in the occupational settings of their most important clients, the nearby office of Imperial Industrial Applications (ICI). SAP used individuals and paid DM 620,000 at the end of its most notable year of operation. The year 1973 saw the completion of SAP's main financial statements, known as real-time financials (RF), which proved to be insufficiently solid places for improvements in the advancement of SAP's succeeding method-based financial statements, known as SAP R/1. Furthermore, the organization expanded from a local to a national level, gaining clients in many parts of Germany, including the tobacco company Rothandle and the Pharmaceutical Corporation Knoll. Over the course of 2 years, SAP gathered assistance from 40 benchmark clients, and the branding began to develop. After 5 years, the corporate affiliations were disbanded, with its assets going to SAP GmbH.1976 was nearing its end when SAP's 25 representatives were paid DM 3.81 million. SAP's history is littered with examples of overcoming the difficulties of growing from a small private company to a global software company. When the R/2 System was introduced in 1978, it was a watershed moment in the organization's history. R/2 was the first structured, adventurous group that ran on focused server PCs.

It was incredible to see such large European MNCs seeking delicate, sound business plans with multi-cash and multinational assistance. As the accommodations neared the DM 10-million-mark, SAP consolidated all of its meetings under one roof in its modern computing center in Walldorf, which is currently the organization's headquarters. SAP was serving 50 of Germany's top 100 firms at the time. SAP introduced numerous components to its R/2 before travelling extensively, working with its clients. By 1982, deals had increased by 48%, and over 236 organizations in Luxembourg, Germany, and Austria were testing SAP projects. SAP AG was established in Switzerland to expand R/2 System configurations worldwide. The progress groups began to oversee newer modules such as personnel administration, engineering services, production schedules, and process control. By 1985, SAP had established itself as a household name in every European country. The organization continues to grow with the addition of additional volunteers in new locations. SAP solutions owes a significant portion of their advancements to their collaboration with educational institutions like the University of Southern California. SAP GmbH evolved into the business-oriented SAP AG and issued stock in 1988 amid typically significant improvements in overall parts. SAP was awarded the "Association of the Year" award by Successful Managers Magazines twice in 1989. Near the end of the 1980s, the globe began to shift toward client–server architecture. SAP introduced its R/3 solutions to deal with some of these client-server configurations, keeping in mind its historical record of far-reaching adaptability. In R/3, "R" stands for clinically insane, while "3" stands for a three-level system.

The three layers are the Presentation Server (GUI), Web Service, and Database Management System. Shipped off in 1992, it was a second hit, particularly in the United States, where SAP's share of general management shot up from basically nothing to an astounding 44% of SAP's general configurations, igniting the confidence of several Fortune 500 organizations. The examination is quite critical, with 8 of the top 10 semiconductor companies and 7 of the top 10 pharmaceutical organizations participating. It contains connections and monsters such as Microsoft. This transportation was primarily intended for the expected business segment. It was organized into distinct, interconnected modules that covered many express limitations in a company, the most significant of which were Financial and Controlling (FICO), Warehouse Management (MM), Production and Service (SD), Human Resources (HR), and Production Planning (PP). SAP has prioritized best practice frameworks in its item processes. It has created industry-specific (IS) modules to deal with particular organizations. By 1997, SAP had established relationships with more than 25 innovative organizations, including MIT, which contributed to its growth. The Web application decodes "Advanced Businesses Application Video Content Generations" (ABAP/4) programs via a bundle of file systems and controls input and output. All types of applications begin and terminate at the same time. A record named Single Connection File keeps track of a number of these rotations in the AS. The service can be standalone or distributed among several servers with predefined constraints, such as lighting servers. AS is affiliated with and promotes data collection sales to a metadata collection server. The database server is responsible for data collection and management, including enhancement, rehabilitation, and revitalization SAP cryptography library encodes all server-to-server exchanges. SAP R/3 had roughly 10,000 tables in the center that regulated connection implementation.

5.8.14   SAP R/3 vs. ERP

The main difference between SAP R/3 and ERP (Enterprise Resource Planning) is that ERP is built on SAP NetWeaver, where focused portions can be completed in JAVA and ABAP and each new instance is populated autonomously and freely. The initial release of MySAP ERP in 2003 included distinct items such as SAP R/3 Enterprise and SAP SEM, among others, and was a significant step toward integrating the online. Client application was bundled with NetWeaver, which was released in 2003. SAP ERP was therefore dubbed ECC (ERP Central Components) in its subsequent conveyances, which were joined by configurational alterations such as the incorporation of SAP SEM and SAP Information Technology Services Server into ECC. Each SAP organization communicates with different customers using SAP expressions and HTTPS. Oracle E-Business Suite, which is close to ECC, has four distinct implementations:

- Management of Client Relationships (CRM)
- Product Lifecycle Management (PLM)
- Inventory Administration (SCM)
- Management of Supplier Relationships (SRM)

5.8.15   Modules for SAP

SAP provides its replies as modules, allowing customers to purchase only the relevant modules. The most visible modules are:

- Controlling
- Financial Accounting
- Financial Logistics Operations
- Human Resources
- System Implementation
- Materials Administration
- Plant Upkeep
- Project Management System
- Creation Planning
- Quality Control
- Dissemination and Scheduling

Due to the organization's versatility, SAP is frequently a massive expansion operation that can last months or even years. The implementation was first known as Expedited SAP (ASAP), but it was eventually renamed Solution Provider Manager. SOLMAN electromechanical assembly is employed for different purposes such as leader designation, structure support, and defect following, all of which are critical for efficient SAP implementation. The entire performance is separated into stages, each with its own set of aims. Finally, customers can begin conducting routine transactions on the new SAP system. SAP implementations can be quite costly. The item is offered on a per-client basis, and the actual cost may vary depending on various factors, such as the number of consumers and packages. There are risks associated with immigration, and a thorough examination of the cost-saving benefits is required before deciding on a course of action. The implementation cost is determined by three major factors:

- Time span: SAP may be completed over many days and may endeavor to anticipate 5–10 years to complete the process and cost comparisons as necessary.
- People: The performance should be possible with in-house personnel or may necessitate many external experts, project managers, and specific individuals.
- Hardware: SAP implementation can take place on three machines: the manufacturing architecture, the test system, and the management framework, or it can execute up to 100 events.

The benefits and drawbacks

- Overall blend without geographical or financial constraints.
- When performing, a single upgrade is appropriate for the entire firm.
- Constant knowledge, less obvious dreariness blunders.
- Extended capability.

Impediments of SAP:

- Bound into a genuine concurrence with the dealer.
- It could be a justification behind determination.
- Profit from starting a capital venture could be unnecessarily extended, which is a tremendous bet.
- Bets with involved like errand dissatisfaction.

However, regardless, in light of everything, SAP is known to have offered amazing kinds of help to its clients, to which the reliably growing client base stands witness. The pace of domains has increased, but they have taken off in terms of development, competition, cash, and regulations. Of course, ERP's capacity for dealing with the consequences of such changes is quite limited. SAP has strongly emphasized in-memory calculating to find a solution to this problem. During the recent SAPPHIRE gathering, the organization presented its initiatives in areas such as in-memory enrollment, inspection, and cells impacting consistent and achievement models, incorporating guidelines and recommendations, and special operations strategies. In-memory management entails parsing, coordinating, and totaling billions of records using sensing such as RFID, allowing every employee of the company to conceptually retrieve and change the repository. Clients might use their

PDAs to get to and reinvigorate the system, focusing on customizing enlistment. With almost 20 RDS shipped since the initial shipment in November 2010, the organization has demonstrated an astonishingly passionate commitment and responsibility. In present situations, when time is unrivaled, packaged organizations offer compensation all the more just as expenses emerge for consulting courses of action, allowing associations to convey benefits faster and enhance their control over establishments. Rather than open-ended plans, which are frequently prone to issues like undertaking related tasks running wild, packaged courses of action can convey quick benefits from advancement adventures. It has been the genuine setting of SAP courses of action that they are sufficiently adaptable to client necessities. SAP should have significant solid areas for several years to come with such powerful market control systems and a commitment to utilizing its massive database.

5.9 Conclusion

The chapter discussed current electronic developments in the financial services sector, with a focus on the banking system, and emphasized some business difficulties handled using big data analytics. It also addressed several cutting-edge technologies that, when combined with big data analytics, resulted in a significant improvement in the standards and profitability of the finance industry. The stock market and healthcare industries were also investigated, since prescriptive analytics play an important role. This chapter finishes with several obstacles to the full-scale application of big data analytics in the banking industry to increase company value.

References

Abbasi, A., Albrecht, C., Vance, A., and Hansen, J. (2012). Metafraud: a meta-learning framework for detecting financial fraud. *Mis Quarterly*, 1293–1327.

AICPA. (1988). Statement on Auditing Standards (SAS). No. 59: The Auditor's Consideration of an Entity's Ability to Continue as a Going Concern. New York, NY: American Institute of Certified Public Accountants.

AICPA. (2011). Statement on Auditing Standards (SAS) Nos. 122–124: No. 122, Statements on Auditing Standards: Clarification and Recodification; No. 123, Omnibus Statement on Auditing Standards; No. 124, Financial Statements Prepared in Accordance with a Financial Reporting Framework Generally Accepted in Another Country. New York, NY: American Institute of Certified Public Accountants.

Alanyali, M., Moat, H. S., and Preis, T. (2013). Quantifying the relationship between financial news and the stock market. *Scientific Reports*, 3, 6.

Alles, M. G. (2015). Drivers of the use and facilitators and obstacles of the evolution of big data by the audit profession. *Accounting Horizons*, 29(2), 439–449.

Alston, C. L., Mengersen, K. L., and Pettitt, A. N. (2012). *Case Studies in Bayesian Statistical Modelling and Analysis*. UK: Wiley.

Amoore, L. (2011). Data derivatives on the emergence of a security risk calculus for our times. *Theory Culture and Society*, 28(6), 24–43.

Appelbaum, D., Kogan, A., and Vasarhelyi, M. A. (2016). Big data and analytics in the modern audit engagement: Research needs. Auditing: A Journal of Practice and Theory. Association of Certified Fraud Examiners. Report to the Nations on Occupational Fraud and Abuse. http://www.acfe.com/rttn2016.aspx.

Baliyan, A., Dhatterwal, J. S., Kaswan, K. S., and Jain, V. (2022). Role of AI and IoT techniques in autonomous transport vehicles. In *AI Enabled IoT for Electrification and Connected Transportation* (pp. 1–23). Singapore: Springer.

Bell, T. B., and Carcello, J. V. (2000). A decision aid for assessing the likelihood of fraudulent financial reporting. *Auditing: A Journal of Practice and Theory*, 19 (1), 169–184.

Benoit , D. F., and Van den Poel , D. (2012). Improving customer retention in financial services using kinship network information. *Expert Systems with Applications*, 39(13), 11435–11442.

Bhattacharya, S., Xu, D., and Kumar, K. (2011). An ANN-based auditor decision support system using Benford's law. *Decision Support Systems*, 50(3), 576–584.

Brown-Liburd, H., Issa, H., and Lombardi, D. (2015). Behavioral implications of big data's impact on audit judgment and decision making and future research directions. *Accounting Horizons*, 29(2), 451–468.

Busta, B., and Weinberg, R. (1998). Using Benford's law and neural networks as a review procedure. *Managerial Auditing Journal*, 13(6), 356–366.

Cao, M., Chychyla, R., and Stewart, T. (2015). Big data analytics in financial statement audits. *Accounting Horizons*, 29(2), 423–429.

Gepp, A., Kumar, K., and Bhattacharya, S. (2010). Business failure prediction using decision trees. *Journal of Forecasting*, 29(6), 536–555.

Gray, G. L., and Debreceny, R. S. (2014). A taxonomy to guide research on the application of data mining to fraud detection in financial statement audits. *International Journal of Accounting Information Systems*, 15(4), 357–380.

Green, B. P., and Choi, J. H. (1997). Assessing the risk of management fraud through neural network technology. *Auditing: A Journal of Practice and Theory*, 16(1), 14–28.

Griffin, P. A., and Wright, A. M. (2015). Introduction: Commentaries on big data's importance for accounting and auditing. *Accounting Horizons*, 29(2), 377–379.

Guerard, J. B., Rachev, S. T., and Shao, B. P. (2013). Efficient global portfolios: Big data and investment universes. *IBM Journal of Research and Development*, 57(5), 11.

Hastie, T., Friedman, J., and Tibshirani, R. (2009). *The Elements of Statistical Learning: Data Mining, Inference and Prediction* (2nd ed.). New York, NY: Springer.

Hoerl, A. E., and Kennard, R. W. (1970). Ridge regression: Biased estimation for nonorthogonal problems. *Technometrics*, 12(1), 55–67.

Hogan, C. E., Rezaee, Z., Riley, R. A., and Velury, U. K. (2008). Financial statement fraud: Insights from the academic literature. *Auditing: A Journal of Practice and Theory*, 27(2), 231–252.

Huang, S. Y., Tsaih, R. H., and Lin, W. Y. (2014). Feature extraction of fraudulent financial reporting through unsupervised neural networks. *Neural Network World*, 24(5), 539–560.

Huang, S. Y., Tsaih, R. H., and Yu, F. (2014). Topological pattern discovery and feature extraction for fraudulent financial reporting. *Expert Systems with Applications*, 41(9), 4360–4372.

Humpherys, S. L., Moffitt, K. C., Burns, M. B., Burgoon, J. K., and Felix, W. F. (2011). Identification of fraudulent financial statements using linguistic credibility analysis. *Decision Support Systems*, 50(3), 585–594.

IAASB. (2016). Exploring the growing use of technology in the audit, with a focus on data analytics. Available at www.ifac.org/publications-resources/exploring-growing-use-technology-audit-focus-data-analytics: International Auditing and Assurance Standards Board (IAASB).

James, G., Witten, D., Hastie, T., and Tibshirani, R. (2013). An introduction to statistical learning: with applications in R. *New York: Springe Philosophical Transactions (1683–1775)*, 53(1763), 370–418 (49 pages).

Kaswan, K. S., and Dhatterwal, J. S. (2020). *Big Data: An Introduction*. Shashwat Publication.

Preety, Dhatterwal, J. S., and Kaswan, K. S. (2021). Securing big data using big data mining. In *Data Driven Decision Making using Analytics*. New York, NY: Taylor Francis, CRC Press.

Smeaton, A. F., Over, P., and Kraaij, W. (2009). High-level feature detection from video in TRECVid: a 5-year retrospective of achievements. In Divakaran, A. (ed.), *Multimedia Content Analysis. Signals and Communication Technology*. Boston, MA: Springer. https://doi.org/10.1007/978-0-387-76569-3_6

Sood, K., Seth, N., Jindal, M., and Sadawarti, H. (2021). Big data: a boon for food and servicepreneurship. In *Entrepreneurship and Big Data* (pp. 55–69). London, UK: CRC Press.

Sood, K., Seth, N., and Grima, S. (2022). Portfolio performance of public sector general insurance companies in India: a comparative analysis. In *Managing Risk and Decision Making in Times of Economic Distress, Part B* (pp. 215–230). Bingley, UK: Emerald Publishing Limited.

Chapter 6

Machine learning and deep learning for financial data analysis

Jagjit Singh Dhatterwal[1], Kuldeep Singh Kaswan[2], Simon Grima[3] and Kiran Sood[4]

Abstract

Supervised learning is commonly used in digital imagery, computational linguistics, and digital sound classification. Deep learning's astounding achievement as an online analytical approach has piqued the curiosity of the scientific establishment. With the rise of Fintech in current history, the application of machine learning (ML) in financial products and activities has become commonplace. However, there is a shortage of a systematic assessment of future research directions in finance and economics in the actual knowledge. This work evaluates the ability of the convolutional neural network in important financial and accounting areas to give a comprehensive study due to the advent, input variables, and parameter estimation. Finally, we address three factors that may impact the results of monetary neural network architectures. This study offers scholars and operators insight and perspective on the state-of-the-art deep teaching methods in accounting and investment banking.

Keywords: Machine learning techniques; Artificial intelligence; Natural language processing; Deep learning; Neural network

6.1 Machine learning and deep learning for financial data analysis

Artificial intelligence (AI) frameworks are machine based with changing degrees of independence that can, for a given arrangement of human-defined goals, make expectations, suggestions, or choices utilising gigantic measures of elective information sources and information examination alluded to as large information. Such

[1]Department of Artificial Intelligence & Data Science, Koneru Lakshmaiah Education Foundation, India
[2]School of Computing Science and Engineering, Galgotias University, India
[3]Insurance and Risk Management, Faculty of Economics, Management & Accountancy, University of Malta, Malta
[4]Chitkara Business School, Chitkara University, Punjab, India

information provides machine learning (ML) models ready to learn from informative sets for persons to self-improve without being explicitly informed (Almahdi and Yang, 2017).

The COVID-19 scenario has expedited and intensified the pre-pandemic digitisation movement, particularly around the usage of AI. Increasing AI adoption in finance, for example, demand forecasting, computational exchange, credit recommendations, and cryptocurrency income organisations, is supported by a wealth of acquired data and a more expanding and more reasonable mathematical restriction (Baek and Kim, 2018).

AI is increasingly being communicated by money-related administration's policies manufacturers across entrepreneurs inside the money-related area: in retail and institutional banking (personalised items, visit packages for consumer loyalty, credit trying to ensure and creating chances, credit unfortunate luck forecasting, AML, misunderstanding examining and proof of identity, client support (Robo-exhortation, claims the board). The authorities sector is also conveying AI in RegTech and SupTech programs [e.g., natural language handling (NLP) and consistency operations; Dhatterwal *et al.*, 2022].

As the implementation of AI and ML employing massive data is intended to fill in importance, the possible dangers arising from its performance in banking advancement are becoming extremely distressing. They may merit further attention from technique developers.

Multiple community agreements in place between manufacturers and global fora have previously kicked off the conversation about how control systems and bosses can ensure that the experiences the effects of the use of AI in banking advancement are mitigated and what could be the best way to deal with the transmission of information of AI in banking advancement from the methodology creator perspective. How can strategy designers support advances in the field while ensuring that buyers and campaign donors are adequately protected, and the industry sectors surrounding such things and activities continue to be fair, organised, and intuitive?

Given AI's possible league season impact on some key sectors and the distinct dangers involved with its deployment, AI has emerged as a rising strategic imperative in recent years. The OECD established the AI Principles in May 2019, the essential global laws approved by legislators for the better management of credible AI, with advice from several co-overseeing batches (Butaru *et al.*, 2016).

The Council on Asset Management has said that AI, ML, and big data research would be included in their training system and priorities for 2021–2022.

This report analyses the way AI/ML and huge information influence specific monetary area regions that have presented such advances almost immediately and how these imaginative components are changing their plans of action; it talks about benefits and related gambles from the arrangement of such innovations in finance; gives a report on administrative effort and approaches of controllers opposite AI and ML in monetary administrations in certain business sectors, as well as data on open discussions by iOS and other strategy producers. Different locations that remain troubling and warrant additional, the Commissioners and its Specialised

Panel discussed it, and it gives significant strategic implications in these domains. The report does not consider the application of AI and big data in the protected sector, which has been evaluated by the OECD Healthcare coverage and Autonomous Pension contributions Commissioners (Cavalcante *et al.*, 2016).

The goal of this discussion and study is twofold: first, to give research to feed the continuing conversation around approaches manufacturers and IOs, and second, to analyse difficulties emerging in the intersection of AI, finance, and approaches that are currently mostly neglected. The last option comprises researching how AI, ML, and huge data affect certain aspects of banking price movements (e.g., resources in the network; computational bartering; credit endorsement; and blockchain-based currency things) and the individual implementation plans; and whether these improvements relate to present hazards (like liquidity, instability, assembly).

6.2   Graph neural networks for investor networks analysis

According to the OECD's AI Technical Committee, an AI framework is a machine-based framework that could generate estimations, suggestions, or decisions influencing digital or physical situations for a given set of human-characterised goals. It utilises machine and human-based contributions to see natural or potentially virtual conditions; dynamic such discernments into models (in a robotised way, e.g., with ML or physically); and utilises model surmising to figure out choices for data or activity in Figure 6.1. Simulated intelligence frameworks are intended to work with changing degrees of independence (Chai and Li, 2019).

(a)   Implementation of strategy, data gathering and transformation, simulation models and understanding
(b)   Verification and authorisation
(c)   Transmission

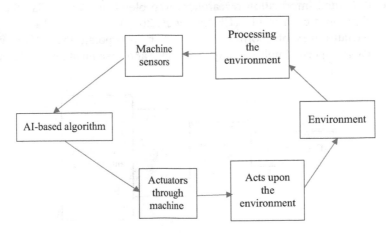

Figure 6.1 AIML framework

(d)   Activities and measuring are the elements of the AI framework's lifespan. An AI study's observational results identify Intelligent systems (e.g., NLP), approaches to illustrate modern evolutionary synthesis (e.g., neurological organisation); advancement (e.g., visual attentiveness); and researchers concerned with cultural factors (e.g., straightforwardness) (Japan *et al.*, 2013).

ML is a subclass of AI that demonstrates that programming's capacity to profit from relevant information indexes improves without being deliberately altered by experienced programming (Chai and Ngai, 2020). The various kinds of ML include managed learning ('old style' ML, comprising of cutting edge relapses and arrangement of information used to develop expectations further) and unaided getting the hang of (handling input information to comprehend the conveyance of data to create, for instance, computerised client sections); and deep and support learning (in light of brain organisations and might be applied to unstructured information like pictures or voice) (Kaswan *et al.*, 2022).

Cognitive intelligence brain enhances the role of how neurons link in the brain with some ('Deep') levels of rebuilt connection in Figure 6.2. These models employ multi-facet cerebral networks to understand and recognise complicated instances in knowledge, which are stimulated by the manner forebrain works. ML techniques can examine incoming data without constructing formal conceptions (no need to concentrate on finding expression tracking systems) and distinguish unique situations that no person could foresee or develop. Such institutions are known for having greater disturbances resilience and the capacity to operate at several levels of engagement from the thread. ML stars heavily use various media producers and related to better, sometimes known as 'big data'. The phrase 'big data' first originated in the early 2000s, when that was used to describe 'the blast in the amount (and here and there, nature) of accessible and possibly significant information, to a great extent the aftereffect of late and phenomenal progressions in the information recording and stockpiling innovation'. The environment of large information incorporates information sources, programming, examination, programming and measurements, and information researchers who blend the data to flag the commotion and produce clear results (Chatzis *et al.*, 2018).

Credited attributes of enormous information incorporate the '4Vs': volume (size of data); speed (high-velocity handling and examination of streaming

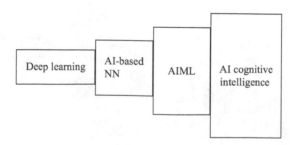

Figure 6.2   Stages of cognitive intelligence

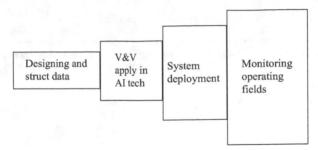

Figure 6.3   AI system lifecycle

information); assortment (heterogeneous information), and integrity (sureness of knowledge, source dependability, honesty), also characteristics including exhaustivity, extensionality, and intricacy. Veracity is of specific significance as it might be hard for clients to survey if the dataset used is complete and reliable, which may need case-by-case evaluation.

Surroundings statistics, geostationary connotations, sophisticated images and audio tapes, change documentation or GPS indications, and identification documents: a name, a stock photo, contact information, bank subtleties, posts on long-distance communication skills sites, patient studies, or a PC IP address are all examples of large data. Such information challenges existing strategies because of size, intricacy, or pace of accessibility and requires advanced procedures, for instance, ML models, to break them down. Expanded utilisation of AI in IoT applications produces critical amounts of information, taking care of once more into AI applications.

More important online learning enables ML algorithms to keep improving as a consequence of their ability to gain from the modelling taken care of into the assumptions in a continuous connection known as the study of the development in Figure 6.3.

6.3   Using ML to predict the defaults of credit card clients

Constantly increasing investments in AI in the finance industry and expanded scientific information about the topic breakthrough demonstrate progress in the delivery of ML and AI (Chen *et al.*, 2018a). Over the next 4 years, global investment in AI is expected to more than double, rising from $50.1 billion by 2023 to over $110 billion in 2024. As per IDC, spending on AI techniques will increase for the next several years at a CAGR of over 20% for 2019–2024 as companies embrace AI as part of their innovative progress initiatives and sustain its effective advantage. On a year-to-year basis, venture capitalists interested in AI new enterprises tripled in 2017 and accounted for 12% of total private value inclinations in H1 2018. Additionally, progress in AI-related investigation is significantly more important than progress in computer programming or research approach

Table 6.1   Fund invest-related AI entities

No. of years	Number of dealings	Fund investing (crores)
2012	18	150
2013	26	420
2014	55	900
2015	77	1,300
2016	81	1,380
2017	95	1,600
2018	101	1,625
2019	91	1,300

distribution patterns, indicating a growing interest in this imaginative invention in Table 6.1.

6.4   Application of deep learning methods for econometrics

Worldwide financial professionals are increasingly examining the potential benefits of using AI pieces of information in 'SupTech' gadgets, for example, FinTech-based apps used by authorities for organisational regulation and supervision. Similarly, managed foundations are creating and embracing FinTech applications for administrative and consistence prerequisites and detailing. Monetary foundations are also embracing AI applications for inside controls and chance administration. A mix of AI advancements with conduct sciences permits enormous financial establishments to forestall wrongdoing, moving the concentration from ex-present goal to forward-looking anticipation (Chen *et al.*, 2017).

The growth of appropriate buttons and SupTech alternatives is mainly attributed to both current assets side cabbies, such as the increased greater increasing prevalence of awareness, along with robot expertise, development of AI operations, and implementation side removalists possibility for an increase in efficiency and supportability of managerial cycles, opportunities for further established interactions into probability and consistency upgrades (Chen *et al.*, 2018b).

Despite the opportunities and benefits of AI for administrative and business reasons, experts remain cautious due to risks associated with utilizing such innovations (resourcing, digital gambling, reputational hazards, quality of information issues, restricted simplicity and interpretability). These are likewise the dangers winning in the arrangement of AI by financial industry players, which are investigated in further depth in this presentation.

6.5   AI and multimedia application in finance

The growing availability of information inside budgetary conditions and the general advantage that AI/ML may provide to monetary administration organisations are driving the application of AI in banking. The eruption of relevant facts and official investigation (enormous knowledge), in conjunction with more experience in data limits (for example, decentralised computing), can be segmented by ML techniques to understand transmissions and catch foundational relationships in data in a manner that people cannot. The use of ML and enormous analytics by banking industry organisations is meant to progressively generate a competitive edge between enhancing company performance by cutting expenditures and improving the implementation of budgeting supplied changes ordered by consumers. This section investigates the possible impact of AI and big data on certain macro-economic market activities, for example, resource allocation and successful financial management, exchange; lending; and cryptocurrency implementations in financing (Chong *et al.*, 2017).

Using AI and ML in resources, the board can expand the proficiency and exactness of functional work processes, upgrade execution, reinforce risk to the executives, and further develop the client experience. Financial advisors can use Natural Language Generation (NLG), a component of AI, to 'adaptive' and learn to improve on information investigation and answers to clients. As ML models can screen many gambling factors consistently and test portfolio execution under a huge number of market/monetary situations, the innovation can upgrade risk the board for resource chiefs and other enormous institutional financial backers. Regarding functional advantages, AI can decrease administrative centre expenses of speculation supervisors, supplant physically concentrated compromises with computerised ones, and possibly diminish costs and speed up (Collobert *et al.*, 2011).

Taking care of ML models with vast information can give resource chiefs proposals that impact decision-production around portfolio designation and stock choice, contingent upon the AI method utilised. Huge information has supplanted conventional datasets, which are currently viewed as a product effectively accessible to all financial backers. Resource directors are using it to acquire bits of knowledge in their venture cycle. Data has forever been critical for the local speculation area, and information has been the foundation of numerous venture methodologies, from crucial investigation to efficient exchanging and quantitative techniques. While organised information was at the centre of such 'customary' methods, tremendous measures of crude or unstructured/semi-organised information are currently encouraging to give another educational edge to financial backers conveying AI in executing their techniques. AI permits resource chiefs to process immense measures of information from different sources and open experiences from the information to illuminate their strategies in exceptionally short periods (Deng *et al.*, 2017).

The utilisation of AI/ML and enormous information might be held to bigger resource chiefs or institutional financial backers who have the limit and assets to put resources into AI advances, potentially presenting a hindrance for the reception of such methods by more modest entertainers. Interest in innovation and ability is expected to change and investigate immense measures of creating new datasets containing massive data to generate ML algorithms. This might be the circumstance if AI and ML are combined with unique algorithms, providing a competitive advantage, and bringing about confined investment by more modest players who cannot embrace in-house AI/ML procedures or utilise huge information data sources. This might build up the pattern of focus on a few bigger players that are being seen in the speculative stock investments industry, as greater gatherings dominate a portion of their more deft opponents.

Confined support by more modest players would drive forward until the business arrives, where such instruments become pervasive/offered as assistance by outsider sellers. Simultaneously, outsider datasets may not be held at a similar norm across the industry, and clients of outsider devices should fabricate certainty concerning the precision and reliability of information utilised ('veracity' of enormous information) to arrive at a degree of solace adequate.

The deployment of equivalent ML algorithms by a huge proportion of commodity managers might result in overcrowding behaviours and first ads, which may enhance possible dangers for the technology's dependability and authenticity, especially during periods of crisis. Industry uncertainty may rise due to large trades or purchases made, resulting in additional sources of vulnerability.

It very well may be contended that sending AI/ML and large information in effective financial planning could alter the course towards passive money management. Assuming the utilisation of such inventive advancements ends up being alpha-producing in a reliable way that proposes some degree of circumstances and logical results connection between the utilisation of AI and the predominant presentation, the dynamic venture local area could use this potential chance to revitalise active financial planning and give alpha-adding amazing open doors to their clients (Chen and Su, 2022).

6.5.1   AI & ML techniques for simulation of markets, economics, and other financial systems

Flexibility investing has been at the forefront of FinTech customers, using massive amounts of data, AI, and ML predictions in exchange executions and administration centre capacity. A new class of artificial intelligent pure-play equity funds have emerged recently, relying only on AI and ML (e.g., Aidiyia Holdings, Cerebral cortex Capital, Taaffeite Asset Management, and Decimal digits) (Dhatterwal *et al.*, 2020).

There has been no conceptual or another free auditing for the representation of ML assets from a non-industry resource, evaluating the many investments guaranteed to be AI-driven until now. Store managers use varying amounts of AI in their duties and operations and are typically cautious about exposing their systems to maintain their advantage. While several assets may promote their products as artificial knowledge managed, the degrees at which such improvements are employed by reserves and the growth of AI arrangement alter completely. They found it tougher to compare the efficacy of several personalities AI objects.

Databases of AI-powered companies were made available in corporate companies. Heavy investment in mutual fund when the closer resource agree for related documents. Independent observer lists are prone to different biases, such as self-reliance and self-propensity of participants to the recording or metal casting, and should be regarded with suspicion.

ETFs driven by AI, wherein investing choices generated and performed by algorithmic, are still in their infancy. By the conclusion of 2019, the aggregate AuM of this ETF companion was estimated to be around USD 100 million. The efficiency of sending AI on highly automated ETFs reduces administration fees (assessed at a typical yearly charge of 0.77% as of the end of 2019). Regarding determining execution, there is expanding proof that ML models outflank regular estimates of macroeconomic pointers like expansion and GDP. These upgrades are generally articulated during financial pressure when gauges make the biggest difference. Proof additionally exists on the prevalence of AI-driven methods in distinguishing significant yet already obscure connections in monetary emergencies, with ML models generally outflanking strategic relapse in out-of-sample expectations and anticipating (Elad and Aharon, 2006).

6.5.2   *Infrastructure to support AI & ML research in finance*

Simulated intelligence can be utilised in exchanging both to give exchanging procedure ideas and to control mechanised exchanging frameworks that make expectations, pick the game plan and execute exchanges. AI-based exchanging frameworks working in the market can recognise and manage trades completely alone, with no human mediation, utilising AI methods like developmental calculation, deep learning, and probabilistic rationale. AI methods can help plan any forthcoming exchange of a systematic design by empowering an 'if' point of view to be carried out as an issue of the system. Given the present interconnectedness between resource classes and topographies, the utilisation of AI considers a prescient limit that quickly outperforms the force of even standard algos in money and exchanging (Feuerriegel and Prendinger, 2016).

A computational intelligence-enabled framework in trading may also assist merchants in managing the evolution of their transactions and their bets on the board. For example, AI-based implementations can implement the game of chance acceptance and transform or leave the location based on the needs of the consumer, completely autonomous and without the need for reconstruction, because they train all by themselves and adjust to the changes in financial specialists environments without (or with relatively insignificant) human intervention. They can assist merchants with dealing with their streams among their representatives for exchanges that are now chosen and control charges or liquidity distribution to various pockets (e.g., provincial market inclinations, cash judgments or different boundaries of a request dealing with). In deeply digitised markets, for example, the ones for values and FX items, AI arrangements vow to give cutthroat estimating, oversee liquidity, and improve and smooth out an execution. Significantly, AI computations sent in trading can increase availability monitoring and processing. Expanding size, length, and demanded magnitude in a robust approach relating to economic situations to place delivery orders with limited market impact (Fischer and Krauss, 2017).

AI and large volumes of data in opinions evaluation to discern subjects, structures, and transmitting indicators are not a novel method for improving instruction. Entrepreneurs have researched news items and company scientifically unsupported remarks in the last several generations to better comprehend the profitability concept of non-data. Gathering and examination of data from web-based amusement posts and funny stories or satellite data using NPL estimations is an example of the resource usage of innovative developments that can help illustrate sending and receiving selections, as they can robotise knowledge of social affairs and independent inquiry and differentiate hardworking examples or behavioural patterns on a scale that a human cannot fathom.

The capacity of the AI system to educate and adapt to new economic situations separates ML investing from efficiency marketing. In contrast, standard purposeful techniques would take more time to modify limitations due to the large manual support needed. Traditional home safety methods based on credible data sometimes fail to produce capital appreciation when freshly identified patterns segregate. ML models shift the study towards dynamic forecasting and evaluation of trends, such as using stroll forward tests instead of additionally noticed. Such tests constantly anticipate and respond to patterns to reduce over-fitting in backtests based on actual knowledge and practices. The application of AI in investing has progressed through numerous small improvements and complexity, providing a level of conventional financial engineering at every point of the interaction.

The first one is that computations consisted of trading operations with basic bounds, followed by calculations that considered dynamic estimates. Second-generation estimates communicated strategies for separating large orders and reducing potential market sway, resulting in lower prices (assumed 'execution algorithms'). Current deep in brain network-based techniques is meant to provide the optimal request positioning and execution style, which can reduce market sway. Central nervous system networks perform and learn by simulating the human cerebral cortex through computations designed to recognise designs. Applying such strategies can aid market manufacturers in improving stock upkeep and minimising the expense of their bank records. As AI improves, AI measures evolve into the machine, and desktop evaluations benefit from new knowledge and require less user mediation (Galeshchuk and Mukherjee, 2017).

More complex types of AI are now frequently used to distinguish signalling from 'low intellectual worth' occurrences in broadcast trading, which includes more nuanced activities that may be harder to differentiate and detach appreciation from. Instead of aiding with computing performance, AI is used to extract the signal from the noise in data and transform this data into transactional decisions. Reduced sophisticated equations are typically utilised for 'strong instructive conditions', these include knowledge of pecuniary occurrences, which are much clearer for all stakeholders to grasp.

ML methods, like high-frequency trading techniques, are not ready for prime time at this stage in technological maturation. They are concentrating on hand-lay transactions and profit from the speed of operation. Overall, they are mostly constrained to be used in isolation, for example, to align calculation borders and further improve calculations' decision reasoning rather than for execution reasons. However, when AI innovations progress and are communicated in different situations, it may improve the abilities of conventional algorithms exchanges with proposals for budgetary company sectors. This is likely to happen when AI operations start to be offered more often during the execution time of businesses. This will increase the ability to automate connection executions and support the entire chain of engagement, from communicating to designing and executing ways. ML-based implementation optimisation algorithms will investigate the uniqueness and adaptability of their chosen rationales during investing. Overall, the basic requirements previously used for evolutionary algorithm transmission of information (e.g., shields ended up working in from before the risk the corporate heads' runtime environments, computer-based control systems to turn off the computation when it goes past the cutoff points implemented in the game of chance model) should be extended to AI-driven computational transmission of information (Mittal and Jhamb, 2016; Mittal *et al.*, 2020).

6.5.3   Chatbots & robot advisors for payment and innovation

The use of the same or similar methods by several brokers may have unanticipated competition may suffer as a result, and this may play a greater role in anxiety in aspects of the economy. For businesses, the proliferation of regularly used designs should limit the number of replacement alternatives open, lowering profits. Finally, it would assist shopkeepers by minimising bid-ask spreads. Concurrently, it may result in unity, aggregating behaviour, and one-way showcasing, with possible repercussions for market reliability and availability circumstances, particularly during extreme pressure. As with any computation, widespread use of competitive Information examination increases the risk of identity input circles, which can result in abrupt price changes.

Such a gathering could similarly enlarge the danger of cybercrime. As it becomes less difficult for electronic crooks to influence professionals acting analogously as appeared differently about self-governing specialists with instantly recognisable actions and attitudes concerning software gamble, when AI is used in a wrong way, it can potentially unpalatably lead to self-governing assaults (without user intervention) on weak architectures in communicating yet additionally broadly in the worldwide financial field of view. The usage of constrained modelling that can then be duplicated is necessary for brokers to preserve any advantages and may induce a deliberate lack of directness, adding to ML algorithms' lack of competence. Companies' refusal to share their modelling techniques, prompted by a psychological prospect of rejection of their edge, causes computational tracking and ML modelling challenges.

Computational investing can also give unfounded conclusions that are easier to maintain but more probable to be detected in computerised marketplaces. This is connected to the concern that ML infrastructures would support illicit activity. Activities aimed at controlling major industries, for example, 'disparaging', by making it more difficult for managers to differentiate such acts presuming a plot

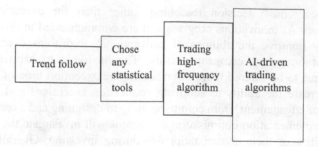

Figure 6.4   Structure of business algorithm

among computers is established. The lack of comparability in the ML models employed to back changing may make modifying the technique difficult throughout awful converting execution. Sending and receiving computations are not often framework sequential circuits (input A caused conversion procedure B to be performed) that can be tracked and evaluated with a clear grasp of which constraints controlled the consequences during such a poor achievement. Business people need to have the option of disintegrating the result into the significant determinants of the conversion choice, adjusting and readjusting moreover rectify as per the circumstances. In any event, clients cannot appreciate why the appropriate swapping decision was made and thus cannot distinguish if the representation is because of the designer's universality and capacity to represent crucial links in understanding or simply because of compassion. In terms of future unanticipated implications on the economy, it may be suggested that AI advancements in trading and high-frequency trading (HFT) might raise market unpredictability through massive transactions or buys carried out all the time, putting up new imperativeness of sensitivity. Furthermore, some HFT tactics appeared to have growing market unpredictability, decreased availability, and exacerbated streak breakdowns, which have been more popular over time. Because HFT is a significant indicator of capital agreements under a typical financial environment, any disturbance in the operation of their algorithms has a substantial effect on the business sector competencies in Figure 6.4.

6.5.4   AI/ML-based evaluating models

Irrespective of their massive possibilities for velocity, effectiveness, and possibility assessment of the 'aggregate score', AI/ML-based algorithms create hazards of differing influence in financial outcomes and the possibility of severe or incorrect penalties (US Treasuries). As with other applications of AI in finance, such examples emphasise important issues related to the concept of data utilised and the designer's lack of clarity/rationality.

Uncomplicated ML techniques may inadvertently provide unequal finishes, persecuting specified groups of individuals (for instance, thinking about race, direction, ethnicity, and religion). Imperfectly organised and regulated AI/ML models communicate the risk of worsening or maintaining present trends while predictable and reliable task partition substantially more sincerely.

Also, similarly as with any technology used in credit intermediaries, the adage 'garbage in, garbage out' applies to ML risk rating algorithms. To say the least, inadequate data could integrate insufficiently stamped or mistaken data, data that reflects fundamental human inclinations, or lacking data. When confronted with 'exceptional' data, a good ML algorithm equipped with insufficient data wagers on producing incorrect answers. However, despite the entirely pre-planned fundamental calculation, a mental network trained on the first data and then confronted with missing data would provide a primitive result. This, along with the lack of sensitivity in ML techniques, makes it more difficult to detect ill-advised data consumption or the use of impermissible data in ML technologies.

Along these lines, using poor-quality or insufficient/unacceptable information could achieve misguided or uneven decision-making. Uneven or biased scoring may not be deliberate as indicated by the perspective of the firm using the model; taking everything into account, estimations could join facially fair snippets of data and deal with them as middle people for extremely durable characteristics like race or direction, thus avoiding existing non-isolation guidelines. For example, while a banking authority may be creative in not incorporating opposite-way variants as a commitment to the models, the approach might change the outcome from speculative trading and utilise such data in the analysis of economic sufficient, circumventing the legislation. Trends may similarly be characterised in the information used as characteristics. Given that the model trains itself on data from external resources that may have deliberately orchestrated explicit preferences, valid predilections propagate.

Like various purposes of AI in finances, ML-based algorithms pose unwavering quality concerns because of their lack of sensitivity, i.e., the barriers to accessing, comprehending, or replicating the positive and significant relationship. Issues associated with sensibility are particularly important in advancing decisions, as moneylenders are liable for their decisions and ought to have the choice to determine the justification for repudiations of charge augmentation. This implies that purchasers have little capacity to recognise and fight erroneous credit judgments and little problem figuring out what activities they should be doing to improve their reputation.

Regulations in emerging nations guarantee that computer systems are not evaluated in reputation risk assessments, for example, the US law regarding race or postal size of the target and the UK rule regarding protected class information. There is rule pushing foes of dissociation rules, for example, the US fair credited requirements, in selected neighbourhoods, and legislators are typically examining the bet of potential predilection and sole risk that AI/ML and calculating an introduction.

In specific domains, relative evidence of different treatment, for instance, beneath credit limits for people from defended packs than for people from various get-togethers, is seen as partition whether or if there was a strategy to isolate. Possible future mitigants against certain dangers include the occurrence of investigating parts that perception checks the models to compare the effects against means of measuring data sources; testing of such goals-scored processes to enhance their bourgeois morality and accurateness; and organisational capabilities for ML thoughts and nonprofits, as well as the assignment of responsibility to the living thing maximum of the undertaking, to name a few examples.

6.5.5 Validation and calibration of multi-agent systems in finance

The use of AI creates difficulties regarding data security and tensions about practices through which operation, storage, and utilisation of private data could well be manipulated for corporate advantage as BigTech dynamically impact their free permission to enormous proportions of client information that feeds into AI-generated algorithms to give monetary types of assistance; whose use of AI creates difficulties regarding data security and tensions about practices through which operation, storage, and utilisation of private data could well be manipulated for corporate advantage. These practices could burden clients, for instance, through one-sided practices associated with credit openness and esteem (Muddumadappa *et al.*, 2022; Chen and Su, 2022).

Induction to client data by BigTech gives them an indisputable advantage over customary money-related organisations' suppliers. This advantage is anticipated to be reinforced by their usage of AI, which provides important opportunities for innovative, modified, but more productive support ways to proceed by these participants. The dominance of BigTech in a certain sector of the economy may result in excessive macroeconomic factors and an increase in the currency market reliance on a small number of massive BigTech businesses, with potential core ideas dependent on their magnitude and enhancement. This, accordingly, could prompt concerns over anticipated risks should financial buyers, who may not be getting the comparative extent of thing decisions, assess or appeal that would be presented through standard money-related help providers. It may also make it harder for authorities to access and investigate the trading transaction provided by such businesses.

Additional associated risk has everything to do with unfavourable to real ways to action and the right locations in the support proposal's improvement portion. The possible improvement of a few fundamental members in business areas for AI courses of action or possibly helps to incorporate AI developments (for instance, conveyed figuring expert communities who in like manner give AI organisations), verification of which is at this point found in a specific region of the planet. Concerns for the unrelenting atmosphere are also prevalent, considering BigTech organisations' leaning approach stance on the issue of customer data. Such organisations, in particular, can exploit their knowledge superiority to create dominating advantages comparable to customer acquisition (for instance, via profitable expenditure segregation) and into the construction of high barriers with segmentation for new inconspicuous competitors.

From around the end of 2020, the European Union and the United Kingdom propagated authoritarian-proposed amendments, the Electronic Marketplace Act, attempting to propagate out an ex bet foundation to monitor 'Newspaper' highly automated different phases like BigTech, to direct a piece of the other possible options and ensure fair and open multiple corporate segments. One of the suggested tasks is for such intermediaries to provide regular customers with access to the data generated by their operations and to provide data adaptation while restricting them from being used for data obtained from enterprise customers to match these regular customers (to address twofold work possibilities).

6.6　Advance ML for financial stability

The implementation of circular record advancements (digital ledger technology—DLT, e.g., the bitcoin protocol) has expanded significantly throughout undertakings, particularly in financials. The shown advantages of speed, effectiveness, and candidness that such innovative improvements might give, pushed by digital transformation and deregulation of markets, keep the rapid development of cryptocurrency apps going. Massive accumulation of DLTs in earnings may be motivated by an effort to increase productivity gains from fragmentation, remembering for the financial sector (declaration and thread and remuneration); parts (governmental bank advanced monetary policies and quantitative easing stablecoins); and going extinct of assets this even more comprehensively, and may keep driving the job groupings and methods are in line with corporate needs (for instance, administrators).

A get-together of the firm is advancing AI and DLTs in cryptocurrency financing to achieve better outcomes in such frameworks since increased digitalisation would improve the efficiency assured by cryptocurrency systems. Regardless, the actual degree of AI accomplishment in cryptocurrency initiatives does not appear to be substantial at this moment to justify occurrences of collaboration with different breakthroughs.

As opposed to a get-together, what is truly being seen essentially is the implementation of ML and AI in specific blockchain technology for typical utilisation (e.g., risk management, see below) and, more broadly, the performance of DLT possible actions in unequivocal AI instrumentation (for instance, for data the leaders). The final option encompasses using such DLTs to negotiate with the knowledge to a ML model, utilising the unchallengeable and uninterrupted character traits of the blockchain technology while additionally contemplating the communication of sensitive data on a negligible supposition without having entered configuration and efficient policy. The use of DLTs in AI components is intended to allow customers of such features to modify data they own, utilised by ML techniques and other automation technologies (for instance, IoT). The ability to provide additional enhancement sufficiency advantages of digital transformation and deregulation of markets in DLT-based constructions and affiliations drives the implementation of such AI utilisation.

The most important role of AI in DLT-based money may be in expanding the robotising ranges of clever agreements. A few implementations of AI can be identified in extremely clear utilisation implemented inside DLT connections, for example, consistency and hazard the committee (e.g., aggressive and hostile to manipulation, acquaintance of mechanisation stumbling blocks with a link); and data strength of character and the advisory council, most of these implementations, are in the early stages of development.

AI may be utilised in cryptocurrency connections to reduce (but not eliminate) security vulnerabilities and assist in guarding against relationship compromise, for example, in percentage implementations. Using the capabilities of technology can help customers of cryptocurrency organisations recognise contradictory actions that might be related to robberies or pranks since such events do occur regardless of a client's requirement for both cryptographic keys to consider. Similarly, intelligent systems can improve an institution's boarding procedures (e.g., fingerprinting for AI noticeable identification) and anti-money laundering and counter-terrorism financing (AML/CFT) verification in the course of any DLT-based financial connected business. Incorporating AI in DLT-based frameworks can also aid consistency cycling and probability organising in such organisations. AI technologies, for example, can provide wallets addressing expected outcomes that can be utilised for legislative consistency or an internal uncertainty appraisal of trade counterparties. In any event, when income representatives are removed from financial transactions, the effectiveness of continual financial management techniques concentrating on restricted drugs may be jeopardised.

Incorporating AI-based possible actions in DLT-based infrastructures at the presentation level might assist professionals in effectively accomplishing their magisterial goals. This might be accomplished, for example, by modifying the delivery of guided elements' data to experts in a consistent and comparable method and by programming administrative requirements into the codes of the operations, accelerating consistency in a customisable approach. The market has explored the importance of authorities as anchor nodes in distributed nodes as one of the options for resolving the difficulties of monitoring such phases that exhibit poor on a single centralised government.

Collaboration on the power of rules addressing and communication as such a circumstance becomes more important as the duty of data content management shifts from impermeable anchoring nodes to self-governing, mechanized ML mechanisms. In specifically, the use of AI might undermine the operation of banished off-chain nodes, for example, confirmed 'Prophets', nodes engaging with contextual information into the relationship. The employment of Oracles in DLT networks introduces the risk of incorrect or missing data transactions in the relationship by failing to meet expectations or even toxic renegade off-chain locations. On a basic level, AI might further accelerate creative destruction by placing AI resolution explicitly on-chain, making unassailable knowledge producers to the chain, such as Prophecies, dull. All else being equal, it might serve as a precaution by evaluating the reliability and authenticity of the information provided by the Oracles and preventing sophisticated methods or manipulation of such undesirable data from proceeding into the organisation.

The use of such AI apps may theoretically increase people's faith in the organisation since they may examine the details available in the database and look for any acceptable vulnerabilities. In today's reality, technology implementation does not assure that the 'trash in, rubbish out' issue is resolved since the problem of poor character or insufficient data outputs is a challenge encountered in AI-based components and systems.

6.6.1 AI-based blockchain in financial networks

The important effect of AI strategy collaboration in cryptocurrency systems could originate from their implementation in rapid provisions, with a good repercussion on the international organisation and possible establishment of such agreements, and various conceptual framework (yet untested) consequences for occupational groups and designs of DLT-based network infrastructure. On a fundamental level, AI may evaluate separate DLT chains interacting with a completely free reason.

Intelligent configurations, which rely on direct computer software, existed long before the arrival of ML and AI. Without a sure, even now, the majority of intelligent arrangements applied substantially do not have links to AI techniques. Many of the suggested advantages of using AI in DLT systems remain hypothetical. Commercial statements about the integration of AI and DLT features in shown objects should be viewed cautiously.

In light of everything, AI use cases are unbelievably helpful in expanding clever agreement limits, particularly concerning taking a risk with the board and the conspicuous evidence of deformities in the code of the splendid understanding. PC-based insight systems, for instance, NLP, may be employed to investigate the occurrences of excellent organisation performance, identify deceptive improvement, and concentrate on the material's protection. More specifically, AI can do code testing to the extent that a human code expert cannot, concerning speed and level of detail/circumstance assessment. Taking into account that such code is the key justification for the computerisation of sagacious agreements, impeccable coding is at the centre of the strength of such arrangements.

6.6.2 Business challenge: deep learning seen as too resource-intensive

Monetary establishments, for example, banks and insurance agencies, are flooded with information. Client information, financial information, outside information, for example, articles and web-based entertainment discussions, call focus information, pictures, etc., hold the tempting guarantee of business bits of knowledge. Direct relapse procedures, with which most firms are natural, function admirably for little informational collections. In any case, the execution of direct relapse examination will crumble as informational indexes become exceptionally huge. Conversely, deep learning – artificial brainpower (AI) discipline that utilises deep brain organisations – is ideal for checking out large amounts of information. Deep learning calculations rapidly make associations between apparently different wellsprings of data, distinguishing new experiences that can be utilised to screen markets, create expectations, and oversee chance; from there, the sky is the limit.

Extricating those experiences from a huge information store that includes both organised and unstructured information has been a restrictively overwhelming errand for some in the business. Hindrances to the huge scope utilisation of deep learning have included secluded information stores, complex instruments, restricted designing assets, a small ability pool of information researchers, and the requirement for a specific registering foundation that can deal with computationally concentrated jobs.

The Intel Nervana arrangement carries deep figuring out how to monetary help associations of each size, opening the business experiences expected to support organisations' misrepresentation anticipation endeavours, client assistance levels, prescient capacities, and information the executives.

6.7   Credit scoring models using ML algorithms

The Intel Nervana stage for DL is easy to use, versatile, and adequately solid to help handle countless crushing troubles defying banks, trading associations, security carriers, and various firms in the financial organisation industry. Coming up next are two or three cases of how these associations can put deep getting to work:

- Distinguish unusual data. Deep learning models use a genuine degree of valid capacity to get the complex quantifiable plan of financial data, often clearly better than other ML procedures. These extraordinary resources can be used to perceive irregularities in many settings, including hailing underhanded Visa trades, recognising peculiar development in an exchange limit-demand book, or expecting surprising changes in power assurance markets.
- Consolidate more data sources. Deep acquiring models can consolidate data from disparate sources, for instance, asset cost time series, Twitter volume and assessment, US Securities and Exchange Commission filings, master reports, satellite imagery, and text, sound, and video news sources. Deep learning reveals associations and causal effects across these disparate sources that individuals or standard ML systems could miss, simplifying it to develop mind network models for data assessment. The Intel Nervana plan can increment business decisions by using new, ground-breaking wellsprings of data. For example, banks can additionally foster client care by checking online diversion discussions, and trading associations can include titles and reports to all the almost certain expected fluctuations in stock and bond costs.
- Money-related associations have meandered aimlessly for IT establishments. A colossal variety of separated structures ordinarily manages processes. Deep learning gives a solid customary perspective to sorting data across these systems. The Intel Nervana stage for deep understanding probably goes as a central resource for conveying deep help acquiring models that can robotise complex cycles from trade and settlement to ideal trade execution and motorised market making.

For example, one tremendous financial establishment with an overabundance of 30,000 specialists is including the Intel Nervana stage for deep sorting out some way to save portfolio bosses opportunity in their regular timetables by refining information from up to 30,000 chronicles every day – messages, internal records, online information, and money-related news. With permission to more lavish examinations, these bosses can quickly seek more definite endeavour decisions.

6.8 Python to implement methods from stochastic

Deep learning handles various financial industry data issues. The Intel Nervana stage offers an all-out response for sending deep progressing as a middle development, probably as a central community where state-of-the-art computations can be applied across different business locales.

By conveying Neon* Deep learning structure and Nervana Cloud, clients can quickly arrange, make, and send state-of-the-art deep learning models – like this, killing the cost and complexities of cultivating their deep learning limits. Express benefits include:

- Speedy results: Neon is among the speediest deep learning frameworks open today, engaging data specialists to set up a model in hours, not days.
- Ease of use: The Intel Nervana stage for deep learning engages associations to focus on the science instead of the course of action. For example, Nervana Cloud has an easy-to-use interface that unequivocally deals with ML cooperation. All value is similarly open through a request line interface.
- Moderateness: Since it is a work with a plan, Nervana Cloud engages associations to get to deep learning models without placing assets into an expensive on-the-spot establishment.
- Versatility: Nervana Cloud maintains stacking and getting ready on record, pictures, sound, time-series data, and other data types conceivable.
- Security: The plan is immovably organised with dispersed capacity providers to help move and store data securely. At the item level, the course of action uses a safeguarded OS and containerisation to develop security further. At the gear level, the game plan uses trusted platform module (TPM) and encryption to shield data extremely as yet, moving and being utilized.

Adaptability: As Nervana Cloud works with the strategy, it adds new features and meets customer commitments. Intel's evaluation libraries support adding gas pedals to Intel devices to give it more handling power.

6.9 Conclusion

Deep learning and intelligent systems (AI) are at the heart of today's technological advancements. Deep understanding may assist financial advisory businesses in generating information from their large data, resulting in fraud protection, increased customer service, greater predictive capacity, and stronger information sharing. The Intel Nervana deep learning approach, available in both dedicated and on-premises versions, enables organisations of all sizes to create and grow AI applications – and obtain insights more effectively – without investing in costly new equipment rapidly and efficiently.

References

Almahdi, S., and Yang, S. Y. (2017). An adaptive portfolio trading system: a risk-return portfolio optimisation using recurrent reinforcement learning with expected maximum drawdown. *Expert Systems with Applications*, 87, 267–279.

Baek, Y., and Kim, H. Y. (2018). ModAugNet: a new forecasting framework for stock market index value with an overfitting prevention LSTM module and a prediction LSTM module. *Expert Systems with Applications*, 113, 457–480.

Butaru, F., Chen, Q., Clark, B., Das, S., Lo, A. W., and Siddique, A. (2016). Risk and risk management in the credit card industry. *Journal of Banking and Finance*, 72, 218–239.

Cavalcante, R. C., Brasileiro, R. C., Souza, V. L. F., Nobrega, J. P., and Oliveira, A. L. I. (2016). Computational intelligence and financial markets: a survey and future directions. *Expert System with Application*, 55, 194–211.

Chai, J. Y., and Li, A. M. (2019). Deep learning in natural language processing: a state-of-the-art survey. In *The Proceeding of the 2019 International Conference on Machine Learning and Cybernetics* (pp. 535–540).

Chai, J. Y., Liu, J. N. K., and Ngai, E. W. T. (2013). Applying decision-making techniques in supplier selection: a systematic review of the literature. *Expert Systems with Applications*, 40(10), 3872–3885.

Chai, J. Y., and Ngai, E. W. T. (2020). Decision-making techniques in supplier selection: recent accomplishments and what lies ahead. *Expert Systems with Applications*, 140, 112903. https://doi.org/10.1016/j.eswa.2019.112903.

Chatzis, S. P., Siakoulis, V., Petropoulos, A., Stavroulakis, E., and Vlachogiannakis, E. (2018). Forecasting stock market crisis events using deep and statistical machine learning techniques. *Expert Systems with Applications*, 112, 353–371.

Chen, C. T., Chen, A. P., and Huang, S. H. (2018a). Cloning strategies from trading records using agent-based reinforcement learning algorithm. In *The Proceeding of IEEE International Conference on Agents* (pp. 34–37).

Chen, L., Qiao, Z., Wang, M., Wang, C., Du, R., and Stanley, H. E. (2018b). Which artificial intelligence algorithm better predicts the Chinese stock market? *IEEE Access*, 6, 48625–48633.

Chen, L., and Su, S. (2022). Optimization of the trust propagation on supply chain network based on blockchain plus. *Journal of Intelligent Management Decision*, 1(1), 17–27.

Chen, H., Xiao, K., Sun, J., and Wu, S. (2017). A double-layer neural network framework for high-frequency forecasting. *ACM Transactions on Management Information Systems*, 7(4), 11.

Chong, E., Han, C., and Park, F. C. (2017). Deep learning networks for stock market analysis and prediction: methodology, data representations, and case studies. *Expert Systems with Applications*, 83, 187–205.

Collobert, R., Weston, J., Bottou, L., Karlen, M., Kavukcuoglu, K., and Kuksa, P. (2011). Natural language processing (almost) from scratch. *Journal of Machine Learning Research*, 12, 2493–2537.

Deng, Y., Bao, F., Kong, Y., Ren, Z., and Dai, Q. (2017). Deep direct reinforcement learning for financial signal representation and trading. *IEEE Transactions on Neural Networks and Learning Systems*, 28(3), 653–664.

Dhatterwal, J. S., Kaswan, K. S., and Preety. (2020). Intelligent agent based case base reasoning systems build knowledge representation in Covid-19 analysis of recovery infectious patients. In *Application of AI in COVID 19*. Springer Series: Medical Virology: From Pathogenesis to Disease Control, July 2020, ISBN No. 978-981-15-7317-0 (e-Book), 978-981-15-7316-3 (Hard Book). DOI: 10.1007/978-981-15-7317-0.

Dhatterwal, J. S., Kaswan, K. S., Jaglan, V., and Vij, A. (2022) Machine learning and deep learning algorithms for IoD. In *Internet of Drones: Opportunities and Challenges*. Apple Academic Press (AAP), Canada, ISBN: 9781774639856

Elad, M., and Aharon, M. (2006). Image denoising via sparse and redundant representations over learned dictionaries. *IEEE Transactions on Image Processing*, 15(12), 3736–3745.

Feuerriegel, S., and Prendinger, H. (2016). News-based trading strategies. *Decision Support Systems*, 90, 65–74.

Fischer, T., and Krauss, C. (2017). Deep learning with long short-term memory networks for financial market predictions. *European Journal of Operational Research*, 270(2), 654–669.

Galeshchuk, S., and Mukherjee, S. (2017). Deep networks for predicting the direction of change in foreign exchange rates. *Intelligent Systems in Accounting, Finance and Management*, 24(4), 100–110.

Kaswan, K. S., Baliyan, A., Dhatterwal, J. S., Jain, V., and Chatterjee, J. M. (2022). Intelligent classification of ECG signals using machine learning techniques. In *Healthcare Monitoring and Data Analysis using IoT*. IET. ISBN No. 9781839534379.

Mittal, A., Aggarwal, A., and Mittal, R. (2020). Predicting university students' adoption of mobile news applications: the role of perceived hedonic value and news motivation. *International Journal of E-Services and Mobile Applications (IJESMA)*, 12(4), 42–59.

Mittal, A., and Jhamb, D. (2016). Determinants of shopping mall attractiveness: the Indian context. *Procedia Economics and Finance*, 37, 386–390.

Muddumadappa, P. M. B., Anjanappa, S. D. K., and Srikantaswamy, M. (2022). An efficient reconfigurable cryptographic model for dynamic and secure unstructured data sharing in multi-cloud storage server. *Journal of Intelligent Systems and Control*, 1(1), 68–78.

Chapter 7

Self-supervised, unsupervised & semi-supervised learning for multimedia banking and financial services

Kuldeep Singh Kaswan[1], Jagjit Singh Dhatterwal[2], Sunil Kumar Bharti[3] and Kiran Sood[4]

Abstract

Qualitative research machine learning (ML) algorithms have been used to discern statements made in online user-contributed texts, with applicability in marketing and advertising, content marketing, and advanced analytics. Computing and data mining are computer programming study topics rapidly evolving due to breakthroughs in data analysis studies, expansion in the database business, and the accompanying commercial need for methods required to retrieve useful knowledge from enormous data stores.

Much research has been conducted in multimedia to address various elements of business intelligence, such as the collection, storage, categorization, mining, and retrieving of big multichannel data. However, quite a few published papers comprehensively assess the entire pine line of ML and data mining methodologies employed in research topics.

This review study provides a thorough overview of the most recent methods, algorithms, pattern recognition, and data mining in application domains.

Keywords: Machine learning; Data mining; Pattern recognition; Multimedia; Supervised learning; Detecting fraud; Predictive modelling

[1]School of Computing Science and Engineering, Galgotias University, India
[2]Department of Artificial Intelligence & Data Science, Koneru Lakshmaiah Education Foundation, India
[3]Department of IT, Galgotias College of Engineering and Technology, India
[4]Chitkara Business School, Chitkara University, Punjab, India

7.1   Supervised learning for money-laundering prevention, document analysis and underwriting loans, trade settlements, high-frequency trading

Almost a while back, the scholar spiritualist Pythagoras asserted that everything could be communicated in numbers. Around then, nobody figured him out. Today, we are seeing an advanced forward leap in which machines examine a lot of information on choices made by individuals in various circumstances, interpret learning calculations into their language, and act by the relationship with people. Today, advancements in machine learning (ML) follow the way of making a PC, the mental elements equivalent to the human cerebrum. The areas of money, banking, and protection are the most encouraging regions to apply these advancements (Arrieta *et al.*, 2020).

Globalization has resulted in a rise in digital payments in recent years and increased fraud. Credit cards are widely utilized for virtually all physical and cyber interactions. Identity fraud is one of the most concerning issues, costing billions of dollars in fraudulent purchases. A physical card purchase requires the cardholder to give his card to the seller for payment. Suppose the cardholders need to realize the card has been lost. In that case, the credit card company may suffer a significant loss because the fraudster needs very little information to make the fraudulent purchase (card number, social security number, etc.). According to financial sources, such thefts resulted in significant losses of roughly $28 billion globally in 2019. In the United States, up to 40% of credit card transactions were detected as illegal (Al-Shabandar *et al.*, 2019).

7.1.1   What exactly do detecting fraud paradigms perform?

ML classifiers are used in detecting fraud platforms to decrease these types of transactions. They employ data mining techniques to identify anomalous trends in a transaction (Coopers, 2021). Credit card fraud detection frameworks are used to reduce and prevent trading company losses due to unauthorized charges. So, how a fraud be detected? To create a pipeline for the same, the following are given in Figure 7.1.

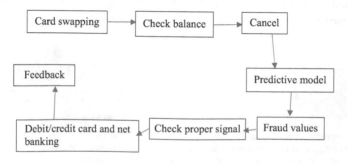

Figure 7.1   Framework of debit and credit cards detection

When an exchange is made using a charge card, a Terminal Check happens. Is the pin, right? Does the individual have good equilibrium? Is it an obstructed card? After acknowledging these prerequisites, the exchange is taken care of as a perception of the visionary ML model (Lokanan, 2019). If the Fraud Score is high or the model distinguishes an irregularity, the exchange is then checked by specialists. They affirm on the off chance that it is a misstep or the exchange is a cheat. The criticism is then taken care of into the model that is rehashed. Here is a ML forward prescient model we have worked to decide the fake exchanges in charge cards: The model can be prepared in a regulated way by utilizing classification models to determine if a business is fake via preparing past information (Ngai *et al.*, 2011).

It can likewise be prepared by solo demonstrating method by anomaly location. We can invest highlights like the energy of the exchange, a measure of cash, the area of the deal, and so on. The inconsistency is identified if any of these highlights show unusual behavior. Utilizing prescient demonstrating, the credit card fraud detection market has expanded immensely. As per Fortune Business Insights, it will grow to $106 billion by 2027. North America is a ML district for this market, yet Europe and Asia are also considered critical players. The developing number of exchanges during the COVID-19 lockdowns might support this number significantly higher than anticipated (Labib *et al.*, 2020).

7.1.2 Customer experience and segmentation

Client division is the methodology of isolating an enormous and various client base into more modest gatherings of related clients that are comparable in some ways and applicable to showcasing items and administrations (Weber *et al.*, 2018). Furthermore, that assists enterprises with further developing the client experience because of the various fragments of clients. Allow us to show you a portion of the instances of ML further extending client experience.

7.1.2.1 ML can approve loans faster

Clients applying for credit or searching for advance application endorsement generally held up weeks. Presently, many firms have diminished this timetable to days. However, assumptions have advanced; over 60% of buyers need a prompt reaction (under 10 min) to deals or administration questions (Paula, 2017).

As indicated by Tech Radar, this has prepared for utilising ML-driven applications approaching learnings and endorsement. With admittance to monetary informational collections, ML apparatuses can assess different credit factors and arrive at a ML choice – and do it much quicker than their human partners. According to Forbes, JPMorgan Chase saved over 360,000 h by examining 12,000 records in seconds (Alsuwailem and Saudagar, 2020).

7.1.2.2 Deep learning and ML to improve authentication

The fast reception of computerized financial advances accompanies an admonition: lost passwords and neglected account subtleties. ML-based menial helpers are presently being tapped to give immediate client care – by providing key subtleties;

clients can rapidly have passwords reset or get key monetary data without looking out for hold or visiting the branch face to face. A few banks send voiceprint, an ML-driven biometric arrangement, to validate clients using their voices. Arrangements like HPE's DL have arisen to assist organizations with speeding up information examination for solid, ongoing outcomes (Irofti *et al.*, 2021).

7.1.2.3   ML helps industries root out fraud

Compelling security is central for monetary client fulfilment – 84% of customers will take their information and business elsewhere, assuming they feel protection is deficient. As indicated by Emerj, banks are presently utilizing ML instruments equipped for recognizing normal client conduct, identifying key deviations and informing bank staff of expected extortion (Leite *et al.*, 2019).

Instruments like Splunk offer the essential speed and scale to deal with the extent of banks' Big Data and further develop data security best practices use cases in Banking, Finance and Insurance medium without compromising client protection. The result is twofold: fewer false exchanges for financial firms to remediate and further develop consumer loyalty with information security endeavors.

7.1.2.4   ML to predict customer demands

A definitive client experience result for banks? Foreseeing what clients need – before they realize they need it. ML devices equipped for investigating enormous informational indexes across classes, for example, purchasing behaviors, socio-economics, exchange volumes and administration solicitations, can assist keeps money by making designated credit, advance or reserve funds offers that are okay for monetary foundations; however, high-incentive for clients (Semenov, 2017).

Client experience currently supports the cutthroat fate of monetary associations. ML can assist money with ML in front of the group on endorsement volumes, administration reaction, extortion discovery and prescient individual co-operations (Shaju and Valliammal, 2019).

7.1.3   Underwriting and credit scoring

In the financial, banking, contract organizations, and different organizations that take part in advance and credit endorsing, innovations, including artificial reasoning and ML, are testing the premises of existing regulations and altering the course of credit and credit guarantees. These advances permit loan bosses to consider a wide scope of elective variables which are undiscovered by customary credit scoring models, with research proposing that they can enable organizations to stretch out good credit to individuals from underserved networks who, as of now, come up short using a credit card history important to take part in the monetary framework completely. Utilizing these apparatuses, organizations can increment productivity while possibly keeping up with or bringing down risk levels and wrongdoing rates (Sudjianto, 2010).

ML, a subset of artificial intelligence, depends on figuring ability to filter through large information to perceive examples and make forecasts without being expressly modified to do such. Over time, ML calculations utilize experience to "self-advance" and further develop how they play out their allocated task. This innovation is promising for banks, contract organizations, and organizations participating in advance and credit endorsing. It can effectively consider elective information that needs to be discovered by current loaning and credit scoring models. Through this interaction, organizations can "work on cross country admittance to monetary open door by making more shoppers 'storable' inside the standard monetary framework," ML new clients while hypothetically keeping up with or bringing down risk levels and wrongdoing rates (Force, 2021).

7.1.4 Difficulties to industry adoption

The principal limits of applying an ML calculation to decide financial assessment are not connected with the calculation's terrible showing or absence of complexity. The ML obstacles are related to everything beyond building this calculation/model (Kitchenham and Charters, 2007).

- One-sided information – all managed ML calculations accept that the future would follow comparative examples as the past. The outcome is that models can make expectations in light of hidden human qualities inconsequential to one's capacity to reimburse an advance, likewise called "predisposition a ML gatherings or classes of individuals." Banks are searching for ways of engaging this test through strategies like "segment visual deficiency" (select uncorrelated arrangement of highlights), "equivalent chances" (pick an equivalent number of true positives and bogus positive for each class), and that's only the tip of the iceberg (Jullum *et al.*, 2020).
- Interpretability – ML calculations are thought of as "discovery" because of the powerlessness of grasping the thinking behind individual choices. In 1974, Congress established "The Equal Credit Opportunity Act (ECOA)," which precludes lenders from going with options because of touchy attributes. A model as a "black box" does not follow those guidelines and may keep quality and strong calculations from truly being utilized practically speaking (Davenport, 2020).
- Notwithstanding ECOA, Congress has passed "The F-machine learning Credit Reporting Act (FCRA)," which intends to keep up with reasonableness in credit announcing and guarantee customer security by safeguarding or utilizing specific data. Nonetheless, it is viewed as far-fetched that profound learning calculations which require information focus that agree with FCRA. Leaders who depend on huge amounts of information to pursue choices frequently dodge these guidelines by denying to uncover any model's debt ML. It is a "proprietary advantage to state they." This is anything but a supportable arrangement, and the two organizations and specialists are investigating elective choices (Jaiswal and Valstar, 2016).
- Versatility – when a model is demonstrated to perform well and obstructs no administrative prerequisites, the test of increasing it should be survived. Decreasing preparation time, incorporating the model into existing items and providing a consistent stream of information are only a portion of the issues each association faces before encountering the maximum capacity of ML.

7.2   Robo-advisors is a tool of supervised learning for optimizing portfolios

Robo-counsels are advanced stages that give mechanized, calculation-driven monetary arranging administrations with practically no human oversight. A regular Robo-counselor poses inquiries about your fundamental policy and future aims using a web-based evaluation; it then employs the data to formulate recommendations and perform adequately.

7.2.1   What is a Robo-advisor?

The best robot guides offer simple record arrangement, strong objective preparation, account administration, and the executives' portfolio. Moreover, they offer security highlights, mindful client care, ML Ning, and low charges.

- Robo-counsels are advanced stages that give mechanized, algorithmic venture administrations with little human oversight.
- They frequently robotize and improve uninvolved ordering techniques in light of the current portfolio hypothesis.
- Robo-consultants are frequently economical and require low opening adjusts, making them accessible to ret ML financial backers (Liang, 2016).
- They are the most appropriate for day-to-day money management and are not the most ideal choices for additional perplexing issues, for example, home preparation.
- Robo-guides have been criticized for their absence of compassion and intricacy.

7.2.2   Understanding Robo-advisors

The first Robo-counsel, Betterment, was sent off in 2008, with the underlying reason for rebalancing resources inside deadline reserves. It looked to assist with overseeing inactive, purchase, and-hold speculations through a basic online interface. In 2022, ML Makara, a robot-guide stage that forms and keeps up with digital money portfolios to extend its contributions to financial backers.

The actual innovation was the same old thing. Human abundance chiefs have been utilizing computerized portfolio distribution programming since the mid-2000s. Be that as it may until Betterment was sent off, they were the ones who could purchase the innovation. Hence, clients needed a monetary consultant to profit from the development.

Today, most robot counsels utilize aloof ordering methodologies enhanced by using some variation of the present-day portfolio hypothesis (modern portfolio theory—MPT). Some robot guides offer improved portfolios for socially capable money management (socially responsible investing—SRI), Halal financial planning, or strategic procedures that copy mutual funds. Also, they can deal with substantially more complex errands, for example, charge misfortune reaping, venture choice, and retirement arranging.

In 2021, the biggest Robo-counsel regarding resources was Vanguard Personal Advisor Services, with $231 billion in resources under administration (assets under management—AUM).

The business has encountered hazardous development; client resources overseen by robo-counsels came to almost $1 trillion in 2020, with the assumption for coming to $2.9 trillion overall by 2,025.34. Other normal assignments for Robo-counselors incorporate a "mechanized speculation guide," "computerized venture the executives," and "advanced exhortation stages." Regardless of the name, everything alludes to fintech (financial innovation) applications for venture the board (Kipf and Welling, 2017).

7.2.3   Portfolio rebalancing

Most Robo-consultants use the current portfolio hypothesis (or some variation) to assemble latent, recorded portfolios for their users. Once settled, Robo-counsellors keep on observing those portfolios. Even if additional selling stations relocate, commodity class weightages must be maintained. Restructuring groups are a technique used by robots-consultants to achieve this goal.

Depending on the resource class or level of security, an observable weight and susceptibility range are assigned to each. For example, a part system may include holding 30% in growing business sector values, 30% in domestic blue chips, and 40% in sovereign bonds, with a flow of 5% for each investment product.

Before, this rebalancing was disliked because it may be tedious and create exchange expenses. Notwithstanding, Robo-counselors are intended to do this consequently with low costs.

This means that the expanding business community and native blue-chip properties may fluctuate between 25% and 35% of the investment, while government bonds should make up between 35% and 45% of the investment. The acquisition is restructured to reflect the fundamental goal synthesizing whenever the weight of an investment exceeds the acceptable range.

One more sort of rebalancing normally found in Robo-counsels – made financially savvy through calculations – is charge misfortune collecting. Charge misfortune reaping is a procedure that includes unloading protections at an inopportune time to counterbalance a capital increases charge responsibility in comparative security.

This system is commonly utilized to restrict the acknowledgement of transient capital increases. Robo-counsellors do this by keeping at least two stable trade exchanged reserves (ETFs) for every resource class. Thus, if the S&P 500 ETF loses esteem, it will naturally offer to secure in a capital misfortune; at the same time, it purchases an alternate S&P 500 ETF (Chen and Xiao, 2018).

7.3   Fundamental advantages of Robo-advisors

The lower cost is the primary advantage of using a Robo-counselor over a definitive guide. Social media platforms may give identical functionality at a fraction of the cost by eliminating the need for human labor. In most cases, automated financial impose annual fees that are less than 5% of the owed amount in full. It is much less than the typical 1–2% fee paid by a human money manager (or something else for commission-based accounts).

Sophisticated supervised learning capabilities are also included in Robo-counselors. As long as you are connected to the Internet, you may reach them anytime or at night. As a result, the initial start-up costs are much lower, often ranging from $300 to $5000 (a typical starting point is between $3,001 and $5,000). Improvement, a well-known Robo-counsel, has no evidence of giving anything less than its regular product.

Numerous human counsellors like to take on clients with more than $100,000 in investable resources, particularly those with ML out in the field. These high-total assets people need different abundance the executive's benefits and can stand to pay for them (Muddumadappa *et al.*, 2022; Chen and Su, 2022).

Proficiency is another huge benefit these Internet-based stages have. For example, before Robo-consultants, if you needed to execute an exchange, you would need to call or genuinely meet a monetary counsel, make sense of your necessities, and hang tight for them to execute your trades. Presently, you can do all of that with the snap of a couple of buttons in the solace of your home.

Then ML, utilizing a Robo-guide, will restrict the choices that you can make as a singular financial backer. For instance, you cannot pick which common assets or ETFs you are putting resources into, and you cannot buy individual stocks or bonds in your record. Normal financial backers frequently see improved results with an ordering procedure (Han, 2015).

7.4 Hiring a Robo-advisor

Opening a robot guide frequently involves facing a short challenge profiling survey and assessing what is happening, the time skyline, and individual speculation objectives. As a rule, you will have the amazing chance to interface your financial balance ML forwardly for fast and simple subsidizing of your Robo-warning account.

The sign of computerized warning administrations is their simplicity of online access. In any case, numerous advanced stages will generally draw in and target explicit socioeconomics more than others – specifically, Millennial and Generation X financial backers who are innovation sharp regardless of aggregating their investable resources.

The Securities and Exchange Commission (SEC) gave a gamble caution to financial backers in November 2021 regarding consistency issues with numerous Robo-counselors. Hence, it assists with keeping yourself informed by checking the FINRA Investor Alerts and the SEC Division of Examination sites for information.

This populace is considerably more open to sharing individual data on the web and entrusting innovation with fundamental assignments, like the abundance of executives. Undoubtedly, many of the showcasing endeavors of Robo-warning firms utilize web-based enter ML channels to arrive at these financial backers (Alarab *et al.*, 2020).

7.5 Robo-advisors and regulation

Legally, Robo-consultants have the same standing as human legal advisors. Traditionally represented vendors must be registered with the US SEC for proper protection.

Financial industry regulators make up most of the Robo-counseling staff (FINRA). As with a human consultancy, you may use BrokerCheck to investigate Robo-counselors.

Since venture capital firms keep these funds rather than banks, they are not covered by the FDIC's deposit insurance program. However, this does not imply that customers are completely exposed since professional merchants may safeguard their resources in several ways. For example, the Securities Investor Protection Corporation (SIPC) protects Wealthfront, a prominent Robo-advisor in the United States (SIPC).

7.5.1 How Robo-advisors make money

The essential way that most Robo-counsels bring in cash is through a wrap charge in light of resources under administration (AUM). While customary (human) monetary consultants regularly charge 1% or more each time of AUM, numerous Robo-guides charge around 0.25% each year per $1,000 in resources under administration.

If the profits on your ventures with a Robo-consultant do not offset the complete expenses related to utilizing it, then you might be in an ideal situation not using one.

Notwithstanding the administration expense, Robo-counselors can bring in cash in more ways than one. One way is the premium on money adjusts ("cash the executives"), which is credited to the Robo-consultant rather than the client. Since numerous Robo-exhorted accounts have little distribution of funds in their portfolios, this can become a huge type of revenue once more, assuming they have multiple clients.

Another income stream comes from instalments for the request stream. Commonly, Robo-counsels will gather supports that have been added from stores, interest, and profits; then, they pack these into huge square requests executed at only a couple of focuses in a day. This permits them to perform fewer exchanges and get better terms because of the enormous request sizes.

At long last, Robo-counsels can bring in cash by promoting designated monetary items and administrations to their clients, for example, contracts, mastercards, or insurance contracts. These are, much of the time, done through essential organizations instead of promoting networks (Feng *et al.*, 2019).

7.5.2 The best-in-class Robo-advisors

There are many Robo-consultants accessible in the United States also around the world; a greater amount of them sends off each year. They all give a blend of venture the board, retirement arranging, and general monetary counsel.

Here is an aggregation of the most aggressive contributions with the biggest portions of the overall industry.

- Independent Robo-advisors
  These organizations are the absolute earliest ML blazers of advanced warning innovation. They have the most cutthroat charges with low to zero record

essentials. Clients with no ongoing contributed resources can begin without preparation with these stages.

- Inheritance offerings of Robo-advisors
  With a rising number of monetary administrations and resources, the board firms are sending off Robo-consultants. These stages commonly have higher expenses and record essentials and are intended something else for refined financial backers. They are helpful choices for clients who utilize these organizations as resource overseers.
- Shortcomings of Robo-advisors
  The passage of Robo-counsels has separated a portion of the conventional boundaries between the monetary administration world and normal buyers. Due to these web-based stages, sound economic arranging is currently a ML label for everybody, not simply high-total assets.

In any case, numerous businesses need more clarification about the practicality of computerized guides as a one-size-fits-all answer for the abundance of executives. Given the general nascence of their mechanical abilities and insignificant human presence, Robo-counsels have been scrutinized for lacking sympathy and refinement.

They are great passage-level devices assuming you have a little record and restricted speculation experience. They may need to be included if you want progressed administrations like bequest arranging, confounded charge the board, trust store organization, and retirement arranging.

Focus on what a Robo-guide puts resources into, as many are presently creating some distance from aloof record systems and putting resources into additional dangerous regions that could ML to meet the market's expectations.

Mechanized administrations must be more prepared to manage startling emergencies or unusual circumstances. For instance, they will only be aware if you are in the middle between occupations or managing an unforeseen cost. If you have set up automatic withdrawals for the automated counsel, you run the risk of having your funds emptied without warning.

A review directed by Investopedia and the Financial Planning Association found that shoppers lean toward a mix of human and innovative directions, particularly when unpleasant. As indicated by the report, 40% of members of ML would not be open to utilizing a robotized contributing stage during excessive market volatility.

Moreover, Robo-guides work with the understanding that you have characterized objectives and an unmistakable comprehension of your monetary conditions. For some financial backers, that is not true. Study questions like, "Is your gamble resistance low, moderate, or high?" expect that you have principal information on venture ideas and the real ramifications of every choice you pick.

7.6 Component of ML

For investigative information accumulation, dimensionality reduction, data pressure, knowledge de-noising, and bounty-free documentation and try yourself at

PCA, principal component analysis (PCA) is one of the most often used solo ML computations.

Before diving into PCA's core activities, let us better understand it. Imagine that we have a two-dimensional dataset. Component sections may be created for each aspect.

The following is the bimodal distribution address for the comparable dataset: PCA's primary goal is to identify principle components that may be used to represent the data of interest using many principal components.

Vectors make up the bulk of the design, although they are chosen sparingly. ML principle components are calculated in a way that makes sense of the best estimate of the difference between the initial data items. Following the primary principle component, the second portion is symmetrical and makes sense of the remaining measure of difference.

Component vectors may be used to address the initial piece of information. Using PCA, we can look at data as direct mixes of primary components. Using major components, information may be directly sent between the feature1 and feature2 hubs.

We only gain a little by using PCA in the little two-layered model above, as an element vector of the structure (feature1, feature2) is practically the same as a vector of the system (PCA1 and PCA2). However, in large datasets (with more variables than 100 distinct ones), principle components reduce agitation by reducing innumerable highlights to a few key ones. Basic building blocks consist of symmetrical informational projections into a lower-layer area.

PCA should return a comparable number of main components for the prepared dataset. We only preserve some of the major sections, however. Just a few key components are needed to get a good approximation of the original dataset. Therefore, there is no need for further highlights. The result is a new arrangement of primary components, each of which may be used in a variety of ways.

7.6.1   What is PCA?

An information cleaning or pretreatment approach may be used before another pattern recognition calculation, or the computation can stand alone.

There are a variety of uses for PCA on its own, including:

- Multi-layered data should be represented graphically detailed information may be effectively conveyed in two- or three-layered plots using knowledge interpretation.
- *Reduce the size of data*. Data is packed using head component analysis to store and deliver additional information efficiently. For example, it is often used to compress images without sacrificing much of their quality or to handle signals. Many pressing concerns in design acknowledgement (explicitly face acknowledgement) and image acknowledgement may be efficiently addressed using the approach, and there is no end. Complications in business decisions are reduced to their simplest forms. PCA has been used to make difficult commercial decisions easier. For example, brokers employ more than 300

financial instruments when managing a client's portfolio. The board of loan cost subsidiaries portfolio has shown the efficacy of the computation by reducing the number of monetary policy instruments from more than 300 to just three or four key components.

- *Untangle confusing logical loops*. There is a lot of use for the calculation in analyzing complex and multidimensional aspects that might lead to agents available in a ML community.

When PCA is used as a preprocessing feature as given below, the computation is used to (1) reduce the number of aspects in the preparation dataset and (2) calm down the information. Due to its ability to recognize patterns in data, PCA can focus on what matters most and ignore what doesn't.

7.6.2   Calculation of PCA

PCA may be calculated in a variety of ways:

- Covariance network Eigen deconstruction
- Degeneration of the informational lattice's singular value
- Power iterative computation is used to estimate the Eigenvalue
- Iterative midway least squares (NIPALS) computation

Let us take a closer look at the Eigen decomposition of the covariance network, which is the primary technique for PCA analysis. PCA may be broken down into the following steps:

- Standardization of features. We normalize each component separately to have an average of 0 and a fluctuation. Later, in suspicions and limitations, we discover that highlighting values of various significance hinders PCA from recording the finest main components.
- Covariance network computation through ML. It is a square lattice of dxd "aspects" in the covariance network, where d signifies "aspect" (or component or section, assuming our information is even). Each component is shown to have a ML-included connection.
- Determine the covariance new framework Eigen decomposed. The covariance network's eigenvalues and eigenvectors (unit vectors and scalars used to replicate the eigenvector) are calculated. It is a good resource if you are looking for ways to enhance your ML variable-based arithmetic and decomposition.
- From highest to lowest, rank the principal components according to their eigenvalue. The deep learning model's primary component is the eigenvector with the highest eigenvalue. Eigenvalues are a better indicator of shared differences than other measurements.
- Decide how many main components you want. For each eigenvector, choose the N main features with the highest Eigen values. Principal components should have a maximum of both abstract and issue subordinate parts. In most cases, we look at the overall amount of shared variation explained by the

combination of primary elements and choose the number of pieces that still substantially explains the common fluctuation. This is standard procedure.

Understand that most investigators do not do PCA the hard way but rather use ScikitLearn or R to do it. These mathematical structures improve our ability to perceive PCA, but they need to be more balanced when implementing it. A better grasp of PCA's advantages and disadvantages allows us to make better decisions.

7.6.3   Benefits and limitations of PCA

PCA has a lot of benefits, but it also has some drawbacks. PCA is very simple to use. ML variables are at the heart of PCA's computations, making it an easy problem for computers to solve.

Other ML computations are sped up as a result. Calculations for ML based on primary components rather than the initial dataset come together more quickly.

Antidotes maximum information difficulties. Relapse-based algorithms need help overfitting with high-layered knowledge. Using PCA to reduce the elements in the pretreatment dataset prevents the prescient computations from generalization.

PCA's drawbacks:

- The lack of generalization ability of primary components. But they are not as easy to understand as ML mixtures of the first information's strengths. For example, it is difficult to identify the ML aspects in the dataset after processing the critical ingredients.

The result of a trade-off between data loss and a dimensionality reduction. Even while dimensionality reduction is beneficial, there are some substantial drawbacks. PCA relies heavily on data mishaps. Unfortunately, while using PCA, we must choose a trade-off between high-dimensional data and data misery.

7.6.4   Assumptions of PCA

A number of the same assumptions and limitations apply to PCA since it is linked to the Pearson connection and its ordering of activities:

- PCA recognizes the existence of a link between two items. No head parts will be determined if the spotlights (or aspects or segments, in pattern recognition information) are not connected.
- The size of the elements has a significant impact on PCA. Let us pretend we have two characteristics, one of which accepts values between 0 and 1,000 and the other of which accepts values between 0 and 1. PCA will be one-sided towards the primary element being the ML guideline part, no matter what the greatest change inside the information. For this reason, normalizing the qualities first is so significant.
- PCA is not a vigorous ML anomaly. The calculation will be one-sided in datasets with solid monsters like the point over. For this reason, eliminating anomalies before performing PCA is suggested.

- PCA accepts a direct connection between highlights. The calculation is not appropriate for catching non-ML connections. That is why it is encouraged to transform non-ML highlights or links between highlights into direct, utilizing the standard strategies, for example, log changes.

Specialized executions frequently expect all the qualities. While processing PCA utilizing factual programming devices, they often hope that the list of capabilities has all the qualities (no blank lines). Make ML to eliminate those lines or potential sections with missing rates or missing credit qualities with a nearby estimate (e.g., the mean of the segment).

7.6.5   Practical working in PCA

- The extent you are acquainted with the whole information science process dictates how you should use PCA realistically.
- Amateurs should begin by showing data from datasets that have already been collected and cleaned. At the same time, experts may scale up their operations by selecting the appropriate programs for the task.
- PCA: a beginner's guide to the technique.
- PCA may be evaluated realistically with an infinite number of high-layered datasets. ML algorithms may be used to predict whether a patient has pneumonia by preprocessing images of X-rays and feeding the information to other algorithms.
- Predicting the outcome of soccer games may be improved by ignoring the noise of little highlights.
- Estimate the price of Bitcoin. Using PCA to analyze the first Bitcoin dataset may improve your prophetic calculation's demonstration.

7.6.6   Production programming for cutting-edge information science

Creation of information science implies spending over 80% of your experience on information assortment and cleaning. If you desire to accelerate the whole information pipeline, use the programming that computerizes assignments to give you additional opportunities for information display.

ML researchers may use Keboola as a staging area to build their models. Jupyter Notebooks, which allow all showings to be done using Julia, R, or Python, are packaged with a single check to express them.

Intense immersion in Keboola's information science methodology

- Gather the important data.
- Find designs by exploring and cleaning up the data.
- Use PCA to prepare the data for analysis.
- It is time to put your ML model to the test.
- A variety of metrics should be used to evaluate the model.

Do you need to take another step forward? Keboola can assist you in orchestrating the flow of all of your data-related activities.

To prepare your data for ML computations, Keboola's information-driven stage allows you to build your ETL pipelines and arrange projects. To construct your work, you may use a variety of models and computations and then determine which ones function best.

7.7   Financial asset clustering using cluster analysis

Apportioning methods k-implies bunching strategy ML to parcel n noticed models into k groups. Every model has a place with one group. All models are treated with the equivalent significance, and along these lines, the centroid of the group's perceptions is calculated as a mean. Using the predetermined k, the computation proceeds by rotating between task and update steps. The task step appoints every guide to its nearest group (centroid). For newly framed groups, the update step calculates new means (centroids) using the aftereffect of the task step. The k-implies computation is fast, but the optimum k value is yet to be known in advance.

To organize shared reserves, the designer makes use of k-implies computation. Self-declared speculation aims to allocate the created bunches, and ML is used to distinguish between assumptions and monetary characteristics. It was also used to determine the number of groups (k) by using Hartigan's hypothesis: where k is the number of bunches, extended support scheme (ESS) addresses the number of squares and the dataset's size, n is the number of squares. A large number of groups is the base k. Hence (1) is false.

- *Density-based*
  Density-based is another method of grouping that does not use the mean centroid but rather uses density-based factual information to properly group knotted, unpredictably molded, but all-around distributed datasets.

  Density-based dispersion in a dataset may be studied using OPTICS, a bunching approach based on density. As a result, the k-implies computation is not affected by the lack of knowledge about the optimum method for selecting the value k. OPTICS provides a vantage point from which to examine the size of groups depending on densities. OPTICS, unlike centroid-based grouping, does not construct a bunching of a dataset from the beginning.

  In light of the appropriation based on density, it raises the need for models. Density-based bunching, such as DBSCAN, may use this group request. A bunch reachability plot in OPTICS visually provides density-based statistics about the dataset, making it easier for the customer to understand its density-based architecture.

  Though there are certain preconditions like the neighborhood range (MaxPts) and the minimum point quantity (MinPts), OPTICS requires some principles like these to be reached and related in a way that is independent of density. ML of MinPts objects in the neighborhood relies on the density-based associated range for DBSCAN. In OPTICS, the request to group objects is stored, not the enrolment of a bunch from the beginning. Center distance and reachability distance make up this set of data. The required datasets for further debt ML on DBSCAN and OPTICS have been provided.

There are no information bounds in the reachability plot, therefore, it suggests that the attributes should be "enormous" enough to produce a good result with no unclear models. MinPts uses values between 10 and 20 and typically achieves excellent results with a large, according to tests. A very natural way to grasp the density-based basis of financial information is via a reachability graphic. Its overall form is independent of the limits that are used.

- *Information stream grouping*

Applied an online advancing methodology for recognizing budget summaries' abnormalities. The online advancing strategy is powerful for bunching information streams. This technique powerfully builds the number of groups by working out the distance among models and existing bunch habitats. Assuming that this distance is higher than edge esteem, another group is made and instated by the model. This grouping calculation can be summed up in three ML steps:

1. Calculate the distance D iJ between information object × I to all current group places Cc J, find the base distance D ik and contrast it with the range R k of bunch C k.
2. If D ik < R k, then × I has a place with bunch C k, find the closest group that can assess S a = D ia + R an ML a limit δ.
3. If S a > δ, then make another group for × I else × I has a place with bunch can and update R a = S a/2. In this calculation, the quantity of bunches isn't predefined.

Notwithstanding, the distance computation and the limit esteem need the master to give earlier information, thus names of the recently framed bunch.

Applied various leveled agglomerative grouping ways to deal with examining financial exchange information. The creators proposed an effective measurement for estimating the likeness between bunches, a central question for various levelled agglomerative grouping techniques. This likeness between two groups C = {C_1, C_2, ...C_k} and C' = {C'_1, C'_2 ...C'_k} is characterized as follows.

As a result, various pre-handling procedures, such as dimensions reduction and standardized, should also be used to work on the implementation. In addition, the Precision-Recall approach was used to improve the group's quality, and its methodology was employed to break down account statements, such as a financial exchange. In addition, the designers defined a second distance measure in light of the potential to include time series data. $sI(t)$ is the value of stock *I* at time *t*, which gives us the distance between stock *I* and stock *j*. According to the designers, the optimal result is achieved by progressive agglomerative grouping with constant rate change after anomalies have been sifted.

Regardless, a determined limit is needed to identify anomalies from the rest of the population. As a result, the researchers combine brain organization and affiliation research with the clustering approach to analyze stock exchange datasets.

7.8 Latent variable modeling for financial volatility

Factual strategies for idle factors have a longstanding practice in both hypothetical and observational explores and cover a wide scope of scholarly and functional fields. Despite recent pertinent advances, the handiness of inactive factors in monetary investigations is still generally neglected. In this chapter, the authors propose investigating the main economic factors by focusing on their static nature. The authors recommend turning to the measurable approach produced for examining static variables to present a creative appraisal of economic peculiarities.

In customary monetary investigations, stocks are broken down based on the gamble and the normal return. In this structure, the commitment of factual philosophy can be applicable since gambling, and expected return is not straightforwardly detectable factors and can be estimated through the various measurable techniques created for dormant characteristics. All the more explicitly, the stock's gamble-expected return profile should be visible as an inactive variable fundamental to the stock's presentation. The noticed return values can be utilized as the marker factors that empower the improvement of an estimation technique. Accordingly, it is essential to characterize a strategic cycle capable of evaluating the idle idea of the gamble and the normal return and directing me to segregate stocks under their gamble and bring the profile back. Assessing the LC models for various upsides of K permits me to characterize the number of classes that can better machine learn the connections among the manifest factors. In my proposition, K addresses the number of gatherings that portrays the new financial information grouping. The LC models are assessed utilizing mutually the EM and the Newton–Raphson calculations and 50 different beginning qualities to keep away from the issue of probability intermingling into a nearby greatest.

7.9 Association rule learning for financial revenue analysis

The overall knowledge data discovery (KDD) process has the subsequent stages: gathering information, preprocessing, applying the genuine information mining errands and post-handling. We particularize these ventures for affiliation rule mining in the loan management system (LMS) do ML.

- Gathering information: Many of the ongoing LMSs do not store logs as text documents. All things being equal, they typically utilize a social dataset that holds every one of the framework's data: individual data of the clients (profile), educational outcomes, the client's cooperation information, and so forth. Information bases are all the more remarkable, adaptable, and bug-inclined than the ordinarily printed log documents for social event detaching learning led to access and significant level utilization Downsides and arrangements of applying affiliation rule mining data from every one of the administration's ML labels in the LMS. The LMSs keep detaching learning-led logs of movements of every kind that understudies perform. Not just every snap that understudies make for navigational purposes (low-level data) is put away, yet additionally, test scores, slipped by time, and so forth (significant-level data).

- Information pre-handling. Most of the customary information pre-handling assignments, for example, information cleaning, client distinguishing proof, meeting ID, exchange ID, information change and advancement, information incorporation and information decrease, are not vital in LMS. Information pre-handling of LMS information is less difficult because most LMS stores the information for investigation purposes, as opposed to the ordinarily observational datasets in information mining, that were produced to help the available setting and not so much for investigation in any case. LMSs likewise utilize an information base and client verification which permits distinguishing the clients in the logs. A few runs-of-the-mill undertakings of the information arrangement stage are information discretization, deduction of new qualities and determining properties, making outline tables, and changing the information design.

7.10   Semi-regulated text mining for environmental, social, and governance

A cryptic structure is assumed to be at the root of the information predictions generated by AI ML for the computational exhibition economy. In which, a bunch of factors go about as data sources. The goal is to track down a standard (calculation) that works on inputs to anticipate or group units, all the more actually with practically no deduced conviction about the connections between factors. The normal component of AI approaches is that calculations are acknowledged to gain from information with negligible human intercession. The run of the mill scientific classification is used to arrange AI calculations depending on their learning style and categorizes them as prescribed or unassisted learning methodologies.

Regulated AI revolves around the problem of predicting a reaction variable, y, given several indicators, x. Instead of examining the fundamental relationship between y and x, such computations aim to make large out-of-test assumptions. These estimates rely on the cross-approval approach. This last option contains the repeated rotation of sample groups of the whole information, in which the investigation is done on one random sample (the ML set), and the outcome is subsequently tested on the other subset(s) (the test set). Such rotating defined variables with the goal are explored with the ML of concentrating on out-of-test uniformity (accuracy) while avoiding concerns of wearing correctly and choosing tendency. This is caused by the twisting caused by accumulating prospective longitudinal tests.

Managed AI strategies incorporate the accompanying classes of algorithms:

- Calculations for decision trees. Choice trees are selection algorithms based on the real credits seen in the researched dataset. The purpose is to identify a sequence of broad principles conceptualized in a binary tree that drives from observations to outcomes presented as expected principles. Choice trees are referred to as relapsing: when the response data is normally distributed, trees are the best; when the response variable is exhausted, we use order trees. In this class, CART (Classification and Regression Trees) is the most often used computation. Arranging (when y is an uncontrollable variable) or relapsing (when y is a continuous variable) tree is formed by dividing the space of indications x into homogeneous and separate regions concerning y.

- Collections of trees are extensions of individual trees based on expectation averaging. ML is better than a single tree in making precise predictions. Gradient Boosted Regression Trees (GBT) and Gradient Boosted Augmented Bootstrapped Amplification (Bagging) are some of the most well-known augmentation approaches (GBRT). Random Forest is another option.

- Calculations on a case-by-case basis, only intelligible examples are used in these approaches to build grouping expectations. A closeness measure is used to locate the ideal outcome among the sample groups. Here is a list of some of the most often used formulas: Examples of ML algorithms include k-nearest neighbors (KNN), learning vector quantization (LVQ), privately weighted learning (PWL), and support vector machines (SVMs). Because they may be used for both order and relapse assessment, SVMs, in particular, are quite adaptable. Extending the vector classifier, these feelings are divided by straight boundaries in a collection of experiences. The nonlinear qualities of SVM are further enhanced by organizing them in a way that adds to high-layered highlight spaces. Using a higher dimensional space is what SVM does, in more technical terms, with a raised layered speed (or a collection of separating hyperplanes, which are only lines in a two-layered space). ML of pieces of information in distinct classes may be used to create hyperplanes, which are used to split rooms into subcategories. These distances are calculated using a bit, i.e., for a comparable effort across MLs, read the following.

- Additionally, batch normalization computations may be found here. Improved prediction ability may be achieved by negotiating better terms models, which provide alternate fitting approaches to the most un-square method. Models like the simple straight one is widely used to show how one variable (y) relates to other variables in a collection of ($x1$-XP). Least Absolute Deformation and Selection Operator (LASSO), Elastic Net, and Edge Relapse (ER) are all built on discovering which elements are more predictive of the dependent attribute out-of-test using ML assessments of demarcation evaluations.

- The backpropagation algorithm is used in Bayesian calculations' identification and relapse challenges. A computer program recognizes patterns ML probabilistic Bayes ML and multinomial distributions. The most well-known Bayesian estimates are Bayes Averaged One-Reliance Estimators (AODE), the Bayesian Belief Network (BBN), and the Bayesian Network.

- Supervised the operation of artificial neural networks (ANNs). Human cognition is modeled after that of ANNs. An ANN is said to be "controlled" if it receives inputs and then uses them to activate "neurons" and produce a result. In order to reduce the amount of evaluation error, the voltages used to link neurons are adjusted based on the difference between their measurement yield and their aim.

7.11   Performance of companies

A company's profitability is a powerful indicator of how well it can use its main commercial resources to develop income. A company's total financial health during a certain time period is also described by the term (Mittal and Jhamb, 2016; Mittal *et al.*, 2020).

Comparing companies in the same sector or evaluating organizations or regions is done using business performance by investigations and financial backers.

- Grasping financial performance
  An institution's partners include exchange lenders, investors, financial supporters, spokespeople, and administrators. In watching an organization's financial execution, each assemblage has its own advantage. The macroeconomic exhibition differentiates how successfully a company's primary function is to make profits while simultaneously overseeing its participants' assets, liabilities, and financial interests.
- Recording financial performance
  Form 10-K is a crucial archive for disclosing business financial performance and is heavily relied upon by researchers. According to the SEC, this annual report is a requirement for all publicly traded companies. Its goal is to provide partners with accurate and trustworthy data that provides an overview of the organization's financial well-being.
  Autonomous accounting professionals review the data in a 10-K, and the company's management approves it and other disclosure files. As a result, the 10K provides financial supporters with the most comprehensive dataset available for ML annually.
- Asset report
  They represent the fact that provides a snapshot of an organization's finances at a certain point in time. An overview of the institution's liabilities and assets is provided. Investigations may find information on long-term vs. short-term financial commitments in the financial record. They may also discover information about the available operations, such as its obligations and the worth of its assets in relation to the value of its shareholders.
- Pay statement
  The paid announcement summarizes the year's work in a single document. The articulation of remuneration starts with transactions or earnings and ends with total income. It is also known as the benefit and deficit declaration; the pay explanation outlines total revenues and expenses and net revenues. Also included is a breakdown of the special offerings and a ML test of the previous year's presentations.
- Income statement
  Both the pay description and the currency record go into the income articulation. Since total profit and income are both taken into account, the income announcement is considered the most important budget report by some investigations. Researchers can see how much money was spent on stock repurchases and other capital expenditures. Also included are details on how money is generated, how it is finished and how it is invested.

7.12   Conclusion

AI is normally a solid match for money, banking and protection enterprises because of the staggering ML ability of very much organized information. In addition, ML models can work with information enlisted continuously. Yet, they can likewise scratch and change tremendous measures of authentic details to discover cycles and occasions. With the force of knowledge and ML, finance organizations have had the option to smooth out their administrations and pass esteem onto clients and clients. Risk is diminished, bringing down the predominance of extortion while allowing real instalments to go on immediately. In the securities exchange, AI is mechanizing the exchange system, empowering incredibly touchy and productive high-recurrence exchanges that destroy manual trading strategies. As figuring power increments, it will be more than just multinationals and other huge organizations that can partake in this mechanical ML, SMEs and new businesses. In any case, while presenting ML calculations and in these ventures, pioneers likewise need to consider an arrangement of security ML digital assaults and ways of giving clients trust in the wellbeing of their information.

References

R. Al-Shabandar, G. Lightbody, F. Browne, J. Liu, H. Wang, and H. Zheng. (2019). "The application of artificial intelligence in financial compliance management," in *Proc. Int. Conf. Artif. Intell. Adv. Manuf. (AIAM)*, pp. 1–6.

I. Alarab, S. Prakoonwit, and M. I. Nacer (2020). "Competence of graph convolutional networks for anti-money laundering in bitcoin blockchain," in *Proc. Assoc. Comput. Machinery*, pp. 23–27.

A. A. S. Alsuwailem and A. K. J. Saudagar (2020). "Anti-money laundering systems: a systematic literature review," *J. Money Laundering Control*, vol. 23, no. 4, pp. 833–848.

B. Arrieta, N. Díaz-Rodríguez, J. Del Ser, *et al.* (2020) "Explainable artificial intelligence (XAI): concepts, taxonomies, opportunities and challenges toward responsible AI," *Inf. Fusion*, vol. 58, pp. 82–115.

J. Chen and T. C. M. Xiao (2018). "FastGCN: fast learning with graph convolutional networks via importance sampling," in *Proc. Int. Conf. Learn. Represent. (ICLR)*, pp. 1–15.

L. Chen and S. Su (2022). "Optimization of the trust propagation on supply chain network based on blockchain plus," *J. Intell. Manag. Decis.*, vol. 1, no. 1, pp. 17–27.

T. Davenport. (2020). The Future of Work Now: AI-Driven Transaction Surveillance At DBS Bank. Forbes. Available: https://www.forbes.com/sites/tomdavenport/2020/10/23/the-future-of-work-now-ai-driven-transaction-surveillance-at-dbs-bank/?sh=4772a6383f7f.

Y. Feng, C. Li, Y. Wang, *et al.* (2019) "Anti-money laundering (AML) research: a system for identification and multi-classification," in W. Ni (ed.), *Proc. 16th Web Inf. Syst. Appl. Conf. (WISA)*, Cham, Switzerland: Springer, pp. 169–175.

F. A. T. Force (2021). What is Money Laundering. Accessed: Feb. 26, 2021. Available: https://www.fatf-gafi.org/faq/moneylaundering/#d.en.11223.

J. Han (2015). "NextGen AML: distributed deep learning-based language technologies to augment anti money laundering investigation," in *Proc. Assoc. Comput. Linguistics (ACL)*, 2015, pp. 37–42.

P. Irofti, A. Pătraşcu, and A. Băltoiu. (2021). "Fraud detection in networks," in *Studies in Computational Intelligence*. Cham, Switzerland: Springer, pp. 517–536.

S. Jaiswal and M. Valstar. (2016). "Deep learning the dynamic appearance and shape of facial action units," IEEE, Lake Placid, NY, USA, Tech. Rep. 7477625, https://doi.org/10.1109/WACV.2016.7477625.

M. Jullum, A. Løland, R. B. Huseby, G. Ånonsen, and J. Lorentzen. (2020) "Detecting money laundering transactions with machine learning," *J. Money Laundering Control*, vol. 23, no. 1, pp. 173–186.

T. N. Kipf and M. Welling. (2017). "Semi-supervised classification with graph convolutional networks," in *Proc. Int. Conf. Learn. Represent. (ICLR)*, pp. 1–14.

B. Kitchenham and S. Charters (2007). "Guidelines for performing systematic literature reviews in software engineering," in *Guidelines for Performing Systematic Literature Reviews in Software Engineering*. Keele, UK.

N. M. Labib, M. A. Rizka, and A. E. M. Shokry. (2020). *Survey of Machine Learning Approaches of Anti-Money Laundering Techniques to Counter Terrorism Finance (Lecture Notes in Networks and Systems)*. Singapore: Springer, pp. 73–87.

G. S. Leite, A. B. Albuquerque, and P. R. Pinheiro (2019). "Application of technological solutions in the fight against money laundering—a systematic literature review," *Appl. Sci.*, vol. 9, no. 22, p. 4800.

Y. Liang. (2016) "State of the art control of Atari games using shallow reinforcement learning," in *Proc. Int. Found. Auton. Agents Multiagent Syst. (IFAAMAS)*, pp. 485–493.

M. E. Lokanan. (2019). "Data mining for statistical analysis of money laundering transactions," *J. Money Laundering Control*, vol. 22, no. 4, pp. 753–763.

A. Mittal, A. Aggarwal, and R. Mittal (2020). "Predicting university students' adoption of mobile news applications: the role of perceived hedonic value and news motivation," *Int. J. E-Serv. Mob. Appl.*, vol. 12, no. 4, pp. 42–59.

A. Mittal and D. Jhamb (2016). "Determinants of shopping mall attractiveness: the Indian context," *Procedia Econ. Financ.*, vol. 37, pp. 386–390.

P. M. B. Muddumadappa, S. D. K. Anjanappa, and M. Srikantaswamy (2022). "An efficient reconfigurable cryptographic model for dynamic and secure unstructured data sharing in multi-cloud storage server," *J. Intell Syst. Control*, vol. 1, no. 1, pp. 68–78.

E. W. T. Ngai, Y. Hu, Y. H. Wong, Y. Chen, and X. Sun (2011). "The application of data mining techniques in financial fraud detection: a classification framework and an academic review of literature," *Decision Support Syst.*, vol. 50, no. 3, pp. 559–569.

E. L. Paula (2017). "Deep learning anomaly detection as support fraud investigation in Brazilian exports and anti-money laundering," in *Inst. Elect. Electron. Engineers Inc.*, CA, USA, Tech. Rep. 7838276.

Pricewaterhouse Coopers. (2021). Explainable AI Driving Business Value Through Greater Understanding. Available: https://www.pwc.co.uk/services/risk-assurance/insights/explainable-ai.html.

A. Semenov (2017). "Survey of common design approaches in AML software development," in *Proceedings of the CEUR-WS*, pp. 1–9.

B. Shaju and N. Valliammal (2019). "Measures for financial fraud detection using data analytics and machine learning," *Int. J. Adv. Sci. Technol.*, vol. 28, no. 17, pp. 270–280.

A. Sudjianto (2010). "Statistical methods for fighting financial crimes," *Technometrics*, vol. 52, no. 1, pp. 5–19.

M. Weber, J. Chen, T. Suzumura, *et al.* (2018). "Scalable graph learning for anti-money laundering: a first look," arXiv:1812.00076. Available: https://arxiv.org/abs/1812.00076.

Chapter 8

Natural language processing and multimedia applications in finance

Jagjit Singh Dhatterwal[1], Kuldeep Singh Kaswan[2], Kiran Sood[3] and Simon Grima[4]

Abstract

The innovation of multimedia apps has accelerated in recent years. Developing technology and techniques enable the construction of massive multimedia archives and the construction of new intervention techniques. This chapter presents an overview of multimodal applications that extensively use natural speech.

Conventional multifunctional systems often do not save explicit reconstructions of user input and merely manage mode integrating in an introductory manner. This chapter demonstrates how expanding techniques and conceptual representation frameworks established for natural linguistic structures can aid in resolving some of these issues.

It examines strategies for developing autonomous multimedia instructional systems based on lessons acquired while creating machine-creating synthesizers. Finally, it contends that using natural language technology can result in a quantitative upgrade of existing approaches for following form and interpretation.

Keywords: Natural language processing; Know you customer; Artificial intelligence; Repetitive brain organization; Artificial intelligence; Machine learning; Named element acknowledgment

8.1 Financial technology and natural language processing

The foundation on the most proficient method to cause PCs to comprehend and utilize normal language gets from different fields including semantics,

[1]Department of Artificial Intelligence & Data Science, Koneru Lakshmaiah Education Foundation, India
[2]School of Computing Science and Engineering, Galgotias University, India
[3]Chitkara Business School, Chitkara University, Punjab, India
[4]Insurance and Risk Management, Faculty of Economics, Management & Accountancy, University of Malta, Malta

neuroscience, math and software engineering, and results in an interdisciplinary region called natural language processing (NLP). NLP is a subfield of man-made consciousness [artificial intelligence (AI)] and with the approach of AI [machine learning (ML)] calculations and expanded computational capacities, NLP has become considerably more adaptable and dependable (Al Nasseri *et al.*, 2015).

As expressed in TechCrunch, over the most recent 3 years, NLP has gained more headway than some other subfield of AI. NLP-based applications are all over the place, beginning from home associates like Amazon Echo or Alexa, to chatbots, etc. The impetus of the NLP unrest has been the open, feasible datasets, instead of the restricted datasets accessible just to a couple of associations.

Likewise, the reasonability of NLP models has widened to numerous dialects, aside from English, empowering close to-consummate machine interpretation calculations on various stages. NLP apparatuses, methods and application programming interfaces (APIs) are currently all-overrunning various enterprises, including finance. There has never been a superior opportunity to fabricate NLP answers for finance, then, at that point, presently (Alostad and Davulcu, 2015).

These days, information is driving money and the most significant piece of information can be found in composed structure in records, texts, sites, discussions, etc. Finance experts invest a lot of energy perusing the investigator reports, monetary press, and so forth. The programmed printed information handling can essentially diminish how much manual routine work and speed up the exchanges.

NLP procedures and calculations help to decipher the crude printed information into significant bits of knowledge across a few regions in finance. Merchants, portfolio chiefs, investigators, banks and other monetary associations endeavor to work on their monetary examination, and NLP and ML have turned into the advancements of decision. NLP is employed throughout the monetarily company, from financial institutions to index funds smart financial management. Such NLP methods as viewpoint assessment, discussion to (chatbots), record grouping and topic bunching are used to deal with uncontrolled financial accounting (AL-Rubaiee *et al.*, 2017).

NLP and ML procedures can be utilized to plan a monetary foundation that can pursue informed choices consistently. NLP can assist with planning such frameworks that can advance monetary streams by following an organization's evolving nature. For instance, NLP can work on the activity of a bank as follows:

- Work on improving operational effectiveness.
- Ensuring that strategy guidelines are more consistent.
- Gaining new scientific expertise.
- Making innovative additions to the body of knowledge.

8.1.1 NLP-based finance

NLP has explicit money applications, including advance gamble evaluations, examining and bookkeeping, opinion examination and portfolio choice. The following are four instances of how NLP changes the monetary administrations field:

Measuring of risk analysis

A credit risk assessment may be used by banks to estimate the likelihood of a successful forward installments. Installment limits are often decided based on previous spending patterns and creditworthiness. However, in certain circumstances, especially for the more disadvantaged, this data is not available. Nearly a quarter of the population does not use financial services, according to a survey (Alvarado *et al.*, 2015).

This problem can be addressed using NLP. To assess credit risk, NLP approaches make use of a wide range of information sources. NLP, for instance, can assess a company's inventive spirit and thinking. Essentially, it can likewise call attention to confused information and take it up for more examination. Significantly more, the unpretentious perspectives like moneylender's and borrower's feelings during a credit interaction can be integrated with the assistance of NLP.

As a rule, organizations catch a great deal of data from individual advance archives and feed it into credit risk models for additional examination. Albeit the gathered data surveys credit risk, botches in information extraction can prompt some unacceptable evaluations. Named element acknowledgment (NER), a NLP strategy, is valuable in such circumstances. NER assists with inferring the pertinent substances removed from the credit understanding, including the date, area, and subtleties of gatherings included (Ammann *et al.*, 2014).

→ Peruse how NLP social diagram strategy assists with surveying patient data sets can assist clinical exploration associations with prevailing with clinical preliminary examination.

Monetary feeling

Data regarding certain equities is essential for successful trading in the financial market. With this knowledge, dealers have the option of purchasing, holding, or selling a stock. You should also know what inspectors are saying about these firms, which you may learn via internet amusement instead of just poring over quarterly financial statements (Kaswan *et al.*, 2022).

Web-based entertainment investigation includes checking such data inside virtual entertainment posts and choosing likely open doors for exchanging. For instance, fresh insight about a CEO abdication ordinarily conveys a negative feeling and can influence the stock cost adversely. Yet, in the event that the CEO was not performing great, the securities exchange takes acquiescence news decidedly and it might possibly expand the stock cost.

DataMinr and Bloomberg are a portion of the organizations that give such data to help in exchanging. For instance, DataMinr has given stock-explicit alarms and news about Dell to clients on its terminals possibly influence the market (Balakrishnan *et al.*, 2010).

The monetary feeling investigation is unique in relation to routine opinion examination. It is different in both the space and its motivation. In customary feeling examination, the goal is to find regardless of whether the data is intrinsically good. Nonetheless, in monetary opinion examination in light of NLP, the intention is to check whether how the market will respond to the news and whether the stock cost will fall or rise.

BioBERT, a pre-prepared biomedical language portrayal model for biomedical text mining, has been very helpful for medical services and presently scientists are chipping away at adjusting BERT into the monetary area. FinBERT is one of those models created for the monetary administrations area. FinBERT works on a dataset that contains monetary news from Reuters. To appoint feeling, a Phrase Bank was used. It comprises of around 4,000 sentences named by various individuals of business or money foundations (Boskou *et al.*, 2018).

In regular feeling investigation, a good assertion suggests a good inclination. However, in Financial Phrase Bank, negative feeling suggests that the organization's stock cost might fall in view of the distributed news. FinBERT has been very fruitful with an exactness of 0.97 and a F1 of 0.95, altogether worked on contrasted with other accessible apparatuses. The FinBERT library is open on GitHub with the important information. This hearty language model for financial feeling characterization can be utilized for various purposes. Find the opinion investigation calculation worked from the beginning by our information science group.

Bookkeeping and inspecting

The primary focus of Deloitte, Ernst & Young, and PwC is to provide thorough and notable analyses of a foundation's annual report. Deloitte, for example, has transformed its Auditing Command – line interface into a more effective NLP tool. Contract archives audits and long-distance acquisitions, notably with governmental material, have been audited using NLP techniques (Bowers and Chen, 2015).

Organizations now recognize the importance of NLP in gaining a significant advantage in the reviewing relationship, especially after handling endless daily transactions and receipts like paperwork for a significant duration. NLP empowers monetary experts to straightforwardly distinguish, center, and picture inconsistencies in the everyday exchanges. With the right innovation, less time and exertion is spent to figure out inconsistencies in the exchanges and its causes. NLP can help with the recognizable proof of critical expected dangers and conceivable misrepresentation, similar to tax evasion. This assists with expanding esteem producing exercises to scatter them across the association (Kaswan *et al.*, 2022).

Portfolio determination and streamlining

Every economic backer's primary goal is to increase their money over the long term without learning about the hidden expenses of shares. It is possible to predict financial security and exchange enterprise processes using knowledge of science, artificial intelligence, and probabilistic insights. The accumulated data from the past may be used to predict the beginning of the exchanging period and an investment. In light of this knowledge, financial supporters will be able to distribute their funds among the available options.

NLP may be used to streamline inventories in a semi-log-normal fashion. Semi-log-ideal portfolio determination is a computational option in contrast to the log-ideal portfolio choice. With its assistance, the greatest conceivable development rate is accomplished when the ecological variables are questionable. Information envelopment investigation can be used for portfolio choice by sifting through alluring and unwanted stocks (Chen *et al.*, 2014).

Stock conduct expectations

Foreseeing time series for monetary investigation is a muddled errand on account of the fluctuating and unpredictable information as well as the long haul and occasional varieties that can cause huge mistakes in the examination. Notwithstanding, profound learning joined with NLP outclasses past approaches working with monetary time series generally. These two advancements joined really manage a lot of data.

Profound advancing without anyone else is certainly not a fresh out of the box new thought. Over the most recent 5 years, an incredible number of profound learning calculations have begun to perform better compared to people at various errands, like discourse acknowledgment and clinical picture examination. Repetitive brain organizations (RNN) are an excellent method for forecasting time series, such as stock prices, in the financial sector. RNNs are naturally capable of determining complicated nonlinear interconnections in financial historical time series data and estimating any polynomial capability with a high degree of accuracy. These strategies are feasible options in contrast to existing ordinary procedures of stock records forecast as a result of the great degree of accuracy they offer. NLP and profound learning procedures are helpful to anticipate the instability of stock costs and patterns, and furthermore is an important instrument for pursuing stock exchanging choices (Chen *et al.*, 2017).

NLP in monetary practice

NLP procedures are utilized to change the unstructured text data into quick investigation. NLP calculations have become significantly more solid and versatile as of late and are furnishing monetary leaders with a far-reaching comprehension of the market (Chen *et al.*, 2017).

The monetary business is using NLP to diminish how much manual routine work and to speed up the exchanges, survey the dangers, grasp the monetary opinion, and build portfolios while robotizing inspecting and bookkeeping. These advances are accomplished with the assistance of feeling investigation, question responding to (chatbots), theme grouping and report arrangement.

NLP and ML have turned into the innovations of decision for monetary investigators, dealers and portfolio chiefs. Protection associations use NLP to handle asserts consequently, while retail banks are smoothing out their client assistance, offering better monetary items to their clients and are better outfitted to manage extortion and tax evasion exercises.

8.2 NLP-based investment management

A new examination by Cerulli Associates, a supplier of worldwide resource the board investigation, of the resources under administration (AUM) and net new progressions of Europe-domiciled AI-drove assets from 2013 to April 2020 shows strong AUM development from 2016 to 2019. Outstandingly, the examination finds that the aggregate return of AI-drove speculative stock investments was around three-times the general returns timed by the mutual fund universe during this period: 33.9% contrasted with returns of 12.1%. The report finds that European AI-drove dynamic value subsidizes added resources at a quicker rate than other dynamic value assets from January to April this year. The exploration fights that there has for some time been doubt of the capacity of AI to respond to startling occasions, for example, the COVID-19 pandemic, yet there is presently a feeling that the innovation has progressed to where it is better ready to adjust to unanticipated situations by means of the steadily developing measure of market information accessible (Chen *et al.*, 2018).

In the effective financial planning world, it used to be the situation that edge depended on admittance to better wellsprings of data and prevalent examination/calculating. Considering that admittance to data is at this point not an upper hand, creating alpha has become a lot harder. In addition, with the expansion of humongous text-based information (unstructured) across media, it is at this point not feasible for human limit alone (nor proficient) to peruse and break down the information. To definitely cut the text-related snort work and catch overabundance returns, the resource administrators are progressively utilizing NLP methods – a vital subset of AI to handle unstructured text into noteworthy experiences for navigation. The NLP has wide applications across different business regions. The COVID-19 pandemic and harder financial environment have just sped up the utilization of NLP in venture executives. Probably the most convincing utilizations of NLP remember help for credit scoring, misrepresentation identification, client care, chatbots, and report search and handling for business knowledge (Kaswan *et al.*, 2022).

8.2.1   Instances of some key NLP applications in asset management

- During the pandemic, Blackrock utilized NLP on research records to gather bits of knowledge from investigators, a considerable lot of whom were moderately delayed to refresh their profit gauges for the main quarter of 2020. The main resource chief fights that while an expert might set aside some margin to refresh a mathematical conjecture, looking at the text of their reports helps catch a genuine image of their general position without a trace of a standard mathematical gauge. In addition, Blackrock has as of late additionally used the NLP model to create opinion signals for getting an early perused on monetary strategy, permitting the speculation supervisor to parse expert language for a feeling of how strategy is getting across nations. The speculation administrator then slants its portfolio choices to incline toward those with facilitating inclinations, like the United States (Chye Koh and Kee Low, 2004).
- Uncovering stowed away market signals in values: Global resource chief American Century Investments utilizes NLP to supplement its examination cycle with a NLP opinion model that means to identify trickery in administration editorial/language during quarterly income calls. The NLP model predicated on brain research and computational etymology has been prepared on Russell 3,000 organizations. It assesses the text for a sign of trickery like

oversight (inability to reveal key subtleties), turn (distortion from the board and excessively prearranged language), obscurity (the executives' utilization of mind-boggling clarifications/narrating for a straightforward idea), and fault (avoidance of obligation portrayed by the utilization of language, e.g., 'misfortune', 'testing climate', and so on.).

- Better sustainability investing: Deutsche Bank saw that commonly huge cap organizations will more often than not get generally speaking higher ESG appraisals, presumably in light of the fact that enormous firms utilize more prominent assets to compose point by point maintainability reports. For example, around 85% of S&P 500 organizations distribute maintainability reports. The bank chose to devise an elective method for assessing maintainability reports utilizing the NLP calculation – to discover whether the responsibilities firms made to decrease fossil fuel byproducts were related with accomplished supportability execution. For surveying carbon-related conversations inside the reports, analysts distinguished five distinct points alongside the top catchphrases related with every theme. The NLP model positioned organizations in view of their attention on the alleviation and variation points. The calculation additionally checked for notices of numeric and quantitative terms (like 'first' and 'half'), and for utilization of dynamic versus inactive language. Overall, a 74% possibility decreasing their future outflows. In addition, organizations that regularly examine relieving or adjusting to environmental change have a 65% higher likelihood of accomplishing decreases.

- The executives are involving NLP in its venture an expected level of investment to identify negative news through perusing and investigating immense measures of archives brought from web crawlers created by its in-house AI-group. The calculation saves long periods of time and consequently opens up the examination group to zero in on other basic assignments. Moreover, UBS likewise involves similar model in its client screening process, where profiles are filtered to distinguish whether elements meet a client's rules.

- Top institutional financial backers, for example, AIG and Citadel, are utilizing experiences from elective information, for example, text in interpersonal organizations, shopping history, transporting data to upgrade dynamic speculation return, and are thinking about how NLP innovation can further develop proficiency and versatility in this training. Besides, a few resource administrators have employed in-house specialized groups or enrolled outsider suppliers for programmed ingestion and investigation of public filings and get signals from opinion in the news and web-based entertainment content.

- Shutting contemplations people are by and large better at significant level cognizance of composed text and have a superior comprehension of the specific circumstance. Be that as it may, with the ascent of heap sources and colossal quantum of unstructured literary information, it seems OK to saddle innovation to handle such information. In the meantime, progresses in AI-like NLP strategies, combined with an enormous expansion in computational power are at an affectation point. This presents tremendous open doors for resource directors to use NLP methods for getting solid experiences from printed datasets and fabricate an upper hand. Later on, there is surely going to be a gigantic split between the organizations that influence innovation and information for an upper hand, and the individuals who are falling behind. Over the long haul, this will reflect in the progression of resources and portfolio execution of resource supervisors.

8.3   NLP-based know your customer approach

Know your client, or know your customer (KYC), alludes to a wide arrangement of against illegal tax avoidance administrative rules that require monetary administrations foundations to confirm and guarantee their clients' personalities, business setting, sources and uses of assets, and related gambles associated with keeping up with business connections. This industry system is utilized to survey the appropriateness and related dangers of every client business relationship. By and large, KYC has been related with the "counteraction" part of against illegal tax avoidance, or AML, rehearses. That's what the thought is in the event that a bank can keep a dubious person from opening a record, then, at that point, the bank has done its part to restrict the illegal development of cash through the monetary framework. Be that as it may, as innovation and criminal way of behaving has advanced, KYC is currently viewed as a nonstop interaction by which monetary establishments audit and assess client risk profiles and reasonableness for the business (Coussement and Van den Poel, 2008).

The lines have been obscuring between organizations that go about as monetary foundations and those that do not. For instance, Venmo began as a credit only shared installment supplier. Be that as it may, as their methodology developed to help and oversee repayments and exchange clearing, the organization fell under administrative requirements expecting it to take part in KYC practices to assist with stemming illegal tax avoidance exercises inside the geographic locales in which it works.

- For what reason is KYC important?
  KYC is involved a bunch of administrative rules that vary by locale (United States versus the European Union, for instance) and require monetary foundations to lead adequate reasonable level of effort on clients to relieve the gamble of unlawful cash development inside the monetary area. KYC casually alludes to the act of checking people's and organizations' ways of life as well as confirming that their assets start from real exercises and not, for example, criminal way of behaving [18].
- How C3 AI helps organizations manage KYC with AI

To stay aware of criminal way of behaving and progressively rigid administrative necessities, monetary foundations should send continuous KYC examinations of clients, exploiting every important datum, including exchange movement, virtual entertainment information, and news data. Be that as it may, the rising pace and size of exchanges and social information require another innovation approach. As well as handling huge amounts of information, monetary establishments are observing that it is basic for KYC officials to exploit new advancements like normal language handling, PC vision, and AI to empower AI-based experiences that drive the most effective activities and constancy.

The C3 AI Anti Money Laundering application gives an all-encompassing survey of client movement that upholds continuous KYC. The application further develops consistence official efficiency with savvy case proposals, robotized proof bundles, and high-level representations of key relevant case information, like negative news, alarms, parties, accounts, exchanges, counter-gatherings, and hazard drivers. The application gives straightforward, simple-to-decipher risk drivers for each chance score. Not at all like inflexible principles-based frameworks, C3 AI Anti Money Laundering models are effectively configurable and adaptable, empowering keen acclimation to changing guidelines and criminal techniques. The application utilizes refined AI procedures, including self-learning in light of consistence official result, to distinguish known and new typologies. Further, improved auditability highlights permit officials and controllers to follow the heredity of client conduct and assets from source to steadiness reports (Dhatterwal *et al.*, 2022).

8.4 Applications or systems for FinTech with NLP methods

For most ventures, staying aware of the speed of innovation and data is a test. The monetary administration industry is the same, and generally, it has been one to embrace change all the more leisurely – and for good explanation. Exceptionally, directed ventures like money cannot stand to think twice about, sit around idly, or make themselves defenseless against the obstacles that accompany incorporating new innovation into as of now existing frameworks. Yet, imagine a scenario where said innovation had the ability to smooth out dreary cycles, filter through monstrous measures of information rapidly and precisely, in this manner giving your representatives and business an upper hand (Duan *et al.*, 2018).

Whether the guarantee of these benefits is sufficient to arouse your curiosity or you are in the 'in the event that it isn't broken, don't fix it' camp, the truth is, monetary organizations are getting covered in information. People cannot keep up, and accordingly, embracing innovation to expand once manual undertakings is a business need, as opposed to an 'ideal to have'. This is the reason savvy monetary organizations are going to NLP to assist them with slicing through the clamor and gain significant industry bits of knowledge. NLP not just can interpret the immense measures of information terminating from all chambers, however, really comprehends its items and how to introduce the data in a reasonable, effectively absorbable way that assists monetary experts with going about their responsibilities.

While NLP is taking incredible steps in ventures from medical services to retail, the following are four different ways the AI-fueled innovation is improving FinTech.

- Understanding algorithms
Whenever we consider finance, the primary thing that rings a bell is numbers. However, one of the most effective utilizations of NLP in finance does not have anything to do with math, and all that has to do with words – understanding perception, to be careful. Truth be told, practically all monetary news is presently coming from calculations, from Bloomberg Terminal to SEC filings, and even tweets. Quite a while back, you needed to peruse all of this data yourself – however, in this age, that is not doable. There is not a moment to spare in the high-speed finance industry. Going from hours to minutes to distil significant data has an immense effect, and NLP is liable for the fast investigation and conveyance of this data to the leaders who need it (Ediger *et al.*, 2010).
- Composing algorithms
What might come as a shock is that most monetary substance today is not recently perused, yet composed by NLP-controlled calculations, as well.

For instance, in previous years, an expert would peruse and expound on S1 filings, yet presently, these are computerized as news composing, writing for a blog, and in any event, tweeting. The calculation peruses the article, chooses what's essential to expound on, and when and where to present it all together on get appropriate data out. Precision and idealness are extremely vital here, and with NLP, you do not need to address whether you're forfeiting one for another.
- Grasping jargon and context
One more helpful utilization of NLP is transforming unstructured information into a more usable structure. For instance, not all information is found in message: some of the time it is introduced during a profit call, show, or from a live news report. NLP can catch this data, interface it to other siloed information sources, and comprehend the setting to give more significant experiences.

Similar as in the clinical field, monetary language presents more prominent difficulties with regard to accessibility, particularly in the event that you consider different industry-explicit terms utilized by various organizations. NLP can wisely interface these to lay out the full image of what's happening, assisting with extending industry information and prevail upon an edge the opposition (Kaswan *et al.*, 2022).
- Surmising relationships with knowledge graphs
Connections among things and text should be perceived for NLP to offer genuine benefit. It is considerably more powerful on the off chance that these associations can be removed rapidly and without any problem. Luckily, propels in information charts have made this conceivable. Information charts address an assortment of interlinked depictions of substances – articles, occasions, or ideas – and put information in setting to give a structure to information reconciliation, unification, examination and sharing. Take a procurement, for instance. You would simply prefer not to realize what organization got gained, yet additionally the date, the sum, on the off chance that it is public,

and different subtleties, which can all be delivered from examining text with NLP.

Also, assuming you are taking a gander at monetary news, leader developments, giving stock, value, and that's just the beginning, you care about additional particular subtleties that expect NLP to comprehend the connection between the two elements included.

With the capacity to give ongoing and exact experiences to monetary experts, NLP innovation is broadly applied across the business. Time is cash and with information becoming continuously, without the right devices, organizations lose their edge to more sharp pioneers. NLP gives an incredible and quick chance for monetary organizations to profit by that staying light-footed and settling on the most ideal choices conceivable with the best and latest data (Feuerriegel and Gordon, 2018).

8.5   Crowdfunding analysis with text data

Crowdfunding is a method of soliciting contributions from a large number of individuals or organizations, usually over the internet, in exchange for a future product or some other kind of compensation, in order to support campaigns with a specific goal in mind. At its center, rather than raising assets from a little gathering of expert or modern financial backers, firms acquire limited quantities of cash from an enormous number of people, ordinarily non-proficient i.e., the "swarm." Along these lines, crowdfunding is a two-sided market that joins capital-searchers (crowdfunders) and capital-providers (financial backers) empowered by a crowd-funding go-between (stages). Crowdfunding stages do not get, pool, or loan cash for their own; however, they empower financial backers to vow reserves, frequently on a go big or go home or keep-it-all premise. The financial model for these stages is normally a commission in light of assets raised or gifts got. These stages provide food for a wide scope of activities, including items, experience products, and social drives. Ordinarily referred to reports gauge the quantity of crowdfunding stages at north of 1,250 overall in 2014, and more than 510 stages working in the European Union in a comparable period.

Crowdfunding can be separated from customary funding ventures by the attributes of financial backers, the speculation model, and for sure the sort of relationship that the financial backers have with the investee. First and foremost, in contrast to conventional speculation, most crowdfunding financial backers are not proficient. For sure, early crowdfunding financial backers, will quite often be loved ones, and affected by signals from these nearby friendly ties as opposed to more expert screening and a reasonable level of investment processes. Crowdfunders contrast fundamentally from customary investment financial backers in their speculation inspiration. Notwithstanding benefit-sharing, they observed that crowdfunders were propelled by ahead of schedule or special admittance to items and other local area benefits, like sensations of connectedness to a local area. Besides, crowdfunding venture models are more changed and various principal classifications exist i.e., gift, reward and pre-buy, loaning, and value based, the initial two are some of the time alluded to as group supporting, while the last two are here and there alluded to as group financial planning. Different variations incorporate receipt exchanging and crossover crowdfunding. The different venture models contrast in speculation inspiration and advantages. For instance, gift-based models might have very issue-focused, individual, or local area benefits. Conversely, pre-buy models have more shopper arranged benefits, like cost separation or potentially confidence. Such more immaterial advantages stand out from the straightforward money model of customary speculation. Third, the connection among financial backers and investees in crowdfunding models varies from conventional venture (Mittal and Jhamb 2016; Mittal *et al.*, 2020; Muddumadappa *et al.*, 2022). There is a deeply grounded writing base on how investors control office issues and relieve risk all through the venture cycle. The speculation interaction while utilizing an ex-risk and ex post approach recognizes various expected contrasts in organization elements among crowdfunding and conventional funding venture. Ex-risk factors incorporate bargain screening, bargain references, data awareness, and a reasonable level of effort while ex post factors incorporate authoritative privileges, board portrayal, esteem adding capacity, monetary life, and leave choices. In every one of these cases, the "swarm" parts of crowdfunding influence the degree to which these variables can be amplified or limited all through the whole speculation process and in certain models e.g., gift and award and pre-buy, may not be significant by any means. For sure, ex-risk vital contribution by financial backers, considered by numerous financial backers as a basic achievement factor for new companies, may not be doable, fitting, or welcome in crowdfunding.

Ongoing investigations in business venture writing center around two principal parts of crowdfunding:

- The impetuses and inspirations for beginning or partaking in crowdfunding tasks.
- Factors related with effective missions observed that initiators and funders are roused by both outward and inherent variables. In particular, outward factors incorporate raising money (initiators) and consuming items or encounters (funders); while, inborn variables incorporate social co-operations, supporting obligation to a thought in light of criticism (makers), and interfacing with a local area with comparable interests and goals (funders). Concentrates on the attributes of effective missions recommend that project quality, spatial vicinity among initiators and funders, and business people's inner social capital assume a basic part in drawing in both early capital and early patrons, henceforth impacting the outcome of crowdfunding efforts. Among these variables, the geology of crowdfunding has drawn specifically consideration, given a few nonsensical discoveries that rise out of past examinations. One of the significant advantages of crowdfunding is that it might possibly kill geological limits among business people and financial backers. At the end of the day, financial backers can support endlessly undertakings can recognize financial backers, in their own country as well as from some other country on the planet

without extra exertion. In any case, experimental proof proposes that the actual distance among financial backers' business visionaries actually assumes a critical part, with nearby financial backers contributing moderately early and exceptionally restricted cross-line exercises (Feuerriegel and Gordon, 2019).

8.6 Text-oriented customer preference analysis

We initially present a purchaser inclination examination strategy, as displayed in Figure 8.1, and afterward acquaint how with work out characteristic qualities from message remarks by means of feeling investigation.

It expects that a customer rates an option in light of its exhibition of qualities and her inclinations over the properties. The options ought to be of similar classification, with the end goal that they are portrayed by similar restricted credits, where the choices can be lodgings, eateries, computerized items, and so on. We accept that the rating upsides of choices are addressed by an added substance utility capacity (Chen and Su, 2022). Accordingly, we total the characteristic qualities and loads to acquire the rating values, where the loads are alluded to as the customer inclinations over traits of choices. In light of authentic audits produced over the long run by a buyer, we can dissect the quality inclinations from each survey. According to the viewpoint of multi add drop multiplexer (MADM), albeit the inherent characteristic inclinations of the customer are consistent, the inclinations got from each survey can be conflicting, because of purchaser blunders (for instance, a low generally speaking a client dated numerous friends while evaluating various restaurants) while making audits, a client dated numerous accomplices. We model the flood of gotten quality inclinations, i.e., the surge of loads, as reluctant decisions (if it is not too much trouble, allude to the following segment for subtleties). The methodology of inclination investigation for a buyer is as per the following:

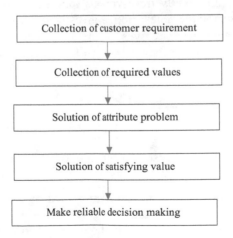

Figure 8.1   Customer preferences analysis framework

1. Stage 1: The audits, comprising written comments and assessments of the selections made by a customer from networking, should be collected.
2. Stage 2: Based on every message remark, use opinion examination to work out the property estimations installed in the remark.
3. Stage 3: Based on the qualities got from a text remark and the rating relating to it, address the characteristic loads by an enhancement model, and afterward settle for a flood of loads in light of all the text remarks and relating evaluations listed by time.
4. Stage 4: Establish reluctant decisions in view of the surge of loads listed by time.
5. Stage 5: Based on the reluctant decisions, utilize the heterogeneous memory management (HMM)to tackle for the delightful loads that fit the purchaser's inclinations over credits at the most elevated fulfilling level.

8.7 Insurance application with textual information

Record-based data mining, also known as messaging mineral extraction, is a more advanced kind of data analysis. Originally intended just as a means of expression, it has now evolved into of late advanced to incorporate strategies ready to order archives as indicated by their dormant theme or to surmise data about the "opinion" of clients or the clients of informal organizations. The methodologies have been helped by the development of both the computational effectiveness of the calculations important to dissect printed information and the innovation expected to store data.

This work is meant to be taken as an attempt to explain a comprehensive and crucial set of references that may be found in the definition of information retrieval. Is what we are attempting to demonstrate the manner by which insurance agency can take advantage of this strategy to remove important data from unstructured information. In protection, as in numerous different settings, there are major areas of strength for a message classifier since organizations gather a colossal amount of message information consistently from various sources, for example, client input, claims agent notes, guarantor notes, police investigate mishaps, clinical records, reviews, e-mail messages, web archives, online entertainment posts, and so forth. Text investigation could assist organizations with refining the accompanying:

• Promoting efforts
• Brand the executives
• Misrepresentation discovery
• Claims the board and pay
• Subrogation
• Connections between the assistance community and clients
• Investigation of agreement statements

To evaluate the conceivable outcomes presented by message mining, a UK safety net provider as of late presented an engine insurance contract that conceded limits to younger drivers who agreed to allow the group access to their online accounts (ongoing changes to information protection guidelines don't permit the trial to be rehashed). Given admittance to the profiles, the organization fostered a calculation that examined all client posts, preferences, and GPS areas to play out a character test. By breaking down every client's way of composing, the calculation could reveal positive and negative attributes. Along these lines, character qualities could be utilized as indicators of a client's life and driving way of behaving and to survey measures for deciding qualification for a protection markdown.

As recommended by this examination, one of the likely upper hands of text investigation in protection is the chance of enhancing client risk profiles in light of the standard organized "Organization DB" client information base. In a perfect world, we are alluding to a system where statisticians accumulate data from a "Cloud DB" that is uncontrolled and managed by a third party (e.g., archives, web sources, and so forth.). It is possible to link consumer segments in the Cloud database with those of an institution's clients, allowing data from the two seemingly disparate systems to be combined.

Text mining is a challenging subject of study. For example, it is necessary to analyze vast volumes of large datasets, as well as the difficulty of finding important words to normalized languages for deductive reasoning reasons. For example, written material from an insurance firm may include language that ranges from informal to professional. A lexical structure that is sometimes stable and unexpected may be found in reports from police officers or claims agents, but this has no bearing on the language that is used in virtual enjoyment, which is always evolving and so cannot be studied using traditional methodologies.

Enormous information, as a rule, might be portrayed as an unstructured, huge, heterogeneous, and temperamental informational collection that frequently conceals idle important data not quantifiable through a standard examining process. Huge information might incorporate records; the tweets on the web; any interpersonal organization; opinion about the soundness of the economy, the situation with a nation, or an organization; or the progression of archives delivered during day-to-day work (e.g., reports, recipes, calls, messages). Utilizing a broad portrayal of a contextual analysis, we intend to show the potential outcomes presented by message mining to extricate dormant data that may be utilized by safety net providers to adjust strategy valuing or to more readily survey client risk profiles.

Recordings are the primary element of text mining. An aggregation of repositories is known as a corpus. Whenever we have selected the record unit, we wish to specify the granularity degree of the examination, after which we may investigate single letters, phrases, expressions, or even groupings of manifestations.

Perhaps the most well-known mechanism used to study a report is the n-gram, a series of n words (or even of characters) gathered from a document. This is a form of movable windows of dimension n: by moving this window by each circumstance in turn, we gain a rundown of new n-grams. For instance, let us consider about the line "The police stopped a car without defense." We may create various n-grams by modifying the length n:

- n = 1 (unigram) returns {"The," "police," "stopped," "a," "vehicle," "without," "insurance"}

- n = 2 (bigram) returns {"The police," "police stopped," "stopped a," "a vehicle," "vehicle without," "without insurance"}
- n = 3 (trigram) returns {"The police stopped," "police stopped a," "stopped a vehicle," "a vehicle without," "vehicle without insurance"}

The size of n-grams is influenced by how complex a problem is and how extensive an investigation is. Using a high n value means include more additional context in the document's units, whereas using a low n value means the most vital piece of data will be more detailed.

8.8   Telematics: motor & health insurance

Telematics is a following innovation that utilizes the standards of telecom and informatics. A telematics framework stores and sends driving-related information. It has three primary parts:

- Telematics control unit – It comprises of a global positioning system (GPS) that tracks the area of the vehicle. This control unit likewise gets and stores data from the vehicle, for example, vehicle speed, fuel utilization, trip distance, trip term, slowing down, flaws, and motor information.
- Cloud server – Information gathered in the telematics unit is communicated to a cloud server utilizing a remote or cell organization. Here, the information is put away as bundles.
- Versatile interface – The cloud server communicates the information to a portable connection point through a web waiter. Here, the information is dissected, and a report is arranged that talks about your driving way of behaving.
- OBD based – A little electronic gadget is introduced in the vehicle to an Onboard Diagnostic port. This gadget stores data from the vehicle and communicates it through a remote organization to an expert information base.
- Application based – It utilizes a cell phone's GPS and telematics application to store vehicle information. It is more reasonable, however, more powerless to misrepresentation.
- Blackbox-based – Blackbox is an electronic gadget mounted in the vehicle to store trip-related information. It is generally utilized in armada following to screen associated vehicles. It has a high establishment cost.

8.8.1   *Telematics and automobile insurance*

Accident protection organizations, with the assistance of telematics, are utilizing clients' driving way of behaving to offer tweaked charges. Telematics gives helpful experiences into two critical parts of driving (Feuerriegel and Prendinger, 2016).

- Vehicle support utilizing motor information.

Utilizing these experiences, guarantors reward dependable drivers by bringing down charges and giving extra advantages. Telematics helps insurance agency to break down the gamble profile of a driver and redo both disconnected and online vehicle insurance contracts with a fitting evaluating model intended for the client. It assists safety net providers with exploring the cases better with ongoing information examination and recognize misrepresentation claims.

8.8.2   Benefits of telematics-based auto insurance

- Offers a similar inclusion as customary vehicle protection at lower costs due to precise gamble estimation.
- Prompts better driving ways of behaving and further develops street security.
- Saves fuel and fix costs.
- Lessens the expense of business with assessment in light of information instead of actual investigation.
- Helps in offering some benefit added administrations in view of driving way of behaving.
- Continuous information is exceptionally helpful in conveying a crisis cautioning message during a mishap.
- Supportive in recognizing misrepresentation claims.
- Decreases vehicle robbery.
- Benefits both guarantor and protected.

Indian scene for telematics-based insurance:

In India, telematics is for the most part utilized by armada the board organizations, for example, taxi administrations, strategic organizations, and so on. It keeps their vehicles associated with a focal framework and helps in checking trip distance, term, course, and driving way of behaving. Following the vehicle helps in overseeing costs, upkeep alarms, and further develops efficiency.

IRDAI's pilot project, which sent off 'pay as you drive' and 'pay how you drive' utilization-based protection for a restricted period, brought about numerous insurance agency carrying out telematics-based vehicle protection designs and free establishment of the telematics gadget. Numerous web-based vehicle insurance agency additionally offers a rebate on charges for vehicles previously introduced with telematics and against robbery gadgets.

8.9   Text-based market provisioning

Clients benefit from text mining since they are able to extract the most valuable information from a document's contents. In recent years, there has been a significant increase in interest in text mining. Text mining is progressing at a rapid pace when it is integrated with extensive data analysis. There are several ways in which this strategy may be used to finance, which is both a need and an advantage to corporations, government, and the general people. This section focuses on some of the most important and broad-ranging methods for analyzing published evidence relevant to funds.

- *Opinion investigation (SA)*
  SA is a common technique used in the field. A wide range of uses may be found for it. Additionally, it is referred to as evaluation mining since it extracts

the concealed attitudes from literary data. Internet business stages, websites, online gaming, and microblogs are just a few of the places where it may be put to the best use. Opinion prosecution's motivations may be broken down into two distinct categories: recognition of feelings and identification of extremes. Classifier-based approaches with distinct findings are more prevalent when it comes to extremities localization than when it comes to sensation identification (e.g., good and pessimistic).

There are two main techniques to SA: vocabulary-based (word reference-based) and artificial intelligence-based (ML). Regulated and solitary learning are further characteristics of the final choice. Dictionary-based techniques make use of Finest quality word maps, while ML views SA as a characterization problem and use methods that are put out for it. To get an overall attitude score with dictionary-based systems, you divide the number of positive and negative views by how often you feel that way. There are two important methods in ML that use named information: the Naive Bayes (NB) classifier and the supporting vector machines (SVMs). SA using ML offers an advantage over the vocabulary method since it does not need word references that are excessively burdensome. No matter how you slice it, ML is constrained by the need for area-specific datasets. Following the pretreatment of data, the highlight selection is carried out in accordance with the requirement, and the end-product is obtained after an assessment of the provided information in accordance with the adopted strategy.

SA has been used to predict future general financial behaviors and expenses from the examination of monetary news articles in the financial services expectations space. SVMs and irregular timberland (RF) fared better than NB in three ML computations. In order to get the most accurate results, the researchers used data from StockTwits (a platform for people to express their opinions on the stock market) and then ran five different calculations, including the NB and the most excessive entropy techniques, as well as a straight SVM, an RF, and a multi-facet recurrent neural network. Analysts have combined traditional AI methodologies (such as the building of an emotion vocabulary) with slow learning tactics, resulting in further promising results.

- *Data extraction*

Extraction of predetermined material from a text record is done using data extraction (IE). Most IE frameworks focus on extracting relevant data from sections and then putting it back together again in an orderly fashion. As a central strategy, DiscoTEX (Discovery from TextEXtraction) is utilized to transform the ordered data into meaningful data in order to discover information from it.

Named-element acknowledgment (NER) is used in finance to extract certain types of information from an archive. Customers' exchanging demand notifications may arrive through fax in the banking industry, resulting in severely disorganized records due to the lack of a logical arrangement and necessitating view of obtaining in order to create an orderly archive.

- *NLP*
NLP is a part of the man-made reasoning space, and it aims to aid in the transformation of confusing and confusing communications into clear and precise ones. A company's existing and future presentations, space standards, and rules may all be evaluated using this method. It is often used to sift through data to unearth insights for new projects. NLP can assist with performing different examinations, for example, NER, which further aides in distinguishing the connections and other data to recognize the key idea. In any case, NLP misses the mark on word reference list for every one of the named elements utilized for distinguishing proof.

As NLP is a common sense examination way to deal with break down the tremendous measure of accessible information, applied it to overcome any barrier among NLP and monetary estimating by considering points that would intrigue both the exploration fields.

There was a thorough examination of NLP's current and future roles in FinTech. Know Your Client (KYC), Know Your Item (KYP) and Serve Your Client (FYC) are the three aspects they examined (SYC). Much printed material is generated throughout the KYC process as customers' data is safeguarded (corporate area and retail). In terms of KYP, salespeople are supposed to know every property of the thing they are selling, which means they are also expected to know about the item's potentials, risks, and opportunities. Selling/merchandising/scientists in SYC aim at making monetary activities more productive to meet the needs of both company and customer groups. NLP was discussed, as was the role it plays in demonstrating money, as well as how it has increased information flow within an environment plagued by data overload.

- *Text grouping*
Text grouping is a four-venture process including highlight extraction, aspect decrease, classifier determination, and assessment. Highlight extraction should be possible with normal strategies like term recurrence and Word2Vec; then, dimensionality decrease is performed utilizing methods like head part examination and straight discriminant investigation. Picking a classifier is a significant stage, and deep learning algorithms have exceeded other AI computations, as has been shown. To better understand the photographer's display, the evaluation stage makes use of several criteria, such as the Mathews compatibility coefficient (MCC), area under the ROC bend (AUC), and accuracy. In terms of difficulty, precision is the simplest of the three. A flowchart of the text-ordering procedure is shown in Figure 8.1.

It looked at how several message order tactics, such as NB, k-nearest neighbors (KNN), SVM, decision trees, and relapse, were presented and found that SVM performed better than the others in terms of correctness, review, and F1 metrics.

- *Deep learning*
AI is preparing a data structure that can be used to generate predictions about incoming data. Layered innovation in information accumulation means that

information enters at the lowest level and outputs at the highest level. Simulations are used to divide the data into segments at various levels of the organization, change highlights into variables, and afterward input the elements into the more profound layer again to acquire changed highlights. It zeroed in on the information, as it assumes a significant part in the exhibition of any calculation. The creator presumed that change of the organization design with profound learning calculations can extraordinarily influence execution and give great outcomes.

In finance, profound learning takes care of the issue of intricacy and vagueness of regular language. It involved predicted financial exchange changes by studying 13,135 German statements in English that had been expressly appointed by the German government. Long-term memory modeling outperformed all existing AI computations when move motion was used to pretrain word representations, according to the results of the experiment.

8.10   Conclusion

Sentiment analysis based on ML has been used to discern views in online texts written by users, having applications in advertising and branding media platforms tracking, corporate analytics, business decision, and many other sectors. This research aimed to examine the feasibility of gathering financial-related emotional data from a wide range of sources, including news, discussion boards, and microblogs. To preprocess casual online text, NLP methods were applied. To decrease noise in casual online writing, the chapter developed a pre-processing technique that included six NLP processing steps. The method was used in three previously published sentiment different classifiers. The results reveal that the suggested text pre-processing strategy outperformed the relevant articles' pre-processing approaches in terms of sentiment prediction performance when applied to four databases. The proposed technique washes to improve the effectiveness of the algorithm, additional non-informative distortions in text data and more reliable input materials for extracting the characteristics are necessary. One possible approach to this topic of research is to analyze domain-specific comprehension in datasets since sentiment categorization is a domain-dependent activity. Statements should include the ability to understand the context in which they are made.

References

Al Nasseri, A., Tucker, A., and de Cesare, S. (2015). Quantifying StockTwits semantic terms' trading behavior in financial markets: an effective application of decision tree algorithms. *Expert Systems with Applications*, 42(23), pp. 9192–9210.

Alostad, H. and Davulcu, H. (2015). Directional prediction of stock prices using breaking news on Twitter. In *2015 IEEE/WIC/ACM International Conference* on *Web Intelligence and Intelligent Agent Technology (WI-IAT)*, pp. 523–530.

AL-Rubaiee, H., Qiu, R., and Li, D. (2017). Visualising Arabic sentiments and association rules in financial text. *International Journal of Advanced Computer Science and Applications*, 8(2), pp. 1–7.

Alvarado, J.C.S., Verspoor, K., and Baldwing, T. (2015). Domain adaptation of named entity recognition to support credit risk assessment. In *Proceedings of Australasian Language Technology Association Workshop*, University of Western Sydney, Australia, 8–9 December, pp. 84–90.

Ammann, M., Frey, R., and Verhofen, M. (2014). Do newspaper articles predict aggregate stock returns? *Journal of Behavioral Finance*, 15(3), pp. 195–213.

Balakrishnan, R., Qiu, X. Y., and Srinivasan, P. (2010). On the predictive ability of narrative disclosures in annual reports. *European Journal of Operational Research*, 202(3), pp. 789–801.

Boskou, G., Kirkos, E., and Spathis, C. (2018). Assessing internal audit with text mining. *Journal of Information Knowledge Management*, 17(2), 1850020.

Bowers, A. J. and Chen, J. (2015). Ask and ye shall receive? Automated text mining of Michigan capital facility finance bond election proposals to identify which topics are associated with bond passage and voter turnout. *Journal of Education Finance*, 41, 164–196.

Chen, W., Lai, K., and Cai, Y. (2018). Topic generation for Chinese stocks: a cognitively motivated topic modeling method using social media data. *Quantitative Finance and Economics*, 2(2), pp. 279–293.

Chen, K., Li, X., Xu, B., Yan, J., and Wang, H. (2017). Intelligent agents for adaptive security market surveillance. *Enterprise Information Systems*, 11(5), pp. 652–671.

Chen, C. L., Liu, C. L., Chang, Y. C., and Tsai, H. P. (2014). Opinion mining for relating subjective expressions and annual earnings in US financial statements. *Journal of Information Science and Engineering*, 29, 743–764.

Chen, L. and Su, S. (2022). Optimization of the trust propagation on supply chain network based on blockchain plus. *Journal of Intelligent Management Decision*, 1(1), pp. 17–27.

Chen, K., Yin, J., and Pang, S. (2017). A design for a common-sense knowledge-enhanced decision-support system: integration of high-frequency market data and real-time news. *Expert Systems*, 34(3), e12209.

Chye Koh, H. and Kee Low, C. (2004) Going concern prediction using data mining techniques. *Managerial Auditing Journal*, 19(3), pp. 462–476.

Coussement, K. and Van den Poel, D. (2008). Integrating the voice of customers through call center emails into a decision support system for churn prediction. *Information Management*, 45(3), pp. 164–174.

Dhatterwal, J. S., Kaswan, K. S., and Balusamy, B. (2022). Emerging technologies in the insurance market. In *Big Data Analytics in the Insurance Market*, pp. 275–286.

Duan, Z., He, Y., and Zhong, Y. (2018). Corporate social responsibility information disclosure objective or not: an empirical research of Chinese listed companies based on text mining. *Nankai Business Review International*, 9(4), pp. 519–539.

Ediger, D., Jiang, K., Riedy, J., Bader, D. A., and Corley, C. (2010). Massive social network analysis: mining twitter for social good. In *Proceedings of 39th International Conference on Parallel Processing*, San Diego, CA, USA, 13–16th September, IEEE, pp. 583–593.

Feuerriegel, S. and Gordon, J. (2018). Long-term stock index forecasting based on text mining of regulatory disclosures. *Decision Support Systems*, 112, 88–97.

Feuerriegel, S. and Gordon, J. (2019). News-based forecasts of macroeconomic indicators: a semantic path model for interpretable predictions. *European Journal of Operational Research*, 272(1), pp. 162–175.

Feuerriegel, S. and Prendinger, H. (2016). News-based trading strategies. *Decision Support Systems*, 90, 65–74.

Kaswan, K. S., Baliyan, A., Singh, J., Dhatterwal, V. J., and Chatterjee, J. M. (2022). Intelligent classification of ECG signals using machine learning techniques. In *Healthcare Monitoring and Data Analysis Using IoT: Technologies and Applications* (pp. 257–272). Stevenage, UK: The Institution of Engineering and Technology.

Kaswan, K. S., Dhatterwal, J. S., Kumar, S., and Lal, S. (2022). Cybersecurity law-based insurance market. In *Big Data: A Game Changer for Insurance Industry*. Emerald Publishing Limited, pp. 303–321.

Kaswan, K. S., Dhatterwal, J. S., Sharma, H., and Sood, K. (2022). Big Data in insurance innovation. In *Big Data: A Game Changer for Insurance Industry*. Emerald Publishing Limited, pp. 117–136.

Mittal, A., Aggarwal, A., and Mittal, R. (2020). Predicting university students' adoption of mobile news applications: the role of perceived hedonic value and news motivation. *International Journal of E-Services and Mobile Applications (IJESMA)*, 12(4), pp. 42–59.

Mittal, A. and Jhamb, D. (2016). Determinants of shopping mall attractiveness: the Indian context. *Procedia Economics and Finance*, 37, pp. 386–390.

Muddumadappa, P. M. B., Anjanappa, S. D. K., and Srikantaswamy, M. (2022). An efficient reconfigurable cryptographic model for dynamic and secure unstructured data sharing in multi-cloud storage server. *Journal of Intelligent Systems and Control*, 1(1), pp. 68–78.

Chapter 9

Digital disruption and multimedia technological innovations in the banking world

Enid Masih[1], Shanti Swaroop Chauhan[1], Vartika Singh[1], Balamurugan Balusamy[2] and Simon Grima[3]

Abstract

Banks may link geographically dispersed areas and their respective financial markets using multimedia communication technology. The task of striking the correct balance between global and local is especially great for international banks. They need to determine what their local consumers want and provide it using global resources. This chapter describes the increasing prevalence of multimedia banking worldwide, illuminating the extent to which the banking sector has adopted and begun to benefit from such technologies. Information technology is crucial in connecting the world's many regions. Banks widely implement multimedia communication technologies to supply consumers with the best financial goods and services. Now more than ever, these networks allow for the coordination of widely scattered teams, sharing relevant knowledge and skills in times of need and establishing new connections with clients. Due to such platforms' proliferation, information technology's function in global banking has evolved significantly.

According to the available literature on multimedia banking, the Internet through a personal computer is the primary multimedia delivery channel in banking at the present moment. The literature frequently uses the words "multimedia banking," "Internet banking," "e-banking," and "online banking" to refer to the same type of technology. Online banking with multimedia features is not required. Mobile phones, personal digital assistances (PDAs; a handheld computer that serves as a tool for reading and conveying documents, electronic mail, and other electronic media over a communications link, as well as for organizing personal information. Like Tabs, i-pad, etc.), and other wireless devices increasingly have it built into their small screens. Customers may check their account balances and

[1]Joseph School of Business Studies and Commerce, Sam Higginbottom University of Agriculture, Technology and Sciences, Prayagraj, India
[2]Shiv Nadar University, Delhi National Capital Region, India
[3]Insurance and Risk Management, Faculty of Economics, Management & Accountancy, University of Malta, Malta

transaction histories, see visual representations of their investment portfolios, make payments or trade orders, and maintain two-way contact with their banks using data analytics, interactive electronic mail, and short message service (SMS). The future delivery platform is predicted to change from wired Internet connections to wireless mobile technologies, which would increase the significance of mobile and TV-based banking even though they do not appear to play a big part in banking at the present moment. This outlines some actual uses of multimedia banking and the opportunities and constraints those institutions confront.

Keywords: Multimedia banking; TV-based banking; Data analytics; Financial products

9.1   Background of multimedia banking

A nation's economy can only function with a strong financial system. Technology today is crucial to the smooth operation of the three pillars of the banking industry. The success and expansion of the industry and economy, made possible by advances in information and communication technology, has increased the importance of the banking sector in developing countries (Goel, 2013). Numerous innovations have been introduced to the banking sector as a result of the incorporation of new policies and the support of new technology and innovation for the client, such as RTGS, mobile banking, Digital Wallets, UPI, Blockchain technology, computing, cloud banking, wearable technology, omnichannel banking, and the point of sale (Chen et al., 2019). And multimedia banking communication systems help link different locations and their respective financial markets. Finding that feasible spot between global and local is a particularly difficult balancing act for national and international banks. They need to figure out what their local consumers want and give it to them, using knowledge and resources from worldwide. Technology in the form of the Internet is crucial in connecting what happens in one place to what happens elsewhere in the world (Stoica *et al.*, 2015). A common misconception is that banking IT is concerned with international money transfers. However, banks aiming to serve their clients with the best financial goods and services will implement multimedia communication technologies. These networks help employees in different locations work together, share knowledge and skills when needed, and forge connections with new clients. The rapid change in the function of information technology in international banking has resulted from introducing such systems (Mansoor Khan and Ishaq Bhatti, 2008). The relationship IT media communication revolutionises the connection between a consumer and a bank. Banks may use cutting-edge Internet technology and information brokerage processes to create novel distribution channels for financial information and services in the multimedia economy (Tidd and Bessant, 2018). The third-dimensional environments for traversing virtual banks or complex financial data to determine the requirements of a new user interface (UT) design for national and international banking systems (Tunay *et al.*, 2015).

Users of multimedia banking services regularly engage in transactions distinct from traditional banks (Chavan, 2013). These features consist of (a) the reliance on technology for all transactions, (b) the remote and impersonal nature of the online world, and (c) the inherent uncertainty of using an open technological infrastructure for transactions (Chavan, 2013; Gulati *et al.*, 2002). To be clearer, consumers engage in extensive technology usage via interacting with the bank's website. This is an example of productive technological utilization. Second, customers' worries about the security of conducting financial transactions when both the product and the customer's identity are unknown are exacerbated by the geographical and temporal separation between them and multimedia banks (Nagaraju and Parthiban, 2015). Third, the Internet delivery route and supporting infrastructure banks use to connect with their customers has their share of reliability issues (Kiljan *et al.*, 2018). As a result, consumers worry more about using online banking and have a lower sense of control over their online activities. Due to these misunderstandings, there is a wider chasm between intended and actual usage.

Consumers must engage with websites and, more generally, employ Internet technology in virtually every stage of the planned procedure for completing online transactions (Shaneeb and Sumathy, 2021a). Given that intentions to transact require using technology, it is reasonable to consider factors to anticipate intentions to utilize Internet technology for online transactions. However, people are beginning to accept multimedia banking, but there is still a significant gap to be closed to achieve the objective. This is because customers acclimate to the conventional financial operations method. Nevertheless, if given enough time, the trend of multimedia banking will become a major component of the delivery channel in a few years. People of all ages, both the tech-savvy younger generation and the more traditional clientele, are adapting to multimedia's new ways of banking. Customers of all ages, including the most senior ones, are gradually adapting to the conveniences of multimedia banking. As time progressed, banking grew increasingly important, and banks themselves became embedded in everyday economic life (Shaneeb and Sumathy, 2021b). In recent years, the trend in banking has been toward using various forms of media to conduct financial transactions. Multimedia banking services have been linked to a wide range of features and products, which have significantly impacted customers' opinions of the bank. Athanasopoulos and Labrouskos introduced multimedia banking in 1999 in Greece, providing valuable insights into how customers responded to the new service. Consumers have distinct mental models for thinking product-specific qualities like cost and turnaround time (Athanassopoulos and Labrouskos, 1999), service fees, pricing, timeliness of delivery, bank reputation, client understanding, and the bank's readiness to assist consumers were all regarded as crucial factors in the spread of multimedia banking. One of the most significant changes in banking is the growing emphasis on selling various financial services (Strieter *et al.*, 1999). The banking services provided to clients were more important in multimedia banking, enticing more people to use the overall banking services (Latimore *et al.*, 2000). Consumers who use multimedia banking services prefer to carry out several financial operations (such as bill payment, statement reading, stock trading, and insurance buying), all from the convenience of a single online location. In addition, tech-savvy clients who use online banking services anticipate having complete transparency in their accounts, lower rates than at brick-and-mortar branches, and a broader selection of products and services from which to choose (Mols, 2000). Bank operations, including communication with and connection with customers, and business procedures in general, have been repeatedly disrupted by technological advancements (Malhotra *et al.*, 2010). Banks must place a greater emphasis on technology as they face rising competitive and regulatory pressures. The Internet, social media, and mobile technologies, in particular, have the potential to completely transform the relationship between banks and their clients (Malhotra *et al.*, 2010). This shift is important for tactical purposes (such as boosting self-service) and long-term planning.

9.2   Phases of multimedia banking

1st Phase: Multimedia banking's initial implementation, including automatic teller machines and telephones: in the beginning, people were mostly concerned with the telephone (which had been around for more than a century) and the automated teller machine (invented a good 30 years old). Because of advancements in communication and computing, traditional distribution channels are giving way to online stores and mobile apps, while in-branch transactions are moving to ATMs and cell phones. By providing ATMs, US banks hoped to get around the McFadden Act of 1927, which limited the activities of national banks with branches in different states from conducting business with one other. Second phase of multimedia banking was equipped with PCs and online services; this phase got the wave of technological evolution; the desktop computers were in demand for managing money and reporting data over the Internet.

2nd Phase: In the second wave of technological evolution, the desktop computer became increasingly important for managing money and reporting data over the Internet. Different forms of multimedia banking emerged due to competition for client attention between content creators, service providers, and gateways, each with unique strategic consequences.

3rd Phase: There were two main tracks in the evolution of cyber cash. The first improvement was a rise in encryption criteria, which allowed for the secure transfer of funds over the Internet. The second is the spread of "electronic wallets," essentially smart cards that can store and transport a small amount of money for routine purchases. Customers can make deposits and withdrawals without having to visit a branch or an ATM when they use a smart card device equipped with advanced digital signature security and connected to any multimedia communication device, such as a computer, PDA, mobile phone, or interactive television.

4th Phase: Simply put, FinTech is using technology in the financial sector to create innovative new services. Financial technology encompasses a wide range of industries, including (i) credit, deposits, and capital-raising services; (ii) payments, clearing, and settlement services (including digital currencies); (iii) investment management services (including trading); and (iv) insurance.

9.3   Challenges and acceptance of multimedia banking

Technology has reincarnated the banking industry completely, and the word "multimedia banking" has been a major leap by human beings in the direction of development. Based on the digital era, many banks have a presence on the Internet, and many others are on the verge of doing so. Banks can use multimedia technology to reach out to their customers and provide better service. There is no doubt that multimedia banking has eased the banking services in India, but everything comes with some cons and pros. In this subheading, the challenges and acceptance of multimedia are discussed.

9.3.1   Safety and security

With customers' growing dependency on mobile banking, safety and security is emerging as a major issue of concern. Multimedia users are more prone to phishing (fraudulent e-mails that track the user's personal information), which may create insecurity in the mind of the users. India saw a significant jump in cybercrimes in 2021. As reported, 52 thousand of cyber-crime incidents were registered. As a result, the majority of the portion resists going with the option of multimedia banking.

9.3.2   System

As much as the banking industry has advanced to make things easier for its consumers, there are still a plenty of people over the age of 40 or 45 who prefer the "pen-paper" method to the "just a click" method of banking. In addition, they have a hard time functioning. Customers' access to mobile banking is hampered by (Sujith, 2017) mobile devices with inadequate hardware for the task, such as small screens, low-resolution cameras, and unfriendly keypads. Especially for consumers who are less well off financially and hence more likely to utilize mobile devices with less functionality, this can make banking apps more difficult to use. Despite the prevalence of mobile devices, banks still need to develop a universal solution compatible with all of them.

9.3.3   Significant charges

The banking sector is exceeding customer expectations to ease the banking facility. Still, they also charge some significant amount which gets accumulated with the regular use of mobile banking services. And bank charges these amounts on a monthly, quarterly and annual basis. No matter how easy it gets, some customers always prefer paying a little extra from their pocket. Because first, consumers have to pay the cost of high-end smartphone devices because mobile banking does not operate on all phones. Second, for their Internet connection, and then further, they lack interest in paying extra charges for the banking facilities.

9.3.4   Internet connection

Multimedia banking requires an Internet connection, leaving customers from rural areas at a great disadvantage. Regardless of the world running on 5G technology, there are still some villages in India where a smooth Internet connection is a dream for many. This still is a major issue for the customers to avail the benefit.

9.3.5   Customer awareness

Rural banking is one of India's fastest-growing industries, and it is critical to the country's economic growth and development. However, many customers from rural areas are still unaware of the facilities provided by the banks other than just the "lending and withdrawing money" functions. Even today the rural customers are relying on manual banking transactions and there is a long way to multimedia banking for the section of people residing in village areas because banking over the Internet is a completely new technology; not all banking customers are acquainted with it and find it difficult to get used to it.

9.3.6   Cash-dominated rural society

Sujith (2017) stated that rural places are still cash-dominated, and their adaption towards mobile money could be much higher. They use cash for day-to-day transactions as they have limited options for buying and selling anything with digital money. The conservative mind of the people can be transformed in just one go. It would take time for customers to adapt to the technology.

9.4   Acceptance for multimedia banking

9.4.1   Convenience

With mobile banking, customers can access any bank-related information at their convenience anytime, anywhere. Mobile banking allows users to perform many financial transactions like funds transfer, balance enquiry, investments, bill payments, loans and insurance. Mobile banking has advanced to enhance the customer experience by adopting the latest technology.

9.4.2   Confidentiality

The success and growth of multimedia banking depend on the trust and confidentiality they can develop among their customers. Customer trust can be developed with the help of privacy and reliability. That is to ensure there is no leakage of personal and financial data (Purohit and Arora, 2021). Mobile banking and its security mean that customers need to be aware and knowledgeable about mobile banking systems and their security. They need to provide a reputable website for downloading these banking applications to strengthen the privacy-related issues of the users.

9.4.3   Communication with customer

Multimedia banking communicates with their user regarding every transaction they make in a day by quoting, for example, credit card transactions (Tiwari *et al.*, 2007). With the aid of mobile technology, online banking facilities inform owners whenever purchases are made beyond the certain limit of the card. Through this, the users are continuously informed when their card is being used and about the transaction amount of the user (Goyal and Goyal, 2012). Internet banking makes it simple to keep track of your accounts and transactions from the comfort of your home. This is useful since it alerts users of suspicious activities or attempts to compromise their accounts.

9.4.4 *Personalization*

Sujith's (2017) personalization refers to the modifications of service as the users require it. Mobile banking is competent enough to offer services on an individual basis, meaning thereby, as per the taste and preferences of the users. This personalization of services helps them create the brand's presence in the market, thus raising customer loyalty. Personalization can also be termed as the readiness of the information.

9.4.5 *Add-on-services*

Users can have a wide variety of add-on services, including buying and selling of mutual funds, buying insurance policies and applying for various types of loans with just one click. And Internet banking also allows users to set auto payments for all recurring expenses making the facility more user-friendly.

9.4.6 *Accessibility*

Multimedia banking saves late fees even if we forget to pay a bill until the very last minute. Buying and selling online is a convenient and a la carte service that can be done at any hour of the day. Additionally, you can transfer money anytime without any fuss or need to be physically there, saving you time and money for the many transactions you would otherwise have to make.

9.4.7 *FinTech*

Investment in the development of new financial products has been demonstrated to be theoretically hazardous but worthwhile because of the considerable returns it provides to investors (Thakor, 2020; Vishnuvardhan *et al.*, 2020). The Financial Stability Board (FSB) defines fintech as "technologically enabled financial innovation that has the potential to result in new business models, apps, processes, or products and that has an associated material influence on financial markets and institutions and the provision of financial services."

9.5 Future of multimedia banking

9.5.1 *Neobanks*

Neobanks is a modern word for a bank which is a wholly virtual organization with no brick-and-mortar locations. Almost immediately, these banks prove themselves to be a reliable alternative to the standard banking system. To date, the Reserve Bank of India has not given the go-ahead to Neobanks in the country. For their services, they must rely on the cooperation of other banks. Exciting offers are common with Neobanks, including higher interest rates and other benefits unavailable at conventional banks. After the pandemic hit, there was an immediate and widespread transition to internet banking, driving up demand for cloud computing and machine intelligence.

9.5.2   Physical decline

The physical decline of the banks would mean that there would be no physical branches of Banks made up of brick and mortar. Slowly but steadily, it will continue to fade away. This would give rise to available digital services in the market. The future of the physical set-up will surely decline. All those who would remain will have to serve niche needs as general financial services are rapidly available over digital media.

9.5.3   Thinner wallets

The paper currency will vanish, and the general public will start preferring electronic transactions over the conventional method, not just because of its convenience and efficiency but also of its significant advantages to businesses, governments and economies at large.

9.5.4   Cardless payments

Many years ago, it was impossible to convince somebody that the payments for buying and selling products would be completed through a small plastic card. Today the same situations returned as it is hard to convince that even those small plastic cards would also be nowhere to be seen in the near future. Asian markets have begun the trend where beyond 50% of the transactions are being carried out through digital wallets.

9.5.5   Competitions with non-banks

In the coming future, the rivalry between banks will end, and the actual competition will be between the banks and the non-banks such as PayPal, Stripe, Monese, and Venmo, which are not even considered as banks, but they serve the customer financial needs as the traditional bank does.

9.5.6   Micro-personalization

Micro-personalization is AI-driven analytics under which the banks will treat each customer as if they are their greatest priority. Customer personalization would include factors like instantaneous borrowing, proactive product suggestions, detailed guidance on purchasing of the product, and budgetary recommendations. In layman's language, the banks will start functioning as per the need and choices of each customer.

9.5.7   Interoperability

The presence of multiple players in the financial field, which includes traditional banks, FinTech apps and related service providers, merchants and customers, leads to privacy and fraud concerns for all the parties involved. Interoperability or technological compatibility allows one payment system to work with others of its kind to assure patrons of their reliability and viability.

9.6 Multimedia banking making a prolific growth

Technology has outshined itself in every way possible. Decades ago, the people that dreamt of doing it are currently hooked to it, all thanks to the technology mushrooming at the international level and in India.

A study by the strategic consulting and market research firm Bluewave disclosed that India's digital banking platform market was worth USD 776.7 million in 2021. And it has been assumed that the market is estimated to grow at a Compound Annual Growth Rate (CAGR) of 9.8%, and by the end of the year 2028, the revenue earned would be near around USD 1,485.5 million. The reason behind the growth of the Indian digital banking platform is rapid digitization and adoption of advanced technologies like cloud computing, the Internet of Things, Artificial Intelligence, etc.

In addition to these, "Digital India," a government initiative, played a major role in expanding the reach of technology to every citizen of India.

Despite various advantages, high data security concerns and risks of cyber-attacks and fraudulent activities may restrain people from moving ahead with multimedia banking.

9.7 Reasons for rapid growth in multimedia banking

9.7.1 Adoption of digital banking by SMEs

The growth of SMEs is rising rapidly in India. A report published by the government of India revealed that there are more than 7.9 million macro, small, and medium enterprises as on March 27, 2022. And these firms are adopting advanced technologies like cloud computing and business efficiency tools, thereby giving rise to the market growth of digital banking at a high pace. SMEs are adopting these technologies for the smooth functioning of business transactions. Options like automatic payments for regular utility bills has enabled better accessibility and flexibility in managing transactions along with better security which has given rise to the use of multimedia banking for day-to-day purpose.

9.7.2 Neobanks boosting the growth of India's multimedia banking

Neobanks are synonyms for the "banks of the future" as these banks are without any physical branches, and they completely rely upon the INTERNET and are called "Digital Banks." The only hindrance these Neobanks are facing currently is that the RBI in India doesn't allow banks to operate 100% digitally, so they merge with their partner banks to offer varied services to their customers. And they even offer higher interest rates and several other benefits which the conventional banking system fails to offer, thereby attracting the attention of their customers towards them. Neobanks like Razorpay, Airtel Bank, Jupiter and Niyo are emerging rapidly and have created a growing demand for multimedia banking in India.

9.7.3 Mushrooming mobile banking sector giving a boost to multimedia banking

The number of smartphone users has increased drastically in recent years, speeding up the growth of multimedia banking in India. Currently, millennials run the world, and these customers prefer instant gratification and demand one-click solutions for everything, including payments and other banking services. Moreover, mobile banking offer services like instant transfer of funds, bill payments, access to transaction history, etc., which is like a brownie point in favor of mobile banking. Thus, the increasing popularity of mobile banking is favoring the growth of multimedia banking in India.

9.7.4 Deployment types – India digital banking platform market

Based on deployment types, the digital banking platform of India is classified into on-premises and cloud segments. The reason behind cloud deployment in market shares is improved efficiency, faster data access, and better traffic monitoring in the cloud. Cloud deployment also facilitates companies to expand beyond their physical capacity along with their financial capacity. Cloud-based deployment allows for faster tracking and rectifying issues, reducing the risk of reputation damage caused by service interruptions.

9.7.5 Regional insights of multimedia banking in India

The overall digital banking platform in India is segmented into four zones, i.e., North India, South India, East India, and West India. And out of all these zones, the western region dominates, and on the other hand, North India is seen as the potential market with a high CAGR in the near future. The emergence of FinTech companies and increasing Internet access are providing growth opportunities to the market, directly impacting India's digital banking platform's positive growth.

9.7.6 The pandemic impacted multimedia banking

The pandemic has hit various industries and devastated them, but the nationwide imposed lockdown has boosted the growth of multimedia banking in India. The inaccessibility of customers to banking services has shifted both customers and employees to operate digitally. It has been seen that COVID-19 has been a blessing in disguise for multimedia banking.

9.8 Customer perspective on multimedia banking in India

According to Aithal and Varambally (2015), the customer perspective towards multimedia banking is examined based on six factors and they are as follows.

9.8.1 Demography of customers

The demographic has been found as an important determinant for the acceptance of multimedia banking. A person with a high income, a relatively young age, and a good education are dominating factors for the acceptance of multimedia banking. And many other studies revealed that older people take time adopting new technologies, and hence they are expected to have negative attitudes towards the invented technology.

9.8.2　Personal banking experience

It is said that people's personal beliefs and attitudes largely depend upon their personal experiences about a given situation. Satisfied bank customers are expected to perceive mobile banking positively and are likely to move online faster. A dissatisfied branch customer may also try mobile banking but will not regularly use it as much as satisfied customers.

9.8.3　Technology experience

The previous studies revealed that if the customer has more experience with the technology, they will understand new technologies in a better way. The one who is a pro of technology fears less than the one who has not adopted the technology.

The non-users negative experiences greatly impact the usage of new channels worldwide. Because negative attitude about the new channel prohibits their usage. Lack of guidance about multimedia banking for financial transactions negatively affects them. And prior mobile phone usage experiences positively influenced the adoption of multimedia banking.

9.8.4　Psychology and culture

The belief that the use of the new electronic channel for financial transaction improves the customer status in society, and more of the services offered by the banks enhances the usage of the channel. And it is also observed that a lack of opportunities, like service areas, mobile devices etc., to use new channels will diminish their usage.

9.8.5　Security challenges and trust

Security has been treated as a major barrier to uptaking online banking worldwide. But in both developing and developed nations, consumers perceive that risk, fraud, and loss are the major obstacles to adopting multimedia. Therefore, security and trustworthiness are services required for switching to new channels, and they also have a positive effect.

9.9　An approach to build customer relationship management (CRM) through multimedia banking

Banks are the country's backbone, and they aim to build long-term relationships with their customers (Khare, 2010). By escalating their marketing strategies, they are trying to expand their service offerings to their customers to retain them.

Years ago, the banks tried their best to maintain their customer relationship by focusing on understanding their individual needs. But with the advent of technology, multimedia banking has increased the interface options between banks and their customers. Multimedia banking is thoroughly changing the face of banking services. New technologies that are completely user-friendly are being introduced with the hope of improving banking services.

To improve the customer interface, the banks are investing a lot more in CRM technologies with the aim of enhancing customer satisfaction and value to the customers. CRM is turning out to favor the banking industry because it helps deliver more personalized experiences to their customers.

The number of customers is increasing rapidly for the banking industry, and it is becoming quite difficult for them to serve personalized experiences to their customers. Therefore, with the help of the Internet and new machines, the banks strive to ensure customer loyalty and customer satisfaction and retain them at a very low cost in the long run. This industry cannot deny that multimedia banking services will help them ensure effective relationships with their customers to get a competitive advantage over others.

With the aid of multimedia banking, the banks are serving quality products to create loyal customers in the market, who may further say some positive words in favor of them in their community, thereby easing their survival in the market.

All the banks offer their customers the same products and services. Thus, the need for attributes can only distinguish them from one another. Multimedia banking or online banking is one such tool for maintaining a speedy and effective relationship with their customers and continuously keeping in touch with them.

9.10   Real multimedia banking fraud in India

Vishal Kumar Pal, February 4, 2021

The complainant gave written information to the police regarding online net banking fraud. The allegations made were that the complainant has two bank accounts in PNB bank, and from both of his accounts, a sum of Rs. 25,74,435/- has been withdrawn, and he was not even aware of it. The complainant went to the bank to withdraw a sum of Rs. 10,000/- from his bank. However, he received a message that the amount had already been withdrawn from his account. The complainant enquired about the same from bank officials, to which he was informed that there must be some mal-functions in the ATM machine. After filing the complaint, a few days later, the complainant got a call from Rahul Sharma from the Head Office of Punjab National Bank. He asked for a 16 digits Pin number from the complainant, required to register his complaint. On August 22, 2019, the complainant went again to enquire about his issue, and he learned that there was no money in his account, and the bank officials asked the complainant to register FIR.

Based on the available information, the police started the inquiry, and the investigation showed that the petitioner had received a phone call from No. 7469980751. Further investigation revealed that the above-written mobile number was traced in West Bengal. And the police got the trails of transactions linked to PNB, India Post Payment Bank, IRCTC-Mudra, Citrus Pay, etc.; all these amounts are deposited in a Private Sector Bank. Further investigation revealed the involvement of the bail petitioner in his online bank fraud. Based on the investigation, the police arrested him, and since February 2, 2020, he has been in judicial custody.

Dr S. Praveen Kumar, November 24, 2017
The complainant was the credit card holder of the opposite party bank, bearing no. 4629864377303005 for 5 years. With the credit limit of Rs. 71,000/-. On September 13, 2011, he noticed that on August 21, 2011, a transaction was done of amount Rs. 27,854/- on www.ebay.com and on August 24, 2011, two transactions were done of amount Rs. 12,394/- and Rs. 388.65/- respectively from the same website and these transactions were not done by him.

After contacting customer care, the amount got credited for the transactions made on August 24, 2011, but the opposite party demanded him to pay for the amount of Rs. 27,854- a transaction dated August 21, 2011, which was not credited to his account.

The respondent party admitted police registered FIR 275/2011 Vide Ex. A-13, but the main rebuttal of the council for the transaction dated August 21, 2011 for Rs. 27,854/-that it has undergone 3D secure authentication. Apart from the card verification, the transactions also require a six-digit 3D secure pin. Therefore, it can only be done by the appellant or any other person aware of the above details, and nobody could find any abnormality in the transaction.

But the respondent requested the bank officials to enquire about the details of the transaction to eBay people, purchases of the product and the delivery address, etc., but the respondent bank admitted that the third party did the transactions and they are not responsible for the same.

So, traditionally the transaction was committed fraudulently by somebody.

9.11   SWOT analysis of multimedia banking

Based on the whole study, the following is the SWOT analysis of multimedia banking:

Atharva Dhamale *et al.* (2019) presented the following SWOT analysis:
Strengths:

1. Practices that are available over multimedia banking are transparent and disclosed clearly.
2. Multimedia banking helps in offering additional services to their customers.
3. Loyalty and customer satisfaction are increasing rapidly due to multimedia banking.
4. Multimedia banking has emerged as a competitive advantage for banks.
5. The cut-throat competition among banks has led to the launching of more and more schemes for their customers.
6. Multimedia banking has reduced the interaction time, cost, and effort of the public.

7. This provides permanent access to the bank.
8. Multimedia banking has evolved as a safe and secure method.
9. Several discounts and offers available through multimedia banking are attracting more offers available in traditional banking.

Weaknesses:

1. People are less aware of multimedia banking.
2. People have a negative perception of security reasons leading people to go for multimedia banking on a very small scale.
3. In rural & some urban areas, low Internet connectivity is an obstacle that is preventing a large section of society from accessing multimedia.
4. Mobile banking has not penetrated sufficiently in rural areas of India.
5. Improper infrastructure, like ATMs in rural areas, is one major point preventing the growth of technology in the banking industry in rural areas.
6. Multimedia banking is costly; everybody cannot afford it.
7. Online payments are not accepted everywhere.

Opportunities:

The following factors may lead to an increase in qualities and decreased cost of services provided in banking:

1. Increased quality of online services.
2. Supporting government policies.
3. Increasing investment in the E-banking sector.
4. Increase competition among companies in the E-banking sector.

Threats:

1. The following are the security threats in online transactions:
   • Card trapping
   • Fake websites
   • Keystroke logging
   • Use of malware programs
2. People often do not deactivate their lost cards; others may misuse them.
3. Customers lose data like phone numbers, e-mail address passwords, and other useful information during online transactions.
4. Multimedia banking is growing rapidly, but it is decreasing the employment of people in the banking sector.

9.12 Conclusion

The banking system has evolved over a period of time with the aid of technology. And the banks have extensively used this technology to supply their consumers with the best financial goods and services. New policies with the assistance of technology and creativity to serve the clients within the banks have introduced the RTGS, mobile banking, digital wallets, UPI, Blockchain technology, computing, cloud banking, wearable technology, and omnichannel banking has given rise to numerous innovations. Multimedia banking has several plus points over traditional banking, like making a payment as per the convenience of the customers, and even the transactions over the net are secured with OTP or 4-digit PIN option. Not only this, but the banks also provide users with the required services. And as today's generations are more tech-savvy, the future of multimedia banking is rapidly growing. In addition, all the stakeholders, like the government and telecom service providers and mobile device manufacturers, need to invest more so that mobile banking reaches high-end to low-end users, and even penetration is required, especially in the middle towns and rural areas. One of the advantages of multimedia banking is its extensive branch network. There is a dramatic shift in the domain of consumer engagement. It follows that even front-desk operations will feel the effects of new media banking. Customers are pleased with the website and use of multimedia technologies in banking services because of their improvements in the service's ease of use, convenience, speed, and availability (and more). Users still worry about their privacy and security, but it is under control. Though there have only been a small number of global internet banking thefts, clients' anxieties appear to be greater. The service's popularity stems from customers' attention to and appreciation of the many factors that led them to make their transaction decision. However, more and more clients are switching to online banking since it is more accessible, faster, and more convenient than traditional banking methods. Even if the multimedia technologies in the banking industry are in the infancy stage, it appears to be a long way off until banks adopt the necessary technology.

References

Aithal, P. S. & Varambally, K. V. M. (2015). Customer perspective on online mobile banking in India – an empirical study. *International Journal of Management, IT and Engineering*, 5(7), 77–97. ISSN- 2249-0558.

Athanassopoulos, A. D., & Labrouskos, N. S. (1999). Corporate customer behaviour towards financial services: empirical results from the emerging market of Greece. *International Journal of Bank Marketing*, 17(6), pp. 247–285.

Chavan, J. (2013). Internet banking-benefits and challenges in an emerging economy. *International Journal of Research in Business Management*, 1(1), 19–26.

Chen, M., Wu, Q., & Yang, B. (2019). How valuable is FinTech innovation? *Review of Financial Studies*, 32, 2062–2106. 10.1093/rfs/hhy130.

Dhamale, A. (2019). A study of E-banking in India: trends of popularity. *International Journal of Innovative Science and Research Technology*, 4(6), 435–480. ISSN No. 2456-2165.

Goel, M. (2013). Impact of technology on the banking sector in India. *International Journal of Scientific Research*, 2(5). 2.

Goyal, V. M., & Goyal, G. (2012). Customer perception towards Internet banking wrt to private and foreign banks in India. *International Journal of Computing & Business Research*, 2012, 2229–6166.

Gulati, V. P., Sivakumaran, M. V., & Manogna, C. (2002). IT framework for the Indian banking sector. *ASCI Journal of Management*, 31(1), 67–77.

Khare, A., Khare, A., & Singh, S. (2010). Role of consumer personality in determining preference for online banking in India. *Journal of Database Marketing & Customer Strategy Management*, 17, 174–187. https://doi.org/10.1057/dbm.2010.18.

Kiljan, S., Vranken, H., & van Eekelen, M. (2018). Evaluation of transaction authentication methods for online banking. *Future Generation Computer Systems*, 80, 430–447.

Latif, S. (2019). Impact of customer relationship management (CRM) through online banking services on customer retention with mediating role of customer perception and satisfaction. A case of Standard Chartered Bank Pakistan. *International Journal of Sciences: Basic and Applied Research (IJSBAR)*, 44 (1), 14–32.

Latimore, D., Watson, I., & Maver, C. (2000). The customer speaks: 3,300 Internet users tell us what they want from retail financial services. Available at URL: http://www.mainspring.com/research/document/view/1,2099,1215,00.html (Accessed 28 May 2001).

Malhotra, P. & Singh, B. (2010). Experience in internet banking and performance of banks. *International Journal of Electronic Finance*, 4, 64–83. 10.1504/IJEF.2010.030786.

Mansoor Khan, M., & Ishaq Bhatti, M. (2008). Islamic banking and finance: on its way to globalisation. *Managerial Finance*, 34(10), 708–725.

Mols, N. P. (2000). The Internet and services marketing – the case of Danish retail banking. *Internet Research: Electronic Networking Application and Policy*, 10(1), pp. 7–18.

Nagaraju, S., & Parthiban, L. (2015). Trusted framework for online banking in the public cloud using multi-factor authentication and privacy protection gateway. *Journal of Cloud Computing*, 4(1), 22.

Purohit, D., & Arora, Dr. (2021). The benefits and challenges of mobile banking at the bottom of the pyramid. *Journal of Contemporary Issues in Business and Government*, 27, 2021.

Shaneeb, P., & Sumathy, M. (2021a). Impact of intellectual capital on financial performance in Indian textile industries. *Academy of Accounting and Financial Studies Journal*, 25(4), 1–14.

Shaneeb, P., & Sumathy, M. (2021b). Impact of intellectual capital on firm performance in Indian it companies. *Journal of Contemporary Issues in Business and Government*, 27(02), 4335–4340. https://doi.org/10.47750/cibg.2021.27.02.459.

Stoica, O., Mehdian, S., & Sargu, A. (2015). The impact of internet banking on the performance of Romanian banks: DEA and PCA approach. *Procedia Economics and Finance*, 20, 610–622.

Strieter, J., Gupta, A. K., Raj, S. P., & Wilemon, D. (1999). Product management and the marketing of financial services. *International Journal of Banking Marketing*, 17(7), 342–354. JIBCfile:////omics-accounts/Accounts/JIBC%20HTML%20TO%20PDF/2004-9-3/Vijayan.HTM[13-02-2015 12:15:24]342-354.

Sujith, T. S. (2017). Awareness of green marketing and its influence on buying behaviour of consumers in Kerala. *International Journal of Scientific Research and Management*, 5(7), 6156–6164.

Thakor, A. V. (2020). Fintech and banking: What do we know? *Journal of Financial Intermediation,* 41(C), Article 100833.

Tidd, J., & Bessant, J. R. (2018). *Managing Innovation: Integrating Technological, Market and Organisational Change.* New York, NY: John Wiley & Sons.

Tiwari, R., Buse, S., & Herstatt, C. (2007). Mobile services in banking sector: the role of innovative business solutions in generating competitive advantage. http://www.tuarburg.de/tim/downloads/arbeitspapiere/Working_Paper_48.pdf.

Tunay, K. B., Tunay, N., & Akhisar, İ. (2015). Interaction between Internet banking and bank performance: the case of Europe. *Procedia-Social and Behavioral Sciences*, 195, 363–368.

Vishnuvardhan, B., Bairam, M., & Naik, R. L. (2020). A study of digital banking: security issues and challenges. In *Proceedings of the Third International Conference on Computational Intelligence and Informatics*, pp.163–185. 10.1007/978-981-15-1480-7_14.

Chapter 10

Fraud and cyber operation countermeasures for multimedia in financial services

Arti Gaur[1], Sweta Bhatti[1], Sanju Verma[1] and Mark Laurence Zammit[2]

Abstract

Cybercrime and malignant hacking have additionally strengthened. In financial wrongdoing, controllers constantly modify rules progressively to represent unlawful dealing and tax evasion, and states have tightened up the utilization of financial authorizations, focusing on nations, public and confidential substances, and even people. Digital empowered assaults are becoming more aggressive in scope and ubiquitous, dissolving the worth of individual data and security assurances. In the area of monetary wrongdoing, in the meantime, controllers consistently overhaul rules progressively to represent unlawful dealings and tax evasion, and legislatures have tightened up the utilization of financial assets, focusing on nations, public and confidential elements, and even people. Foundations find their current ways of battling such wrongdoings cannot agreeably deal with the numerous dangers and weights. The study includes the conceptual research of cyber frauds with multimedia technologies in the financial sector. Cybercrime in finance is becoming volumetric mostly using scams and the biggest reason for the downfall of the country's economy. This study shows the measures to overcome these terrible problems and technologies playing a major role in decreasing fraud. Cybersecurity is most important to save confidential data and information. Cybersecurity can vary from system to system. It depends on the information held by that particular system. So, this study helps to know about methods to reduce cyber fraud related to finance.

Keywords: Cyber crime; Frauds; Finance; Measures; Multimedia technologies

[1]Department of Business Administration, Chaudhary Devi Lal University, India
[2]Department of Insurance and Risk Management, University of Malta, Malta

10.1   Introduction of cyber fraud

Cyber fraud is the most well-known and undermining sort of fraud which happens universally. Through the expansion and development of the cyber world throughout the twenty-first century, fraudsters can access victims' financial and personal information in various ways. Fraudsters can utilize the data they assemble to store themselves later monetarily, or worryingly they could use this cash to sponsor psychological warfare. Therefore, individuals and organizations must understand how to protect themselves from online fraud. Any fraudulent activity that involves a computer or computer information is regarded to be a sort of cyber fraud. The infractions range widely. Fraudsters can use the internet to gain a close enough look at victims' personal information, online accounts, and ledgers. They can then use the money and knowledge they earn from this to fund psychological oppression. There are more opportunities than at any other time in recent memory for criminals to commit cyber fraud thanks to the widespread and well-known use of web banking and portable financial. It is intense wrongdoing – one that should be gotten serious about.

10.2   Fraud and cyber operation countermeasures for multimedia in financial services

As we become progressively dependent on advanced monetary administrations, the quantity of cyberattacks has significantly increased over the past 10 years, and financial administrations remain the most designated industry. Cybersecurity has turned into a danger to economic strength. Given solid monetary and mechanical interconnections, an effective assault on a significant financial establishment, or a center framework or administration utilized by quite a few people, could immediately spread through the whole monetary framework causing far and wide disturbance and loss of certainty. Exchanges could flop as liquidity is caught, and families and organizations could lose admittance to stores and instalments. Under outrageous situations, financial backers and contributors might request their assets or attempt to drop their records, administrations, and items they routinely use. Since, as the saying goes, "that is where the money is," the financial administration business is particularly concerned about cybersecurity. Today's world is brimming with complex and contemporary schemes to relieve people of financial obligations. Whatever the case, nothing engages a criminal's mind more than electronically transferring assets from one person's record to another that they control.

As assaults increment, controllers get to notice and take lengths to press the business to track down arrangements. Immediately, administrative and consistence necessities are a huge test for the monetary area and the absolute most significant explanation that shoppers entrust the business with their cash. Controllers watch out for cyber occasions in this area and stand prepared to apply more difficult guidelines. Clients expect a consistent, frictionless, credit-only experience utilizing the web and versatile applications. Also, like all businesses, monetary administrations experience the ill effects of worldwide cybersecurity abilities.

These realities finish in what could be named the amazing coincidence of conditions for cyber dangers. Under the prevailing circumstances, this area ought to be commended for giving a degree of security that most clients see as OK. Be that as it may, at what cost? Many think that the hidden expenses of consistency and strength may, eventually, be a lot for some monetary specialist co-ops. If this occurs, hands down, the biggest may make do, diminishing rivalry in the area. This does not look good for purchasers over the long haul. This market is ready for development that will rise above the ongoing circumstances and give a safer strategy for giving monetary exchanges safely [1].

10.2.1   The top cyber threats to financial services

- **Phishing**: A way to trick individuals into providing account information so they may get close to a net connection. E-mail phishing is the most prevalent sort of fraud, in which a message that appears to be genuine correspondence is delivered to victims. Speaking with any of the dubious organizations or organizations mentioned in phishing communications may lead to the establishment of a virus on the user's computer network or weight a phoney Internet site that gathers account information. In the case of the clueless beneficiary, the trick messages appear to be exceptionally persuading, particularly when they are given a need to keep moving. Here is an illustration of a phishing e-mail acting like a dire Coronavirus pandemic asset from the World Health Organization [2].

- **Ransomware:** Another basic digital threat to financial organizations is ransomware. Cybercriminals use malware to scramble their PCs during a ransomware attack to prevent setbacks. If payment is made in full, the damage could be mitigated. Attackers who use ransomware often use coercion to force victims to make a payment. The most common being the dissemination of other unmistakable bits of misleading information held on to illegal social occasions till payment is made. Such coercion strategies are, tragically, exceptionally compelling against monetary organizations because their weighty guidelines expect commendable cyberattacks and information break flexibility. With ransomware now developing into information break an area, an effective assault could have more extensive ramifications on administrative consistence norms.

- **Dispersed denial of service (DDoS) attacks:** The most widespread dispersed denial-of-service attacks in 2020 targeted the financial industry. The loss server is overloaded with fictitious affiliation requests during a DDoS attack, forcing it to disengage. DDoS assaults are a well-known digital danger for financial businesses because of their specific attack surface, which includes banking IT infrastructure, customer accounts, portion entries, etc. DDoS attacks are now more likely to target financial resources as a result. Cybercriminals could exploit the following disorder in two ways: While security forces are occupied with a DDoS attack, more cyberattack missions can be launched [3].

- **Supply chain attacks:** A setback is introduced via a retail network attack by a hacked pariah dealer in their stock management. Attacks on retail networks enable online attackers to get beyond security measures by creating access routes to critical resources through an objective's untouchable vendor. Because vendors would not consider cybersecurity as carefully as their clients, making a trade-off for them is typically much easier. However, because outside sellers keep sensitive data on behalf of their customers as a whole, a single trade may have an impact on many different businesses. Financial administrations are advised to practice a safe and advantageous authentication mechanism and host security framework techniques to protect against production network attacks. These drives included in Biden's cybersecurity chief request attests to their sufficiency in reducing network attacks on retail establishments.

- **Bribery and corruption:** Extensively, bribery is the proposition, guarantee, giving, demand or acknowledgement of a monetary or another benefit as prompting or prize for an activity which is unlawful, exploitative or a break of trust. For instance, a payoff could be a commitment of anything of significant worth, the proposition or receipt of any profit, credit, charge, reward, or other benefit or even the giving of gifts or magnanimous guidance regardless of where it is intended to apply ill-advised impact (e.g., in the honor of a deal) [4]. Corruption, extensively, is the abuse of public office or power for private addition; or abuse of personal power corresponding to business outside the government domain. Demonstrations of bribery or corruption are intended to impact the person in the presentation of their obligation and grade them to act viciously. For the motivations behind this approach, whether the payee or beneficiary of the demonstration of bribery or corruption works in people in the general or confidential area is unimportant. The individual being paid off is, for the most part, somebody who will want to acquire, hold or direct business. This might include deals drives or advancements (e.g., in the honor of a deal), or it might consist of the handling of regulatory errands like licenses, customs, expenses, or import/trade matters by a public authority. It does not make any difference whether the demonstration of bribery is committed previously or after the offering or grant of an agreement or the finish of a regulatory errand by a public authority [5].

Bribery and corruption conduct can be committed by:

1. a worker, official or chief;
2. any individual following up in the interest of the company; or
3. individuals and associations where they approve another person to complete these demonstrations.

Bribery is a criminal offence in many nations and punishments can be serious. The UK Bribery Act 2010 makes bribery and corruption unlawful. Yet, it also expects UK organizations to take responsibility for not executing good techniques to forestall such demonstrations by those working for the organization or its sake, regardless of where the demonstration happens. Also, current US regulation offers comparable preclusions and expected punishments and is upheld with life by the US specialists. It is subsequently to your greatest advantage, as well as those of Conti's (Anti-Bribery and Corruption Policy), that you act appropriately and consistently. Degenerate demonstrations committed abroad, including those by colleagues or partners dealing with our benefit, may well bring about an indictment at home.

10.2.2   Tax evasion and tax fraud

Tax evasion to the necessary open experts' exaction from the general public for public purposes. Charges come in various forms, such as personal expenses, business obligations, local fees, and legacy obligations, and they can be made immediately or gradually. Singh and Sharma (2007) focused on the opinions of financial specialists about the Indian Income System [6]. They noted that the high level of tax evasion in India was anticipated to be caused by incompetent assessment gatherers. India's main causes of tax evasion were excessive expense rates, easily bankrupt charge gatherers, social acceptance of assessment instalment default, a low possibility of recognized tax avoidance, and a low ethical standard. In a non-industrial country, tax evasion is also explained by a wasteful duty collection system [7].

Tax fraud goes beyond simply an oversight; it is a determined effort to avoid filing taxes. The allegation of tax fraud must be supported by evidence that the defendant continued to engage in or deliberately did conduct designed to evade paying taxes. Even though the punishment for a simple error could seem severe, the consequences of a tax fraud conviction are much more powerful. Within the IRS, the Criminal Investigation (CI) unit looks into tax fraud, tax-related tax evasion, and illegal returns obtained by legitimate businesses using various fraudulent methods. Among the wrongdoings that CI is pursuing are some of the following:

- **Work and finance tax fraud**: Tax problems with payroll are common. The IRS is interested in several strategies, including underreporting the labor force, collecting finance taxes (such as federal retirement benefits, unemployment insurance, and keeping taxes) without paying them to the IRS, and paying representatives in real money off-budget.
- **Discount fraud**: Most people know that filing a false personal tax return could result in a tax case. Individuals and tax preparers engage in discount fraud and even wholesale fraud to receive an unauthorized tax discount. In this case, the most significant factor may be operating expense, exceptions, and counterfeit derivations.

The IRS may become involved if tax fraud or tax avoidance is committed. Remember that the IRS is currently understaffed and underfunded. Planning is a big element of any tax offence. To agree with a late taxpayer instead of trying to prosecute the same taxpayer for a crime would entail less time and money [8].

10.2.2.1   Third-party risk management

This type of risk management (TPRM) is the most widely recognized approach to taking apart and restricting dangers related to moving to outsider merchants or expert centers.

Many kinds of cutting-edge take a chance inside the outsider gambling class. These could consolidate financial, normal, reputational, and security chances. These hazards occur because merchants handle protected health information, sensitive information, by and large, recognizable data (PII), and licensed invention (PHI).

Third-party risk management is essential to all cybersecurity programs since third-party connections are critical to business operations.

Third-party risk management is significant in light of using third gatherings, whether straightforwardly or in a roundabout way, to influence your cybersecurity. Third parties increment the intricacy of your data security because of multiple factors:

1. Every business depends on third parties as it is not unexpected to move to a better specialist in a given field.
2. Third parties are not regularly influenced quite a bit, nor do you have total straightforwardness into their security controls. Some merchants excel at risk management and have solid security policies, but others fall short.
3. Every third party represents a possible attack channel for a data breach or online attack. If a merchant has a weak attack surface, they might be able to access your company. Your attack surface will be larger, and you may run into more weaknesses the more merchants you employ.
4. The SHIELD Act, the LGPD, the GDPR, the CCPA, and other general data affirmation and data breach notice rules have all significantly increased the status and regulatory significance of inadequate outsider gamble the board programs. For instance, assuming a third-party approach your client data, an information break at that third party could bring about your association having to deal with administrative fines and damages regardless of whether you were not straightforwardly liable for the holiday. A well-known illustration of this is the point at which one of Target's HVAC project workers prompted the openness of millions of Visas [9].

10.2.2.2   Fraud and insider threats

It is a serious risk to a company regarding insiders who know the firm's data encryption, records, and application servers, such as officials, former employees, temporary personnel, or company associates. The threat could mean fraud, theft of confidential or financially valuable information, robbery of authorized technology, or damage to computer systems.

Insiders may have access to legitimate computer systems through accounts initially given to them to help them fulfil their obligations; however, these accounts could be misused to harm the organization. The knowledge and licensed invention of the association, as well as the safeguards put in place to protect them, are frequently known to insiders. This makes it easier for the insider to go around any security measures they know. Actual proximity to information suggests that the insider is already inside the structure, frequently with direct access to the firm's internal structure, and does not need to breach firewalls to gain access to the hierarchical organization. Since an insider already has legitimate access to the organization's data and resources, insider threats are harder to prevent than attacks from outsiders [10].

An insider could try to steal things or information for their benefit or to aid another group or nation. The association could also be in jeopardy from malicious software that previous employees may have left running on their PC systems, a so-called "rational bomb" [11].

10.2.3 Retail cybersecurity: challenges and threats

10.2.3.1 Threat 1: payment skimmers

Realizing that traffic and exchanges are at a new high during the middle of shopping seasons, programmers try to take important payment information from accidental clients and retailers the same. This should be possible by compromising existing POS frameworks with malware. The devices may be unable to fend off known attacks if retailers still use outdated POS systems or have not updated them in a while. Programmers know this would be a good time to launch an attack to steal crucial Visa information because PoS frameworks and terminals will likely be submerged in a flood of customers.

10.2.3.2 Threat 2: SQL injection

Hackers should also be wary of using shop websites to collect payment information before an online purchase. This is typically accomplished through a SQL infusion, which injects malicious code into a website and steals and conceals information. This enables hackers to steal payment information entered into a field without the customer or the hacker being aware of it. One of the most well-known attack techniques employs an unpatched version of Magento to install malicious code that steals payment information, reroutes connections to harmful websites, or, more recently, mines bitcoin invisibly.

Although this attack can be carried out at any time, cunning hackers may choose a time when the flurry of activity on websites and in stores makes it likely that no one will detect the attack. Suppose the merchant is overwhelmed with warnings and other serious issues. In that case, any preparation that has a potential problem may be ignored, justified as deceit, or may not be attended to promptly.

10.2.3.3 Threat 3: fraudulent transactions

There are two main ways that cybercriminals might use shopping deception to try to gain quick money. They can either engage in payment extortion, which involves using a stolen credit card to make a purchase (either through one of the two methods mentioned above or through information theft). As a result, since victims are likely to report fraudulent purchases, retailers may suffer. The merchant will still be charged for the entire transaction, but the Mastercard business will give the buyer a discount and exclude the retailer's cost. Return misrepresentation is another trick that cheaters and con artists frequently employ. Tricksters can get a sizable refund for something they never bought by returning stolen goods or using falsified documents (that the retailer will never obtain). This can be done in person or online. Tricksters can continue to fake returns and collect money until the trick is exposed if the proper confirmation or check processes are not in place.

To avoid being detected, hackers know to carry out these attacks during the busy holiday shopping season. Without the proper setting or conditions, sorting through the massive expansion of transactions can be challenging to spot a fake one.

10.2.3.4   Threat 4: DDoS attacks

Rush hour congestion at retail locations is worsening during the holiday shopping season. A malicious programmer can launch a DDoS attack on a retailer's website if they want to harm the site, hurt the business, or influence increased traffic to launch another attack. A botnet, a collection of compromised devices, is widely used in DDoS attacks to spam a site with inquiries to overburden it. On the off chance that the webpage does not have the right insurance, the overflow of questions can dial back or in any event, cut down the site [12].

10.2.3.5   Non-retail threats

● Consumer trust

  Gaining customers' trust is one of the hardest things for online retailers. In actuality, it usually tends to be more difficult for those new competitors who have no prior market renown. Undoubtedly difficult to get the business moving for a company with hardly any physical presence.

● Advertising costs

  Although an online retailer may not need a physical location, it must advertise its products to attract customers. Computerized advertising can be expensive and typically uses the pay-per-click model. Regardless of the arrangement, the publicist should pay for every photograph on its notice.

● Structural costs

  A non-store retailing operation may have high structural costs. A business will first need a location and a stockroom. Additionally, having a virtual entertainment presence is as important for non-store retailing; therefore, you may need to hire professionals to create and manage your website and online entertainment profiles.

● Security and legal requirements

  Hackers frequently target sites and other online platforms. Things can be extremely untidy for you if a programmer gets into your business site or web-based entertainment profiles. Plus, you should know about and consent to eCommerce regulations connected with maintaining a non-store retailing business [13].

10.2.3.6   Market abuse and misbehavior

Market abuse may be as old as the capital markets themselves, but the introduction of computerized trading has increased the likelihood that it will happen. Regulators and market players are already retaliating by utilizing cutting-edge trade surveillance tools to curate data, identify illegal trading, aid investigations, and minimize false positives.

According to EU standards, there are two distinct components of market abuse:

1. Insider dealing: the use of information for one's benefit by someone who has access to information that other investors do not (for instance, a director who is aware of a takeover proposal).
2. Market manipulation: When someone purposefully disseminates inaccurate or misleading information (such as information regarding a company's financial situation) to affect the price of a share for their benefit [14].

Market misbehavior is a conscious effort to obstruct the market's ability to function. Market misbehavior can take many different forms, including fake trading, insider selling, the revelation of knowledge about illegal transactions, and other similar behaviors when market meddling generates profits. The end objective of the intervention, however, might range from financial gain to averting losses. Examples of market misbehavior include fraudulent practices, completely bogus buying and selling, predatory pricing, disclosing details of transactions that are prohibited, telling false data to induce transactions, manipulating the financial markets, and other things of that nature where real economic overreach reaps earnings [15].

10.2.3.7 Credentials management

Through the lifecycle of credentials, the resources they provide for entry will change and adapt. Credential changes can result in security issues for various reasons, including lost or stolen devices or passwords, employee needs for updated access, and even simple organizational departures. Organizations need user credentials to restrict access to sensitive data. As a result, effective credential management is crucial for these changes, and it should cover every phase of the lifetime, including access updates, resets, and revocations. A reliable credential management system – or numerous credential management systems – must be implemented to safeguard all systems and data. As consumers and workers come and go, change positions, and as corporate procedures and regulations change, authorities must be able to issue and revoke credentials.

Additionally, enterprises must be able to confirm the identification of internal privileged users and online customers due to the expansion of privacy rules and other security demands. By integrating with a corporate directory, credential management solutions may further simplify the revocation process, lighten the administrative burden, and protect IT systems from unauthorized or expired users. Up to the end of the life cycle, strict credential security must be used, along with effective deactivation [16].

10.2.3.8 Use of technology in addressing cybersecurity issues

Cybersecurity is the study of securing critical systems and confidential material against Internet attackers. Information security precautions, sometimes known as IT protection, are designed to fend against assaults on networked services and devices, regardless they originate from within or without a business [17]. Cybersecurity threats affect people, non-profit organizations, the government, and enterprises. Researchers and information security professionals are always developing proactive strategies and technologies to increase cybersecurity. Some new dangers include ransomware attacks and flaws brought on by rising cloud service usage. Security issues are also posed by the development of the Internet of Things (IoT), which includes smart home gadgets and potential flaws in 5G technology. Cybersecurity threats can encourage the creation of new cybersecurity technology. Further information on some of the most exciting new solutions developed to counteract current cybersecurity threats are discussed later in this paper [18].

Cybersecurity specialists use the following tools to protect against cyber threats.

10.2.3.9   Behavioral analytics

Data is examined using behavioral analytics to analyze user behavior on websites, mobile applications, systems, and networks. Cybersecurity experts may use platforms for behavioral analytics to identify possible threats and weaknesses. Finding unexpected occurrences and behaviors that point to cybersecurity vulnerabilities can be accomplished by analyzing activity patterns. For instance, behavioral analytics may discover that a single device is producing abnormally significant volumes of data. This might indicate that a cyberattack is imminent or already underway. The odd timing of occurrences and unusually ordered acts are two more signs of nasty behavior.

- *Blockchain*
  A blockchain database is a safe way to store data in blocks. Through cryptography, it links the blocks together. Data collection is possible with blockchain, but not editing or deletion. Cybersecurity professionals may use blockchain technology to safeguard computers or other hardware, create industry-standard security protocols, and make it nearly impossible for hackers to access databases. Better user privacy, a decrease in human error, increased transparency, and cost savings due to the elimination of third-party verification are all advantages of blockchain technology. In addition, blockchain addresses the security issue associated with centralized data storage. Data storage across networks results in the creation of a decentralized system that is less vulnerable to hackers. The problems with using blockchain technology are its cost and inefficiency.
- *Cloud encryption*
  Cloud services help businesses save money while increasing efficiency and providing better remote services. However, the cloud's remote data storage can make data more vulnerable. Before entering the cloud, data is transformed using cloud encryption technology into an incomprehensible code. Cybersecurity experts use a mathematical formula to finish cloud encryption. Data can only be decrypted and readable again by authorized users with the encryption key. This restricted access reduces the likelihood of data breaches by unauthorized attackers. According to experts, cloud encryption is a fantastic cybersecurity tool for protecting data in the cloud. Cloud encryption can stop unauthorized users from accessing data that is useful. Further, cloud encryption can boost customer

trust in cloud services and make it easier for companies to comply with legal requirements.

- *Context-aware security*
  Context-aware security is a cybersecurity technology that aids companies in real-time security decision-making. It is less likely to reject access to a legitimate user when security is context-aware. Context-aware security determines whether a user is real or not using various supporting data, such as time, location, and URL reputation, as opposed to replies to static yes/no questions. Data access procedures are streamlined by context-aware security, which facilitates work for authorized individuals. But there is a problem: end-user privacy issues.

- *Defensive artificial intelligence*
  Cybersecurity experts may use artificial-defensive intelligence (AI) to find or block cyberattacks. Deep fakes, faked photos, personalities, and films that convincingly represent individuals or events that have never occurred or do not exist are examples of offensive AI. Malicious actors may use adversarial machine learning to deceive computers into malfunctioning by feeding them false data. Cybersecurity experts may use defensive AI to identify and thwart attempts by offensive AI to measure, test, and understand how the system or network operates. Algorithms can be strengthened by defensive AI, which makes it harder to compromise them. Researchers in cybersecurity can subject machine learning models to more rigorous vulnerability evaluations.

- *Extended detection and response*
  Advanced cybersecurity technology, known as extended detection and response (XDR), is used to identify security threats and incidents and take appropriate action. XDR responds across networks, endpoints, and the cloud. XDR offers a more comprehensive view by connecting data from many sources. Cybersecurity experts can now detect and evaluate threats at a higher, automated level thanks to technology. This can assist in preventing or minimizing existing and upcoming data breaches across the whole ecosystem of assets inside a business. Cybersecurity experts can respond to and identify targeted assaults using XDR. They can also automatically check and correlate warnings and produce extensive analytics. Automation of tedious operations, powerful automatic detection, and a decrease in the number of occurrences requiring inquiry are all advantages of XDR.

- *Manufacturer usage description*
  The Internet Engineering Task Force created the Manufacturer Usage Description (MUD) to increase security for IoT devices on networks in homes and small companies. Network-based assaults can affect IoT devices. A machine may malfunction or lose confidential data due to these attacks. IoT devices should be safe without being overly expensive or difficult.

- *Zero Trust*
  Traditional network security adhered to the principle of "trust but verify," presuming that users residing inside a company's network perimeter were not potential security concerns. On the other hand, the slogan of Zero Trust is "never trust, always verify." Zero Trust is a methodology for handling network

security that requires all users to verify themselves before allowing access to a company's data or apps. Zero Trust is that no one on the network is more trustworthy than any other. Greater overall information security for the firm may be the outcome of this closer examination of all users. Cybersecurity experts may utilize Zero Trust to cope with difficulties like ransomware attacks and remote workers more safely. Multi-factor authentication, data encryption, and endpoint security are some of the techniques that may be combined in a zero-trust architecture.

10.2.4   Security-operations center and network-operations center, which enable monitoring

Security-operations center (SOC): A SOC, which acts as its command center, is where a group of digital technology experts with experience in data protection collaborate to monitor, analyze, and protect a business from cyber-attacks [19]. An information security team is housed in a SOC facility, which is responsible for regularly assessing and monitoring an institution's cyber resilience. Utilizing a mix of technological solutions and a solid foundation of procedures, the SOC team's objective is to identify, investigate, and respond to cybersecurity issues. Security engineers and analysts, as well as managers who direct security activities, are frequently employed by security operations centers [20]. SOCs play a crucial role in reducing the expenses associated with possible data breaches since they assist firms in promptly responding to incursions and continuously enhance methods for detection and prevention. Although most big organizations have in-house SOCs, smaller businesses may outsource part or all of their SOC-related responsibilities to a managed service supplier, the web, or a virtualized network. SOCs are extensively used in the high-tech, financial, public, armed forces, medical, and academic industries [21].

Network operation center (NOC): Computer, telecommunications, or satellite network systems are continuously monitored and managed at this single location. It acts as the first point of defense versus transmission loss and outages [22]. A NOC, which is a single place, allows an IT team to track the operation and security of a network continuously. The initial source of protection regarding network disruptions and outages is the NOC. The NOC (prominent "knock") gives organizations total network awareness, allowing them to see anomalies and act quickly to either stop them from happening in the first place or deal with them as soon as they do. The NOC manages the network's hardware, including servers, firewalls, and wiring, as well as wireless systems, databases, dashboards, and reporting. It also deals with linked network devices such as smartphones and IoT devices. NOC's management services significantly impact the provision of top-notch customer service since they also entail monitoring helpdesk inquiries, support station devices and platforms, and contact with users' Internet protocols. The task can be farmed out to a third party with experience in network and infrastructure monitoring and administration. NOCs can be created internally and locally, typically inside the data center. Employees of the NOC are in charge of recognizing problems and acting quickly to remedy them, regardless of the design [23].

10.2.5   Cyber security costs, cyber breaches; confidentiality, integrity, systems availability

Cyber security costs: Many variables affect how you create a cybersecurity budget, just like any other aspect of a company. Here are a few things to take into account:

- The size and industry of your business.
- The delicate nature of the data you gather, utilize, and share.
- Requests from customers or other stakeholders in the enterprise.

The IT budget of businesses is typically connected with their spending on cybersecurity, which helps account for elements like company size and IT infrastructure. According to estimates, firms currently spend between 5.6% and 20% of their IT budget. Not that you need to pay a large sum of money all at once. If you have not had one before, consider adding a small cybersecurity budget to your 2020 estimates. You can undertake a crucial cybersecurity risk assessment and start working on upgrades critical to a relatively minimal cost, proving that a little bit can go a long way. Small firms may have limited resources; occasionally, the individual creating and approving the budget may not understand the need for cybersecurity. A basic risk assessment may be a great approach to explain to leadership, stakeholders or the board of directors where your firm is and how an investment could strengthen protection if you are encountering resistance from them. Administration, whether the board, the C-suite, or the business owner, must steer the organization in the proper path, including safeguarding the organization from dangers [24].

Cyber breaches: A data breach is a cyberattack in which private, sensitive information that should have been kept secret has been accessed, used, or disclosed. Any company size, from tiny companies to large multinationals, is susceptible to data breaches. Personal information, personally identifiable information (PII), protected health information, and other confidential information may be included. Data breaches routinely disclose corporate information, client lists, source code, card details, PII, vehicle registration number, and other private details [25]. A data breach is considered to have occurred when someone not authorized to do so views or steals personal information from the entity responsible for keeping it secure. The offending organization may be subject to penalties, legal action, reputational damage, and even loss of the ability to conduct business if a data breach leads to identity theft and a violation of government or industry compliance rules.

Data protection regulations provide for mitigation of breaches of personal data due to cyber breaches and attacks. The General Data Protection Regulation (GDPR) put requirements for companies (large or small) within the EU and non-EU/EEA countries which possess personal data of EU citizens to do annual Privacy Impact Assessments on all data storage applications, systems and hardware.

Confidentiality: While doing business with clients and prospects, collecting and preserving their personal information is customary. Names, e-mail accounts, and contact information are a few examples of personal information. It is your company's responsibility to maintain and protect this private information. Relying on and having faith in your internet or customer relationship management provider is insufficient. To ensure that the privacy of your clients and future consumers is safeguarded, your business must put additional security measures in place. Determining and regulating information access levels internally and externally can be the first step in protecting confidentiality. For instance, employees in the IT department who don't frequently deal with customers or potential customers should not have access to client information. Someone should not have access to certain information if they do not require it to carry out their job. Restrictions on data accessibility significantly lessen the possibility of information being leaked accidentally or on deliberately [26].

Integrity concerns safeguarding data or information on your system from unauthorized alteration or erasure. This is crucial to the dependability, correctness, and cleanliness of data. Backing up your data, using access controls, monitoring your electronic record, and encrypting your information are the easiest approaches to maintain data integrity. Cyberattacks that affect data integrity include electronic mail deception (which compromises the accuracy of interactions), accounting scams and embezzlement by modifying accounting statements, and even assassination attempts like Stuxnet, which influences the data integrity of remote monitoring mechanisms information flows to cause physical harm.

Availability: The CIA Triad's third and last instalment is this one. It means that users have access to systems and data at all times, in any environment – including during power cuts or environmental catastrophes. Even if you meet another two CIA Triad requirements, your company may suffer if you are not readily available. Your business may use alternative networks, processors, and applications to ensure availability. They can be configured to become available if the main system fails. In addition to having backups, the IT architecture is crucial. For instance, if your IT systems have high availability built-in, you will be able to continue operating at a given degree of performance even under unforeseen conditions. Attacks on availability include denial of service attacks, extortion (which encodes computer documents and information to make them inaccessible to authenticated persons), and even screaming operations, which could also impair business operations.

10.2.6   Customer identification and authentication

Customer identification occurs when a user (or another person) asserts an identity. The title may be in the shape of a login, procedure identification, digital certificate, or any other means specifically designating a subject or individual. Security systems examine whether a person has the authority to enter a certain object using this type of documentation. Identification includes understanding someone's identity despite their reluctance to provide information. Numerous methods, such as fingerprints, DNA samples, and remote monitoring, can be used to identify someone. Multiple processes, such as fingerprints, forensic evidence, and remote monitoring, can be used to identify someone. However, the same function is served in the modern era by device fingerprinting or other biometrics. By their writing style, keyboard patterns, or gaming habits, people can also be recognized online [27].

Customer authentication: Authentication is ensuring that an individual or entity is actually the person or thing it purports to be. Identification software examines whether users can use the network by comparing their credentials to those kept on a data identity provider or in a directory of legitimate personnel. Authentication ensures safe systems, procedures, and business information security; it does just that. Authentication can take several different forms. User authentication occurs when a user inputs credentials, such as a password, that match their user ID. Users are frequently given user IDs for identifying purposes. In single-factor authentication, a user ID and password are required (single factor authentication—SFA). Recently, businesses have strengthened authentication by asking for additional authentication factors, such as a unique code delivered to a user's mobile device during an attempt to sign on or a photographic identification like a thumbprint or facial scan. In this case, two-factor authentication (2FA) is applied. SFA, which requires login credentials, and 2FA, which requires an id number, login, and biometric signature, are only two examples of more sophisticated authentication techniques. Using three or more additional authentication factors for verification, such as an id number, passphrase, photographic identification, and sometimes a relevant statement the individual must answer is known as multifactor authentication (MFA) [28].

Monitoring and detection of anomalies
Identifying already recognized cyber risks has long been the primary emphasis of standard IT security and monitoring ideas. However, they are susceptible to external elements that might harm an IT network or industrial control system (ICS) and cause failures. The threats to networks have expanded in variety and complexity, particularly in businesses' rising digitalization and component networking. New ideas are required to solve these new issues to maintain network security and stability. These issues are methodically addressed via anomaly detection. Anomaly detection is identifying pieces of information, items, comments, or situations that do not follow the orderly sequence for a certain group. While certain abnormalities are extremely rare, they might indicate a serious concern, including cyber invasions or IT systems fraud. To learn about the detection, identification, and prediction of the phenomena of these anomalies, anomaly detection is employed in behavioral analysis and other types of research [29]. Anomaly detection is a novel technique for IT and OT security and condition monitoring. Contrary to conventional security measures, anomaly detection is not constrained to identifying known dangers or operating following a broad allow list. The method's objective is to find any network anomalies. Any modification to the network's established standard communication is an abnormality. Malware, cyberattacks, malformed data packets, and communication changes brought on by network issues, capacity constraints, or device failures can all be considered anomalies. So, anomaly detection ensures

comprehensive digital transparency, safeguards productivity, and allows for holistic malfunction avoidance [30].

10.3   Cyber security tools and technologies

10.3.1   Cybersecurity monitoring tools

- **Site Lock:** Site Lock offers extensive site security to watch your webpage against vindictive digital dangers, including web applications and your webpage code. Contingent upon which paid plan you buy into, each offers a 30-day free preliminary you can utilize Site Lock to direct daily sweeps of your site for malware, infections, and other security dangers before exploiting the stage's programmed malware expulsion including.

Features:

- Weakness the executives
- Site checking and reinforcement
- Content conveyance network empowers high traffic with zero slack time
- Web application security
- Upholds different CMS conditions, including WordPress, Drupal, Magento, and WooCommerce, and that's just the beginning.

10.3.2   SolarWinds security event manager

SolarWinds offers many online protection answers for tackling many capabilities, including network traffic security and investigation, information-based administration, frameworks for the executives, IT security and IT administration for the board, application for the board, and more. Security event manager is the organization's lightweight and reasonable network protection instrument, natural and clear enough that you can support your PC security without expensive and complex elements you will not be guaranteed to require.

Features:

- Computerized danger recognition and reaction
- Brought together log assortment
- Simple-to-utilize dashboard
- Inherent document trustworthiness checking
- Consistency announcing
- Legal examination
- Cyberthreat insight

10.3.3   Heimdal® security

Heimdal offers a full set-up of network safety arrangements. Organizations have the choice to one or the other single out individual security items or put resources into Heimdal's Unified Threat Platform, which has the advantage of working on your IT tasks and smoothing out various network safety activities, including endpoint assurance, access the executives, and email security. Heimdal additionally offers digital danger counteraction and antivirus programming for individual home use.

Features:

- Far-off-work area control
- Email extortion anticipation
- Weakness evaluation
- Ransomware encryption assurance
- DNS sifting
- Authoritative freedoms the board
- Strong investigation through Heimdal's dashboard

10.3.4   Packet sniffer software

Wireshark: The world's most famous organization convention analyzer, Wireshark, provides a little perspective on your organization's activities. Utilizing Wireshark, you can investigate many conventions and peruse your caught network information using a graphical UI (GUI) or the TTY (teletypewriter) mode TShark utility.

Features:

- Live catch and disconnected investigation
- Rich VoIP investigation
- Trade result to XML, PostScript, CSV, or plain text [31]

10.4   Tools for cyber fraud

Kali Linux:
Open-source software called Kali Linux is supported and updated by offensive security. It is a specially designed program for computerized infiltration and criminology testing.

Ophcrack:
This tool is mostly used to decrypt hashes generated by documents comparable to windows documents. It provides a secure GUI framework and enables you to run on several platforms.

EnCase:
An agent can photograph and examine data from hard plates and releasable circles with this product.

10.4.1   Safe Back

SafeBack is typically used to image the hard drives of PC systems powered by Intel and restore these images to a few other hard discs.

Data dumper:

This is a legitimate order line PC gadget. It is freely accessible for the UNIX Operating System, which may create accurate copies of circles suitable for sophisticated legal inquiry.

Md5sum:

A gadget to look at helps determine whether information has been successfully copied to another capacity [32].

10.4.2   The Dark Web

The US Naval force first developed an unofficial section of the Internet as a task to allow intelligence agents to communicate covertly. Over time, the Navy made its Tor program "open source," making it available to everyone – including you and me – for no charge. That has proven to be a big gamble for criminals. Due to its capacity to maintain clients' secrets, tech specialists instruct con artists on how to utilize it for communication, data sharing, purchasing stolen labor and goods, and planning crimes.

10.4.3   Telegram

That is the name of a secure, encrypted, private information-sharing application that Russian billionaire Pavel Durov uses. Due to its reputation for being difficult for law enforcement to monitor, Wire has emerged as the new favorite hangout for online scammers and criminals.

10.4.4   PII

Data fraud is a part of all financial cybercrimes. Enhanced innovation is required to create a retail front for this data that policing can infiltrate effectively. Criminal websites are notorious to law enforcement and challenging to take down, such as Robo-check, which collects millions of Americans' Social Security numbers and dates of birth. However, hackers also use several legitimate websites, such as AnnualCreditReport.com, Delvepoint, TLO, Intelius, and Been Verified, to obtain information that is in the public domain about you.

10.4.5   Your Internet browsing "fingerprints"

Rich company websites collect a lot of unique information about the device you use when you visit. Those characteristics are sufficiently distinctive to set you out from potentially a lot of other clients. The current generation of criminal tech masters regularly tries to obtain your program's fingerprint. These fingerprints are sold on the black market for just $3 each to various hoodlums. That could make it possible for thugs to trick online merchants like Amazon and Walmart into thinking they are logging in using your mobile device.

10.4.6   Burner phones

Trickers occasionally require an organization's phone number to execute a trick (express, set up another financial balance in your name). Even though specialized automated methods may be successful, real prepaid cell phones are frequently used by thieves. What is the price of one of these burner phones? About $40.

10.4.7 Spoofing tools

Cybercriminals have access to websites like Phone-Gangsta and Spoofmycalls that allow them to mimic various phone numbers on a guest ID. They may appear to be the police, the IRS, the financial establishment, or even you. Cost: one cent per minute of a phone conversation

10.4.8 SOCKS5 proxies

Through this invention, criminals can hide their online location. They can make it appear as though they are in Florida, California, New York, or anywhere else they choose, even though they may be in Ghana, Nigeria, or the United Kingdom. The cost to enter the intermediate is about 30 cents.

10.4.9 Fake driver's licenses and documents

Successful Internet-based crime typically calls for the perpetrator to provide proof of identity or residence. As in the movies, there are, therefore, illegal organizations that can carry out these demands. The cost of a fake driver's license is $40. Fake reports with address verification (charging articulation) typically cost $25.

10.4.10 Remote desktop protocols (RDPs)

A coder gains access to and control over a target's computer. The individual can then permit various criminals to exploit that admission to commit harm. RDPs are used to provide a perfect, undetectable connection for illicit purposes. For each meeting where the programmer signs in remotely, the cost is typical $5 [33].

10.5 Tools for financial crime (anti-money laundering tools)

10.5.1 SEON – Block bad users and stop fraud

Made by extortion chiefs for misrepresenting supervisors, SEON is progressively well known as a consistent help with fintech, instalments and iGaming – particularly because of its computerized impression location capacities. So, it can assist you with telling whether a client is lying about their character by looking at elective information, for example, their web-based entertainment profiles, without bringing any grating into the cycle.

Although not an anti-money laundering (AML)-compliant platform, SEON offers features that can aid businesses in their AML efforts. These include synchronizations with various devices to alert you to suspect transactions and personalized guidelines to allow you total control over the hailing settings. You may greatly support your AML efforts by setting things up such that they function for you, either with our customer success group's guidance or on your own.

10.5.2   Active – smarter digital decisioning

Actico, a pioneer in computerized decision-making processes, claims to offer a complete suite used for extortion prevention, dynamic estimating, endorsing, and consistency. Great clientele includes, among others, Volkswagen Financial Services, ING, and Santander. The deliberately intended consistency apparatuses include the Money Laundering Detection System (MLDS) module, which fights against illicit tax avoidance. The module supports the management of crucial client data, exchange verification, and risk management. It enables you to process data according to risk guidelines, which might help you concentrate on high-risk exchanges.

10.5.3   AML check – smarter digital decisioning

The Madrid-based company AML check has some experience performing manual and automated checks of customer data against PEP and authorization records. The lists are provided by their main partner, Dow Jones Risk and Compliance, and are regularly updated. Additionally, you can cross-reference your results with other public records and any private data you approach. Following the fourth EU Anti-Money Laundering and Terrorist Financing Directive, you can also run similar data via risk ratings as a component of a KYC interaction. Their customers remember numerous Spanish companies for iGaming, luxury goods trade, banking, land, and protection.

10.5.4   Dow Jones – risk and compliance

Beginning around 1982, Dow Jones has made it its central goal to guarantee that top-notch and very much kept up with information abilities its screening motor, particularly regarding work processes connected with AML and counter-psychological oppression supporting. With Dow Jones, you get exhaustive gamble screening, including PEP sanctions, high-risk enterprises, improved expected level of effort reports, and progressing checking to guarantee your information is generally state-of-the-art.

10.5.5   Feedzai – fight financial crime with AI

Feedzai, a market leader in reducing financial wrongdoing for FIs, fintech, processors, and shippers, supports all components necessary to minimize extortion and adhere to AML requirements. In addition to conventional and self-administration rules and scenarios created specifically for AML checks, you may convey a full shakedown of the board and detailing stage. You can use Feedzai to include outsider mixes and pre-made SAR files to hasten your responses to the right offices.

10.5.6   HM treasury – official UK and EU sanctions lists

The UK's AML sanctions records are managed by the Office of Financial Sanctions Implementation (OFSI), a division of HM Treasury (a.k.a HMT). Fortunately, you may check their list to confirm that it complies with UK internal counterterrorism system regulation regarding AML. It also includes records from the EU and the UN, which is crucial. You should avoid using 26 HMT financial authorization systems when writing if you do not want to pay fines of up to £1 million (or half of the amount) [34].

10.6   Risk severity matrix

A risk assessment matrix, also known as a possibility and intensity solely on cost, is intended to assist you in lowering the likelihood of potential risks when working on an updated project. Essentially, it visualizes the relevant threats to a venture and allows associations to establish a balanced structure. Murphy correctly predicted that things would get serious and that when they did, project bottlenecks would have an impact on both the main issue and the flow of events. While the majority of task managers might roam around looking for opportunities. I was amazed when I created my rating scale because task managers now regularly use it.

Even at the beginning of work, normally the worst time of my life, it was there, but it was handled so skillfully that I could not tell if it was genuine. I will admit that I had to put in a few extra efforts to ensure that something so simple remained feasible and legal. The advantages of a risk assessment matrix will be obvious to those of you who enjoy creating and using them, but for those who are new to the concept or want to sharpen their perception, we should explain it.

10.7   Benefits of risk severity matrix

- Recognize occasion results that ought to be focused on or gathered for additional examination.
- Give a decent graphical depiction of dangers across an undertaking/task.
- Works on the gamble the executive's cycle.
- Help to recognize regions for risk decrease.
- Give a fast and somewhat economical gamble examination.
- Empower more nitty gritty examination to be centered around high-risk regions [35].

10.7.1   Cybersecurity as a pressing concern for financial organizations

Trust is the underpinning of monetary administrations. To win and maintain clients' trust, financial establishments should exhibit devotion to protecting secrecy, affirm the accessibility of frameworks and administrations, and keep up with the respectability of information. Trust has never been particularly difficult to maintain. Attacks on particular institutions have grown into attacks on the global financial system due to network security vulnerabilities. Additionally, financial institutions are transforming due to new electronic channels, computerization, and other cutting-edge advances, which bring with them new opportunities and threats. Accordingly, controllers are vigorously cantered around foundational digital gamble and the virus across firms and outsiders. Controllers additionally anticipate that monetary organizations should upgrade security assurances for clients who request their private data to be safeguarded across carefully open items and administrations.

Another way to deal with addressing online protection is required. Seeing digital gamble as a data innovation issue just misses the mark. What is called for is a coordinated network safety risk the board system, including assets and exercises of the whole association.

Our view is that online protection begins with individuals. Moreover, a fruitful methodology ought to be ability-driven, spotlight on a mindful network protection culture, and incorporate preparation and attention to be imparted in the association.

Past mindfulness, everybody plays a functioning part to play, including business leaders, chance, consistency and review experts, functional groups, lawful and others. Network protection risk the executives is a group activity and is everybody's liability, from the meeting room to the forefront.

A successful cybersecurity risk management strategy should be the following:

- **Vital and imaginative**: Having a solid navigational foundation and being prepared to adapt to and take advantage of extraordinary development
- **Risk-oversaw and focused on**: Driven by a comprehensively managed risk arrangement, risk awareness, and chance prioritizing throughout the project.
- **Astute and coordinated**: Capable of communicating real threat differentiation evidence and reactions through sound situational awareness and danger understanding.
- **Strong and adaptable**: Minimize disruptions' impact while remaining current with business development [36].

References

[1] https://cybersecurityguide.org/industries/financial/, accessed on July 11, 2022.
[2] https://gomindsight.com/insights/blog/7-cyber-security-threats-to-financial-services/, accessed on July 15, 2022.
[3] https://www.upguard.com/blog/biggest-cyber-threats-for-financial-services, accessed on July 5, 2022.
[4] https://www.contis.com/anti-bribery-and-corruption-policy/, accessed on July 4, 2022.
[5] https://www.principal.com.my/en/bribery-and-corruption, accessed on July 16, 2022.
[6] Singh, J. and Sharma, P. (2007). Tax professionals' perception of the income tax system of India: an empirical evidence.. *IUP Journal of Public Finance*, no. 1, 45–56.
[7] https://acadpubl.eu/hub/2018-119-17/1/21.pdf, accessed on July 8, 2022.
[8] https://www.fedortax.com/en/understanding-tax-fraud, accessed on July 5, 2022.

[9]   https://www.upguard.com/blog/third-party-risk-management, accessed on July 10, 2022.

[10] https://en.wikipedia.org/wiki/Insider_threat, accessed on July 9, 2022.

[11] https://www.cisa.gov/defining-insider-threats, accessed on July 14, 2022.

[12] https://www.indiaretailing.com/2022/02/17/retail/retail-cybersecurity-common-threats-and-how-to-avoid-them/, accessed on July 10, 2022.

[13] https://www.marketingtutor.net/non-store-retailing/, accessed on July 17, 2022.

[14] https://en.wikipedia.org/wiki/Market_abuse, accessed on July 21, 2022.

[15] https://www2.deloitte.com/us/en/pages/regulatory/articles/market-abuse-and-misconduct.html, accessed on July 2, 2022.

[16] https://blog.hidglobal.com/2021/06/why-credential-management-key-your-cybersecurity-strategy, accessed on July 4, 2022.

[17] https://www.ibm.com/in-en/topics/cybersecurity, accessed on July 13, 2022.

[18] https://www.cyberdegrees.org/resources/hot-technologies-cyber-security/, accessed on July 22, 2022.

[19] https://www.techtarget.com/searchsecurity/definition/Security-Operations-Center-SOC, accessed on July 19, 2022.

[20] https://digitalguardian.com/blog/what-security-operations-center-soc, accessed on July 9, 2022.

[21] https://www.techtarget.com/searchsecurity/definition/Security-Operations-Center-SOC, accessed on July 6, 2022.

[22] https://www.ibm.com/cloud/learn/network-operations-center, accessed on July 12, 2022.

[23] https://www.splunk.com/en_us/data-insider/network-operations-center.html, accessed on July 23, 2022.

[24] https://www.mdsny.com/the-cost-of-cybersecurity-and-how-to-budget-for-it/, accessed on July 8, 2022.

[25] https://www.techtarget.com/searchsecurity/definition/data-breach, accessed on July 18, 2022.

[26] https://kobalt.io/blogpost/confidentiality-integrity-and-availability-in-cyber-security/, accessed on July 6, 2022.

[27] https://imageware.io/identification-authentication-authorization-difference/, accessed on July 16, 2022.

[28] https://www.techtarget.com/searchsecurity/definition/authentication, accessed on July 2, 2022.

[29] https://www.xenonstack.com/use-cases/anomaly-detection, accessed on July 20, 2022.

[30] https://rhebo.com/en/service/glossar/anomaly-detection-en/, accessed on July 13, 2022.

[31] https://brainstation.io/career-guides/what-tools-do-cybersecurity-analysts-use, accessed on July 1, 2022.

[32] https://www.guru99.com/cybercrime-types-tools-examples.html, accessed on July 11, 2022.

[33]   https://www.aarp.org/money/scams-fraud/info-2022/tech-tools-used-by-cyber-criminals.html, accessed on July 19, 2022.

[34]   https://seon.io/resources/aml-software/, accessed on July 8, 2022.

[35]   https://www.ntaskmanager.com/blog/risk-assessment-matrix/, accessed on July 21, 2022.

[36]   https://www.ey.com/en_gl/innovation-financial-services/cybersecurity, accessed on July 15, 2022.

Chapter 11

Blockchain technology for the financial markets

*Neeti Misra[1,2], T. Joji Rao[3], Sumeet Gupta[1]
and Luke Grima[4]*

Abstract

After gaining a thorough understanding of blockchain technology's many features, such as the sound foundation of the underlying technology, its benefits, wide range of applications, as well as the security, privacy, and scalability that such technology offers, there is a clear opportunity for its adoption in India and financial markets around the world. Despite its benefits, there still exist several barriers to the technology's mainstream adoption. Moreover, there still exists a great deal of skepticism in the investing world, making it understandable that seasoned investors and hedge fund managers would choose to take a "wait and see" approach with respect to the blockchain. Nonetheless, it is clear that cryptocurrencies (and thus the underlying blockchain technology) are here for the long haul. The technology addresses many of the requirements customers desire in currency today (e.g. decentralisation, transparency, and flexibility) with potential efficiency gains that extend beyond the possibility of traditional *"fiat"* currency. Moreover, the potential benefits extend beyond its role as an alternative currency, but offer applications across a range of industries and professions over and above financial markets, including the banking and insurance sectors. Major stock exchanges are also looking at the integration of blockchain solutions into their operations, and the potential to provide virtually instantaneous settlements and automate compliance through *smart contracts*, all while providing increased security and transparency. In Banking, for example, the use of distributed ledger systems could help to develop new business models through the automation of traditional processes, reduction in potential compliance, duplication errors and thus effectively reduce costs.

This study seeks to uncover and identify some of the most fascinating aspects of blockchain technology that have paved the way for the digital currency revolution. Moreover, this study also looks into the key features and applications of such

[1]School of Business, University of Petroleum and Energy Studies, India
[2]Uttaranchal Institute of Management, Uttaranchal University, India
[3]O.P. Jindal Global University, India
[4]Department of Insurance and Risk Management, University of Malta, Malta

technology, considering the potential it offers to disrupt a wide range of businesses in both the commercial and public sectors. This was done within the context of researching how the applicability of the blockchain can be improved and help to uncover the underlying reasons causing inefficiencies or barriers to entry for the technology within the fields of financial markets, banking, and other sectors.

Keywords: Blockchain technology; Cryptocurrencies; Financial markets; Banking and insurance

11.1   Key features and main applications of blockchain technology in the financial world

A *blockchain* is a distributed digital ledger that stores data records that are constantly being updated or increasing (Fanning & Centers, 2016). A list like this is made up of numerous data blocks that are structured in Cryptographic proofs, which link and protect the data, in chronological order. In the early 1990s, computer scientist Stuart Haber and physicist W. Scott Stornetta developed the first blockchain prototype, who used cryptographic techniques in a chain of blocks to protect digital documents from manipulation (Saguato, 2017). Haber and Stornetta's work undoubtedly influenced Dave Bayer, Hal Finney, and a slew of other computer scientists and encryption aficionados, ultimately leading to the establishment of bitcoin, the world's first decentralised system of electronic money (or simply the first cryptocurrency). Under the pseudonym Satoshi Nakamoto, the Bitcoin whitepaper was published in 2008.

Although blockchain technology predates bitcoin, it serves as a working example of a decentralised, distributed, and public digital ledger that maintains a permanent record (chain of blocks) of all previously validated transactions in most cryptocurrency networks (Rodrigues *et al.*, 2015).

Transactions by blockchain take place in a globally distributed network of peer-to-peer computers (nodes). Each node maintains a copy of the blockchain and contributes to the network's security and operation (Rajnak & Puschmann, 2021). This is what distinguishes bitcoin as a decentralised digital money with no borders, no censorship, and no need for intermediation by a third party. The blockchain, as a distributed ledger technology (DLT), is purposefully designed to be very resistant to tampering and fraud (such as double-spending). This is due to the fact that the bitcoin blockchain, as a database of records, cannot be manipulated or tampered without using an excessive amount of electricity or computing capacity. Further, the network can enforce the concept of "original" digital documents, ensuring that each bitcoin is a one-of-a-kind and uncopyable type of digital cash. The consensus technique known as Proof-of-Work is what allowed bitcoin to be created as a Byzantine fault tolerance (BFT) system, this means that even if some of its members (nodes) engage in dishonest or wasteful behaviour, the blockchain can continue to function as a distributed network. The bitcoin mining process relies heavily on the Proof-of-Work consensus mechanism (Handayani *et al.*, 2020).

Blockchain technology could be adopted and used in a variety of other fields, including healthcare, insurance, supply chain, IoT, and so on. It was meant to work as a distributed ledger (on decentralised systems), but it can also be used on centralised systems to ensure data integrity or save operational costs.

The blockchain is a digital ledger of transactions that are replicated and dispersed over multiple systems, the whole network of computer systems that make up the blockchain (Yaga *et al.*, 2019). A number of transactions are contained in each block of the chain, and each time a new transaction occurs on the blockchain, a record of it is added to each participant's ledger. DLT is a decentralised database that is administered by various people.

Blockchain is a DLT in which transactions are recorded using a hash, which is a cryptographic signature that cannot be changed (Agbesi & Asante, 2019). This means that if one block in a chain is modified, it would be evident that the entire chain would have been tampered with, and therefore rejected. If hackers wanted to take down a blockchain system, they would have to modify every block in the chain, across all distributed versions of the chain.

Blockchains such as Bitcoin and Ethereum are constantly expanding as new blocks are added to the chain, drastically boosting the ledger's security.

Many attempts have been made in the past to create digital money, but they have all failed. The issue of trust is the most pressing. How can we believe that if someone invents a new currency (for the purposes of the argument, we shall refer to it as the "X dollar"), that it can be relied upon as a store of value and unit of transaction?

Bitcoin was intended to solve this problem by allowing users by utilising a blockchain, which is a type of database. A person in control of most regular databases (i.e. not a DLT), such as a SQL database, can manually make entries into such databases that could lead to fraud or misreporting (e.g. giving themselves a million X dollars). Blockchain is unique in that no one is in charge; instead, the individuals who use it, run it. Bitcoins (or other cryptocurrencies for that matter) cannot be faked, hacked, or double-spent.

11.1.1 *What is the process for a transaction to be added to the blockchain?*

A transaction must go through a number of steps before being added to the blockchain as shown in Figure 11.1. Today, we will discuss cryptographic key authentication, proof of work authorisation, the importance of mining, and the more recent use of proof of stake protocols in later blockchain networks (Nguyen *et al.*, 2019).

11.1.1.1 **Authentication**

Although the original blockchain was supposed to function without a central authority (i.e., no bank or regulator deciding who can transact), transactions must still be validated (Yaga *et al.*, 2019). This is done using cryptographic keys, which are a string of data (akin to a password) that identify a person and grant access to their "account" or "wallet" of value on the system.

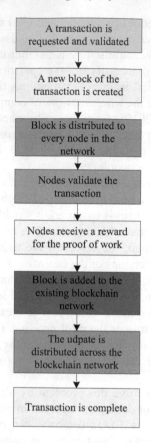

Figure 11.1   Flowchart explaining how a transaction is entered into the blockchain (Euromoney Learning, 2020).

Every user has a private key and a public key that everyone can see. When you combine the two, you have a secure digital identity that can be used to authenticate users and "unlock" transactions.

11.1.1.2   Authorisation

Before a transaction can be added to a block in the chain, it must first be authorised, or authorised, by the users. On a public blockchain, the decision to add a transaction to the chain is made by consensus. This means that the majority of "nodes" must agree to the transaction (or computers in the network). The owners of the network's equipment are compensated for confirming transactions. This approach is known as "proof-of-work."

11.1.1.3   Proof-of-Work

Proof-of-work asks the people who own the machines in the network to answer a difficult mathematical problem in order to add a block to the chain

(Yaga *et al.*, 2019). Mining is the process of finding a solution to a problem, and miners are usually paid in bitcoin.

Mining, on the other hand, is a challenging task. With a 1 in 5.9 trillion chance of winning, the mathematical challenge can only be solved through trial and error. It demands a large amount of computer capacity, which uses a large amount of energy. Because a single computer would take years to solve the mathematical problem, the benefits of mining must outweigh the expense of the computers and the electricity necessary to run them.

11.1.1.4   The Power-of-Mining

Because it would take a single computer years to solve the mathematical problem, the advantages of mining must balance the cost of the computers and the electricity required to run them. According to CIA data from 2016, Ireland (ranked 68th) utilises little over a third of bitcoin's energy use, or 25 TWh, and Austria (ranked 42nd) uses 64.6 TWh every year.

11.1.1.5   The problem with Proof-of-Work

To achieve economies of scale, miners usually pool their resources through firms that aggregate a large group of miners. The blockchain network's revenues and fees are subsequently distributed among these miners.

When more computers are added to the blockchain to try to solve the issue, the difficulty becomes harder to solve, as the network expands, further scattering the chain and making it more difficult to destroy or hack (Yaga *et al.*, 2019). However, mining power has become concentrated in the hands of a few mining pools in practice. These massive corporations now have the computing and electrical resources required to operate and build a blockchain network based on Proof-of-Work certification.

11.1.1.6   Proof-of-Stake

Later blockchain networks employed "Proof-of-Stake" validation consensus procedures, in which members must have a stake in the blockchain – generally in the form of cryptocurrency ownership – in order to be eligible to choose, verify, and validate transactions (Tosh *et al.*, 2018). This saves a large amount of processing power because no mining is necessary.

Furthermore, blockchain technology has evolved to include "Smart Contracts," which automatically execute transactions when certain criteria are met.

Blockchain is the technology that underpins the cryptocurrency bitcoin, but it is not the only distributed ledger system that uses it. Other cryptocurrencies have their own versions of the blockchain and distributed ledger. Meanwhile, the decentralisation of the technology has resulted in various schisms or forks inside the bitcoin network, resulting in offshoots of the ledger in which some miners use one set of rules and others use a different set of rules.

Bitcoin Cash, Bitcoin Gold, and Bitcoin SV are all variants of the original bitcoin cryptocurrency. These cryptocurrency blockchains are more vulnerable to hacking attacks, such as the one that damaged Bitcoin Gold in 2018.

11.1.2　Types of blockchain

There are four different types of blockchain structures to choose from the following.

11.1.2.1　Public blockchains

Public blockchains are permissionless and entirely decentralised, allowing anybody to participate (Chen & Bellavitis, 2019). All nodes of the blockchain have equal rights to access the network, create new blocks of data, and validate blocks of data in public blockchains.

Currently, public blockchains are mostly utilised for bitcoin exchange and mining. Popular public blockchains like Bitcoin, Ethereum, and Litecoin may be familiar to you. On these public blockchains, nodes "mine" for cryptocurrency by solving cryptographic equations to create blocks for the transactions requested on the network. The miner nodes are compensated for their efforts with a tiny amount of bitcoin. The miners are essentially modern-day bank tellers who formulate transactions and are compensated (or "mined") for their labour.

11.1.2.2　Private (or managed) blockchains

Governed blockchains, sometimes known as private blockchains, are permissioned blockchains managed by a single entity (Dinh *et al.*, 2017). In a private blockchain, the central authority selects who can be a node. Furthermore, the central authority does not necessarily provide each node the same permissions to perform functions. Private blockchains are only partially decentralised since public access to them is restricted. Private blockchains include Ripple, a business-to-business virtual currency exchange network, and Hyperledger, an umbrella project for open-source blockchain applications.

Blockchains, both private and public, have drawbacks: the validation of new data takes longer on public blockchains than on private blockchains, while private blockchains are more vulnerable to fraud and bad actors. To address these issues, consortia and hybrid blockchains were developed.

11.1.2.3　Consortium blockchains

Unlike private blockchains, consortium blockchains are permissioned blockchains managed by a group of organisations rather than a single one. As a result, consortium blockchains are more decentralised than private blockchains, increasing security (Dib *et al.*, 2018). However, forming consortiums can be a difficult process because it necessitates collaboration among a number of firms, which poses logistical obstacles as well as the risk of antitrust violations (which we will examine in an upcoming chapter). Furthermore, some supply chain participants may lack the appropriate technology or infrastructure to implement blockchain technologies, while others may determine that the upfront expenditures of digitising their data and interacting with other supply chain members is too high a price to pay.

R3, a corporate software company, has created a popular set of blockchain consortia solutions for the financial services industry and beyond (Zachariadis *et al.*, 2019). The Global Shipping Business Network Collaboration was founded by

ArgoSmart as a non-profit blockchain consortium with the goal of digitising the shipping sector and allowing maritime industry operators to communicate more effectively.

11.1.2.4 Hybrid blockchains

Hybrid blockchains are those that are managed by a single entity but have some oversight from the public blockchain, which is necessary to conduct certain transaction validations (Di Silvestre *et al.*, 2020). IBM Food Trust is an example of a hybrid blockchain, which was created to improve efficiency across the whole food supply chain. In a subsequent piece in this series, we will go through IBM Food Trust in further depth.

11.1.3 Features of blockchain technology

To truly comprehend the main characteristics of blockchain, we must first deconstruct the hype and go into the details. What exactly is a blockchain? Blockchain, according to the majority of observers, is the technology that underpins Bitcoin. In January 2009, the mysterious Satoshi Nakamoto launched the revolutionary cryptocurrency, dubbed "digital gold" (Goforth, 2019). By January 2018, it had risen to an all-time high of USD 19,783, equivalent to 15 ounces of real gold.

The first successful application of blockchain is to power cryptocurrency. Let us take a look at some of the characteristics that make blockchain ideal for digital currency and maybe many other applications. A blockchain is a cryptographically hashed linked list in computer engineering jargon (Pilkington, 2016).

11.1.3.1 As a data structure, blockchain technology

A blockchain is a growing database of data that is organised into virtual blocks. Bitcoin transactions are recorded in the blockchain of bitcoin. The genesis block, which is the first block in the structure, is the starting point. More blocks are added to the system as the amount of data captured on it grows (Boons *et al.*, 2013). Each block in the series is linked to the one before it, all the way back to the beginning. The ingenious name for this sort of data structure comes from the "chain" of blocks (Di Silvestre *et al.*, 2020).

It is worth noting that linked list data structures like this have been explored and utilised in information technology for decades. Many word and photo processing apps produce progressively linked stacks of data, allowing users to "undo" the most current state and return to the prior state (Deuber *et al.*, 2019).

However, as we will see in the following section, the blockchain is often meant to be immutable, irreversible, and tamper-proof.

11.1.3.2 Blockchain immutability and tamper detection

Cryptography is used to make data on the blockchain safe and unchangeable. A cryptographic hash function generates a unique string of characters that is used to refer to each block. This function can take any amount of data as input and produce a string of a certain length (Apostolaki *et al.*, 2017). A hash is a fixed-length output. Each block is linked to the one before it by storing the parent block's hash (known as the parent block). The fact that even little changes in the input result in completely different hash outputs is one of the most apparent properties of the hash function. As a result, any changes to the contents of a block will affect the hash of the block (Hartmann *et al.*, 2019). Also keep in mind that each block, all the way to the genesis block, stores the hash of the parent block. As a result, tampering with data in any block on the blockchain will alter the hash of all following blocks. An observer may detect manipulation at any point on the blockchain in this fashion, without having to verify the contents of every single block (Aheleroff *et al.*, 2021). Beyond digital currencies, we can see how this may be quite useful. Tamper detection like this can be beneficial in checking an online database of valuable physical assets like real estate and art. As we will see in the following part, data recorded in blockchain is further secured by employing private/public pairs of digital keys.

11.1.3.3   Data security in the blockchain

Every unit of bitcoin is saved on the blockchain itself, rather than in a physical or online account that must be managed by a third party (such as a bank) (Mıhçak & Venkatesan, 2001). Users may access bitcoins using their private/public key pairs in a safe manner. Only a customer's private keys may be used to spend or transfer bitcoins, but a merchant's public keys can be shared with the consumer to receive bitcoins (Handayani *et al.*, 2020). The transaction is deemed permanent once it has been propagated over the internet and put in a block. After that, the merchant may unmistakably claim possession of bitcoins. She can also spend those bitcoins and other digital assets using her own private keys.

In most cases, the blockchain is saved and maintained on many devices. The bitcoin blockchain is stored on thousands of machines throughout the world (Hossain *et al.*, 2015). As a result, even if one or more of the devices are compromised due to an attack or network faults, the data remains safe (Ducas & Wilner, 2017).

In the next part, we will go over this important element of the blockchain in more detail.

11.1.3.4   Technology based on distributed ledgers

We will now discuss the distributed ledger of data, which is possibly the most well-known feature of the blockchain. The ledger can be shared with a small group of users over a local area network, or with thousands of people via the internet (Ali *et al.*, 2016). Every time a new block is created, a message is sent out to guarantee that all users have the most recent version of the ledger. This feature is useful for more than just digital currencies since it eliminates the requirement for a trusted central entity to keep track of the data. Stock markets, real estate transactions, personal identity, and many more areas are ready for decentralisation (Hegde *et al.*, n.d.).

Because the ledger is maintained on many storage devices, maybe in separate locations, it protects the system against data loss in the event that one or more devices or servers fail (Goforth, 2019). Other users can continue to view and upload information to the blockchain as long as there is at least one online device running the most recent version (Rajnak & Puschmann, 2021).

Next, we will look at how cryptography helps blockchain attain relative user anonymity.

11.1.3.5   User anonymity

On the blockchain, just the digital addresses with associated units are typically displayed, keeping user identities private. The blockchain may be disseminated around the globe while keeping relative anonymity thanks to the usage of pub public cryptography. Because all transactions are forever recorded on the block-chain, we use the term "relative" (Handayani *et al.*, 2020). Because the bitcoin blockchain is public, if a user's bitcoin address is known, her transaction history may be tracked. Other digital currencies have dealt with this problem by employing a variety of algorithms, each of which provides a varying amount of anonymity to its users (Novo, 2018).

Since the 1970s, public-key cryptography has been utilised in digital currency. Nonetheless, for the first time in history, the intelligent use of encryption in conjunction with the blockchain-enabled viable decentralised currencies (Pakhchanyan, 2016).

11.1.3.6   Solution to double spending using blockchain

The possibility of a user spending the same units twice is known as double spending. This is similar to sending a message to numerous people on Whatsapp (the popular messaging software) (Yaga *et al.*, 2019). It is possible that the recipients have no idea how many others have received the identical letter. While this is not a problem in Whatsapp (in fact, it is a feature), it might be disastrous when sending money or stocks. If we could sell the same painting or residence to several bidders, those assets would be practically useless. This is why clearing houses have been permitted to settle stock market deals (Nguyen *et al.*, 2019).

Bitcoin came up with a clever solution by combining a decentralised ledger with a consensus mechanism that allows users to vote on whether legitimate transactions should be included in the most recent block (Dagher *et al.*, 2018). After the block has been sent around the network, anybody may check to see if the user genuinely possesses the money they want to spend.

It is simple to see how the blockchain's distributed ledger feature may assist disrupt a wide range of industries that presently rely on massive, inefficient central machines (Baier & Breitinger, 2011).

11.1.4   Blockchain technology's power and its revolutionary applications in the financial sector

Even in its infancy, blockchain technology has demonstrated its power to revolutionise various industries. Decentralisation, transparency, and immutability are appealing to businesses all across the world, but finance is leading the way in terms of implementation.

In the financial industry, this underlying technology enables cash transfers to be made with the assurance that the transaction is safe and secure.

The banking and finance industries profit from features in a variety of ways. Here are some examples of how businesses are using blockchain to their advantage:

11.1.4.1 Money transfers

Consumers and financial institutions face numerous obstacles and challenges when transferring money to other countries. Every year, people transmit billions of dollars throughout the world, yet the procedure is frequently costly, time-consuming, and error-prone.

All of this could change thanks to blockchain technology. Many large banks have used blockchain technology for international payments, which saves time and money. Consumers can also use blockchain money transfers to perform electronic transactions with their mobile devices, bypassing the time-consuming practise of visiting a money transfer facility, waiting in line, and paying transaction fees.

11.1.4.2 Inexpensive, direct payments

The majority of money passes through financial institutions like banks and credit card processing centres. Each of these stages adds a degree of complexity to the process, as well as expenses that may mount up quickly.

The following are some of the advantages of blockchain-based transfers for merchants:

Reduced fees: When customers pay with a credit card, businesses are charged processing fees, which eat into their profit margins. By simplifying the transfer procedure, blockchain payments cut or eliminate fees.

Insufficient funds were eliminated: Customers occasionally pay for goods or services with a bad check, resulting in a loss and additional penalties for merchants, as well as the prospect of a legal battle to reclaim the cash. Merchants can have confidence in blockchain-based payments because they can know the transaction is complete in a matter of seconds or minutes.

Individuals profit from blockchain-based transfers in the following ways:

Fewer online scams: While many people are concerned about online scams, blockchain-based payments are instantaneous and reversible. They are also less expensive than banking services, particularly for expensive things.

Cash, wire transfers, and cashier's cheques are the safest payment options, however cash is untraceable, wire transfers are time-consuming, and cashier's cheques can be falsified. All of these issues are eliminated with blockchain-based payments, resulting in increased trust.

11.1.4.3 Transaction details

Blockchain can revolutionise banking in more ways than just money transfers. Blockchain is a fantastic way to keep track of transactions and ensure accurate, secure data, such as:

Details on the title: It is practically impossible to change a distributed ledger, making it easier to track ownership. Transfers of ownership and liens can use the ledger to check information, resulting in increased trust.

Smart contracts: Transactions can be expensive, complicated, and time-consuming, but blockchain allows for automation. Smart contracts can keep track of when a buyer pays and when a seller delivers, as well as any issues that arise along the way. Automated systems also eliminate human mistake and are available 24 h a day, 7 days a week.

11.2   Modern banking ledger with blockchain technology

In this part, we examine topics that may be relevant to the banking and insurance industries, as well as how blockchain technology might assist them.

The blockchain technology has the ability to replace the role of third parties involved in the financial transactions in various sectors like stock markets, insurance intermediaries such as custodian, payment providers, risk poolers, and insurers, in a variety of financial activities (Kshetri, 2017). Remember that the primary functions of such trusted third parties are to provide functionality such as trade transaction validation, prevention of duplicate transactions, the so-called "double spending" issue, transaction recording in the event of contract settlements or deliverables disputes, and acting as agents on behalf of associates or members (Boons *et al.*, 2013). Through the provision of a verifiable public record of all transactions that are distributed and may be decentralised in its administration, the blockchain can give alternative ways to fulfil these functions (Pilkington, 2016). When considering the possible applications of blockchain technology in the banking sector, there are a number of alternative options to consider that go beyond traditional remittance services. Back-end accounting systems, which store client account data, transaction processing systems, such as cash machine networks, all the way through trading and sales, over-the-counter transactions, and interbank money transfer systems are all part of banking systems, which are big and complicated (Ducas & Wilner, 2017). The following are some of the domains where blockchain technology can be used:

- financial ledgers that are automated, decentralised, and distributed;
- Over-the-counter (OTC) contracts/products that are automated and disseminated, as well as clearing and settlement;
- account reconciliations for clients that are automated; and
- loss data reporting that is automated and disseminated.

The decrease of overhead and expenses associated with audit and regulation is one of the possible incentives for financial institutions, banks, insurers, and banking regulators to create distributed blockchain technology for these sorts of applications (Christidis & Devetsikiotis, 2016). Furthermore, increased automation and efficiency in transaction processing, clearing, and reconciliation can assist to mitigate counterparty credit risks.

Before we get into particular instances, there are a few key characteristics that all blockchain initiatives have in common, which may be both advantageous and destructive. As we have seen in earlier discussions on data integrity preservation, they demand careful attention while creating the applications to be presented.

11.2.1   The blockchain's itemised components are immutable

A blockchain is an immutable distributed transaction database or ledger, in which data saved in the blockchain cannot be updated, erased, or amended (Liu *et al.*, 2017). However, certain blockchain systems, such as the Enigma project mentioned above, are beginning to emerge that challenge the notion of immutability. This solution tackles the irreversibility of the conventional blockchain architecture by only allowing reversible and regulated access to data for safe calculations. They also ensure that the raw data is never seen by anybody other than the original data owner(s).

11.2.2   The blockchain's data is transparent

Several blockchains being developed are open to anybody with an Internet connection and are duplicated many times on participating nodes in the network, while private versions or limited blockchain networks are also emerging, as previously noted. The question is how much private vs. public functionality is required by the application (Aheleroff *et al.*, 2021). There are numerous competing constraints in modern regulatory changes on banking and financial institutions that emphasise both the importance of financial disclosure, such as Pillar III of Basel III banking regulations, which requires financial institutions to demonstrate transparency in their reporting and relationships with regulators, and there are also fiduciary duties that institutions maintain in upholding data privacy on behalf of their customers (Kosba *et al.*, 2016). As a result, alternate ways to private vs. public blockchain networks are being investigated, in which data on a public ledger may have varying degrees of data integrity structure protocols that enable features like data encryption in blockchains.

11.3   Blockchain and banking business models

In management studies, business models (BMs) are a relatively recent notion. Despite the lack of a precise definition, a BM has been defined as the "narrative that describes how an enterprise works" or the "how businesses do business." A BM, according to Osterwalder and Pigneur, is "the logic of how an organisation generates, delivers, and acquires value." In addition to the notions of value, strategy, and process, BM research has revealed a strong link with technology. Technological advancements by themselves do not guarantee a firm's success. A BM is essential for gaining a competitive edge and mediating between technological advancements and the creation of economic value, as well as business performance. Capturing the value of an innovation and ensuring its commercial success are both vital. When evaluating the introduction of technological innovations in a certain industry, the link between BMs and technology becomes even more important (Berdik *et al.*, 2021). The financial services industry's present BMs are expected to be reshaped by blockchain technology. Despite the fact that blockchain is frequently regarded as a strategic technology, research on its impact on BMs is still scarce This study develops a hypothesis model that links IT innovations to three generic bank value disciplines: "operational excellence," "customer intimacy," and "product leadership," as well as four generic BM elements: "what," "who," "how," and "value." A BM serves as a bridge between IT innovation and the rest of the world (Mavilia & Pisani, 2020).

In a nutshell, a BM is a company's plan or strategy for selling a product or service and profiting from it. A blockchain BM embodies all three key characteristics of blockchain technology: it is decentralised, based on peer-to-peer transactions, and operates within a trusted and secure network. The same is true for blockchain-based financial BMs.

Building on the BM Canvas framework developed by Osterwalder and Pigneur (*Business Model Generation: A Handbook for Visionaries, Game-Changers, and Challengers*. John Wiley & Sons, 2010). Blockchain technology has the potential to impact all aspects of a bank's BM and perhaps lead to new banking BMs.

The research is required which develops a hypothesis model that links IT breakthroughs to banks' three generic value disciplines: "operational excellence," "customer intimacy," and "product leadership" as well as the four generic elements of BMs "what", "who", "how," and "value." A BM serves as a bridge between IT innovation and the rest of the world.

The implementation of blockchain's distributed ledger system could uncover benefits by automating procedures and decreasing compliance errors. A blockchain-based registry would not only eliminate duplication of effort in performing KYC, but it would also allow for encrypted updates to client information to be sent in near real-time to all banks. In addition, for each client, the ledger would give a historical record of all papers shared and compliance activities completed. Should authorities seek clarifications, this record could be used to show that a bank behaved in compliance with the obligations imposed on it. It would also be useful in recognising entities that are attempting to build false histories. The data within it may even be analyzed by banks to discover abnormalities or foul play—may directly targeting criminal activity—subject to the provisions of data privacy rules.

11.3.1 The top 5 blockchain applications in banking

Blockchain is a decentralised, open ledger that records transactions between two parties (Hamilton, 2020). A blockchain is made up of individual data blocks that include a series of linked transactions in a specific order. All parties involved can share a digital ledger across a computer network without the need for a centralised authority or middlemen. As a result, blockchain transactions are executed more swiftly.

11.3.2 Benefits of blockchain for banking

Blockchain technology has the potential to change the way people do business all around the world (Tapscott & Tapscott, 2017). It can increase trade efficiency by automating and streamlining manual and paper-based processes. Because it is decentralised and cannot be possessed by a single individual, a public blockchain can be an excellent tool for collaboration. As a result, blockchain is more than merely the technology that underpins cryptocurrencies such as Bitcoin and Ethereum.

11.3.3   Five blockchain application examples in banking

11.3.3.1   Funds raising

Today, raising funds through venture capital is a difficult task. The typical situation is as follows: entrepreneurs develop decks, meet with partners on multiple occasions, and engage in extensive conversations about value and equity—all in the hopes of selling their firm for cash.

Companies that use blockchain technology can speed up the process by acquiring capital in a variety of methods. Initial Exchange Offerings (IEOs), Equity Token Offerings (ETOs), and Security Token Offerings (STOs) are all examples of this (STOs). Because of its legal protection, STO has been the most preferred alternative (Di Silvestre *et al.*, 2020).

11.3.3.2   Payment in a shorter time

Improved client satisfaction is a guaranteed thing when it comes to faster payments and lower processing fees. As a result, BFSI institutions should rely on developing technologies by providing a decentralised payment channel. Banks may be able to provide better service, develop new products, and eventually compete with innovative fintech start-ups by offering better security and reduced payment fees. Furthermore, banks will be able to decrease the need for third-party verification and speed up the processing of typical bank transactions by integrating blockchain.

11.3.3.3   System of settlement and clearance

Traditional technologies such as SWIFT have the potential to allow banks to settle transactions immediately and keep better track of them than blockchain (Deuber *et al.*, 2019). Because of the way our financial system is set up, a regular bank transfer takes a few days to settle.

Many banks face logistical challenges when it comes to moving money around the world. Before reaching its destination, a simple bank transfer must transit through a complex chain of middlemen, such as custodial services. Bank accounts must also be reconciled across the global financial system, which includes a vast network of funds, asset managers, dealers, and other companies.

11.3.3.4   Finance for international trade

Trade financing is another area where blockchain is predicted to have a large impact. Trade finance encompasses all financial activities connected to international trade and commerce. Did you know that many trade finance transactions still employ invoices, letters of credit, and bills? You can accomplish this work online with several order management systems, but it takes a long time.

By digitising and removing the time-consuming manual method, blockchain can help to streamline the trading process.

11.3.3.5 Credits and loans

To underwrite loans, traditional financial institutions use a credit reporting system. With the help of blockchain, we can see the future of peer-to-peer lending, as well as faster and more secure loan processes in general, and even complicated programmed loans that mimic syndicated loan structures or mortgages (Dashottar & Srivastava, 2021).

Credit scores, homeownership status, and debt-to-income ratio are used by banks to assess risk while processing loan applications. To acquire all of that information, they will require your credit report from specialised credit agencies.

11.3.3.6 How will blockchain transform the future of the banking sector

If we talk about the working of the conventional banking system, all banks have their private portal for online banking and Internet banking, all user details are secured in the core bank solution portal. NPCI has made an online platform named NFS (National Financial Switch). For all online transactions, the data has got transferred through NFS and it is a kind of verifying decoder and transferred to the core banking portal.

For ECS, NEFT, RTGS, Credit cards transactions, or UPI transactions, all methods are following the same system. So, in this situation, all banks maintain their own private portal servers that may lead to issues such as the problem of duplication of maintenance cost of these systems, as well as bandwidth and speed issues. Further, should the NFS get hacked, it would compromise the data of the entire system. In turn, this would result in much higher data recovery costs and difficulties. Alternatively, through blockchain technology, all that data will be saved at one public ledger where old data cannot be deleted, new entries would be secure, decentralised, and can be used by multiple stakeholders.

DLT is a kind of public record where anyone can enter and others connected to that system will know about that change. So, in banking, the blockchain is beneficial in many aspects which include remittance, loan, finance, stock exchange, credit rating, for record tracking decentralised system is available, time will be reduced, it will enhance security.

In 2016, the ICICI started cross-border remittance with Emirates Bank using blockchain, later the same will be used by Yes Bank and Axis Bank.

Blockchain must meet a number of criteria before becoming a mainstream banking technology. It is critical to start by putting in place the infrastructure required to run a global network using matched solutions. Blockchain will only be able to disrupt the industry if it is widely used.

The investment, on the other hand, will pay off handsomely. Blockchain is expected to help banks to process payments more rapidly and accurately while also cutting transaction processing costs once fully adopted.

11.3.3.7   Enhanced information payments

Payment for enhanced information banking institutions can gain important insights by supplementing payment data. As shown in Figure 11.2, how the payment transaction could be completed with the help of blockchain technology. In both commercial and retail banking, rich data directly associated with payment can provide streamlined processes (e.g., automated reconciliations for net settlements of multiple invoices in wholesale banking, known as information settlement), KYC (e.g., linking key regulatory documents associated with an individual to his payment history), and many other use cases where any type of document can be associated with payment (payslips, contracts, invoices, etc). It is now possible to upload a file during a payment transaction thanks to the improved data use case. The sender will upload the file along with the payment information. A hash of the encrypted data is formed once the file is encrypted. The hash reference is preserved in a shared distributed file system, while the encrypted file is saved on the blockchain transaction. The hash pointer allows the transaction to stay "light" on the blockchain and provide high throughput because the file data is stored outside of the blockchain ledger. Boost information payments can be used as the foundation for a range of more complex use cases, such as domestic trade finance, where a transaction and associated documentation are handled together, and it can be expanded to a variety of other scenarios.

New services, revenue arrangements, and, eventually, new BMs are all being influenced by blockchain. Blockchain technology illustrates disruptive market characteristics because it now provides features that may appear unusual or inconvenient at first, but which in the long run, In the long run, will transform and

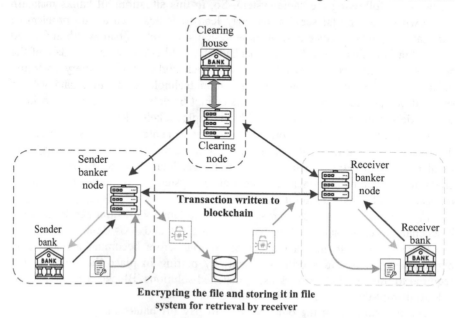

Figure 11.2   Example of blockchain technology in use for settlement and clearing (IDRBT White Paper, 2017).

impact the industry. New technologies have the potential to upset industrial equilibria, particularly by undermining the service logic and revenue structures that have been developed (Pakhchanyan, 2016). Banks and other financial institutions in the payments industry must reconsider their existing BMs and make room for experimentation. In order to prepare for the coming of blockchains, these companies must better examine the effects on their current services and products, based on the technology's ongoing development. Incumbent financial institutions may be better equipped to benefit from Fintechs' dynamism by collaborating with them, avoiding the need for significant and risky investments until a clear path for the technology's development has developed. A few financial institutions have already implemented such a method, as evidenced by the first cross-currency transaction executed by some international banks and the fintech Ripple (Goel *et al.*, 2019). The impact of technology will be seen in the business processes of the companies.

11.3.3.8   Benefits of blockchain technology in finance

Following are the various benefits of blockchain technology in the finance sector.

Inclusion of financial resources

The low costs of blockchain allow startups to compete with large banks, boosting financial inclusivity (De Filippi & Lavayssière, 2020). Because of constraints such as minimum balance requirements, limited access, and banking fees, many consumers are looking for alternatives to banks. Blockchain could give a hassle-free alternative to traditional banking that relies on digital identity and mobile devices.

Fraud is less prevalent

Blockchain keeps track of transactions in a ledger, with each block including a unique hash that links to the preceding block. Every member of the network gets a copy of the transactions as well. Blockchain technology is resistant to distributed denial-of-service attacks, hackers, and other sorts of fraud because of these qualities.

Without the possibility of cyber assaults, the cost of doing business is decreased, saving money and stress for all parties involved.

Cryptocurrency

Digital currencies are the latest wave of blockchain-based assets (Sandner *et al.*, 2020). Despite the fact that digital currency is already in use, blockchain businesses are decreasing the entry barrier by allowing for a seamless exchange of the most popular cryptocurrencies as a banking alternative.

Despite the numerous rules and regulations that govern banking, more and more financial organisations are recognising the promise of blockchain technology and cryptocurrencies. We will see more blockchain-based solutions for transparent, accessible, and dependable financial transactions as the big players in these industries perform experiments to uncover fresh use cases and opportunities.

11.4   Inherent drawbacks of digital currencies such as bitcoin

Recognise the dangers connected with digital currencies, both in terms of currency and in terms of business. A digital currency's distinguishing feature is the fact that it is not issued by a centralised authority, making it potentially immune to government intervention or manipulation. However, this also implies that it may be subject to higher levels of risk in that it is not backed by any singular physical asset and retail depositors are not insured against the loss in value of the cryptocurrency or default of an exchange. To comprehend the dangers of digital currency, one must first comprehend the characteristics of the platform (blockchain) on which it is built. All cryptocurrency transactions are recorded on a blockchain, which is a digitised, decentralised public ledger. It lets market participants keep track of digital currency transactions without having to rely on central recordkeeping since it is constantly increasing as "completed" blocks (the most recent transactions) are recorded and added to it in chronological sequence. A copy of the blockchain is sent to each node (computer linked to the network) obtains a copy of the blockchain, which is automatically downloaded.

11.4.1   Drawback 1: scalability

The scalability issues that cryptocurrencies pose are probably the most serious ones. While the number of digital currencies continues to grow, and their usage is fast growing, it is still dwarfed by the number of transactions processed each day by payment behemoth VISA. Furthermore, unless the infrastructure delivering these technologies is widely scaled, cryptocurrencies will not be able to compete on the same level as players like VISA and Mastercard in terms of transaction speed. It is tough to carry out such an evolution in a smooth manner. However, several have already offered many solutions to address the scalability issue, including lightning networks, sharing, and staking.

11.4.2   Drawback 2: issues with cybersecurity

Digital technology is vulnerable to security breaches and may fall into the hands of hackers. We have already seen proof of this, with many ICOs being hacked this summer, costing investors hundreds of millions of dollars (one of these hacks alone resulted in a $473 million loss). Mitigating this will necessitate ongoing security infrastructure maintenance, but several firms are already dealing with it head-on and employing advanced cybersecurity measures that go beyond those employed in traditional banking.

11.4.3   Drawback 3: price fluctuation and a lack of inherent value

Price volatility, which is related to a lack of intrinsic value, is a major problem and was noted by Buffet a few weeks ago when he called the bitcoin ecosystem a bubble. Although it is a real issue, it can be resolved by expressly tying the value of cryptocurrencies to both tangible and intangible commodities (as we have seen some new players do with diamonds or energy derivatives). Consumer confidence should increase as adoption increases, and volatility should decrease.

11.4.4   Drawback 4: regulations and policies

It does not make sense, Mr. Buffet said in his speech, which was the finest way to put it. There are no regulations for this. There is no control over it. The United

States Federal Reserve or any other central bank are not in charge of overseeing it. I have no faith in anything about this. It is going to implode, in my opinion.

Investment in this technology will be riskier until it is adopted by federal governments and regulated, even if we perfect the technology and resolve all of the issues mentioned above.

Most of the other technology difficulties are logistical in nature. For instance, updating protocols, which is necessary as technology advances, may take a while and obstruct daily operations.

The drawbacks and obstacles that can limit the widespread adoption of blockchain technology and digital currencies like bitcoin and Ethereum must be understood and acknowledged.

11.5   Potential drawbacks to using cryptocurrencies and DLTs

There are drawbacks to using bitcoin, just as there are to any other currency.

11.5.1   Bitcoins are not accepted across the board

Bitcoin is still only accepted by a modest handful of Internet businesses. As a result, it is impossible to rely only on bitcoins as a medium of exchange. Governments may even force merchants to cease taking bitcoins in order to track their customers' transactions.

11.5.2   Wallets can be misplaced

If a hard drive crashes or a virus corrupts data, and the wallet file is corrupted, bitcoins are effectively "lost." There is nothing that can be done to reclaim it. These coins will be orphaned in the system for the rest of their lives. This has the ability to wipe out a large Bitcoin investment in a matter of seconds, with no way to recover. The investor's coins will also be orphaned for good.

11.5.3   The value of bitcoin fluctuates

Bitcoin's value is continually fluctuating based on demand. On June 2, 2011, a popular bitcoin exchange site valued one bitcoin at $9.9. It was only 6 months ago that it was valued at less than $1. Because of the frequent fluctuation, Bitcoin accepting sites will have to adjust their prices on a regular basis. If a product refund is issued, it will also cause a lot of uncertainty. For example, if a t-shirt was purchased for 1.5 BTC and returned a week later, should 1.5 BTC be refunded despite the fact that the value has increased, or should the new amount (calculated according to the current value) be sent? When evaluating valuations, which currency should BTC be pegged to? These are still critical issues that the government must address.

11.5.4   There is no buyer protection

When products are purchased using bitcoins and the seller fails to deliver the goods, there is no way to reverse the transaction. This difficulty can be handled by employing a third-party escrow service such as ClearCoin, however escrow services would then take on the role of banks, making bitcoins more like traditional currencies.

11.5.5 Technical flaws that are not known

The bitcoin system may have weaknesses that have yet to be discovered. Because this is a relatively new system, if bitcoins were extensively accepted and a fault was discovered, it might result in enormous wealth for the exploiter at the expense of the bitcoin economy.

11.5.6 Deflation is built-in

Because the total quantity of bitcoins is limited to 21 million, deflation will occur. As the overall number of bitcoins reaches its limit, each bitcoin will become increasingly valuable. Early adopters will be rewarded under this scheme. The dilemma of when to spend bitcoins becomes more significant as the value of each bitcoin rises with each passing day. This could result in spending spikes, causing the bitcoin economy to change swiftly and unpredictably.

11.5.7 There is no physical form

Bitcoins cannot be used in physical stores since they do not have a physical form. It would have to be converted to other currencies on a regular basis. There have been proposals for cards that contain bitcoin wallet information, however, there is no consensus on which approach to use. Due to the many competing systems, shops would find it impossible to support all bitcoin cards, forcing consumers to convert bitcoins anyway unless a universal method is suggested and implemented.

11.5.8 There is no guarantee of valuation

Because bitcoins are not governed by a central authority, no one can guarantee their minimum value. If a substantial number of merchants decide to "dump" bitcoins and abandon the system, its value will plummet, hurting users who have huge sums of money invested in the currency. Bitcoin's decentralised nature is both a blessing and a burden.

The following are the features of this technology platform:

Immutable: There is no way to undo a transaction after it has been confirmed; there is no safety net. Anonymous transactions and accounts are not linked to real-world identities; instead, everything is digitalised and accessible via the internet.

Global speed: In the network, transactions are almost instantaneous and confirmed in a matter of minutes. They are absolutely unaffected by your actual location because they take place in a global network of computers. Verification and validation are carried out without the involvement of any third parties.

Secure: This system is impossible to break due to strong encryption and the magic of large numbers.

No Gatekeeper: The software is available for free download to everyone. You can receive and transmit bitcoins and other cryptocurrencies once you have installed it.

As a result, we understand that the currency's inherent unique material risks result as follows:

Business risk

Loss of faith in digital currencies: Because of their embryonic nature, digital currencies are fraught with risk. Speculators wanting to benefit from the short- or long-term holding of digital currencies have flocked to online platforms in droves. Cryptocurrencies are not backed by a central bank, a national or international organisation, assets, or other forms of credit, and their value is solely determined by the value that market participants place on them through their transactions, which means that a loss of confidence could result in a drop in value.

Cyber/fraud risk

Because cryptocurrency is effectively a cash currency, it has attracted a significant number of criminals who can hack into cryptocurrency exchanges, drain cryptocurrency wallets, and infect individual computers with malware that steals money. As more and more transactions take place over the Internet, hackers use spoofing/phishing and malware to target people, service handling, and storage regions. To protect purchased cryptocurrencies from theft, investors must rely on the strength of their own computer security systems, as well as security measures provided by third parties.

Furthermore, bitcoin relies heavily on unregulated businesses, some of which may lack adequate internal controls and hence be more vulnerable to fraud and theft than regulated financial institutions. In addition, the software must be updated on a regular basis and may be questionable at times. Buying blockchain technology from suppliers could expose you to a lot of third-party risk.

There is very little that can be done if the keys to a user's wallet are taken. The thief may fully mimic the original owner of the account and has access to the same funds in the wallet as the original owner.

Once the bitcoins have been transferred out of the account and the transaction has been committed to the block chain, the original owner will never see those funds again.

Operational risk

With a centralised clearing house ensuring a transaction's authenticity comes the power to reverse a monetary transaction in a coordinated manner; with a cryptocurrency, this is not feasible. This lack of permeance is further proven by the fact that bitcoin accounts are cryptographically encrypted, which means that if the "keys" to an account are lost or stolen, and then erased from the owner, access to the funds in the account is almost certainly lost or stolen as well.

Regulatory/compliance risk

Despite the worldwide implications, certain nations may prohibit the usage of the currency or declare that transactions violate anti-money laundering legislation. A single AML strategy does not exist due to the complexity and decentralised structure of bitcoin, as well as the large number of participants—senders, recipients (potentially launderers), processors (mining and trading platforms), and currency exchanges.

Market risks

Because the currency trades only on demand, the market risks are unique. Because the currency is limited in supply, it may face liquidity issues, and low ownership may render it vulnerable to market manipulation. Furthermore, due to its limited acceptance and lack of alternatives, the money can appear to be more volatile than other real currencies, with speculative demand fueling volatility and hoarding exacerbating it. Therefore, posing an inherent material risk to the business.

Many of the currency's particular intrinsic hazards appear and harm the business, creating an additional layer of risk.

Additional hazards include the costs of risk mitigation in terms of regulatory risk compliance. Anti-money laundering and privacy rules would have to be followed on a local as well as a global level, requiring a complex system of checks and balances. Moreover, institutions may be prosecuted by a variety of jurisdictional law enforcement agencies, each with their own agenda, for failing to comply with the numerous municipal and state laws.

The competitiveness risk is high since firms will need to accommodate and expand their offering to include all payment transmissions, which would necessitate a significant adjustment to all existing systems and infrastructure. Furthermore, these system changes would need to be kept up to date on a regular basis and be compatible with the company's delivery system as well as that of its various third-party providers.

The tax risk is significant because US citizens may attempt to avoid tax requirements such as the FBAR (Report of Foreign Bank and Financial Accounts) submission by keeping funds abroad in an unusual manner. Institutions that enable this circumvention, whether knowingly or unknowingly, may face sanctions and/or fines. The conversion or de-conversion of currency, as well as the reporting of these instructions, could result in additional company liabilities.

Cryptocurrencies are undeniably here to stay as technology progresses (Hassani *et al.*, 2019). It will take time for the public to adopt and trust the currency, but the risks will stay the same, with some looking to be more serious and elevated than previously for both the currency and the business.

11.6 Fraud detection and claims management using blockchain management

The term "blockchain" refers to a decentralised shared ledger that is impenetrable to alteration (Rajnak & Puschmann, 2021). It allows certified contributors to store, examine, and exchange in a secure environment, digital data which aids in the development of trust, accountability, and transparency in business relationships. To take advantage of these mentioned advantages, businesses are now looking at how blockchain technology may be utilised to avoid fraud in a variety of industries.

11.6.1 Three features of blockchain which prevents frauds

The following are the three primary aspects that make blockchain technology an excellent alternative for combating fraud.

11.6.1.1 Distributed networks

A distributed digital ledger, or blockchain, is a system for storing data that is shared among computers and reconciled on a regular basis (Ducas & Wilner, 2017). There is no centralised authority that does not provide a single point of failure. There is no place to attempt fraud because the management and permission data dispersed across the network is transparent. Members of the business network or supply chain management can check and verify procedures from start to finish swiftly. For the network's participants, not only current data but also historical data on asset transfers is generally always available. To make changes to the data on the block, one must first gain command of the vast majority of the network's systems.

11.6.1.2 Immutable

A data or transaction that has been registered on the blockchain cannot be changed, making it immutable. Additionally, a block is generated before and to the chain it is added, all network participants must validate the contents. Consensus is the term for this type of verification. After the consensus is reached, the block is approved and given a timestamp, before being connected to the chain's previous block (Karthika & Jaganathan, 2019). As a result, via blockchain, one can obtain information about an asset's origin, journey, and owner.

11.6.1.3 Permissible

Permission or non-permission blockchain networks are established depending on the nature and construction of the blockchain. Permission-based blockchain networks are excellent for mitigating fraudulent activity since they limit system access. A private blockchain is another name for this.

11.6.2 What types of frauds are detected?

11.6.2.1 Financial fraud

Financial fraud can be thwarted with the use of blockchain technology. Financial transactions can appear to be more complicated due to a variety of factors. The time required for any settlements, collateral requirements, and the differences in currency denominations are just a few of these tasks. Some operations are multi-staged and, in most situations, need reasonable levels of human contact. By allowing real-time information exchange and updating the ledger with all parties' consent, blockchain can aid in fraud detection (Peters & Panayi, 2016). This will not only prevent fraud, but it will also cut down on overall costs and time spent on the procedure.

11.6.2.2 Identity frauds

Identity theft is one of the most serious problems that has plagued customers around the world in recent years. Blockchain protects the protection of an individual's digital ID in a way that is tamper-proof (Di Silvestre *et al.*, 2020). When identifying data is held in a permission-required framework, only allowed parties have access to a single version of the true information, and only a known party can verify transactions. This ensures that the records are safe and, more importantly, valid.

11.6.2.3   Supply chain frauds

Supply chain fraud has also become a serious problem for a number of businesses in recent years. The supply chain networks are highly complex, involving a significant number of people in the process. By making things more transparent and easy to trace, blockchain helps to avoid fraud. The blockchain products cannot be easily altered, and verification and updating only happens when all allowed parties have agreed. The blockchain's digitisation aids in tracing things back to their origins.

11.6.3   *Identity fraud cases*

11.6.3.1   Facebook security scam

The Facebook Security Scam is a type of social media fraud that was created with the intent of separating social media users from their money. In the year 2012, a Facebook scam was created in an attempt to obtain financial information from Facebook users. Hackers gained access to user accounts by imitating Facebook's security measures. These compromised accounts were used to send bogus messages to other users, informing them that their accounts were about to be terminated and urging them to verify their accounts by clicking on a link. Following this, the users were redirected to a fake Facebook website that requested their account passwords as well as credit card details in order to safeguard their accounts.

11.6.3.2   Supply chain fraud case: supply and distribution of seafood

For a long time, the seafood supply chain has been in the news for all the wrong reasons. The present seafood supply chain includes time-consuming operations such as manual record-keeping, making it more susceptible to mistakes. Improper food storage conditions, mislabelling fraud, and the availability of deregulated prices are all concerns that contribute to the supply chain's inefficiency. As a result, the quality and safety of the food that reaches the final consumer are jeopardised. Throughout addition, numerous sorts of fraud are present in the chain, resulting in a lack of confidence between customers and sellers. Blockchain technology can help with seafood verification since it can track the seafood from the point of production to the point of distribution.

11.7   Cryptocurrency in the financial markets

The banking sector has taken an interest in blockchain, the technology that underpins the much-hyped bitcoin ecosystem (Hartmann *et al.*, 2019; Raskin & Yermack, 2018). The business, which handles billions of dollars in transactions every day, is now experimenting with blockchain to see if the concept of a "decentralised record of all transactions across the network" may be used to alter the global financial system.

A tamper-proof system that can run concurrently on millions of devices over a network, making it failure-tolerant, is defined as blockchain. Smart contracts are a type of technology that automates the act of registering and carrying out transactions, potentially cutting processing costs in half (Raskin & Yermack, 2018).

The democratisation of trading is anticipated to be another significant influence of blockchain on the stock market. The relationship between distance from the stock exchange and entry price has deteriorated as a result of decentralisation, rendering closeness to exchange servers meaningless. The need for market middlemen will be reduced, transaction costs will be reduced, and the share settlement process will become more transparent.

The NASDAQ already employs blockchain technology to issue and manage private securities, and the London Stock Exchange is working with a cross-industry group of institutions to overhaul the way securities are traded in Europe. Other stock exchanges, like the Tokyo Stock Exchange, the South Korean Stock Exchange, and India's National Stock Exchange, are investigating the potential benefits of blockchain.

Cryptocurrencies are no longer considered to be on the outskirts of the financial system. Despite significant volatility, the market value of these innovative assets surged to almost $3 trillion in November from $620 billion in 2017, thanks to surging popularity among individual and institutional investors.

Virtual money markets have a favourable impact on regional stock market performance, and investors tend to diversify their portfolios as a result of these markets, which encourage investors to speculate and invest.

However, there are other types of cryptocurrencies. "Crypto can be classified into different categories, like DeFi, NFT, utility tokens, store of value tokens like Bitcoin and Litecoin, and yield farming tokens like Aave," CEO of Crebaco, a research of crypto organisation, Sidharth Sogani says.

On the basis of utility, cryptocurrencies are broadly divided into four types.

11.7.1 Currency

Bitcoin, the world's first cryptocurrency, was created for this purpose. The goal was to make cross-border payments less expensive and speedier. It has shown to be a reliable store of value over time. According to data from coinmarketcap.com, the value of one bitcoin has increased from around $1 in 2009 to $48,000 today.

"Crypto(s) can be used on any public decentralised blockchain. It is like the Ethereum blockchain has Ether as its token. Solana Blockchain has Sol as its token. So, the tokens have enabled the developers and the public to use that particular blockchain using its native tokens," says Sogani.

11.7.1.1 Asset

Because the value of stable coins is derived from the value of an external item, they can be classified as assets. The value of USDT, for example, is derived from the US dollar. Gold GLC is a cryptocurrency that is linked to the price of gold. Previously, investors could trade any cryptocurrency for any other cryptocurrency (which may or may not be superior) or fiat currency. Because stable coins are now available, they can choose to stay in the crypto ecosystem by swapping their cryptocurrency for more stable crypto while deciding on the next best option.

"It (cryptocurrency) includes features of a commodity as well as currency, sort of like a hybrid. Commodities can also be used to settle a transaction. They do not impact the economic structure of a country directly, so considering them as a commodity is fine," Sogani says.

11.7.1.2   Object

Many investors believe that this is where cryptocurrencies will go in the future. These kinds of cryptocurrencies were designed to fund specific projects aiming at resolving global issues (Helo & Hao, 2019). Siacoin (SIA), for example, tries to address the issue of costly cloud storage. According to their official website, "Sia is the leading decentralized cloud storage platform. No signups, no servers, no trusted third parties. Sia leverages blockchain technology to create a data storage marketplace that is more robust and more affordable than traditional cloud storage providers."

Another example is Decentraland, an Ethereum-based application that allows users to purchase virtual land (NFT-based) with their cryptocurrency (MANA). Similarly, there are a slew of other crypto coins that serve the same purpose.

Terra (LUNA) is striving to establish itself as a stable coin for e-commerce payments and to make decentralised finance (Defi) more accessible to the general public. "Terra is a public blockchain protocol deploying a suite of algorithmic decentralized stable coins which underpin a thriving ecosystem that brings DeFi to the masses," a website says.

11.7.1.3   Is it a meme or a joke coin?

Despite the fact that they were made solely for fun and with no clear objective in mind, they are now worth millions of dollars. Dogelon Mars (ELON), for example, as a joke.

It is meant to make things easier. "InterPlanetary Money Transactions" when it becomes economically viable means, that after the use of blockchain technology, the financial transactions on global level will become easy and more cost effective. According to coinmarketcap.com, it has a market capitalisation of over $500 million as of December 13.

"Meme coins don't have any purpose and are very speculative assets which work on the simple idea of community-based pumped-up trading. Most of them have no use case. Nascent investors should stay away from such risky crypto(s). They can go bust, which means their value becomes zero at any time. Like what happened recently with the Squid crypto. Its owner ran away with millions of dollars of investor's money," Sogani says.

However, for the time being, some have stood the test of time. In their early days, both Dogecoin and Shiba Inu were meme currencies, but today they are part of the crypto race. "Working with Doge devs to improve system transaction efficiency. Potentially promising," Elon Musk, the CEO of Tesla, sent out a tweet this week. Developers of Dogecoin are now attempting to make their coin a genuine competitor to bitcoin.

Ryoshi, the originator of Shiba Inu, has disclosed that the Shiba Inu Core Devs (SICD) is working on constructing its "Oshiverse" metaverse. According to a

Yahoo Finance storey, the unnamed developer remarked, "We are working on so many aspects of Shiba Inu, including Shibarium, Shi, Shibanet, The Decentralized Shiboshi Game, Incubator and much more that won't become evident until the near future."

However, like with any cryptocurrency, investors should exercise caution. Today, there are over 15,000 cryptocurrencies, with more on the way.

11.8   Regulation of blockchain technology

The government of many countries have developed blockchain as the base platforms and services, and many vendors of these countries are delivering Blockchain-as-a-Service to clients as mentioned below:

1. China's blockchain-based service network (BSN) program aims to make it easier and more affordable for enterprises and individuals to develop blockchain applications (Zheng *et al*., 2019). BSN provides a number of developer tools to aid in the development of smart city and digital economy apps.
2. For smart city infrastructure, China is developing a blockchain-based identification system. This technology will provide each of China's smart cities with a unique worldwide digital ID, allowing them to communicate and share data more easily. A blockchain-enabled Notary Service is also in the works in China.
3. The European Blockchain Partnership (EBP) aims to create a European Blockchain Services Infrastructure that is reliable, safe, and robust (EBSI) that meets the highest interoperability, privacy, cyber security, and other standards policy implementation using blockchain and distributed ledger technologies.
4. Keyless Signature Infrastructure (KSI) in Estonia is a form of blockchain. The Government of Estonia uses this technology to verify the legitimacy of records related to electronics.
5. They have also put in place X-Road, an open-source data interchange layer. X-Road allows two organisations to securely exchange information.
6. The Smart Dubai program in the United Arab Emirates seeks to make Dubai the first city to be totally by 2021, everything from healthcare and education to traffic control and environmental sustainability will be enabled by blockchain.
7. Food and Drug Inspection in the United States is implementing blockchain to solve the lack of transparency and security in the processing of health data. In order to improve food traceability, the Food Standards Agency in the United Kingdom is using blockchain to track the circulation of meat.
8. The government of Brazil is concentrating its efforts on the platform of Ethereum for the development of numerous applications, as well as voting. Brazil is also concentrating on public contract bidding, employing the government's on-line bid system to provide secure and transparent negotiations

for agribusiness applications, student credentials, and student performance tracking.

9. Ethereum network is adopted by Chile to improve energy transparency of the system is achieved by keeping track of data and funds. The Ethereum platform in Switzerland is now giving digital IDs.

10. The Ethereum network is being used by Canada to increase openness in government grant expenditure. Sweden focuses on real estate transactions, but Ghana is developing a blockchain-based land register and to collect property taxes, cadastral records are used.

11. Singapore's Monetary Authority (MAS) is a government-run financial institution in Singapore, concentrating on the financial and technological applications of blockchain technology. Cross-border payments are made possible by blockchain technology. They are working on a solution for safeguarding healthcare data, and insurance firms are also adopting smart contracts.

12. The Swiss city of Zug was the first for tax reasons, it is the first country in the world to accept bitcoin payments. They built a blockchain-based voting mechanism and formed a Blockchain Taskforce to assist businesses in deploying the blockchain architecture.

13. CosmeeDApp was designed by Samsung Blockchain Wallet, which is powered by COSMOCHAIN Blockchain, a cryptocurrency-based content buying app. Customers that contribute or produce information are rewarded for using in a completely transparent fashion, blockchain if their information is used by a company.

14. LG has released a blockchain platform that includes applications for digital identity, community tokens, and supply chain management.

15. Amazon Managed Blockchain, Microsoft Azure Workbench, IBM Blockchain, Oracle Blockchain, and Blockapps Strato, and other Blockchain services are among the options.

11.8.1   National efforts: applications developed and piloted

With C-DAC, Institute for Development & Research in Banking Technology (IDRBT), Hyderabad, and Veermata Jijabai Technological Institute (VJTI), Mumbai as executing agencies, Meity has supported a multi-institutional initiative titled "Distributed Centre of Excellence in Blockchain Technology." In various domains, agencies have performed studies on the usage of blockchain technology and generated as part of this program, proof-of-concept solutions will be developed.

In Telangana's Shamshabad District, a blockchain-based property registration solution has been developed and is being tested. A blockchain-based property registration solution has been developed and is being tested in Telangana's Shamshabad District and has all been enabled with proof-of-concept solutions.

Proof-of-Existence (PoE) on the blockchain in general

The framework for digital objects such as academic credentials, sale deed documents, and memorandums of understanding was built. A solution for the purpose of verifying academic qualifications has been built utilising the PoE framework and is being piloted at the C-DAC Advanced Computing Training School (ACTS), as well as for issuing certificates of participation during online seminars and workshops. MeitY has started a project to design and develop a National Blockchain Framework (NBF) in order to create a common blockchain infrastructure and provide Blockchain as a Service (BaaS).

In India, there are no particular regulations governing blockchain. The general laws of India, especially the laws relating to contracts, govern blockchain in India. According to Vijay Pal Dalmia, December 2021, blockchain technology is being utilised practically by all, including government and private parties, including banks.

The Ministry of Electronics and Information Technology (MeitY) has identified blockchain technology as an important research subject with applicability potential in a variety of areas, including governance, banking and finance, cybersecurity, and so on.

In 2016–2017, RBI deputy governor H.R. Khan proposed the IDRBT, a body of the RBI that released a white paper after conducting a pilot study. IDRBT has taken the initiative to investigate the application of BCT to the Indian Banking and Financial Industry by hosting a workshop that included academics, bankers, regulators, and technological partners. The workshop participants got together to produce this White Paper, which details the technology, concerns, worldwide experiences, and potential areas of adoption in the Indian financial sector. With the active cooperation of NPCI, banks, and solution providers, the Institute tried a Proof-of-Concept (PoC) on the applicability of BCT to a trade financing application, the details of which are described in the White Paper.

The IDRBT coordinating team organised the inputs and study findings into five chapters. The first chapter covers the cryptography components, protocols, and blockchain ledger categories. The second chapter discusses the benefits of BCT, while the third chapter discusses the potential applications of BCT in both currency and non-currency fields. Security, privacy, traceability, and scalability are all key elements in the banking and financial industries, according to the fourth chapter. In the fifth chapter, the Working Group recommends a projected pathway for BCT adoption in Indian banking and finance, based on the basis of the analysis offered in the first four chapters and global experiences (A.S. Ramasastri Director, IDRBT, 2017).

In December 2016, the Watal Committee for Digital Payments proposed blockchain for low-cost transaction monitoring. They also stated that if the central bank produced "Digital Currency," it would incur lower costs, increased tax vigilance, and anti-counterfeiting.

Legal and regulatory by national strategy on blockchain by Meity (December 2021)

1. Initial use cases may be chosen so that contractual responsibilities and legal aspects do not need to be altered. The primary goal should be to use technology to improve transparency and openness in the beginning.

2. As the national blockchain framework grows and based on the lessons learned during implementations, changes to existing legislation and policies may be made. As the framework evolves to meet the needs of diverse application domains, MeitY and other ministries in the Indian government may work on particular legislation and policies for it.
3. Relevant stakeholders may be consulted to address the legal problems of making Smart Contracts admissible in courts.
4. Cross-border legislations are long-term objectives that could be explored as use cases develop.

11.8.1.1   NIC

A Blockchain Technology Center of Excellence (CoE) has been created by NIC and NICSI. The CoE's goals are to execute initiatives, accelerate the adoption and use of blockchain technology in government, focusing on a variety of use cases in order to test deployment, to provide Blockchain Platform-as-a-Service to help with solution design and development, as well as consulting and capacity building (Agbesi & Asante, 2019). The government, the public sector, and the private sector are all working together at the Center of Excellence. Some of the application areas discovered and developed by CoE include the blood bank, Digidhan, Public Distribution System, land registration, GST Back Office, and Excise Management System.

11.8.1.2   NeGD

The National Strategy for blockchain has been published by NeGD, which defines the blockchain application domains, technology adoption obstacles, societal impact, government role, and national strategy concepts, and is now leveraging blockchain to develop e-Attestation for the state of Karnataka.

11.8.1.3   C-DAC

C-goal DAC's to design and create blockchain technology solutions to enable trusted and auditable shared infrastructure for cross-domain application development and large-scale deployment has been validated by successful pilot deployments and Proofs of Concept (PoCs) on blockchain. The C-Blockchain DAC's technology mission includes: (a) performance, scalability, interoperability, security, and privacy challenges in a national blockchain framework for cross-domain applications, (b) integration of eSign with a blockchain-based proof-of-existence system (PoE), and (c) application development and deployment on a huge scale.

11.8.1.4   Academia

IIT Kanpur is developing e-governance solutions based on blockchain technology. The project is divided into three phases: a report on the technology's feasibility, protocol development, and research on confirming the tamper resistance property, which is widely employed in blockchain and application development. The University Blockchain Research Initiative has been founded by Ripple (UBRI). Ripple has selected IIIT Hyderabad as one of the first university partners to support blockchain research and establish a Blockchain Center of Excellence. Through this COE, IIITH is tackling security-related blockchain research, experimenting with game-theoretic methodologies, and developing next-generation blockchain. Machine learning is also being considered by the team for use in blockchain.

11.8.1.5 NITI Aayog

NITI Aayog is working on a number of blockchain applications. The NITI Aayog has created a blockchain-based fertiliser subsidy scheme in partnership with Gujarat Narmada Valley Fertilizers & Chemicals Limited (GNFC). The company has also teamed with PwC and Intel to streamline the fertiliser subsidy supply chain. The application demonstrates how to use blockchain characteristics like tamper-proofing and transparency to transfer fertiliser more efficiently across the value chain and reduce the time it takes to activate subsidies. In this blockchain application, several transactions pertaining to challans, claims, and invoices are recorded on a ledger.

11.8.1.6 Govt. of Telangana & Govt. of Tamil Nadu

The policy documents for Telangana and Tamil Nadu's adoption of blockchain technology have been released. The government of Telangana is a proponent of blockchain technology as well. Several use cases have been established successfully, as part of Telangana State's Blockchain District programme. The Avasant India Blockchain Report 2019 by NASSCOM, several Indian states have begun to implement blockchain-based use cases. Land registry, agricultural insurance, and digital certifications are the top three application cases.

11.8.1.7 Banking sector

The Reserve Bank of India (RBI) is looking into how blockchain technology can be used in banking. IBM and Mahindra are working together on supply chain management solutions. In the case of a blockchain-based application prototype, the State Bank of India (SBI) Commercial banks and financial organisations have cooperated with us. Yes Bank, Axis Bank, and ICICI Bank are also using blockchain in their financial operations.

11.8.1.8 IDRBT

The IDRBT has published a whitepaper outlining a three-step roadmap for BCT implementation in finance and banking in India: (1) intrabank—a private blockchain for banks' internal use, (2) interbank—proof-of-concept installation and testing; (c) central bank—commencing appropriate initiatives to digitise the Indian Rupee via BCT. They have also developed a Blockchain Platform Blueprint for the Banking Sector, which focuses on the architectural, governance, and technological aspects of a blockchain-based business network.

11.8.1.9 Capacity building

Through NIELIT and C-DAC, the Indian government has launched the Future Skills Prime initiative (https://futureskillsprime.in/standalonetechnology/blockchainspecifically)

through NIELIT and C-DAC, for upskilling and reskilling in the domain of blockchain to fulfil the requirement for strengthening the talent pool in the country.

Multiple messages from various stakeholders have caused major confusion in India about crypto assets: the central bank has flagged risks from cryptocurrency to the financial system, while North Block is attempting to regulate' the asset class rather than enforcing an outright ban in its new crypto bill. The blockchain and crypto businesses, according to Harishkarthik Gunalan, CEO of Singapore-based Coin fantasy, are essentially an interplay between technology and mathematics, two topics in which Indians have historically excelled, so it's natural for them to be drawn to it. "The huge number of Indians trading digital assets, as well as the fact that, despite the lack of legislative support, India has developed two crypto-focused firms in the previous eight months, demonstrates this fascination. If the regulatory environment is supportive, many more people will be able to engage in this once-in-a-generation new asset class." The huge number of Indians trading digital assets, as well as the fact that, despite a lack of legislative support, India has developed two crypto-focused firms in the previous 8 months, demonstrate this fascination. If the regulatory environment is supportive, a much larger number of individuals will be able to engage in this once-in-a-generation new asset class. "Even as most other governments struggle to create crypto regulations, regulators, and the crypto sector around the world are eagerly awaiting the crypto bill to lay down rules for digital coins, tokens, and virtual currencies.

11.9   Conclusion

All the players or the participants have equal access to blockchain technology, no intermediary is involvement is required, which makes very low or almost zero transaction cost. It allows new BMs to reach out to unbanked clients in both developed and developing countries, and new BMs can provide a wide range of services to those customers. The technology is still in its early stages, and many more trials, prototypes, and tests are required. Despite this, the technology has gotten a lot of press, and it was just added to Gartner's hype cycle of upcoming technologies in 2016. But, the entire potential of the technology is still unknown, and blockchain applications are still very context dependent.

Blockchain technology is still in its infancy, and research into it is limited. We can easily find out that blockchain technology can be applied in BMs. As a result, intra-firm research of business processes is promising, allowing for the study of blockchain technology implementations within fintech or early prototypes generated by incumbents. The BM and the overarching business strategy have interactions. As a result, as blockchain technology affects BMs, it has strategic consequences. As a result, researching the impact of blockchain technology on BMs and corporate strategy will help us better understand how business and IT strategy interact.

As a result of our findings, a study agenda in the realm of blockchain technology has been developed. It appears critical to gain a deeper understanding of new, customer-centric services provided by blockchain technology, as well as how these services could be applied in existing and new payment-related BMs. The services will also enable researchers to look at the interactions between new and established players. Cost benefits are a primary motivator for the adoption of new technology and changes to other sectors, it is critical to examine changes in the cost structure and, as a result, the financial benefits of blockchain.

Summarised, the chapter delivers the concept and features of blockchain technology. The main applications of blockchain technology in the financial world, the impact on the modern banking BMs. It also covers the drawbacks related to digital currencies. In this finance world, the technology also causes frauds, for which also the blockchain application is finding the ways. But most importantly, the formulation of regulations for the proper application of blockchain technology is required, so that the decentralised ledger technology should get adoption acceptance by all sectors in the world uniformly. In the end, it is mentioned that as per the requirements in the sectors for the upgradation, the adoption of blockchain technology proves its demand day by day.

References

Agbesi, S. and Asante, G. (2019). Electronic voting recording system based on blockchain technology. In *2019 12th CMI Conference on Cybersecurity and Privacy (CMI)*, pp. 1–8.

Aheleroff, S., Mostashiri, N., Xu, X., and Zhong, R. Y. (2021). Mass personalisation as a service in industry 4.0: a resilient response case study. *Advanced Engineering Informatics*, 50, 101438.

Ali, M., Nelson, J., Shea, R., and Freedman, M. J. (2016). Blockstack: a global naming and storage system secured by blockchains. In *2016 USENIX Annual Technical Conference (USENIX ATC 16)*, 181–194.

Apostolaki, M., Zohar, A., and Vanbever, L. (2017). Hijacking bitcoin: routing attacks on cryptocurrencies. In *2017 IEEE Symposium on Security and Privacy (SP)*, pp. 375–392.

Baier, H. and Breitinger, F. (2011). Security aspects of piecewise hashing in computer forensics. In *2011 Sixth International Conference on IT Security Incident Management and IT Forensics*, pp. 21–36.

Berdik, D., Otoum, S., Schmidt, N., Porter, D., and Jararweh, Y. (2021). A survey on blockchain for information systems management and security. *Information Processing & Management*, 58(1), 102397.

Boons, F., Montalvo, C., Quist, J., and Wagner, M. (2013). Sustainable innovation, business models and economic performance: an overview. *Journal of Cleaner Production*, 45, 1–8.

Chen, Y. and Bellavitis, C. (2019). *Decentralized Finance: Blockchain Technology and the Quest for an Open Financial System. Stevens Institute of Technology School of Business Research Paper*.

Christidis, K. and Devetsikiotis, M. (2016). Blockchains and smart contracts for the internet of things. *IEEE Access*, 4, 2292–2303.

Dagher, G. G., Mohler, J., Milojkovic, M., and Marella, P. B. (2018). Ancile: privacy-preserving framework for access control and interoperability of electronic health records using blockchain technology. *Sustainable Cities and Society, 39*, 283–297.

Dashottar, S. and Srivastava, V. (2021). Corporate banking—risk management, regulatory and reporting framework in India: a blockchain application-based approach. *Journal of Banking Regulation, 22*(1), 39–51.

De Filippi, P. and Lavayssière, X. (2020). Blockchain technology: toward a decentralized governance of digital platforms? In *The Great Awakening. Punctum Books*, pp. 185–222.

Deuber, D., Magri, B., and Thyagarajan, S. A. K. (2019). Redactable blockchain in the permissionless setting. In *2019 IEEE Symposium on Security and Privacy (SP)*, pp. 124–138.

Di Silvestre, M. L., Gallo, P., Guerrero, J. M., *et. al.* (2020). Blockchain for power systems: current trends and future applications. *Renewable and Sustainable Energy Reviews, 119*, 109585.

Dib, O., Brousmiche, K.-L., Durand, A., Thea, E., and Hamida, E. Ben. (2018). Consortium blockchains: overview, applications and challenges. *International Journal on Advances in Telecommunications, 11*(1 and 2), 51–64.

Dinh, T. T. A., Wang, J., Chen, G., Liu, R., Ooi, B. C., and Tan, K.-L. (2017). Blockbench: A framework for analyzing private blockchains. In *Proceedings of the 2017 ACM International Conference on Management of Data*, pp. 1085–1100.

Ducas, E. and Wilner, A. (2017). The security and financial implications of blockchain technologies: regulating emerging technologies in Canada. *International Journal, 72*(4), 538–562.

Fanning, K. and Centers, D. P. (2016). Blockchain and its coming impact on financial services. *Journal of Corporate Accounting & Finance, 27*(5), 53–57.

Goel, U., Ruhl, R., and Zavarsky, P. (2019). Using healthcare authority and patient blockchains to develop a tamper-proof record tracking system. In *2019 IEEE 5th Intl Conference on Big Data Security on Cloud (BigDataSecurity), IEEE International Conference on High Performance and Smart Computing, (HPSC) and IEEE International Conference on Intelligent Data and Security (IDS)*, pp. 25–30.

Goforth, C. (2019). The Lawyer's cryptionary: a resource for talking to clients about crypto-transactions. *Campbell Law Review, 41*, 47.

Hamilton, M. (2020). Blockchain distributed ledger technology: an introduction and focus on smart contracts. *Journal of Corporate Accounting & Finance, 31*(2), 7–12.

Handayani, I., Supriati, R., and Aisyah, E. S. N. (2020). Proof of blockchain work on the security of academic certificates. In *2020 8th International Conference on Cyber and IT Service Management (CITSM)*, pp. 1–5.

Hartmann, F., Wang, X., and Lunesu, M. I. (2019). A hierarchical structure model of success factors for (blockchain-based) crowdfunding. In *Blockchain and Web 3.0*. Routledge, pp. 270–308.

Hassani, H., Huang, X., and Silva, E. S. (2019). Fusing Big Data, blockchain, and cryptocurrency. In *Fusing Big Data, Blockchain and Cryptocurrency*. Springer, pp. 99–117.

Hegde, S., Ashwini, B. V, and Madasu, S. (n.d.). A virtual energy trading platform for smart homes. *International Journal of Computer Science Trends and Technology (IJCST)*, 7(4), 30–34.

Helo, P. and Hao, Y. (2019). Blockchains in operations and supply chains: a model and reference implementation. *Computers & Industrial Engineering*, 136, 242–251.

Hossain, M. M., Fotouhi, M., and Hasan, R. (2015). Towards an analysis of security issues, challenges, and open problems in the Internet of Things. In *2015 IEEE World Congress on Services*, pp. 21–28.

Karthika, V. and Jaganathan, S. (2019). A quick synopsis of blockchain technology. *International Journal of Blockchains and Cryptocurrencies*, 1(1), 54–66.

Kosba, A., Miller, A., Shi, E., Wen, Z., and Papamanthou, C. (2016). Hawk: The blockchain model of cryptography and privacy-preserving smart contracts. In *2016 IEEE Symposium on Security and Privacy (SP)*, pp. 839–858.

Kshetri, N. (2017). Blockchain's roles in strengthening cybersecurity and protecting privacy. *Telecommunications Policy*, 41(10), 1027–1038.

Liu, Y., Li, R., Liu, X., *et al.* (2017). An efficient method to enhance Bitcoin wallet security. In *2017 11th IEEE International Conference on Anti-Counterfeiting, Security, and Identification (ASID)*, pp. 26–29.

Mavilia, R. and Pisani, R. (2020). Blockchain and catching-up in developing countries: the case of financial inclusion in Africa. *African Journal of Science, Technology, Innovation and Development*, 12(2), 151–163.

Mıhçak, M. K. and Venkatesan, R. (2001). A perceptual audio hashing algorithm: a tool for robust audio identification and information hiding. In *International Workshop on Information Hiding*, pp. 51–65.

Nguyen, C. T., Hoang, D. T., Nguyen, D. N., *et al.* (2019). Proof-of-stake consensus mechanisms for future blockchain networks: fundamentals, applications and opportunities. *IEEE Access*, 7, 85727–85745.

Novo, O. (2018). Blockchain meets IoT: an architecture for scalable access management in IoT. *IEEE Internet of Things Journal*, 5(2), 1184–1195.

Pahlajani, S., Kshirsagar, A., and Pachghare, V. (2019). Survey on private blockchain consensus algorithms. In *2019 1st International Conference on Innovations in Information and Communication Technology (ICIICT)*, pp. 1–6.

Pakhchanyan, S. (2016). Operational risk management in financial institutions: a literature review. *International Journal of Financial Studies*, 4(4), 20.

Peters, G. W. and Panayi, E. (2016). Understanding modern banking ledgers through blockchain technologies: future of transaction processing and smart contracts on the internet of money. In *Banking Beyond Banks and Money*. Springer, pp. 239–278.

Pilkington, M. (2016). Blockchain technology: principles and applications. In *Research Handbook on Digital Transformations*. Edward Elgar Publishing.

Rajnak, V. and Puschmann, T. (2021). The impact of blockchain on business models in banking. *Information Systems and E-Business Management, 19*(3), 809–861.

Raskin, M. and Yermack, D. (2018). Digital currencies, decentralized ledgers and the future of central banking. In *Research Handbook on Central Banking*. Edward Elgar Publishing, pp. 474–486.

Rodrigues, A., Montague, K., Nicolau, H., and Guerreiro, T. (2015). Getting smartphones to talkback: understanding the smartphone adoption process of blind users. In *Proceedings of the 17th International ACM SIGACCESS Conference on Computers & Accessibility*, pp. 23–32.

Saguato, P. (2017). The ownership of clearinghouses: when skin in the game is not enough, the remutualization of clearinghouses. *Yale Journal on Regulation, 34*, 601.

Sandner, P., Gross, J., and Richter, R. (2020). Convergence of blockchain, IoT, and AI. *Frontiers in Blockchain, 3*, 522600.

Tapscott, D. and Tapscott, A. (2017). How blockchain will change organizations. *MIT Sloan Management Review, 58*(2), 10.

Tosh, D., Shetty, S., Foytik, P., Kamhoua, C., and Njilla, L. (2018). CloudPoS: a proof-of-stake consensus design for blockchain integrated cloud. In *2018 IEEE 11th International Conference on Cloud Computing (CLOUD)*, pp. 302–309.

Yaga, D., Mell, P., Roby, N., and Scarfone, K. (2019). Blockchain technology overview. *ArXiv Preprint ArXiv:1906*.11078.

Zachariadis, M., Hileman, G., and Scott, S. V. (2019). Governance and control in distributed ledgers: understanding the challenges facing blockchain technology in financial services. *Information and Organization, 29*(2), 105–117.

Zheng, X., Zhu, Y., and Si, X. (2019). A survey on challenges and progresses in blockchain technologies: a performance and security perspective. *Applied Sciences, 9*(22), 4731.

Chapter 12

Automation to handle customer complaints: a grievance handling system

Kuldeep Singh Kaswan[1], Jagjit Singh Dhatterwal[2], Avadhesh Kumar[3], Simon Grima[4] and Sharon Seychel[5]

Abstract

Effective and rapid responses to client complaints are crucial indicators of the success of a service-oriented business, particularly for a chain of upscale restaurants. Food flavour, quality and amount, service speed, pricing, and attitude of the staff, as well as the atmosphere and hygienic element, are some factors that may be improved upon in a restaurant. Nowadays, customers want prompt redress to their grievances. Method reengineering was used in this article to solve the shortcomings of the present (as-is) complaint management process. A framework for a complaint management system for a Japanese fast-food chain is examined and built in this research. The interactions between the corporate headquarters and the regional offices are scrutinised to demonstrate the advantages of the suggested complaint-handling procedure. The as-is complaint reporting method is presented in the study's first phase. Models and processes for managing complaints will be developed in the second phase utilising an INCOME approach. Complaint registration, compensation diagnosis, and complaint analysis are part of the new structure. In addition, this chapter analyses the benefits of using an automated system to resolve customer complaints and demonstrate how this compares to present procedures: customers' happiness, complaint handling, and information retrieval.

Keywords: Automation; Customer complaints; Grievance handling system; Service-oriented business; Restaurants; Quality; Service speed; Pricing

[1]School of Computing Science and Engineering, Galgotias University, India
[2]Department of Artificial Intelligence & Data Science, Koneru Lakshmaiah Education Foundation, India
[3]School of Computing Science & Engineering, Galgotias University, India
[4]University of Malta, Malta
[5]Faculty of Economics Management & Accountancy, University of Malta, Malta

12.1   Introduction

The simplest way to tell whether a service-oriented firm is doing its job well is to look at client complaints. Negative customer feedback may significantly impact a company's bottom line if they are not handled appropriately and quickly. Complaint handling in a business directly affects customer loyalty and patronage. Customer complaints are an essential source of feedback for companies like the restaurant chain in this research. Neglecting to address these issues may significantly impact a company's ability to compete. Some customer complaints at a restaurant chain's branch outlets must be promptly submitted to the chain's headquarters for quick complaint resolution. In the past, faxed statements and phone calls were used for reporting purposes, which created a communication gap and informational imbalance.

Without real-time decision assistance from the headquarter authority, specific problems may not be dealt with correctly. Another issue is that when a large number of complaints are received at a certain time (say, once a month or once a week) rather than spread out continuously over a period (e.g., every day or every hour), there is a considerable time lag between receiving the required advice and making it available to the client. Complaint reporting, compensation diagnosis, complaint searching, and analysis will all be included in the paper's suggested structure for a customer complaint handling system. Complaint data from each branch of the restaurant chain may be found and shared throughout its many locations. The new procedure also incorporates effects and real-time statistical analysis.

A happy and productive work atmosphere can only be maintained if grievances are handled correctly. All that matters in grievance management is how well the issues are dealt with (and solved). In today's world, it is vital. Many firms nowadays claim that their people resources are their most valuable assets and that it is no longer permanent staff but rather Human Capital. As a result, the veracity of these claims must be established. To achieve this, tracking the speed at which workers' issues are handled and resolved is possible. If it is completed more quickly, it is safe to claim that employee concerns are well-represented in the company (Kerr and Anderson, 2002). Many issues working with their employers involve contractual obligations, work rules and regulations, policies and procedures, health and safety laws, historical practices, changes made unilaterally to social norms, and personal victimhood. Keeping a high-performing culture is more likely when management takes a more open-minded approach to learning about their workers' concerns and finding solutions that everyone can agree on. An effective grievance procedure and a positive working relationship with the union need managers to be well-informed. Positive work relations and a fair, prosperous way for an organisation can only be achieved via effective grievance processing. It is a two-way street to foster a positive work environment. Successful employment relations can only be reached via the development of strong working relationships (Kim and Kim, 2009).

12.1.1   E-complaint

The complaint is defined differently by every company. They formally represent user complaints about the services they provide. Because organisations offer a wide range of services, there is no universally accepted definition (Ueno, 2006). Customer complaints, which are described as "the results of consumer unhappiness" (Hoots, 2005), have been recognised for a long time as a valuable source of market feedback. In other words, the ability to effectively handle customer complaints is rapidly becoming an essential component of corporate success in the modern day. A complaint management system is an online tool for gathering consumer opinions on a specific business. Organisations that follow best practices see customer complaints as feedback for making changes. These businesses appreciate the importance of swiftly addressing simple issues with their customers to maintain their loyalty. The researcher also thinks that the government or any system requires user input to identify difficulties after implementing a new system. The organisation may use user complaints and ideas to fine-tune its offerings (Faed *et al.*, 2010).

12.1.2 Service-oriented architecture

SOA, or service-oriented architecture, is an approach to programming that emphasises collaboration and communication between different parts of a system. Designing a system on services rather than steps (Ueno, 2006). Decomposing an application into "services" that can be used by other applications—both internal and external to the organisation and independent of the applications and computing platforms on which the business and its partners rely—is an essential step in the process of application modernisation. As a result, the system is more adaptable. Using SOA will drastically reduce the cost of making changes to a system, as the administrator will only have to make adjustments to the services necessary for the new configuration. Although there are several definitions of SOA, the researcher believes they are all essentially the same. Although each system has its data type, they must be able to communicate with one another in SOA-based systems by using a common bus and data type (Ueno, 2006). According to their findings, SOA-based e-complaint discusses the design of a system that incorporates several services rather than just one.

12.1.3 Examination of the system

The growth of the suggested model depends on more than just how the system functions. The working flow method that has been determined will also need to be put into place and adhered to. A technique, platform, or web-based application is suggested for addressing complaints. This would guarantee that complaints are dealt with appropriately (Robinson *et al.*, 2011).

The primary operations of the proposed model's workflow process. The process begins with validating the citizen, then creating the complaint, and finally searching the knowledge base for a similar case or related reference that can help speed up the solution-finding process with the help of the responsible staff who will be dedicated to identifying the rules on how to solve and get the appropriate solution (Chaudhry, 2007).

This chapter provides a framework for electronic complaints that may facilitate reporting service quality and delivery issues. The benefit of this technique is a straightforward approach to addressing citizen concerns.

12.1.4   System architecture

The primary department for managing customer complaints has been eliminated, thanks to this new paradigm. As a result, it established a dedicated sub-section inside each division to field customer complaints. Concerned individuals might reach out to these compact complaint-processing divisions for assistance. Because every company has its system for dealing with customer complaints, different divisions within the company may provide different approaches to processing customer feedback (Lawson Body and Limayem, 2004).

The researcher disagrees with the previous model because decentralising the complaint process goes against the spirit of e-CRM, which is to coordinate and share a standard view of all processes about the customer. Instead, the researcher has proposed the following SOA-based architecture for a complaint system. The investigator improved upon the traditional concept by centralising the complaint management system.

In the suggested model's three levels, we have the following.

12.1.5   SQL server database layer

Information about system users, citizens, resources, and social network accounts are all included.

Tier 1: Business: The heart of the system is contained inside it. This deals with comments and complaints and the level of presentation. The interface is entirely web-based. The suggested approach might be used with any electronic complaint system that operates via the Internet.

Modelling the deployment process: Following a description of the workflow process and the suggested model, the following steps constitute the system's actualisation:

- The administration is the users who control the access to File a Complaint About the Services, Received.
- The agent enters the complaint into the Web-Based System and Notifies Appropriate Personnel to Follow Up.
- Staff-manage the root causes and systemic responses to complaints, and provide resolutions.
- The "Civil Registry" contains everyone's name, social security number, etc.
- Social solidarity—information on citizens who should get assistance.
- Staff information—this contains complete information on all employees involved with Social Solidarity and who may be tasked with handling Complaints.

12.1.5.1   Overview of the scenario

When a citizen has a complaint about Social Solidarity, he may either fill out a new complaint form online or speak with an agent over the phone. The agent then logs the issue, accesses the complaint system, and adds a new complaint entry while simultaneously performing updates to the complaints and entering details about each linked failure. Subsequently, the service department's personnel take over and assigns each complaint to the appropriate individual. Complaints are handled by the fair division, which then analyses the measures taken and their root causes to determine the outcomes. The next step is to provide an acceptable answer to the citizen's issue. The formal complaint is closed if the citizen is happy with this resolution. If that is not the case, the relevant division revises the first complaint, and the procedure is repeated. A new Complaint Management System is essential for these processes to be more efficient and for each division to participate in resolving citizen concerns (Kaswan *et al.*, 2022).

12.1.5.2   Flowchart of events

12.1.5.2.1   Three-point-one-system evaluation

The growth of the suggested model depends on more than just how the system functions. The working flow method that has been determined will also need to be put into place and adhered to. A technique, platform, or web-based application is suggested for addressing complaints. This would guarantee that complaints are dealt with appropriately (Ngai *et al.*, 2009).

12.2   Literature review

Customers' complaints are a way of expressing their displeasure when their expectations are not met. The behaviours of complaints occur during or after a customer's visit when they are displeased with the restaurant's food, service, and/or other elements. Heung & Lam (Chen and Popovich, 2003) found that Chinese guests' complaint intentions were low, and they were reluctant to express their displeasure with restaurants. Even if consumers may express displeasure but do not make a formal complaint, the employees may be able to identify the issue and take the necessary steps to fix it.

In the case study, we discovered that complaint handling ends unhappiness and takes remediation and compensation to improve customer satisfaction. Apologies and explanations are included in the emotional path. When a consumer is dissatisfied with the service, the physical directive is to compensate them financially. Customer unhappiness may be alleviated in one of two ways: emotionally or physically, by managing customer complaints. Davidow (Frow *et al.*, 2011) outlined six elements of organisational reactions, including timeliness, facilitation, redress, apology, credibility, and attentiveness, to better understand how to respond to incidents. Because of managing client complaints, the corporation might develop a customer loyalty strategy. Service recovery is another term for the process of resolving complaints. When a service provider has a service failure, Gronroos (Chen and Sockel, 2004) believes that the best technique for service recovery is to take some recovery action. When clients are dissatisfied, this involves taking action to alleviate their discomfort. Complaint information is critical to a firm because it may be used to alter its service approach. Staff might then use this idea to fix service faults. Complaints are more likely to occur if consumers are unsatisfied

(Mendoza *et al.*, 2007). According to the findings, bringing in a new client costs six times as much as keeping an existing one happy.

Customers who have had a terrible encounter with a company's customer service might be turned from enraged to loyal by an effective complaint management strategy. Thus, consumers who have had a positive customer service experience are more likely to stick with a company than those who haven't (Ueno, 2006). In Christo's (Özgener and Iraz, 2006) view, the response time is inversely proportional to how satisfied the customer is. Hoffman *et al.* (Hoots, 2005) devised eight ways to compensate restaurant workers. Meal changes and proper servings are also included in the strategy of apologies without reward and free of charge.

12.3   Grievance handling through integrated grievance management system (IGMS)

Shintori, a Taiwanese high-end restaurant brand, was founded in Taipei in 1996. Thanks to their efforts, there are now five branches of the eateries Shintori and People in Taipei City. In Shanghai, China, there are four more branches. Shintori and People extensions use various tactics. As a result, each location's interior décor and food are distinctively different. Both Shintori and People provide unique Chinese/Japanese cuisine (Payne and Frow, 2005).

Complaint acceptance, cause investigation, handling action, analysis and improvement, and record keeping are part of the restaurant group's customer complaint handling procedure. It is the responsibility of the store's branch manager and department managers to handle client complaints. Quickly reporting certain unique circumstances to the HQ is necessary to seek timely advice and support. Complaint management is a vital and interconnected activity between branch shops and the corporate headquarters.

12.3.1   As-is complaint handling process

Customer complaints and displeasure are common in restaurants when diners vent their resentment against wait staff over things like substandard food, subpar service, inadequate facilities, and a less-than-perfect dining experience. No matter how they are made, all complaints should be taken seriously and handled appropriately. Complaints should be accepted by workers and supervisors, who must apologise and console consumers emotionally before attempting to understand why they are unhappy. The managers are responsible for apologising and explaining the reasons to dissatisfied consumers after the inquiry. As a result, the supervisors implement corrective and compensatory measures to address the complaint. There are numerous flaws in a restaurant's quality control, including food taste, number of items, speed of service, spoiled food, foreign matter, price, reservation service, meal service, service attitude, the environment, and sanitary conditions. These are just a few examples of the myriad problems restaurants face.

Once the cause of the incident has been identified, management must implement the appropriate compensation techniques, such as not charging, giving a discount, providing a voucher, apologising, altering the meal, presenting the right food, and not blaming. Managers and employees must evaluate customer feedback and corporate policy to choose the appropriate course of action for remuneration. Customers must be reimbursed for whatever portion of the meal cost, no matter how much they paid or how little. After that, they begin filling out the customer complaint form with all the procedure details. In addition, they must continue monitoring whether consumers are satisfied after the resolution. For the management to understand why the consumers are still dissatisfied, they should ask them directly. If the consumers have already left the shop, they must follow up on the situation and take the required steps to ensure they are happy. Every month, the managers of each shop are required to collect data on consumer complaints and then present the findings at the appropriate meeting. Finally, monthly customer complaint data should be communicated to the department manager and the general manager for final approval (Bose, 2002).

12.3.2 The disadvantage of the as-is module

As it is, the module for handling complaints has several flaws. Customer complaints are directed on a case-by-case basis by each branch rather than being consolidated and cross-referenced across outlets. When complaints are received monthly, the time it takes for the issue to be resolved is significant. When dealing with client complaints, the level of customer service suffers because of this predicament. Third, historical and statistical data on complaints are not effectively maintained and repurposed. We offer a new method for handling complaints and illustrate its full process models to minimise these inadequacies (Furuholt and Skutle, 2007).

12.3.2.1 The value of complaint policies and procedures

Conflict at work may come in many forms. The absence of complaints is a necessary condition for the survival of almost every business. However, the organisation's future harmony, productivity, and performance may be inferred from how quickly and effectively problems like these are resolved (King and Burgess, 2008). Therefore, deciding management's faults and weaknesses depends on treating grievances via acceptable processes. When handled with care, complaints may spark good changes inside a company, raising both productivity and morale. An organisation's productivity, confidence, and culture may be hit if employees cannot air their grievances and get closure. Therefore, having a formal grievance mechanism in place is so crucial. The purpose of establishing legal channels for resolving complaints is to encourage each company to maximise the quality of its services and the effectiveness of its workforce. However, he noted that these methods often favour management and may not encourage people to raise concerns about their working conditions (Reinartz et al., 2004).

When there is no apparatus for properly resolving of complaints the organisation's operation may be disrupted. An effective grievance process aids in resolving grievances as soon as feasible and near the point of origin. Employees may feel demoralised, lose dedication to their job, and even resort to sabotage as a form of retaliation against their superiors or upper management. A formal grievance system is essential for maintaining harmony in the workplace, encouraging open communication between management and employees, and preventing conflicts from escalating. This is because it is well-documented that repressed worker complaints lead to increased workplace accidents, absenteeism, increased strike activities and other industrial sabotage, decreased morale and commitment among employees, and so on (Goldsmith, 2010).

Having formal channels for resolving employee complaints is crucial to maintaining high employee satisfaction and productivity levels.

Management may learn more about employees' perspectives on the organisation's policies, procedures, and regulations via an effective grievance system. It's a way for workers to vent their frustrations and share their concerns with the higher-ups in the company, which helps them understand what their employees want from them. Therefore, assist the worker in letting go of the stress brought on by the grievance. It helps management keep the lines of communication open with their staff, pinpoints trouble spots and areas where workers are dissatisfied so they can implement solutions, and reduces the likelihood of arbitrary action by supervisors because workers know they can voice their displeasure with the behaviour to higher-ups and possibly get a warning (Lindgreen *et al.*, 2006).

12.3.2.2   The elements of a successful employee complaint procedure

Management of workplace complaints, or "grievance management," is a crucial aspect of every company's human resources department. By resolving complaints to everyone's satisfaction, including management and staff, employee grievance management fosters a more friendly workplace and aids in creating rules and processes that are well received by workers. Therefore, it is crucial to utilise an efficient strategy to resolve workers' discontent fairly while handling an employee grievance. One may make the case that managers are better able to make judgments by ethical standards if they have access to information on the most successful methods for handling employee complaints (Kaswan *et al.*, 2022).

12.3.2.3   Negotiation between employees of a company

In collective bargaining, union employees, management, or employers negotiate to establish working conditions. It is the method through which employers and employees settle differences about such things as pay, benefits, and working conditions.

When negotiating on behalf of workers, unions often act as a unified front that management has a hard time rejecting. A standard collective bargaining agreement addresses working conditions, pay, benefits, training, overtime, grievance procedures, and employees' rights to engage in the workplace. Collective bargaining is an organised negotiation process between an employer and a group of employees to establish terms and conditions for employment, including pay, hours, benefits, and other monetary and legal protections for workers. Members of the workers' trade union often advocate on their behalf (Iriana and Buttle, 2007).

It was pointed out that workers have an unfair disadvantage when negotiating or making demands individually. Therefore, collective bargaining helps to level the playing field. When workers engage in collective bargaining, their trade union often presents their interests. For this reason, collective bargaining is crucial to effective industrial relations. Collective bargaining helps preserve the peace between workers and their employers, ensures that workers' tenures are secure and stable, protects all workers, limits the influence of abusive workers, and fosters a sense of unity and solidarity among workers (Foss *et al.*, 2008).

An "open door policy" is a kind of corporate communication that allows workers unrestricted access to the offices of upper-level managers to voice any concerns they may have or provide suggestions they feel will benefit the company. Francis (2018) argues that an open-door policy encourages workers to bring up any problems they have with upper management, whether it is related to their performance or that of the firm, their coworkers, or any suggestions they have for how to better the organisation. An open-door policy also promotes open contact lines between employees and upper management. When workers communicate with their supervisors face to face, there is less chance of misunderstanding. Moreover, it stimulates good communication at the workplace and allows the workers to seek their boss's support and openly discuss topics with them for greater clarity. Furthermore, an open-door policy develops an atmosphere of collaboration and respect between the top management team and staff (Chan, 2005).

12.3.2.4 Concept of organisational performance

Organisational performance may be considered the actual output or outcomes that an organisation has accomplished creation (or goals and objectives) (or goals and objectives). Success may be measured by how well a business meets or exceeds its objectives, targets, or proposals relative to its competitors. An organisation's success may be measured in terms of its profitability, market share, asset return, and investment return. To rephrase, "organisational performance" is measured by the company's profitability, market share, and returns on its assets and investments. Companies' performance is defined as their performance compared to rivals and the market norm. The accomplishments of individuals and collectives inside an organisation contribute to its overall success. A company's overall success is a direct result of the efforts of its members, which in turn reflect positively on the overall success of each unit and department (Cho *et al.*, 2003).

That "organisational performance may be operationalised in numerous ways," including "profitability," "market share," "return on assets or investment," "changes in market share or profitability," and "new product success" was claimed. They also recognised customer loyalty, revenue growth, and long-term viability.

Depending on the level of performance, a company may be deemed satisfactory or dissatisfactory. It proposes that corporate performance is the equilibrium between all aspects of production (human and materials) that will offer the maximum output for minimal efforts. Organisational performance is defined as the "conversion of inputs into outputs to accomplish predetermined objectives," as stated by. Organisational performance is defined as the degree to which an organisation is successful in achieving its objectives. According to Daft (2000), organisational performance is "an organisation's capacity to fulfil its objectives by employing resources effectively and efficiently."

12.3.2.4.1   Profitability

Making a profit is crucial for the survival of any firm. Obiekwe (2012) emphasises that profitability is any business operation's fundamental objective. Businesses have very little chance of lasting without profit. To maintain the human resources (the "engines") that drive their companies and to keep providing their products and services in the most efficient manner possible, businesses of all sizes and types are experimenting with different strategies to obtain a competitive edge. According to Enekwe *et al.* (2013), a company is profitable if it generates a positive return on the investment of money and the efforts of its workers. "Profitability is assessed by revenue and objectives of all company operations," says Obiekwe (2012). As Marianne (2013) points out, in a competitive business environment, profitability is the companies' primary focus and the best performance indicator (Reinartz *et al.*, 2005).

12.4   Measuring the efficiency and effectiveness of IGMS

An informational platform that combines expert systems and decision-making systems is developed in this study to address the problem of managing complaints as-is. The information provided here facilitates the connectivity between a branch and the headquarters. Various tools are available on this site, including the ability to look up comparable past situations and track open complaints' progress. In the subsequent section, we will go through the platform's primary functional components in further depth. The following sections explain how the new dispute management creativity and better workers and supervisors handle complaints (Heung and Lam, 2003).

12.5   Transforming customer experiences and leveraging AI solutions

Complaint management, complaint summary, and complaints confirmation are all included in the complaint, characterised by a specific. As soon as employees accept a company's objections, they may use the new web-based system to file a report about it before leaving the office. The headquarters might get the communication the next day and investigate the situation. Depending on the situation, they might advise how to improve how information is handled online. The grievance summary interface allowed the headquarter to see each location's most recent grievance cases (Ndubisi and Ling, 2006).

12.5.1   Compensation diagnosis

Complaint records, reimbursement advice, and keyword diagnostic are all included in the compensatory diagnosis module. Managers might benefit from the new system if the compensation diagnostic is used to begin troubleshooting. Managers might use the diagnostic compensation system to compare the complaint characteristic and keyword to a reference case, and a correct suggestion could be made. In addition, a search for "similar cases" may bring up all of them. A customer's apologies might be determined by reading through these situations. Furthermore, the information might be used in training new employees to improve their skills in addressing complaints. Because of this, the managers could use their past expertise to make the proper judgment when dealing with the complaint (Dhatterwal *et al.*, 2022).

12.6   Achieving customer service excellence in claims management through technology intermediation

Complaint analysis is critical to the branch head's appraisal of the quality. When doing an exception analysis, comparing monthly data for accumulative statistics by categorisation and person responsible is beneficial. The technology might automatically create comparative information for each complaint categorisation. The complaint process may be compared between regular time intervals and the annual cumulative average. This way, as well. It is also possible that it will produce recommendations all on its own. To prevent this from occurring again, all personnel might effectively evaluate the categorisation of exceptions at the monthly teleconference (Muddumadappa *et al.*, 2022; Chen and Su, 2022). The branch head might educate employees on unusual circumstances and make announcements about them. The examination of the system might also serve to recall the individual who has made an excessive number of mistakes. The daily approval on the web might be replaced with monthly permission on a paper document by the General Manager. A comparison of the monthly frequency with the annual accumulative average and an automated suggestion are two features provided by the complaint analysis module. Table 12.1 summarises the handling system structure discussed before (Cho *et al.*, 2001).

Table 12.1   The to-be modules of the complaint handling system

Module	Function
An option to submit a complaint has been added	Reporting of grievances
	Compilation of a complaint
	Approval of a complaint
The mechanism for diagnosing compensating	Thesaurus term: Diagnosis
	A suggestion for remuneration
	A record of complaints
Complaint investigation software	A comparison between the estimated weekly recurrence and the annual total
	Predictive advice

12.7   Customer protection – building a robust complaint management system

The platform might be used by everyone involved in the complaint management process at any retailer. Management at headquarters can respond quickly and know exactly what's going on in each instance once handled by the manager or other relevant staff members instead of relying on paper documentation. In this way, the system might improve accessibility and productivity.

In addition, it is frequently challenging to apologise to young employees or bosses in case of a problem. As a result, they should enlist the aid of others. They may seek the advice of a seasoned supervisor or management at the corporate headquarters. Keywords in the diagnostic function may hint at the system in the to-be model. The remediation and compensation procedure as it now is and how it should be. It was clear that supervisors and employees had various approaches to apologising. The term in the to-be model might automatically generate recommendations and compensation principles. Complaint information was therefore put to good use. It was possible to locate significant historical reference instances quickly. This ensured the quality of complaint processing. It was possible to locate significant historical reference instances quickly. In the following sections, you will find information on the product's current and anticipated future state (Tables 12.2–12.4).

It is simple for the branch manager to examine quality via complaint analysis using the system to collect accumulated data by categorisation or by the responsible employee. Each complaint categorisation in the system automatically generates an "exception scenario," which the manager may also refer to. A comparison of regular time intervals and the annual cumulative average may also be made in the

Table 12.2   The activity details for the remedy and compensation process (AS-IS)

Activity	Description
Corrective actions	When an employee receives a complaint and determines the source of the problem, they must next think about how to resolve it
Think and examine through the lens of your own experiences	By studying the complaint material, the team can identify a remedy
Use training guidelines to help you think and analyse	Based on the complaint information, the company's personnel may determine the approach by studying the regulations that have been set
Complaint records may help you think and evaluate	Because of complaints, employees might use existing complaint data to identify a solution
The activity must be integrated and determined	After analysing potential corrective methods, the team may decide on the best course of action

Table 12.3   *The activity details related to the remedy and compensation process (to-be)*

Activity	Description
Corrective actions	There must be a cure for the problem when it is received and understood by the workforce
Publish data on the Internet	Complaint records are retrieved from the Web system
Create a Computer Program and Methodologies Subject	Complaint diagnosis and management may be identified in instances with the same complaint keyword, categorisation, and training rules
Insertion value	Substitute the word "complaint"
Connect	The proposed compensation action is supplied electronically after evaluating the complaint management system

Table 12.4   *The objects (details) related to the remedy and compensation process (to-be)*

Object	Description
Get to the bottom of why you are here	There must be an understanding of the complaint's root cause among the personnel and the management
Experiencing	Complaint management experience
Training requires protocols	Company-adopted guidelines for complaint management training
Acknowledgement phrase for complaints	The history of how complaints have been handled in the past
Requesting for excuse	Customers' apologies in the correct language
Compensatory measures	Customers may be compensated using this approach
Initiation of the action	The consumer gets compensated as a result of this action

complaint analysis module. Additionally, the management may use the results of this investigation for restaurant enhancements (Florenthal and Shoham, 2010).

The business operates like any other conventional business by hiring locals to work around its site. Higher-level staff is educated and chosen through interviews. However, the information from the contractors is used to appoint staff in lower cadres. They hire folks to work there. These workers lack a solid educational foundation. As a result, the organisation can implement "Training on Communication, Body Language (concerning behavioural characteristics)," "Education and training on Employee Morale," and other similar initiatives.

Program to raise awareness of various labour regulations and employee welfare programs, including ESI and PF advantages.

Discuss the company's mission, vision statements, and strategies for success.

Clarity regarding the tasks and responsibilities that each person must fulfil (duties and rights).

12.7.1   *Education regarding workplace safety and knowledge of the value of education*

The supervisor should encourage employee engagement, suggestions, and ideas because doing so will undoubtedly inspire them and increase their level of job satisfaction. This cannot be done right away, and employees would not all start supporting it at once; it will take time for everyone to get on board. However, the corporation and the employees benefit significantly from it (Liu and Shrum, 2002).

A suggestion box system can be implemented to enable employees to offer suggestions for enhancing the organisation and their performance.

Since most workers at the production and manufacturing levels lack formal education, open-door sessions can be held so that they feel comfortable discussing their issues.

Fixing the time barrier will encourage employees to voice their complaints and solve problems at various levels.

The issues should be resolved considering their significance, urgency, and repercussions.

Employee counselling must be conducted regularly to help the organisation identify and address employees' problems, improving job satisfaction, and worker productivity.

Informal counselling aids in addressing and handling workplace complaints. Management and employees get along well when there is an issue or complaint. The employee will be forced to explain the problem as a result fully. This should be done without regard for opinions or favours (Goodman, 2006).

Job descriptions and responsibilities must be as explicit as possible. The company's objectives and expectations should be made clear to everyone, including what is expected of each employee.

12.8   Conclusion

An enhanced (to-be) customer complaint handling procedure is presented in this chapter based on the existing (as-is) customer complaint management architecture. Three things have been learned because of this study. As a first step, it offers staff members with real-time data and instructions that allow them to communicate effectively and accurately. Second, in terms of organisational management, the new complaint-handling method assures that the cases' data, history, and progress reports are well controlled. It also offers information mining and sharing mechanisms throughout the chain's hierarchical components on the continuous learning front. This initiative at a fast-food chain will realise improvements in consumer relations and overall management of client relationships.

References

Bose, R. (2002). Customer relationship management: key components for IT success. *Industrial Management & Data Systems*, 102, 89–97.

Chan, J. O. (2005). Toward a unified view of customer relationship management. *Journal of American Academy of Business*, 6, 32–38.

Chaudhry, P. E. (2007). Developing a process to enhance customer relationship management for small entrepreneurial businesses in the service sector. *Journal of Research in Marketing and Entrepreneurship*, 9, 4–23.

Chen, I. J. and Popovich, K. (2003). Understanding customer relationship management (CRM). *Business Process Management Journal*, 9, 672–688.

Chen, K. and Sockel, H. (2004). The impact of interactivity on business website visibility. *International Journal of Web Engineering and Technology*, 1, 202–217.

Chen, L. and Su, S. (2022). Optimization of the trust propagation on supply chain network based on blockchain plus. *Journal of Intelligent Management Decision*, 1, 17–27.

Cho, Y., Im, I., and Hiltz, R. (2003). The impact of e-services failures and customer complaints on electronic commerce customer relationship management. *Journal of Consumer Satisfaction Dissatisfaction and Complaining Behavior*, 16, 106–118.

Cho, Y., Im, I., Hiltz, R., and Fjermestad, J. (2001). Causes and outcomes of online customer complaining behaviour: implications for customer relationship management (CRM). In *Proceedings of the 7th Americas Conference on Information Systems*, pp. 900–907.

Dhatterwal, J. S., Kaswan, K. S., Preety, D., and Balusamy, B. (2022), Emerging technologies in the insurance market. In Sood, K., Balusamy, B., Grima, S., and Marano, P. (eds.), *Big Data Analytics in the Insurance Market (Emerald Studies in Finance, Insurance, and Risk Management)*, Emerald Publishing Limited, Bingley, pp. 275–286. doi: 10.1108/978-1-80262-637-720221016.

Faed, A., Ashouri, A., and Wu, C. (2010). The efficient bond among mobile commerce, CRM and E-loyalty to maximise the productivity of companies. In *2010 3rd International Conference on Information Sciences and Interaction Sciences (ICIS)*, pp. 312–317.

Florenthal, B. and Shoham, A. (2010). Four-mode channel interactivity concept and channel Preferences. *Journal of Services Marketing*, 24, 29–41.

Foss, B., Stone, M., and Ekinci, Y. (2008). What makes for CRM system success— Or failure? *Journal of Database Marketing & Customer Strategy Management*, 15, 68–78.

Frow, P., Payne, A., Wilkinson, I. F., and Young, L. (2011). Customer management and CRM: addressing the dark side. *Journal of Services Marketing*, 25, 79–89.

Furuholt, B. and Skutle, N. (2007). Strategic use of customer relationship management (CRM) in sports: the Rosenborg case. In *Advances in Information Systems Development*. Springer, pp. 123–133.

Goldsmith, R. E. (2010). The goals of customer relationship management. *International Journal of Customer Relationship Marketing and Management (IJCRMM)*, 1, 16.

Goodman, J. (2006). Manage complaints to enhance loyalty. *Quality Control and Applied Statistics*, 51, 535.

Heung, V. and Lam, T. (2003). Customer complaint behaviour towards hotel restaurant services. *International Journal of Contemporary Hospitality Management*, 15, 283–289.

Hoots, M. (2005). Customer relationship management for facility managers. *Journal of Facilities Management*, 3, 346–361.

Iriana, R. and Buttle, F. (2007). Strategic, operational, and analytical customer relationship management. *Journal of Relationship Marketing*, 5, 23–42.

Kaswan, K. S., Dhatterwal, J. S., Kumar, S., and Lal, S. (2022). Cybersecurity law-based insurance market. In *Big Data: A Game Changer for Insurance Industry*. Emerald Publishing Limited, pp. 303–321. doi:10.1108/978-1-80262-605-620221018

Kaswan, K. S., Dhatterwal, J. S., Sharma, H., and Sood, K. (2022). Big data in insurance innovation. In *Big Data: A Game Changer for Insurance Industry*. Emerald, pp. 117–136. doi:10.1108/978-1-80262-605-620221008

Kerr, C. and Anderson. K. (2002). *Customer Relationship Management*. New York: McGraw-Hill.

Kim, H.-S. and Kim, Y.-G. (2009). A CRM performance measurement framework: its development process and application. *Industrial Marketing Management*, 38, 477–489.

King, S. F. and Burgess, T. F. (2008). Understanding success and failure in customer relationship management. *Industrial Marketing Management*, 37, 421–431.

Lawson Body, A. and Limayem, M. (2004). The impact of customer relationship management on customer loyalty: the moderating role of web site characteristics. *Journal of Computer-Mediated Communication*, 9.

Lindgreen, A., Palmer, R., Vanhamme, J., and Wouters, J. (2006). A relationship management assessment tool: questioning, identifying, and prioritising critical aspects of customer relationships. *Industrial Marketing Management*, 35, 57–71.

Liu, Y. and Shrum, L. (2002). What is interactivity, and is it always such a good thing? Implications of definition, person, and situation for the influence of interactivity on advertising effectiveness. *Journal of Advertising*, 31, 53–64.

Mendoza, L. E., Marius, A., Pérez, M., and Grimán, A. C. (2007). Critical success factors for a customer relationship management strategy. *Information and Software Technology*, 49, 913–945.

Muddumadappa, P. M. B., Anjanappa, S. D. K., and Srikantaswamy, M. (2022). An efficient reconfigurable cryptographic model for dynamic and secure unstructured data sharing in multi-cloud storage server. *Journal of Intelligent Systems and Control*, 1, 68–78.

Ndubisi, N. O. and Ling, T. Y. (2006). Complaint behaviour of Malaysian consumers. *Management Research News*, 29, 65–76.

Ngai, E. W. T., Xiu, L., and Chau, D. C. K. (2009). Application of data mining techniques in customer relationship management: a literature review and classification. *Expert Systems with Applications*, 36, 2592–2602.

Özgener, S. and Iraz, R. (2006). Customer relationship management in small-medium enterprises: the case of Turkish tourism industry. *Tourism Management*, 27, 1356–1363.

Payne, A. and Frow, P. (2005). A strategic framework for customer relationship management. *Journal of Marketing*, 69, 167–176.

Reinartz, W., Krafft, M., and Hoyer, W. D. (2004). The customer relationship management process: its measurement and impact on performance. *Journal of Marketing Research*, 41, 293–305.

Reinartz, W., Thomas, J. S., and Kumar, V. (2005). Balancing acquisition and retention resources to maximise customer profitability. *Journal of Marketing*, 69, 63–79.

Robinson, L., Jr, Neeley, S. E., and Williamson, K. (2011). Implementing service recovery through customer relationship management: identifying the antecedents. *Journal of Services Marketing*, 25, 90–100.

Ueno, S. (2006). The impact of customer relationship management. *USJP Occasional Paper*, 6, pp. 6–13.

Chapter 13

Robotic process automation applications area in the financial sector

Kuldeep Singh Kaswan[1], Jagjit Singh Dhatterwal[2], Simon Grima[3] and Kiran Sood[4]

Abstract

The world is becoming more and more digitally sophisticated. Transformation is a process that is always changing. Robotic process automation, or RPA, was added to the remodeling process. RPA is becoming a very useful tool in banks and other financial organizations. RPA has helped a variety of different organizations in many ways. The main goal of Robotic Process Automation in banking is to cut down on processes that are done again and over again. In banks and other companies, RPA has helped save operational expenses by 30–70%. RPA helps minimize the number of employees by putting Bot workers in charge, which lowers operational costs and makes jobs more efficient and accurate. Lenders are often put under pressure to cut their charges and speed up the process. So, the lender turns to automation to improve service speed and accuracy. With automation bots, lenders may automate loan processing by gathering information about customers, approving loans, keeping an eye on loans, and setting prices for loans on their own. With the aid of rule-based software bots, this can be done. Also, many lenders execute part of the procedure automatically and part of it by hand. To keep up with the newest security changes, banks and other financial institutions are turning to automation and training. This helps keep an eye on how payment habits change over time. For example, fraud is always a danger. This innovative RPA technology is used by banks, insurance firms, and other financial businesses. This is to find and stop fraud by gathering data from many service lines instead of making a lot of economic macros. The article speaks about how RPA may reduce the risk of fraud by doing things like reevaluating present procedures, getting rid of human mistakes, improving trade monitoring, automating threat identification, looking for outliers, and a lot more.

[1]School of Computing Science and Engineering, Galgotias University, India
[2]Department of Artificial Intelligence & Data Science, Koneru Lakshmaiah Education Foundation, India
[3]Insurance and Risk Management, Faculty of Economics, Management & Accountancy, University of Malta, Malta
[4]Chitkara Business School, Chitkara University, Punjab, India

Similarly, a big banking institution does much of the engagement in a relatively robotic and some in a tactile manner. Banking and macroeconomic establishments are transitioning to automation and preparing to keep steady over recent security advancements. This assists with watching out for the developing patterns in the instalment space. Extortion, for example, is a constant danger. Banks, insurance agencies, and other monetary establishments utilize this new period of RPA innovation. This is to distinguish and counter fake pulling information from different assistance lines instead of making many financial macros. The paper discusses how RPA can moderate misrepresentation and takes a chance through various strategies, for example, reconsidering momentum processes, wiping out human blunders, upgraded exchange observing, robotized danger identification, looking for inconsistencies, and substantially more.

Keywords: Humanoid robot; Machine learning; Intelligent robotic process automation

13.1   Introduction contact centre optimization

Progress in innovations has had a profound influence on how organizations operate. Planning operations have been redesigned to be much more efficient and modern to enhance consumer interactions while lowering operating expenses. Companies can increase these objectives with the help of robotic process automation (RPA). RPA is a tool that interacts with a computer's graphical interface PCs like experienced professionals do. Entire banking establishments, health and security, marketing communication tool and commodities, retailing and industry are the primary industries that encourage workflow automation accomplishment. The marketplace is a great open door for equipment and programming worldwide.

Bots can work daily, every day (Vijai *et al.*, 2020), another benefit that individual professionals do not have. RPA transferred boring, repetitive tasks from individuals to bots, assisting account managers in reducing the working population and preventing unnecessary engagement. We can avoid arbitrary potential mistakes via RPA. RPA can then provide better customer engagement. Present-day examples of wide-range hacking and social designing are marks of innovation. Fraudsters generally stay one stride ahead by growing better approaches to execute modern extortion conspires that seem testing to recognize or forestall (Muddumadappa *et al.*, 2022; Chen and Su, 2022). To remain on the ball, banks must put resources into the up-and-coming age of computerized misrepresentation and risk the executive's measures to guarantee wellbeing. Driving "banks in India, including Federal Bank, ICICI Bank, Axis Bank, and HDFC, likewise executed robotic process automation for quicker and more powerful."

13.2 Trade finance operations

The preceding are some strong ideas for mechanical interface automated processes.

- *Effective cost execution*
  Effective execution of robot process automation assists, manages an account with lessening functional expenses. Observations done by different specialists show that implementing RPA in financial establishments assists work by limiting working expenses and saving time.
- *RPA better functional value*
  Bankers that use RPA bots require higher effectiveness. RPA speeds up tasks and provides processes more valuable and productive.
- *RPA chatbots*
  RPA bots may operate 24-h shifts a day, 8 h a week, and finish all delegated tasks on schedule. Furthermore, they could eliminate operational errors created by internal employees and can accomplish high precision. For example, account conclusion in financial establishments is an extremely tedious interaction. Banks need to look at the client's notable credits, speak with them, demand important archives, and drop the immediate charges and future orders. This exceptionally extensive interaction carves out the opportunity to achieve this errand. Furthermore, it really can lead to human weaknesses. RPA chatbots can be used to function efficiently in this circumstance (Gupta *et al.*, 2019).
- *RPA maintenance*
  RPA implementation and administration need no/minimal code. Advocates can be capable of establishing, running, and supervising RPA bots. Because of its UI equipment and programming skills, RPA in financial businesses does not require any advancements. Cloud-based RPA reduces technology expenses even further.
- *Develop customer demand*
  RPA improves customer engagement by responding to customer requirements and enquiries more quickly and with good accuracy, using RPA chatbots or programmable e-mail conversations. RPA enables employees to understand their customers and develop excellent and meaningful contact with them.

13.3 Literature review on customer on-boarding

The Universities of Mississippi where Louis' Mary Lacity led an analysis (2015) in which they addressed the robotic process automation adventure in Telefonica O2. It began the RPA coordination trail on two high-volume, low-intricacy processes. The principal interaction was sim trades in which the client's current sim card is supplanted with a new sim by keeping their existing number. The other cycle was using predetermined credit to a client's record. They arranged blue crystal (a global corporation programmer business that does humanoid robot lifecycle automated). Specialists assisted in the development of the machine for hypothesis testing. The preliminary foundations of "Telefonica O2's architectures were quite strong. With the support of RPA, the machines completed several transactions and raised alarms in the IT security model to differentiate fakes (Lacity *et al.*, 2015). Yara Rizk of University Research AI, Boston, MA, investigated the executions and usage situations of RPA in their assessment task (2020). This depicts the lending registration process, in which the customer submits the advanced approach. At the same time, a bank representative passes through the solicitations and decides either to uphold or disapprove the loan modification. Clients enter data and sometimes decide to approve or reject the advanced registration based on business standards (Rizk *et al.*, 2020). Sandeep Vishnu, Partner, and Capco (2017) describe how RPA configurations can satisfy a few criteria of the banking sector north of some few relationship collaborations, such as bank, financial institution, financial institution, and capital adequacy. Various leading banks are taking serious steps to use RPA in their organizations (Vishnu *et al.*, 2017)."

"In their research study (2018), Kevin C. Moffitt displays automation of reviewing activities implementing RPA. These few RPA executing phases that reviewing businesses should study, for example, differentiating the evaluation engagement that should be automated, how the cycling may be separated into little steps for the computerized system, and the outcome of the evaluation with the help of RPA (Moffitt *et al.*, 2018)." According to the Public Company Accounting Oversight Board (PCAOB) evaluation briefings (2017), business process management for earnings verification has a strength training to increase the strength of the individual. The primary area of evaluation that is routinely evaluated is income (PCAOB, 2017). According to Appelbaum *et al.* (2017), the operational power of examining might be used to authorize intelligence demonstrated by machines. Processing is being used to populate the whole population of transactions. This will help the reviewers end different dangers in the examining system and assess gambles all the more precisely (Appelbaum *et al.*, 2011).

Annette Stolpe studies (2017) show mechanization of the link between Brønnøysundregistrene, a Norwegian public agency for supervisory reporting, and the banking to begin resources and conventional data processing the bot's function rather like humans and are prepared to take on any type of duty (Stolpe *et al.*, 2017). Devarajan (2018) mentions many relevant bankers that regularly trade in their study. It is particularly considerate of banking to maintain exceedingly sensitive and confidential information with great precision and promptly. Technically, increased efficiency may reduce manual errors in manufacturing. Information handling via computerizing process (Mittal and Jhamb, 2016; Mittal *et al.*, 2020). This incorporates customer administrations, creditor liabilities, accounts receivables, general records, credit guaranteeing, consistency, charge card handling, purchaser advance handling, extortion location, reportage, and account opening/conclusion (Devarajan, 2018).

"Wasique Ali Ansari mentions in their research study (2019) that RPA is collaborating toward the Intelligent Robotic Process Automation (IRPA)." Everything opens up various innovations of RPA like AI, information insightful voice acknowledgement, savvy optical person acknowledgement, design examination, etc. It specifies that the foundation of IRPA will excuse low-esteem occupations and assist with sending off new professions for making and overseeing (Ansari *et al.*, 2019). Robots in his assessment (2018), Karippur Krishna Krishna attributed the issues to fortify different client encounters by executing RPA in the financial business. The components are referenced as security protection, unwavering quality, and human-like connection. The examination model and hypothesis area take care of the paper. He proposed four theories concerning security and safety in the financial business (Kumar and Balaramachandran, 2018).

According to PWC (2017), just 5% of businesses are considered professional in their advanced computer engagement and 15% in their use of machine learning and artificial intelligence. Currently, just 5% of firms feel they are fully utilizing AI, while 15% say they are fully utilizing RPA (PWC, 2017).

The review led by PWC (2019) in the December quarter gives us a short overview of the current state of systems engineering innovations. Approximately 15 questions were addressed, encompassing research and processing, various risks and challenges, administration and regulations, and usage areas. According to the perspective, 80% of the firms had mathematical competence, and others were from economics, IT, the administration, or robotic cycle computerization focus of greatness capacities (PWC, 2019).

Max Gotthardt led an assessment of UiPath Studio (2020), where transaction administration is completed with digital transformation. In this case, the customer confronted difficulties like perusing, confirming, approving, enrolling, and posting the solicitations. Two thousand solicitations are handled daily, and, as a result, they decide to automate this engagement by using the RPA technique to engage and publish the soliciting. They reduced the amount of physical labour by 65% to 75% (Gotthardt *et al.*, 2019). According to Gary Barnett (2015), Barclays, another of Europe's greatest banks, has used RPA in its administrative centres to quickly loop customers' needs based on distinct client requirements. For roughly ten years, the bank has used blue spectrum to digitalize numerous cycles, such as fabrication detection and recording retrieval automation. Other financial institutions have automated about 130 cycles with Microsoft Azure and RPA. Innovation includes complex processes, such as VISA chargeback, CHAPs, and different administrative centre cycles (Barnett, 2015).

When cybersecurity is the primary concern of a banking institution, they are extremely vulnerable to a breach of protocol. Cryptocurrency technology is advancing assuming an essential part in reviewing and protection, particularly regarding trading cash or agreement more safely (Anwar *et al.*, 2019; Gupta *et al.*, 2020a, 2020b) With the assistance of the nonstop association of innovation in banking and money, it is likewise conceivable to limit the fakes in different kinds of credit handling (Beena *et al.*, 2021). Mechanical cycles are not just restricted. Besides banking, with a focus currently on the tourism sector and human kindness (Petiwala *et al.*, 2021; Trayush *et al.*, 2021), modern medicine (Suhel *et al.*, 2020) is emerging as among the primary areas to adopt this development.

Skoller, Andrew understands that systems engineering aids in the creation of findings when any investigators or focused financial authority must begin with each of these documents. RPA is beneficial in the era of notifications. The automated programme contributes to the production of investigator's information to check without having the expert quest for the required data (Madana *et al.*, 2021).

According to a study conducted by Carmo, Gonçalo Pires de Carvalho Mota (2020), financial institutions in Portuguese have not implemented robotic, intelligence administrative centres even though most of them know about the idea of RPA. Many of them have RPA, their fundamental methodology, for the future, yet it has not been carried out yet. Even though a couple of banks have previously begun embracing robotization in their workplaces. According to the tests, the front business has witnessed more digital transformation than the managerial centres (Verma *et al.*, 2021). According to Hannah Valgaeren's (2019) research, the banking industry "is one of the most important business sectors for the use of Automated Technology." This segment was expected to account for 34% of the entire systems engineering market by 2022. The study includes a prototype of a British bank implementing RPA in its accounting and macroeconomic cycles. It was discovered that before the use of RPA, each transaction took around 15 min. The exchange duration in the institution has been set at 10 ms for each transaction (Shukla *et al.*, 2020).

The intelligent machine transform the capability of object, according to Dipak Pimpale (2019), to shorten the conversion time, the bank hired a Bot developer to create and operate the robot. Following the completion of RPA, items, for the most part, comprise of not many major components, designer devices to demonstrate the business processes, Bots regulator to work a wide range of work processes and direct the bots, programming young men to deal with an assignment (Nanda *et al.*, 2020).

13.4   Anti-money laundering (AML)

Systems are actively digitizing aspects of their operations via electromechanical cycling computer technology (RPA; Verma *et al.*, 2021). RPA robotizes specific human errands using PC-coded, programmable robotics (i.e., bots). RPA contrasts with intelligent machines, such as cognition mapping or AI, while it can make decisions based on data points. In this basic form, a bot is a multimedia corporation meant to duplicate the gestures that somebody would do to perform a PC-based task while employing equivalent multifactor authentication as the observer (Goel *et al.*, 2021). Bots function at the intermediate user layer, automating operations while causing damage to the fundamental data technological (IT) framework. Bots precisely adhere to authorized conventions and techniques, enhancing uniformity and efficiency improvements (Figure 13.1).

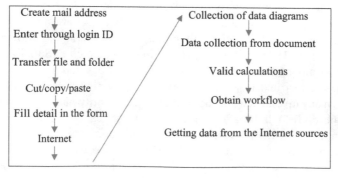

Figure 13.1   The capabilities of RPA

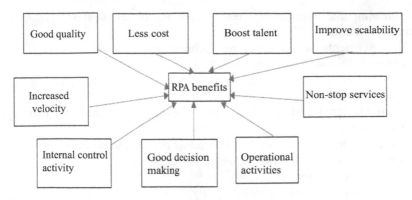

Figure 13.2   RPA benefits

RPA may be inexpensive to implement compared with other automation technologies and can quickly provide financial and non-financial benefits that affect the most common performance measures. Figure 13.2 illustrates RPA benefits.

13.5   Bank guarantee closures

According to Deloitte's 2017 RPA analysis, business dynamics indicate a close all-inclusive absorption of RPA in the next two decades. The typical budget for RPA prototypes was $2 billion, with comprehensive operations costing at least $3 million. This quick increase in domestically consumption and spending is helping to develop a diverse biological ecosystem of RPA vendors and RPA arrangements targeted at assisting organizations in achieving technology innovation. Modern media is increasingly employed exceptionally as businesses seek effective ways to deploy RPA around their organizations. So, wherein do we require to look? The greatest use of digitalization? Autonomous mobile and intellectual computation check by Mckinsey scientist to improve the quality of autonomous system (Shukla and Verma, 2019a).

Bookkeeping record in RPA messaging among consumers. This commercial job is ideal for equipment and programming for several goals, including:

- The need for a high level of performance and predictability.
- Transaction management is repetitious and laborious.
- Data accumulated from divided frameworks.
- Reliance on information section, information control, and reportage.
- Due to these qualities, countless jobs in administrative centre bookkeeping and fund capacities can be computerized. The realistic beneath features explicit cycles inside the bookkeeping and money work and the practicality of robotization inside those cycles (i.e., low, medium, high).

Usually, maintain bookkeeping records and fund capacities include

- Request to money and records receivable.
- Creating and refreshing client ACE information.

- Reviewing and supporting client orders are placed against predetermined credit limitations.
- Client payments authentication and submission.
- Responsibilities of creditors.
- I am entering requests into an enterprise resource planning (ERP) infrastructure.
- We are changing customer orders and renewing the enterprise resource planning system.
- Connecting inquiries with related customer orders and reimbursements.
- Monetary shutting and announcing process.
- Journal section approval.
- Low-risk account compromises.
- We are generating reports and stacking them into announcing/union formats.

13.6   Bank reconciliation process

- Effective organizations constantly attempt to identify combinations that result in enhancing efficiency. A regular pattern everywhere in recent years has been to seaward gifted and nonskilled fill-in as a type of work exchange to lessen costs (Khan *et al.*, 2021). Endeavours are currently turning toward computerising specific business errands (e.g., account compromises, receipt handling, recalculations, source information coordinating, edge application) to upset the human resources influence and model. In particular, RPA might supplant or upgrade specific errands recently performed by people with less expensive, more productive, and solid bots.
- Even though RPA might lessen accidental or purposeful human blunders, the execution of the use of bots creates extra hazards that organizations must be aware of and manage the inability of a business to assess the consequences of these genetic design changes on its increased capability over financial disclosures (ICFR), especially those powers over IT, which is a substantial concern generated by the quick embrace of bots (Wanganoo, 2020). The inability to appropriately study and control these worldwide concerns may disintegrate or limit the benefit provided by the automation exchange. When additional technology, company websites, and collaborative tools are used, malware hazards may grow.

To understand the benefits of organizations ought to consider what RPA take initiative to chance in various classes, including:

- Development phase: Adhering to the laid-out process choice guidelines and advancement techniques (from test to creation) is fundamental for the computerization apparatus to accomplish the ideal result. After a bot is placed in the process to establish (i.e., the terminal stage of evolution of the entire lifespan in which functional advancement is automatically triggered), involvement programs are expected to minimize the effects that the manufacturer bot is not properly configured or that the previously planned digital revolution does not begin to operate to acquire the known and accepted main goal (Shukla and

Verma, 2019b). In these circumstances, it is critical to contrast the use of RPA enhancements in monetary reporting contact with the formulation and execution of computerized constraints that promote a firm cycle. Considering the increasingly automated technique, direct authority incorporates a vicious baseline circle over the algorithms and type of relationship settings (as applicable) while behind digital transformation to ensure that it comprehends the firm's strategy requirements of the organization, which would include methodologies for information examination and highlighting of deductions. Bots should be programmed to detect potential errors and raise unusual instances for bot commanders to deal with constantly. When RPA development is complete and available to pursue attempts are completed, general data improvement controls (GITCs) will ensure that the chatbots continue to perform as expected (Wanganoo, 2021a, 2021b).

- RPA implement phase: In the implementation, enterprises should consider RPA's impact on their IT hazard analysis. The usage of RPA brings additional risks related to proper implementation of the bots' privileged accessibility and surveillance of any technological improvements to guarantee it remains effective as expected. As a consequence, it is vital to have a full grasp of the IT infrastructure's procedures. (e.g., data set, runtime environment, organizational) designed to aid mechanized innovations and GITCs over those features, comprising limitations over:
- Comprehension of clients' activities and foundation and knowledge transfer requirements for chatbots interacting with central foundations will prevent unauthorized clients from accessing RPA's knowledge managing fuzzy rules and the ability-related providers. It is critical to avoid such unauthorized since it might be used to get accessibility to classified knowledge and modify robots, as well as conduct programmed activities, job-based admission rules enable organizations to prevent access and validate clients, accordingly isolating robotization-related obligations among representatives. The capacity to create or control bots' activities can be appointed based on a representative's situation inside the organization. Client access controls, by and large, comprised of (a) occasional audits of client access privileges and (b) validation controls over client ID.
- System change: We, by and large, suggest that accountants adhere to their current management approach for computer program improvement pupal stage tasks. Modification of the managers' plans must depict bots that use the program that is transforming. A solid modify the leadership software will also have an engagement for directly performing modifications to the machines.
- Computer farm and management responsibilities: Protecting the integrity of data accessed, stored, or sent by critical components. The integrity of the IT model is fundamental to compliance with the ICFR related to chatbots. Additionally, enterprises may need to examine external security problems when a bot saves data on the cloud.
- RPA surveillance phase: Developing techniques for determining bot effectiveness is crucial for monitoring and promoting commercial advancements.

Sufficient implementation and management procedures are also essential to the commission's capacity to assess the long-term viability of bots adopting ICFR and, as a result, strengthen the competence to conform to Section 404(a) of the Sarbanes-Oxley Act of 2002. As a result, organizations may consider a variety of monitoring approaches, as well as the initial controlling strength training:

o   Schedule evaluation and consistency norms for including mechanized components.

o   I am continuing with human company monitoring to acknowledge the successful completion of the automated job.

o   Examining logs from the RPA market(s) to ensure the authenticity and acceptability of each measure taken by the automation firms may also analyze and address obstacles encountered by bot faults or harmful code. Tasked with implementing an objective analysis of the information technology algorithm(s) (i.e., retrieving the thermometer) to check conformity with the established strategic planning (Jhamb, 2020).

o   She is keeping a complete uniformity goal to meet statutory duties.

o   As RPA functionality improvement and long periods of bot performance are guaranteed, organizations may consider decreasing the size of diagnostics operational processes. For example, if the administration gains confidence in the overall performance of the RPA programme, organizations may opt to eliminate extremely laborious horizontal scrolling and depend solely on automation. Organizations may also identify and address difficulties caused by bot faults or harmful code and tasked with conducting an annual examination of the information technology algorithm(s) (i.e., restoring the speedometer) to ensure compliance with the established business plan (Jhamb *et al.*, 2020).

• Information gathering by RPA: Notwithstanding the executives' yearly evaluation of the organization's ICFR, remembering outside review necessities is significant. Progress in this space requires proactive correspondences with inspectors throughout the excursion to create and carry out RPA. Holding arranging gatherings and everyday update conversations about the ICFR recommendations are encouraging procedures to aid practitioners and assessors in adapting performance reasoning in regards to gamble with appraisal and the distinguishing proof of significant controls, which will smooth out the review cycle and assemble examiners' trust in the adequacy of the bots. A few unexpected themes to think about while getting ready for outer reviews include:

o   Those accused of inside consistency (e.g., interior review work, IT consistency) ought to keep a refreshed updating of chatbots and establish a protocol to ensure that adjustments to mechanisms are incorporated in both strategies whenever needed.

o   Financial statements, organizational charts, the corporate governance documentation should specify explicitly what but also how chatbots are utilized inside the accountants and monetary institutions.

o   Strict limits on bot strategies and functioning do not suggest that a company should disregard the administration of news suppliers and repercussions. Appropriate power structures should contain restrictions across every exchange cycle, including the original dataset, consequences, and where a performance management process is required, such as reviewing deviations or voicing an attitude. This is particularly essential when bots immediately modify financial information.

Certain bots might be simply functional and utilized on the outskirts of the monetary detailing process, though different bots may easily influence book-keeping and fiscal summary survey control exercises. Reviewers should comprehend the nature and effect of bots utilized by the bookkeeping and money association to zero in on their methods on those generally applicable to the fiscal reports (Singh *et al.*, 2019).

Issues emerging inside any of these dangers might prompt monetary misfortune. For instance, inappropriate execution or computerization of some unacceptable cycles (i.e., functional hazards) may bring prompt economic troubles to an association. Bot-related blunders influencing the honesty of online protection projects or consistency with information security guidelines may not just outcome in that frame of mind to the business; they may likewise lead to reputational worries in the commercial centre. In this way, associations must survey how these progressions illuminate their gamble appraisal, especially those emerging IT dangers, and whether significant improvements in cycling and architecture (i.e., regulating environment) are necessary to meet their current criteria. When assessing the adoption of RPA advancements, it is vital to exploit the controller designing environment whenever feasible and to examine those spots where the current administrations built may not be sufficient to aid these improvements. Controls in the next levels may be considered by enterprises as far as the lifetime of a bot from conception and creation to performance and observation (Shukla and Bhandari, 2019).

13.7 Loan application process

Borrowing treatment began with acquiring the applicant architecture and printed reports from the users, such as ID card electronic communications and so on (Figure.13.1). The bank's task begins here, when the registration is being processed, to proceed to the endorsement engagement.

Based on the probability analysis, the bank decides whether it should approve or deny the extension applications. Following the dynamic stage to endorse or dismiss the advance, the bank then, at that point, sends letters to the client concerning the choice.

13.7.1 RPA abilities

RPA bots operate the same way humans do and therefore have almost the same range of talents. These chatbots function as a computational working population that may interact with various foundations and programs. RPA bots may conduct multiple sophisticated computations, activating a certain event coordinator or document located in the program, analyzing communications, interacting with

APIs, and other tasks. Bots are simple to establish, operate with, and provide in management and artificial intelligence.

13.8   Automated report generation

Automated systems by reconsidering the current procedure, you should eliminate deception and misbehaviour. RPA algorithms assess and analyze the clients' preceding interactions state-of-the-art and choose lopsided and dubious examples indicating fake exercises. If the bots learn about such questionable occasions, they send warnings to banks. Computerization bots can evaluate reasonable deceitful practices and banner high-esteem exchanges in vulnerable segments. Automated systems can discriminate between data from different sources. As a result, they can deal with such situations and basic circumstances with brilliant unwavering quality and exactness, which is superior to any representative (Shukla and Verma, 2019c).

Banks can deal with and work various records at the same time. Large numbers of the stores stay latent for a drawn-out period, and when banks figure out any dubious exercises with such documents, they are put under an impermanent square. These transitory squares would not be removed until the bank experts physically unblocked them (Athota *et al.*, 2020). Automated managed services robots are utilized in this circumstance even though they can recognize personalities created underneath transitioning boundaries, protect their prior actions, and eliminate the shorter geometric shapes and limits. In any case, it is conceivable if the documenting operations are dealt with the rules and standards of organizations to eliminate the obstruction.

13.9   Account closure processing

The first step in beginning the crediting lifecycle is obtaining the overview of the system, ID information, and from before the details. During this stage, the aspirant must provide different data like the candidate's work data, compensation, bank explanations, family pay, and assessment forms. Previously, submissions were delivered on parchment; now, current technology allows applicants to be provided remotely using structured or flexible programs. When the financial department receives the applications, they review them for reliability and approval process completion. The registration is forwarded to the customer or the appropriate bank institution if the mandatory documents are not completed.

When the applications' participation is full, the bank conducts the implementations via several phases of the progression process, such as benefits and disadvantages. This technique can be computerized permanently or temporarily. The bank may now encourage or refuse the application interactions and the decision, as well as supplementary data regarding the option, such as lending sum; borrowing expenses can be communicated to the advancing applicant based on the confirmations and qualifications verification (Agarwal *et al.*, 2019).

13.9.1   RPA programming

Technology in credit management machines can also be automated by various chatbots, which can help with the robotization of the cycle. Multiple online tools aid in the automation of business procedures for diverse factions. The operations centre will be cloud-based, or it will be individually implemented on a web server. The bots we create will be transported and housed in the central controller, from whence they will be dispatched to Bot Marathon. A Bot Runner performs the RPA code. Digital technology can be both monitored and unsupervised.

The experience of going to automated processes is a collaborative effort of chatbots and people, whereas unsupervised autonomous bots function freely. In managed industrialization, bots collaborate with professionals to help with front-of-house duties. We should be able to build a bot and organize it in the software and hardware terminal by providing it with directions or instructions depending on our needs and company requirements.

RPA chatbots are typically layered on top of RPA systems, a software's Windows Environment (GUI), whereas native development is based on the platform's programming interface (API). Advance management implementation, where the bank utilizes mechanization to separate the credit application structure, has been put together by the client and put away in an information (succeed/CSV) document. The breakthrough used in this case is an advancement in OCR. The bot used OCR to inspect the inspected picture; after interpreting the edge detection, the oddities are recorded to a conspicuously highlighted one. RPA is regulation, so we teach the bots specifically what they want to perform. We instruct bots on what to do at each stage of the journey. Variations, such as dependent explanations, are always possible.

In mechanization, with the assistance of a control room, we can get to every one of the apparatuses for controlling, making, recording, changing/refreshing, and sending computerized processes. Before making mechanization, one must download and install bot professionals on their smartphone, authorize the equipment, and upgrade customized specifications. A bot specialized is a little software that, once installed, allows your equipment to be closely correlated with and interface with the RPA police headquarters. When engaged, the gadget may connect with the command centre with no consumer action—maintaining the bot accessible on the switching monitors to ensure smooth operation.

Procedures to segregate the programmes and save them in a data item: in digitalization, the OCR instruction is used to retrieve the relevant data from the particular experimental application, which is kept in the enrolling smartphone's particular enclosing. We can extract pictures with designs, .jpeg, .jpg, .bmp, .gif, .png, using the OCR bundles in the digitalization anyplace. It also enables us to separate text from the windows of a program, collect text from a specified portion of an activity, transmit completely separated text, and store it as a parameter.

With automation technology, it is possible to fully automate a large portion of credit administration, from accumulating individual application structures to delivering communications to clients about forwarding acceptance or elimination per bank laws and procedures. Consequently, loan managing is advantageous for RPA and can provide crucial benefits for banking initiatives.

13.10   Credit card application processing

The fourth modern upheaval, famously known as Industry 4.0 advancements, also assumes a vital part in robotization in roughly all spaces. Web of Things (IoT) and FIR innovations are taking an important part continuously information investigation, in practically all fields, for example, transport the board the travel industry (Zaidi *et al.*, 2021), shrewd horticulture, the executives, medical services, the executives, home computerization, store network the executives, instruction the executives, educating and learning and numerous different areas as well. The RPA cycle and multiple different credit-handling cycles will be more refined and better with these banking and advanced handling advances. This is particularly expected for emerging countries and remote spots, where versatility is a test. There, with this innovation's assistance, a huge populace can be given advantages.

13.11   Conclusion

Banking institutions continue executing RPA innovation, in practically their associations in general. RPA is an off-the-late-started invention. It proceeds to cross and grow out of its creation to upgrade the client experience, facilitate functional efficiencies, and limit the expense where this can be accomplished with the assistance of RPA. Large numbers of banking and different associations keep carrying out RPA to achieve the enormous advantages of executing RPA, including upgraded information quality, quicker and secure administrations, diminished manual human mistakes, further developed business results, and decreased extortion chances.

Executing RPA in financial foundations for advancing it is fruitful to process and misrepresentation identification. Its execution has developed the economic cycles into an exceptionally progressed approach. In the ongoing advances, associations plan to diminish functional expenses and offer better types of assistance to their clients. Subsequently, in the following couple of years, we will see the execution of RPA in the more significant part of the business areas where robotization bots assume responsibility for office work rather than human labourers.

References

Agarwal, P., Shukla, V.K., Gupta, R., and Jhamb, S. (2019). Attendance monitoring system through RFID, face detection and ethernet network: a conceptual framework for sustainable campus. In *2019 4th International Conference on Information Systems and Computer Networks (ISCON)*, 2019, pp. 321–325, doi:10.1109/ISCON47742.2019.9036209.

Ansari, W.A., Diya, P., Patil, S., and Patil, S. (2019a). A review on robotic process automation – the future of business organizations. In *2nd International Conference on Advances in Science & Technology (ICAST) 2019 on 8th, 9th April 2019* by K J Somaiya Institute of Engineering & Information Technology, Mumbai, India, Available at SSRN: https://ssrn.com/abstract= 3372171 or http://dx.doi.org/10.2139/ssrn.3372171.

Anwar, S., Shukla, V.K., Rao, S.S., Sharma, B.K., and Sharma, P. (2019b). Framework for financial auditing process through blockchain technology, using identity based cryptography. In *2019 Sixth HCT Information Technology Trends (ITT)*, pp. 099–103, doi:10.1109/ITT48889.2019.9075120.

Appelbaum, D., Brown-Liburd, H., Cho, S., Kogan, A., Rozario, A., and Vasarhelyi, M.A. (2011). Response to the IAASB in exploring the growing use of technology in the audit, with a focus on Data Analytics. *A Journal of Practice & Theory*, 30(1), 75–99.

Appelbaum, D., Kogan, A., and Vasarhelyi, M.A., (2017). Big data and analytics in the modern audit engagement: research needs. *AUDITING: A Journal of Practice & Theory*, 36(4), 1–27.

Athota, L., Shukla, V. K., Pandey, N., and Rana, A. (2020), Chatbot for health-care system using artificial intelligence. In *2020 8th International Conference on Reliability, Infocom Technologies and Optimization (Trends and Future Directions) (ICRITO)*, 2020, pp. 619–622. doi:10.1109/ ICRITO48877.2020.9197833.

Barnett, G. (2015). Robotic process automation: adding to the process transfor-mation toolkit. White paper IT0022–0005, Ovum Consulting.

Beena, F., Mearaj, I., Shukla, V.K., and Anwar, S. (2021), Mitigating financial fraud using data science – "A Case Study on Credit Card Frauds". In *2021 International Conference on Innovative Practices in Technology and Management (ICIPTM)*, 2021, pp. 38–43. doi: 10.1109/ICIPTM52218.2021.9388345.

Chen, L., and Su, S. (2022). Optimization of the trust propagation on supply chain network based on blockchain plus. *Journal of Intelligent Management Decision*, 1(1), 17–27.

Devarajan, Y. (2018). A study of robotic process automation use cases today for tomorrow's business. *International Journal of Computer and Information Technology*, 5(6), pp. 12–18.

Goel, M., Goyal, A.H., Dhiman, P., Deep, V., Sharma, P., and Shukla, V.K. (2021). Smart garbage segregator and IoT based waste collection system. In *2021 International Conference on Advance Computing and Innovative Technologies in Engineering (ICACITE)*, 2021, pp. 149–153. doi:10.1109/ICACITE51222.2021.9404692.

Gotthardt, M., Koivulaakso, D., Paksoy, O., Saramo, C., Martikainen, M., and Lehner, O.M. (2019). Current state and challenges in implementing robotic process automation and artificial intelligence in accounting and auditing. *ACRN Oxford Journal of Finance Risk Perspectives*, 8, pp. 31–46.

Gupta, D.R., Avila, C.S.R., Win, J., *et al.*, (2019). Cautionary notes on use of the MoT3 diagnostic assay for Magnaporthe oryzae wheat and rice blast isolates. *Phytopathology*, 109(4), 504–508.

Gupta, N., Sharma, P., Deep, V., and Shukla, V.K. (2020a). Automated attendance system using OpenCV. In *2020 8th International Conference on Reliability, Infocom Technologies and Optimization (Trends and Future Directions) (ICRITO)*, pp. 1226–1230. doi:10.1109/ICRITO48877.2020.9197936.

Gupta, R., Shukla, V.K., Rao, S.S., Anwar, S., Sharma, P., and Bathla, R. (2020b). Enhancing privacy through smart contract using blockchain-based dynamic access control. In *2020 International Conference on Computation, Automation and Knowledge Management (ICCAKM)*, pp. 338–343. doi:10.1109/ICCAKM46823.2020.9051521.

Jhamb S. and Shukla V.K. (2020). The role of teacher and technology in foreign language acquisition. *IUP Journal of English Studies*, 15(3), 7–14.

Jhamb, S., Gupta, R., Shukla, V.K., Mearaj, I., and Agarwal, P. (2020). Understanding complexity in language learning through data visualization using python. In *2020 International Conference on Computation, Automation and Knowledge Management (ICCAKM)*, pp. 268–274. doi:10.1109/ICCAKM46823.2020.9051512.

Khan R., Shukla V.K., Singh B., and Vyas S. (2021). Mitigating security challenges in smart home management through smart lock. In: Singh T.P., Tomar R., Choudhury T., Perumal T., and Mahdi H.F. (eds.), *Data-Driven Approach Towards Disruptive Technologies. Studies in Autonomic, Data-Driven and Industrial Computing*. Springer, Singapore. https://doi.org/10.1007/978-981-15-9873-9_7.

Kumar, K.N. and Balaramachandran, P.R. (2018). Robotic process automation – a study of the impact on customer experience in retail banking industry. *Journal of Internet Banking and Commerce*, 23(3), 1–27.

Lacity, M., Willcocks, L.P., and Craig, A. (2015). Robotic process automation at Telefonica O2. In *The Outsourcing Unit Working Research Paper Series* (15/02). The London School of Economics and Political Science, London, UK.

Madana, L., Kumar Shukla, V., Sharma, R., and Nanda, I. (2021). IoT enabled smart boarding pass for passenger tracking through Bluetooth low energy. In *2021 International Conference on Advance Computing and Innovative Technologies in Engineering (ICACITE)*, 2021, pp. 101–106. doi:10.1109/ICACITE51222.2021.9404602.

Moffitt, K.C., Rozario, A.M., and Vasarhelyi, M.A. (2018). Robotic process automation for auditing. *Journal of Emerging Technologies in Accounting*, 15(1), 1–10. doi:https://doi.org/10.2308/jeta-10589.

Mittal, A., Aggarwal, A., and Mittal, R. (2020). Predicting university students' adoption of mobile news applications: the role of perceived hedonic value and news motivation. *International Journal of E-Services and Mobile Applications (IJESMA)*, 12(4), 42–59.

Mittal, A., and Jhamb, D. (2016). Determinants of shopping mall attractiveness: the Indian context. *Procedia Economics and Finance*, 37, 386–390.

Muddumadappa, P. M. B., Anjanappa, S. D. K., and Srikantaswamy, M. (2022). An efficient reconfigurable cryptographic model for dynamic and secure unstructured data sharing in multi-cloud storage server. *Journal of Intelligent Systems and Control*, 1(1), 68–78.

Nanda, I., Sahithi, C., Swath, M., Maloji, S., and Shukla, V.K. (2020). IIOT based smart crop protection and irrigation system. In *2020 Seventh International Conference on Information Technology Trends (ITT)*, 2020, pp. 118–125. doi:10.1109/ITT51279.2020.9320783.

Petiwala, F.F., Nawazish, H.N., Shukla, V.K., Sharma, R., and Nanda, I. (2021). Halal food benefits and challenges: a mobile application based technical review. In *2021 International Conference on Advance Computing and Innovative Technologies in Engineering (ICACITE)*, 2021, pp. 139–144. doi:10.1109/ICACITE51222.2021.9404588.

Pimple, D., (2019). Robotic process automation: a revolution in business process automation. *International Journal of Information Technology Insights & Transformations*, 3(1).

Public Company Accounting Oversight Board (PCAOB) (2017). Proposed Amendments to Auditing Standards for Auditor's Use of the Work of Specialists. PCAOB Release No. 2017-003. Washington, DC: PCAOB.

PWC (2017). Robotic process automation: a primer for internal audit professionals. Retrieved from https://www.pwc.com/us/en/risk-assurance/publications/assets/pwc-robotics-process-automation-a-primer-for-internal-auditprofes-sionals-october-2017.pdf. Accessed on February 2021.

PWC (2019). PwC's 2019 actuarial robotic process automation (RPA) survey report. https://www.pwc.com/gx/en/industries/financial-services/publications/pwc-2019-actuarial-robotic-process-automation-survey-report.html. Accessed on February 2021.

Rizk, Y., Isahagian, V., Boag, S., *et al.* (2020). A conversational digital assistant for intelligent process automation. In *International Conference on Business Process Management*. Springer, Cham, pp. 85–100.

Shukla, V.K. and Bhandari, N. (2019). Conceptual framework for enhancing payroll management and attendance monitoring system through RFID and biometric. In *2019 Amity International Conference on Artificial Intelligence (AICAI)*, pp. 188–192. doi:10.1109/AICAI.2019.8701316.

Shukla, K., Kohli, A., and Shaikh, F.A. (2020). IOT based growth monitoring on *Moringa oleifera* through capacitive soil moisture sensor. In *2020 Seventh International Conference on Information Technology Trends (ITT)*, pp. 94–98. doi:10.1109/ITT51279.2020.9320884.

Shukla, V.K. and Verma, A. (2019a). Model for user customization in wearable virtual reality devices with IOT for "low vision". In *2019 Amity International Conference on Artificial Intelligence (AICAI)*. IEEE.

Shukla, V.K. and Verma, A. (2019b). Enhancing user navigation experience, object identification and surface depth detection for "low vision" with proposed electronic cane. In *2019 Advances in Science and Engineering Technology International Conferences (ASET)*. IEEE.

Shukla, V.K. and Verma, A. (2019c). Enhancing LMS experience through AIML base and retrieval base chatbot using R language. In *2019 International Conference on Automation, Computational and Technology Management (ICACTM)*, pp. 561–567. doi:10.1109/ICACTM.2019.8776684.

Singh B., Shukla V.K., and Singh S. (2019). An empirical study of shift from SMS to chat-apps among university student. *International Journal of Recent Technology and Engineering*, 7(6), 1–6.

Stolpe, A., Steinsund, H., Iden, J., and Bygstad, B. (2017). Lightweight IT and the IT function: experiences from robotic process automation in a Norwegian bank. In *Norsk konferanse for organisasjoners bruk at IT,* 25(1).

Suhel, S.F., Shukla, V.K., Vyas, S., and Mishra, V.P. (2020). Conversation to automation in banking through chatbot using artificial machine intelligence language. In *2020 8th International Conference on Reliability, Infocom Technologies and Optimization (Trends and Future Directions) (ICRITO)*, Noida, India, pp. 611–618. doi:10.1109/ICRITO48877.2020.9197825.

Trayush, T., Bathla, R., Saini, S., and Shukla, V.K. (2021). IoT in healthcare: challenges, benefits, applications, and opportunities. In *2021 International Conference on Advance Computing and Innovative Technologies in Engineering (ICACITE)*, 2021, pp. 107–111. doi:10.1109/ICACITE51222.2021.9404583.

Verma, A., Shukla, V.K., and Sharma, R. (2021). Convergence of IOT in tourism industry: a pragmatic analysis. *Journal of Physics: Conference Series*, 1714 (1), 012037. IOP Publishing.

Vijai, C., Suriyalakshmi, S.M., and Elayaraja, M., 2020. The future of robotic process automation (RPA) in the banking sector for better customer experience. *Journal of Commerce*, 8(2), 61–65.

Vishnu, S., Agochiya, V., and Palkar, R., 2017. Data-centred dependencies and opportunities for robotics process automation in banking. *Journal of Financial Transformation*, 45(1), 68–67.

Wanganoo L., Shukla V.K., and Panda B.P. (2021a) NB-IoT powered last-mile delivery framework for cold supply chain. In: Singh T.P., Tomar R., Choudhury T., Perumal T., and Mahdi H.F. (eds), *Data Driven Approach Towards Disruptive Technologies. Studies in Autonomic, Data-driven and Industrial Computing.* Springer, Singapore. https://doi.org/10.1007/978-981-15-9873-9_22

Wanganoo, L. and Shukla, V.K. (2020). Real-time data monitoring in cold supply chain through NB-IoT. In *2020 11th International Conference on Computing, Communication and Networking Technologies (ICCCNT)*, 2020, pp. 1–6. doi:10.1109/ICCCNT49239.2020.9225360.

Wanganoo, L., Prasad Panda, B., Tripathi, R., and Kumar Shukla, V. (2021b). Harnessing smart integration: blockchain-enabled B2C reverse supply chain. In *2021 International Conference on Computational Intelligence and Knowledge Economy (ICCIKE)*, pp. 261–266. doi: 10.1109/ICCIKE512 10.2021.9410677.

Zaidi S.F.N., Shukla V.K., Mishra V.P., and Singh B. (2021). Redefining home automation through voice recognition system. In: Hassanien A.E., Bhattacharyya S., Chakrabati S., Bhattacharya A., and Dutta S. (eds), *Emerging Technologies in Data Mining and Information Security. Advances in Intelligent Systems and Computing*, vol. 1300. Springer, Singapore. https://doi.org/10.1007/978-981-33-4367-2_16

Chapter 14

Multimedia sustained benefits for financial services

Aradhana Sharma[1], Dhiraj Sharma[2] and Christian Bonnici West[3]

Abstract

Technology plays a huge role in financial services and allows financial institutions to constantly attain new information to gain competitive advantages. The function of MMTs (Multi-Media Technologies) in financial services also enables clients to quickly execute online transactions, which improves confidence in finance, enables the growth of information technology, and at first results in a more quick and effective service. The rationale behind this study is to underline the sustained benefits of multimedia in financial services.

The study is based on secondary data. In this study, secondary data were used to supplement the published and unpublished studies as well as the current literature. The most efficient way to start a literature search for the most up-to-date overview is to use electronic databases.

Findings show that ICT and MMTs have brought a significant transformation in the financial services. MMTs are transforming how the financial sector does business. New business opportunities are being created by rapidly advancing technical advancements. The use of MMTs in the financial services offers several advantages, including enhanced client satisfaction, security, speed, and convenience. Different MMTs and ICT technologies have been applied in the sector. These include blockchain, big data and AI, cybersecurity tools, and digital banking.

Keywords: Multi-media technologies; Financial services; Blockchain; Digital banking; Big Data; Information and communication technologies (ICTs); Sustained benefits

[1]Department of Commerce, Gobindgarh Public College, India
[2]School of Management Studies, Punjabi University, India
[3]Insurance and Risk Management, Faculty of Economics, Management & Accountancy, University of Malta, Malta

14.1   Introduction

Over the past decades, banks and financial institutions, as the service providers, have increasingly adopted emerging information and communication technologies (ICTs) and multi-media technologies (MMTs), such as computer networks, the Internet, video conferencing, the block chain, distributed ledgers, smart contracts, cryptocurrencies, robotic process automation, mobile access, data digitization, machine learning, Artificial Intelligence (AI) assistants, and AI data capture.

Such exploitations enabled the creation of new distribution channels for financial services and financial data, and the development and adoption of novel business strategies and types of client–service provider interactions. As a result, such adoptions also transformed the dynamics of the relationships between the service providers and their clients, and enabled the reaping of various benefits, including cost reductions, sustained and improved competitive advantage, the provision of improved financial services, both locally and globally, and enhanced collaborations between geographically scattered individuals, such as through the sharing of knowledge and skills.

As a result of such changes, the nature of the finance function has evolved across firms. Also, nowadays, service providers hope to accelerate their growth and innovation, by investing further in ICTs and MMTs. For example, AI and predictive intelligence technologies continue to assist users in their decisions, and to support financial service professionals in making better informed decisions about cash flows and forecasts.

14.1.1   Concept of MMT

The term 'multimedia' combines the terms 'multi', which means 'at least two', and 'media', as the plural of 'medium', which in this context refers to 'the mode of communication or transmission of information'. Hence, 'multimedia' refers to the communication of information in forms such as text, braille, graphics, images, audio, animation and moving pictures, through communication channels enabled by such ICT (and other) artefacts as network cables, radio waves, microwaves, visual display units, 3D printers, projectors, virtual reality headsets, and paper (Vaughan, 2008). The term 'Multimedia technology' refers to computer-based applications that enable the communication of ideas and information digitally or involving concrete elements, such as printing. Within the realms of ICT, MMTs are among the most exciting and rapidly expanding areas, leading to various achievements, such as those relating to virtual reality and 3D printing.

Some of the main features of multimedia technology:

- ICTs must be used to control multimedia systems.
- Systems for multimedia are integrated.
- They must be able to represent the information they handle digitally.
- Usually, there is an interactive interface for the media's ultimate display.

14.2 Billings and account receivables

Most accounts receivable (A/R) accounting still depends on manual, paper-based versions of receivable processes. These outdated practices have shortcomings that reduce a company's liquidity and working capital. The techniques for collecting receivables are being revolutionized by MMTs. Accounting activities are now easier, thanks to multimedia and A/R software for businesses. The market for A/R software provides a wide range of options for dealing with various business types. A/R has undergone a metamorphosis due to the integration of several MMTs.

Benefits of MMTs in billing and receivables management

- **Good documentation:** The amount of paperwork involved in A/R accounting is enormous. Customers may request to view statements, purchase orders, invoices, and other documents to decide when paying their bills. The speed of customer payments would undoubtedly increase with software that can access those papers and attach them to emails.
- **Effective e-mail management:** A service that automates the sending of e-mails to multiple recipients is a nice addition to any A/R software. It improves, for example, the efficiency of the otherwise time- and labour-intensive process of reminding consumers to pay their bills.
- **E-Bill payment:** The ideal A/R software should also include functionality that enables the clients to view and pay their bills online rather than through the phone (e.g. reading their credit card numbers) or by sending checks through e-mail.
- **Help in managing working capital:** It will be simpler to manage and boost working capital once organizations have improved their A/R performance and cash position. Organizations may obtain the insights they need to make investment choices, such as equipment purchases, facility expansion, staff recruitment, and other investments to enhance the business's growth using MMT and A/R software.
- **Better cash flow management:** Every firm has employees and debts to pay. MMTs enable businesses to identify bills early in the accounting process, remind consumers to pay, and give simple payment options while providing a clear view of their cash position. Additionally, A/R software programs provide statistical cash forecasts based on past payment data (Russo, 2022).
- **Less administrative cost:** Delivering statements and bills by snail mail or fax is archaic in this digital age. Applications for MMT are made particularly to automate most tasks that don't require human involvement. By automating all client communications, businesses may reduce the expenses involved in employing someone to type, print, fold, and ship envelopes (Mina, 2022). Additionally, companies may save money on missed time, paper, envelopes, printer consumables such as ink, and postage.
- **Quick payment cycle:** One of the secrets to commercial success is the ability to quickly receive payments for services rendered. With sophisticated A/R

software in place, bills can be delivered immediately to clients, and customer portals, equipped with electronic payment features, enable the clients to make fast and direct payments.

- **Increase the proactiveness in the collection process:** Manual dunning is a frantic and time-consuming operation in the absence of a prioritized work list. Thanks to the automation made possible by MMTs, organizations may construct prioritized work lists with reference materials for analysts to follow up on at-risk client accounts. In addition, tools like automatic correspondence and a common repository for backup papers might support the collection team in developing proactive collection plans.
- **Better customer services:** MMTs enable businesses to offer better customer services, particularly when it comes to customer data for augmented reality (AR). This is particularly true in the case of lost or incorrect bills, which can be resolved quickly and effectively when organizations integrate A/R automation into the mix. Organizations should expect improved customer retention and decreased time spent addressing customer service issues (Russo, 2022).

14.3   Account payable

The procedures for paying bills are intricate, cross-departmental, and multi-tiered. Accounts payable automation is another name for this practice. MMMTs are crucial in this scenario, and the AP process is performed digitally rather than physically. The account payable department has faced many challenges, such as lost invoices, late invoice payments, lots of paperwork, cash flow problems, and multiple formats. MMT aids firms in streamlining, automating, and managing their accounts payable procedures while also increasing visibility and cash flow. The primary goal of MMTs is to support and enhance the creation, submission, approval, matching, payment, and recording of documents like invoices.

Companies use AP technologies for the smooth running of the invoice approval process. The following are three prime AP technologies (Matre, 2022):

- Document imaging/scanning is a technique that enables the scanning and digitization of hard-copy documents, such as invoices.
- Optical Character Recognition (OCR) and Intelligent Character Recognition (ICR) are examples of data capture and extraction technologies used for the streamlining of business operations, also supporting the automation of accounts payable processing, and boosting accuracy, while enabling the lowering of costs, by decreasing the number of personnel required for manual data inputting. ICR is an advanced form of OCR that enables the processing of different handwriting slants.
- Automated routing and approval workflow technologies can be used to standardize the invoice handling process, including by establishing the parties responsible at each phase, up to and including the 'final approval' stage.

Benefits of MMTs in AP technologies:

AP software and MMTs can streamline business operations, e.g.:

- **Enhanced productivity:** Automatic data handling (e.g. data entry, data capture and data processing) is better than manual data handling, insofar as it is faster, less costly and contributes to reducing error rates.
- **Shortened approval cycles:** Automated AP workflows, including the automatic forwarding of documents for approval, and the forwarding of needed reminders, enable faster and more efficient approval cycles (Research's, 2020).
- **Less physical handling:** Intelligent AP systems also reduce the need for physical invoice handling; e.g., printing, the capture and recording of handwritten signatures, scanning, physical filing, and bookkeeping (Rai, 2021).
- **Cost reduction:** Process automation reduces the costs involved in processing invoices, including by shortening the time taken and the resources needed to process them, such as by paying less for storage, printing, and paper.
- **Better human resources management:** AP automation can also free workforces from tedious and repetitive tasks, enabling more focus on more worthwhile jobs, and leading to better human resource management and more contented workers.
- **Better business intelligence:** Most AP technology includes data analytics and reporting tools that increase AP visibility and allow for better business intelligence and strategic cash flow management.
- **More accuracy:** AP automation software can also simplify the identification of duplicate payments since it enables the checking of invoice data against data maintained within Enterprise Resource Planning (ERP) systems (Craine, 2018).
- **Enhanced fraud protection:** By controlling access to the approval of invoices and release of payments, and thus enforcing duty segregation, AP automation software lowers the possibility of fraud and facilitates the double-checking data.
- **Improved controls:** AP automation software provides various document management facilities, enabling the recording and linking of the documents and messages associated with transactions and the generation of audit trails, thus enhancing accountability, reducing risks, and supporting audit procedures.

14.4   Collections

MMTs also support the streamlining of collecting processes, insofar as they enable the development and use of improved tactics for communications with debtors, e.g., via e-mail, text messages, digital collection mechanisms and other online tools, supported by cutting-edge technologies like AI and machine learning (ML). By implementing efficient customer interaction techniques, MMTs support the reduction of customer arrears and enhanced overall cash flows and, ultimately, improved financial standings.

Benefits of MMTs in collections:

- **Better portfolio management:** By supporting the automation of follow-ups on payments, the creation of alarms and reminders, and prioritization during the collection process, MMT improves portfolio management and the proportion of debt recovered (Chedayan, 2021).
- **Personalized processes:** The use of multiple channels for collection tasks is advantageous because it enables the creation of tailored procedures, targeting specific debtors and types of debt.
- **Enhanced communications:** Supporting collection procedures by MMTs, lenders may optimize communications across all channels and shift attention from pre-written scripts to unique client-centric services (Chedayan, 2021). For example, they can use preset borrower profiles to understand consumer situations and alter communication to rely more on empathic concern, avoiding passive-aggressive collection notifications.
- **360-degree information regarding customers:** By backing collection procedures by MMTs, lenders can gather sufficient information that enables them to better understand the borrowers' behaviour, and thus to foresee future trends and implement changes based on historical data.
- **Speed and efficiency:** Digital data collection shortens the time needed for data gathering and analysis and for the dissemination of the data collection results.
- **High data quality:** MMT-enabled data collections can also reduce data collection errors, and support the quicker discovery and fixing of such errors. It can also support data audit automation, increase data transparency and visibility, enhance governance and improved risk mitigation, and alter the likelihood of data leaks.
- **Automated collection:** The use of MMTs enhances collection follow-ups and payment procedures. For example, they made it possible to save each client's debt information online, enabling collection managers to access such data from their personal devices and to suggest tactics based on the circumstances of each customer. MMTs also enable managers to evaluate their productivity and the effectiveness of their collection strategies.

14.5   Cash flow management

Collecting and analyzing financial data is a challenge for many firms. With reliable information, MMT may aid cash flow planning. Businesses may assess their cash on hand and better understand their financial status. Digital Cash Management Solutions have improved liquidity and cash management due to their cutting-edge technology, clever functionality, and high usability. A company may strategize more effectively and make more informed decisions by coupling these technologies with a strong cash management policy that facilitates the firm's collection, management, and distribution of cash. Systems for managing money that use such cutting-edge technologies unquestionably outperform conventional methods.

Many types of cash flow management software and technologies assist in improving cash flow efficiency:

Customer relationship management software: By enhancing sales records and ensuring that the company continuously spends resources on the most lucrative activities, customer relationship management (CRM) software may strengthen cash flow. For instance, proactive measures may be taken to maintain current consumers, or new customers may be attracted and converted.

Data analytics: Data analytics may inform organizations' cash flow management decisions. For example, it can be used with big data analysis to enable more precise cash flow projections based on payables and receivables data patterns. Businesses may also dive down and understand how certain activities—e.g. creating a new product, or changing prices—might affect cash flow. Data analysis can also assist the business in locating unusual activities that may negatively affect cash flow or in identifying seasonal troughs in cash flow, enabling better preparations for future events.

Benefits of MMTs in cash flow management:

- **Fraud prevention:** Companies can track every transaction that occurs within their organizations. The cash management system is aided by MMTs that include analytics and monitoring capabilities to look for errors, fraud, and unlawful activity. It has the ability to monitor the behaviour and spot any odd deviations from the norm. Optimizing the cash management system in banks and companies is crucial, given the growth in fraud and loss. A higher level of trust may exist with these systems when using protected gateways.
- Given the various cyber risks and the potential for other criminal actions that might jeopardize a financial institution's service and reputation, the integration of cash management systems within financial institutions is a strict need.
- **Better customer services:** Contemporary MMT and cash management services have improved customer satisfaction. Customers nowadays are actively engaged and tech-savvy, and anticipate that financial assistance would complement and align with their fast-paced lifestyles. Customers expect prompt and efficient solutions. Digital money also enables rapid long-distance transactions.
- Digital cash management leverages databases so customers can be served to their fullest pleasure. It is possible for organisations to use such services to grow their consumer base and create customer loyalty.
- **Reduce cost:** The MMT-enabled digitalization of cash management is proven to be cost-effective, reducing the strain on employees, and helping to avoid needless, time-consuming infrastructure requirements.
- **Effective planning:** The advantage of choosing MMTs in cash management services is that they provide a clear and precise picture of the cash flowing into or out of a business. This enables finance departments to create more effective business expansion, growth, and development strategies, and therefore also better forecasting (Sloop, 2022).

- The available digital tools and technologies can also provide insights regarding businesses' financial balances, revenues, costs, and other crucial data, as well as enable the periodic generation of accurate financial reports.
- **Process simplification in cash management:** The digitization of cash management systems has shown to be more efficient than recruiting and training staff to handle cash in these procedures. Backed by MMTs, these cash solutions offer the ability to troubleshoot and to perform diagnostic tasks. They also enable greater openness because reports are easily accessible, and they enable the expansion of operations and improvement of corporate performance (Trovata Team, 2021).

14.6   Tax preparation

Before the advent of MMT, the tax division in India was only thought of as a compliance department. Traditionally, tax departments submitted returns and manually entered most of the data needed for tax compliances, reconciliations, etc. Today, there are a variety of MMT solutions that may assist tax functions in automating monotonous and repetitive tasks. This lessens the strain on the tax function and enables it to concentrate on activities that create value. Technology is a game-changer in the transformation of the tax function, assisting with accuracy, speed, convenience, and transparency in tax procedures, compliances, and monitoring (Ashima).

The tax environment has changed considerably due to taxpayers and tax officials looking forward to greater technological innovation and improvement in the field of the taxation system, which is primarily utilized to improve the efficiency and relevance of the arduous process. The tax authorities also take advantage of the capacity of new technologies like big data, to enhance tax administration, facilitate e-filing for the taxpayers, and provide many other services. Such authorities primarily started with the e-filing of returns that were IT-enabled and dealt with digital technologies connected to source data input.

Following are the MMTs and other technologies used in tax preparation (Watson, 2018):

AI: Their functions have begun to shift due to the advent of cutting-edge technologies. They have the chance to progress from being a responder to playing a crucial part in the company's development processes now that data is readily available. AI is already used for voice recognition and OCR, and it is easily adaptable to other aspects of tax compliance. Applications with AI capabilities may handle more difficult jobs like detecting fraud or resolving cunning tax questions from a paper (Krishnan, 2022).

Social media: Tax preparers may simply utilize social media as a relationship-building tool to help them become more visible, be acknowledged as experts, expand their online network, enlighten their clients, and offer better and quicker customer service.

Mobile apps: Tax preparers can benefit from on-demand data, thanks to mobile accounting. Even when on the road or in a different location, tax preparers can better serve their customers with real-time access to data. Numerous smart-phone applications exclusively used for tax preparation are available immediately.

Automation: Automation offers several advantages for accounting businesses and tax experts, including freeing their time, enabling the acceptance of more customers and the expansion of their companies.

Following are the benefits of MMTs in tax preparation:

- **Quick services:** Tax preparation businesses can immediately assist their clients, thanks to MMT. Additionally, e-filing a tax return will make it easier for the assessor to pay their taxes quickly and easily (Sutar, 2021). Big Data and simple-to-use digital encouraged Indian enterprises to abandon the onerous manual tax payment method, thus avoid the imposition of harsh penalties due to late tax payments.
- **Less risk involves:** Accounting businesses can provide clients with risk-free services by utilizing MMTs in the tax system. Companies may lessen the danger to their client's business when they receive accurate and prompt findings. Businesses that provide clients with problem-free services will be able to increase their company during tax season since customers simply want their accountants to do their taxes quickly and without danger.
- **Track the status:** Taxpayers can easily access their accounts, return records, Tax Deducted at Source (TDS) records, date of filing return and tax, and similar records.
- **High process efficiency:** With tax technology, data may be safely gathered and collected from any source, and effortlessly transferred to tax provision work papers. Even when book numbers continue to change, assesses may submit unified and harmonized trial balance data for all tax procedures and maintain its accuracy. They can also fulfil those ever-shrinking deadlines, with fewer resources, if data is easily available to compute accurate tax accruals and to generate reports and work papers that substantiate the booked amounts (bdo.com, 2019).
- **Transparency:** Globally, tax authorities grow more aggressive and targeted, and this impacts the business community by raising the bar for disclosure and openness. Tax technology provides unmatched insight into how computations are connected across tax areas, allowing for a comprehensive perspective of tax actions. The administrative burden brought on by the more stringent reporting and transparency standards, globally, is significantly absorbed by technology, which also strengthens audits (Reuters, 2021).

14.7   Cash disturbance

MMTs can also improve the efficiency of the spending process by reducing the use of paper. In cases where the business decides to rely on paperless mechanisms, it becomes essential to secure all data (e.g. invoices and other supporting documents) against breaches of confidentiality, integrity and/or availability, by implementing technical, physical and procedural security controls. For example, it would be useful to confirm that the organization's document destruction policy covers both soft and hard copies.

- **Quick services:** Transactions may be performed more rapidly and with less processing and cash handling. MMTs used in cash disbursements are intended to assist businesses in lowering expenses and shortening the time it takes to transfer money to customers and employees.
- **Easy to administer and cost effective:** Contactless payments reduce costs. People will merely pay what they normally would for card purchases. Several packages are available to accommodate organizations of different sizes, financial situations, and transaction rates.
- **Low risk:** Due to the processing of business transactions through secure gateways that are difficult to tamper with, they are far more secure than traditional ones. Only MMTs make this feasible. Most platforms are strictly monitored and guarded for the safety of expensive transactions.
- **Transparency:** When it comes to payments, transparency becomes a crucial aspect. Transparency in transactions is necessary when employing MMT for payment acceptance. In the case of electronic payments, keeping track of the payment information is not required. The likelihood of confusion will decrease while using MMT.

14.8 Budgeting process

Nowadays, businesses have automated their accounting procedures. The process of company budgeting and financial forecasting is improved via automation and MMT. Technology can incorporate systems that automatically sync with the general ledger during the budget-generating process. Maintaining data accuracy to the minute rather than merely the week significantly lowers the possibility of errors. The field of budgeting is one where ICTs are being increasingly incorporated (Kark, 2020).

Following are the reasons why organizations should implement MMTs or budgeting software in the budgeting process:

- **Time-saving:** With the appropriate software and multimedia tools, organizations may streamline the process of creating an annual budget and more effectively track and enhance their financial performance.
- **Flexible reporting:** Managers must be able to analyze important financial data swiftly. While offering more flexibility and reporting efficiency than spreadsheets, budgeting and forecasting systems simulate a similar environment. MMTs, as opposed to conventional reporting systems, help speedy reporting by reducing labour-intensive manual operations.
- **Improve the overall performance of the budgeting process:** It will enable anything from increased departmental coordination to data collection, modelling, and forecasting. All of this can significantly reduce the tedious tasks involved in budgeting and forecasting, allowing more time for analysis and development (Alade, 2014).

- **Increased reliability:** By connecting with other back-office systems, budgeting and forecasting tools take the guesswork out of determining an organization's financial situation. The most recent project costs and statistics on service consumption are readily available so departmental budget managers may make decisions based on correct data.
- **Trusted procedures**: With MMTs and integrated budgeting and forecasting systems, we can ensure that data is consistently delivered in the appropriate format. Processes can be defined in advance, deadlines can be specified, and reminders can be sent when it is time to submit financial data (Dewell, 2015).
- **Elimination of errors during budget preparation:** When trying to add up some numbers, human error frequently produces inaccurate values, which may not produce the desired result. The authorities will have to spend a lot of resources trying to verify data and repeat computations. Still, a summation error is substantially less likely when MMTs are used (Kalish, 2022). The development of MMT has simplified the process of maintaining figure accuracy.

14.9   Financial analysis and reporting

MMTs enable modern businesses to improve the quality of their financial reports and strategic, tactical and operational decision making. Understanding the capabilities of today's sophisticated technologies, and how these can aid in the collection, management, analysis, and delivery of financial data, with greater speed, reliability, and utility than ever before, is the first step in recognizing how the use of technology can improve financial reporting.

Following are the key benefits of MMTs in financial analysis and reporting:

- **Gathered data from multiple sources:** MMT enables businesses to quickly consolidate data from as many sources as needed. This is a necessary function in financial reporting software.
- **Streamlined reporting process:** The reporting process can be shortened and enhanced with MMT in the financial services industry. Analysts now have better access to reports at a faster rate, thanks to the rapid pace of technological progress, making it possible to create accounts more quickly and with a smaller margin of error. The financial sector has reaped the rewards of such technological advancements.
- **High-quality reporting systems:** MMTs also improve auditors' efficiency, e.g., as a result of higher quality reports and the ability to send more regular notifications.
- **Standardized quantitative data:** Investors seek standardized quantitative data to track the growth of their investments. Advancements in financial technology enable them to access more accurate research, quicker, and in real-time. This enables analysts to conduct more precise forecasting analyses, which may ultimately assist businesses and investors in determining the best course of action. Investors can then use the updated analyses for better investment choices, benefiting the market.

- **Timely and quick information:** Regulators and policymakers also need to collect data about current events to enhance society. Data can now be readily extracted and presented in more relevant formats, thanks to modern break-throughs, such as big data and the Internet of Things (IoT), which can assist policymakers in better comprehending the circumstances inherent in society. Using natural language technologies, cognitive computing, and AI will also play an increasingly significant role in reporting in the future. Such technolo-gies will enhance the users' experience, including by enabling discoveries about their requirements.

14.10   Payroll administration

Human resource (HR) functions play an important role in organizations. They handle the recruitment of the best talent, as well as the management of benefits paid to employees, the resolution of workplace disputes, the addressing of compliance challenges, and payroll management.

Automated payroll systems enable the efficient and effective management, upkeep, and automation of employee payments, including the related administration functions, such as tax preparations and record keeping. They ensure that payments are made in time and in line with the applicable national and international laws.

Benefits of MMT in payroll administration:

- **Tracking of working hours:** Automated systems enable the effortless capture of information about employees' working hours, e.g., by recording information about their login and logout times and their break periods. This enables management personnel to concentrate on more crucial aspects of the business (Shalini, 2022).
- **Efficient handling of errors:** One of the key shortcomings associated with traditional (paper-based) payroll systems was their susceptibility to expensive errors. The use of payroll software (e.g. cloud-based payroll platforms) enables the more efficient identification and management, or even complete avoidance, of such errors.
- **Data security:** Technological advancements have enabled reputable payroll service providers to ensure the secure handling of the data stored and processed within their systems, in line with applicable laws, regulations and standards.
- **Salary structure management:** MMTs also support the creation and imple-mentation of appropriate compensation plans, as well as the identification and resolution of compensation irregularities (Shalini, 2022).
- **Cost-effective:** Payroll software can enable businesses to reduce the costs associated with manual processing. Companies like sumHR provide high-end cloud-based payroll software that handles accounting procedures and can be inexpensively connected with employee attendance and Human Resources Management System (HRMS) software (Jain, 2021).

- **Quick generation of pay slips:** Digital payroll systems can also help HR employees avoid the manual generation and management of payslips, thus shifting their attention away from tedious and time-consuming tasks, and towards more important business issues.
- **Efficient management:** Automated payroll systems can also simplify some of the most difficult tax computation tasks, while minimizing errors, securing data, and lowering the likelihood of data theft. Additionally, they help in keeping workers informed about the organization's payroll rules, and raise their job satisfaction.

14.11   Compliance

Due to recent developments in state and federal securities legislation, banks and other financial institutions are compelled to use MMTs to enhance their risk and compliance management frameworks and activities. Various emerging technologies play a significant role in this. For example, AI enables the automation of workflows and the continuous reviewing of applicable rules and regulations, and big data allows companies to assess vulnerabilities and threats in real time, thus preventing, rather than just identifying, or reacting to, the materialization of risk.

Benefits of MMTs in compliance:

- **Risk assessment and management:** MMTs facilitate various risk management activities, including the identification and assessment of legal and regulatory concerns, the risk-based mapping of operational units, the control of internal risk management responsibilities, the implementation of controls, and the prioritization of corrective measures (Tippins, 2022).
- **Training and development:** MMTs also enable the management—including the generation, scheduling, delivery and control—of compliance training intended for employees and relevant third parties (Tippins, 2022).
- **Effective policy and control management:** MMTs can also simplify and speed up the management—including the creation, analysis, reviewing, updating, approval, distribution, and archiving—of organizational policies. They can also facilitate the management of access to such documentation.
- **Performance measurement:** MMTs can introduce useful metrics that were difficult to adopt in the past, such as regarding the average time taken to resolve compliance concerns, the overall number of open issues across a firm, and many more.
- **Improve employee collaboration:** Beyond enhancing the monitoring and collection of risk- and compliance-related data, the use of dashboards available within risk and compliance systems enables better employee interactions—e.g. for the assignment of tasks and the monitoring of their progress—when compared to the use of more traditional information systems, such as e-mails.

14.12 Conclusion

This chapter outlined how ICT and MMT technologies have, over the past decades, enabled important changes within the financial services and banking sectors. For example, we explored how they transformed the way we manage cash flows, payments, debts, risk and compliance, and how we perform tax preparations, financial analyses, how we generate financial reports, and how we manage payrolls. We have also mentioned emerging technologies, such as big data, AI and IOT, which are likely to continue to transform how we do business in these sectors.

References

Alade, M. E. (2014). Assessment of the impact of ICTs on budget processing in MDAs of Ondo State, Nigeria. *IOSR Journal of Humanities and Social Science (IOSR-JHSS)*, 19(12), 01–09.

Ashima. (n.d.). *How Is Technology Influencing Various Dimensions of the Taxation Process*. Retrieved from https://legalserviceindia.com/legal/article-7904-how-is-technology-influencing-various-dimensions-of-the-taxation-process.html

bdo.com. (2019). *What Is Tax Transformation? Four Benefits For Companies*. Retrieved from https://www.bdo.com/insights/tax/what-is-tax-transformation-four-benefits-for-companies

Chedayan, B. (2021). *Technology Advancements in Debt Collection that Every Business Should Know*. Retrieved from https://www.linkedin.com/pulse/technology-advancements-debt-collection-every-should-know-chedayan#:~:text=One%20of%20the%20benefits%20of,the%20relationship%20with%20the%20customer.

Craine, K. (2018). *4 Key Benefits to Digital Transformation in Accounts Payable*. Retrieved from https://www.parascript.com/blog/4-key-benefits-to-digital-transformation-in-accounts-payable/

Dewell, M. (2015). *10 Reasons to Implement Budgeting and Forecasting Technology*. Retrieved from https://www.oneadvanced.com/news-and-opinion/advanced-offers-ten-reasons-why-businesses-should-implement-budgeting-and-forecasting-technology/

Jain, R. (2021). *Is Technology Making Payroll Management Better or Worse?* Retrieved from https://www.linkedin.com/pulse/technology-making-payroll-management-better-worse-rakesh-jain?trk=public_profile_article_view

Kalish, B. (2022). *How Technology is Impacting the Planning, Budgeting & Forecasting Function*. Retrieved from https://www.financealliance.io/how-technology-improves-planning-budgeting-forecasting/

Kark, K. (2020). *Reinventing Tech Finance: The Evolution from IT Budgets to Technology Investments*. Retrieved from https://www2.deloitte.com/us/en/insights/focus/cio-insider-business-insights/tech-finance-technology-investment-budgeting-processes.html

Krishnan, K. (2022). *5 Technologies that Will Transform Our Lives*. Retrieved from https://www.weforum.org/agenda/2022/08/these-five-key-technologies-will-transform-our-lives/

Matre, P. (2022). *The Most Common Accounts Payable Technologies*. Retrieved from https://www.mastersindia.co/blog/accounts-payable-technologies/

Mina. (2022). *Benefits of Accounts Receivable Management Software*. Retrieved from https://blog.peakflo.co/en/learning-center/benefits-of-accounts-receivable-management-software

Rai, V. (2021). *Role of Technology in Accounts Payable Function*. Retrieved from https://www.linkedin.com/pulse/role-technology-accounts-payable-function-veekshith-rai

Research's, L. (2020). *2020 Payables Insight Report*. Retrieved from https://www.levvel.io/resource-library/2020-payables-insight-report

Reuters, T. (2021). *7 Reasons to Transform Tax with Technology*. ONESOURCE.

Russo, K. (2022). *Top 11 Benefits of Accounts Receivable Automation*. Retrieved from https://www.netsuite.com/portal/resource/articles/accounting/accounts-receivable-automation-benefits.shtml

Shalini. (2022). *Top 6 Advantages of the Automated Payroll System*. Retrieved from https://www.betterplace.co.in/blog/benefits-of-automated-payroll-system/

Sloop, B. (2022). *Ways Technology Can Improve Business Cash Flow*. Retrieved from https://b-scpa.com/2022/07/26/ways-technology-can-improve-business-cash-flow/

Sutar, P. K. (2021). *How Technology is Transforming Tax Functions Across Organisations*. Retrieved from https://www.businesstoday.in/opinion/columns/story/how-technology-is-transforming-tax-functions-across-organisations-312574-2021-11-17

Vaughan, T. (2008). *Multimedia: Making it work* (7th, ed.) New Delhi: McGraw Hill.

Tippins, K. (2022). *What Is Compliance Technology?* Retrieved from https://contractbook.com/blog/what-is-compliance-technology

Trovata Team. (2021). *3 Ways Technology Can Improve Cash Flow Analysis and Management*. Retrieved from https://trovata.io/blog/3-ways-technology-can-improve-cash-flow-analysis-and-management/

Watson, J. (2018). *Top 5 Technologies to Improve Your Tax Practice*. Retrieved from https://www.acecloudhosting.com/blog/technologies-improve-tax-practice/

Chapter 15

Extensive use of multimedia technologies: real-world case studies of multimedia banking

Monica Gupta[1] and Priya Jindal[1]

Abstract

The relationship between a consumer and a bank is redefined through multimedia communication as it helps to link distant locations and combine all their diverse market, which also improves international interaction and collaboration. Banks can create brand-new channels for distributing financial data and services in the multimedia market that use cutting-edge Internet tools and information exchange systems. Finding new clients might be challenging in today's cutthroat market. The in-branch banking process has become automated due to the introduction of advanced computing web application technology. Multimedia applications are used these days to notify bank consumers about transactions and other crucial financial information. The banks should determine the needs of client's requirements and float various financial schemes by exploiting the expertise and technology available worldwide. This chapter will highlight real-world case studies in multimedia banking across the globe, along with a detailed description of the extensive use of multimedia technologies in the banking sector. With the help of this chapter, we will find out the impact of multimedia technology on the banking sector of the economy. We will discuss real-world case studies where multimedia technology had some effect.

Keywords: Multimedia technology; Banking sector; International collaboration; Financial data

15.1 Introduction

Multimedia platforms allow users to interact, communicate, and create digital information through computer systems. It is a digital form of communication that uses textual data, audio, visuals, graphics, and animation to represent information visually and interactively. Generally, email service, video conferencing, and system-generated

[1]Chitkara Business School, Chitkara University, Punjab, India

SMS "Short message service" are multimedia services in the banking system. As a result of a wave of technological advancements like big data, artificial intelligence, and machine learning, the market has been disrupted. Therefore, banks are influenced by technology and use digital tools in the financial services industry.

15.2   Multimedia technologies in the banking sector

15.2.1   Social media in banking

Social media has become the main tool for interacting with people through online platforms; thus, the "banking sector" started to use it to influence potential customers. Social media marketing for the "banking industry" rapidly transformed from a simple "social tool" into a crucial solution to nurturing customer relationships and providing customer solutions to improve user satisfaction. Banking organizations use different social media sites to connect investors, lenders, and potential users to develop strong relationships outside the existing sales process (Bedi *et al.*, 2022). It significantly improves the operations related to marketing, sales, and advertising, as well as user experience. It is important to build intangible customer loyalty besides focusing on ROI to ensure healthy user retention. Thus, banking companies use social media tools such as Facebook, Twitter, and Instagram to interact and provide customer assistance services to maximize user engagement.

15.2.1.1   Social media marketing for banks

- Enables the organization to expand your touchpoints.
- Aids in lead building.
- Create trust by exchanging information and value.
- Establishes emotional bonds.
- Social media is essential for Omni channel strategy.

Banks may utilize social media as a useful marketing tool to foster customer relationships and create tangible and intangible value. However, "social media marketing" related to banks is still in its infancy. It assists banks in becoming more individualized, forging stronger bonds with clients, and providing more specialized goods and services than ever before.

15.3   Mobile banking

"Mobile Banking" enables users to conduct different financial activities and transactions through smartphones and the internet. Mobile-based banking applications make it easier to pay bills, transact money with clients, and check available balances or payment receipts from a remote place (Jhaveri *et al.*, 2022). From the users' perspective, the "mobile banking" service offers all banking access to the users at any time, any place. The widespread adoption of mobile banking and mobile payments in places without access to conventional brick-and-mortar banks and financial institutions has been made possible by the boom of smartphones.

Financial inclusion rates have increased with the popularity of mobile payments and mobile banking applications (Agarwal *et al.*, 2020). However, the data security and lack of reliability on the utilized encryptions can be considered the major drawbacks of this service (Shalender, 2021).

- **Knowledge about mobile banking**
  Using "mobile banking" has become easier daily due to the user-friendly interface design to assure user convenience. People use "mobile banking" through smartphones to pay bills, send amounts, locate the nearest ATM, deposit cheques, and check transaction history. Maximum "mobile banking" applications use a confidential login ID and password to ensure personal data security.
- **Internet security and mobile banking**
  The importance of cyber security has grown in many mobile banking operations. Damage and theft can be protected with the help of a cyber security process. The process is also used to ensure that data, ranging from sensitive personal data to intricate government systems, is not exploited. There are three primary categories of cyber-attacks. The criminals take advantage of these backdoors and develop attacks that gain control over the regulation checks (Yaacoub *et al.*, 2022). The process of human error ensures an increase in the growth of cyber-attacks.
- **Remittances and mobile banking**
  Remittances are sums of money sent back to a foreign country by using wire transfers, postal mail, or mobile banking (online transfer). For many nations that receive these peer-to-peer cross-border financial transfers, the economic impact is creating a sense of fairness in the minds of different economic organizations that are forced to incite a tracking system. Remittances to developing nations are projected to have earned $529 billion in 2018, approximately a 9.6% gain from the previous record high of $486 billion set in 2017 (Chen *et al.*, 2022).
- **Phone payment**
  The convenience and speed of banking transactions have grown thanks to mobile banking. Mobile banking applications have become increasingly popular as smartphone usage has increased. With established banks offering various mobile products and new FinTech companies competing for a seat at the table, mobile banking has become a major part of our financial system. Even mobile B2C investment solutions are available, completing the full range of financial services accessible to the general population (Datta *et al.*, 2020).

15.3.1 Cases of customer experience in banking and FinTech design

15.3.1.1 UXDA is a banking design team including UX architects and UI designers

It took a long process to design Light Bank. The result is based on several experiences gained by solving financial design challenges daily and driven by their passion for disrupting the financial world to fulfilling their needs. The success story of the light bank can ensure banking consumer experiences that are beneficial for reaching 50,000 views in this medium alone. It has been awarded by globally famous international awards such as International Design Awards (IDA), London Design Awards, and DNA Paris Design Award, and this is also nominated for one of the world's biggest and most valuable design awards, the Red Dot Award 2019 and the iF Design Award 2019 (UXDA, Financial UX design architect).

15.3.1.2 ITTI digital back-office: complete digital transformation

Intelligent Tech & Trade Initiative (ITTI) was developed when they started working with UXDA to disrupt the banking industry by creating a never-before-seen core-banking solution 100% focused on the employees – a solution that would take into account all bank employees' pain points, needs, and daily tasks, thus making their job easier, enjoyable and more meaningful from a banking end-customer perspective. During this project, ITTI digital has learned to make users their main priority, and their perception changed drastically. The users can ensure growth that is important for gaining to grow that is developed visibility (UXDA, Financial UX design architect).

15.4   Google Pay

Payment software called Google Pay stores the user's total debit and credit cards, loyalty cards, tickets, and discounts, just like a physical wallet would. Like a traditional debit card, you can use the digital wallet to make contactless payments in stores and online. However, the software only requires an Android phone or tablet to complete these transactions. With Google Pay, you can travel light by only bringing your phone and still make transactions without using cash or a credit card.

15.5   PayPal

PayPal provides financial services and goods that may meet some people's banking needs. Anyone can use PayPal to pay expenses online or through the PayPal app. Suppose you are seeking a simple method to maximize the advantages of your PayPal account. In that case, it does not provide the same variety of financial services and products as a full-service bank. For example, Paper cheques, which are frequently a regular service supplied with checking accounts found at banks, are not available through PayPal. Additionally, PayPal is not an option for you if you want the in-person atmosphere of a physical bank. PayPal does not offer other services and products that you may get at a full-service bank, such as wealth management, home equity lines of credit, vehicle loans, and mortgages (Alam *et al.*, 2019).

15.6   24/7 Gadgets

Proper technological skill development is beneficial to gain progress with the help of information to gain communication and develop different managing information.

The creation, storage, and spread are developed with appropriate communicational technologies. Information and communication technology (ICT) is helped to develop, display, and transition data electronically (Roztocki *et al.*, 2019).

15.6.1 Banking development with ICT

Banks are developing the ICT, including fundamentals of different electronic databases and Web portals, and creating an informative management system aiming to increase productivity. Information and communication technology are used with different acts as a stimulant for economic development. To this purpose, the Asian Development Bank emphasizes that different information and communication technology development has succeeded in bridging rural and urban areas, improving information availability, and resulting in more modern agricultural practices that raise the farmers' incomes. The different ICT involvement in growing progress in the banking sector includes developing community connections and providing access to contemporary technology as its real goal or objective.

15.7 Artificial Intelligence (AI) in banking

AI improves banks' efficiency, dependability, helpfulness, and comprehension. AI in banking speeds up the digitization of the entire banking and financial process. Applications of AI enhance customer service while helping banks identify and stop fraudulent activities. The value of digital banking services is increasing with AI chatbots, voice assistant technologies, facial recognition banking apps, and applications. AI has significantly changed this landscape, with biometric authorization now the standard at large financial institutions. One of the important applications of AI in the banking business is the usage of chatbots. The innovation of "Artificial technology" (AI) has remarkably changed the operation management approaches in different industries. AI is based on a "neural network algorithm" (NLA) that enables a computer or system to make effective decisions without any manual influence. As a result, AI technology is widely used to automate different business operations to improve the quality of problem-solving and "decision-making" by eliminating the possibility of human errors. "AI technology" is commonly used in the banking sector to transmit essential information and take records of transactions with the help of NLA and blockchain encryptions. It has been observed that AI is utilized in many pilot projects to solve real-life industrial issues.

15.7.1 Uses of AI in banking

- **Customer involvement through AI-based chatbot**
  Chatbot technology is used in the banking industry for its advantage related to automated activities and offers a significant "return on investment." Chatbot technology is used frequently in banking services such as fund transfers, checking mini statements, and monitoring balance inquiries. Banks such as Ally and Capital One use AI chatbots to assist customers 24*7 and give accurate

responses to their queries. Ally, situated in Detroit, Michigan-based bank with over a century of experience, uses AI in its mobile banking platform. A chatbot powered by machine learning helps consumers on the bank's mobile platform.

- **Robo-counsel**
  Automated "system-generated" guidance in the financial sector has become very common and improves customer convenience in investment and other financial activities. A Robotics-based financial counsellor analyses customers' data and history of financial statements to get the actual financial situation of clients.

- **Predictive analytics**
  AI technology is used in two specific segments for the banking purpose, one is "predictive analytics" and another includes "natural or semantic language applications." Correlation between financial data and the patterns of data can be identified by AI, which was previously undetectable by using a manual process and traditional technology.

- **Cyber security**
  It is essential to prevent unauthorized interruption, malpractice of hacking, and data breaches to ensure data security in the financial sector. AI has significantly reduced the possibilities of exterior threats by making the encryption system resilient and more protective (Khan *et al.*, 2022).

- **Direct lending and credit scoring**
  AI also helps alternative lenders in assessing their clients' creditworthiness. It enables people or organizations to create strong "credit scoring models" even after having a short "credit history". For instance, the business of GiniMachine is an example of successful "Lending" and "credit scoring" (Dagar and Vishwakarma, 2022).

15.8 Metaverse in banking

Banks were once the place where banknotes were deposited and withdrawn. The requirement for visiting banks or even carrying cash was eliminated when ATMs with debit and credit cards entered the picture. The metaverse has exploded in popularity over the past 1–2 years across a variety of businesses, with banking being one of them. What is the next step regarding the utilization of metaverse in banking, given that the "banking industry" is one of the main industries affected by every wave of digitalization? With virtual banking experiences gaining centre stage, the sector is poised for yet another enormous revolution.

15.8.1 The progression that resulted in metaverse in the banking sector

The fourth stage of the banking sector's transformation has begun with NFTs and cryptocurrencies taking centre stage. A few banking organizations have simultaneously moved into the fifth stage, the metaverse.

- **Standard banking**
  In the "Standard banking" system, all the "in-person transactions" with customers are monitored by central banks, and the whole system works as a

"two-tiered" banking system. Previously, the process was labour-intensive, paper-based, and employed with insufficient personalized "financial products."

- **Web-based banking**
  The "banking industry" has completely transformed in the last decade due to the implementation of advanced technologies. It converts the whole "banking process" digitalized so that customers can access it comfortably with the help of the internet and mobile applications. Accordingly, "web banking" improves the "customer journey" with a fast and digital experience to maximize consumer satisfaction.

- **Bank in full**
  The banking sector has opened up in the previous 3–5 years to connect with external services via APIs. As a result, there are now several "neo-banks" and bank-offered "cross-industrial marketplace" services, including automobile, health services, procurement, and energy services.

- **Electronic banking and finance**
  A new secure, international, and quick banking economy has been born with the introduction of Web3, NFTs, and cryptocurrencies which have completely new assets like art, gaming, and real estate to the financial system and play a significant part in this.

- **Banks can benefit from the metaverse**
  Banks that have entered the market are still trying to find their place, despite the technology's enormous potential for the banking sector and its capacity to deal with varied customer concerns.

15.8.2   Real-world financial use cases for the metaverse

- **JP Morgan**: They have established an Onyx lounge in the Decentraland metaverse where they make it easier to make international payments, create financial assets, store them safely, and engage in trade.
- **HSBC**: has invested in a plot at The Sandbox metaverse that will be created for interacting with gamers and sports fans.
- **Standard Chartered**: The financial institution has also purchased a property in the Sandbox, which it intends to use for metaverse experimentation and the development of fresh client experiences.

15.8.3   Global case studies of real-world multimedia banking

1. **Enhanced self-service banking with software from Diebold Nixdorf: a case-based approach of first Citizen National Bank**
   First Citizens of National Bank (CNB), established in 1889 and had its corporate office in Dyersburg, Tennessee, provides services to clients at 26 financial centre sites around the state of Tennessee. To offer the best customer journeys, the bank will adopt its cloud-based Vynamic TM software suite across all branches with core integration. May 6, 2021, North Canton: First

Citizens National Bank is extending its commitment to technology by implementing cutting-edge, cloud-enabled self-service advancements throughout all branches utilizing Diebold Nixdorf's Vynamic TM Software package. As a 132-year-old, powerful, and prosperous community bank, First CNB is aware of how crucial it is to give customers a satisfying and more individualized branch experience. The bank uses Diebold Nixdorf's Vynamic technology, which offers an API-based interface to the bank's FIS core banking system in an easy-to-deploy, as-a-servicing approach to enable new transaction types. By linking to First CNB's banking core, Diebold Nixdorf's Vynamic Transaction Automation will enable more teller-like transactions at the ATM, expanding the range of self-service choices for customers who are "on-us" to include the capacity to in-house processing of credit and debit transactions, access to deposits, and the ability to distribute funds among various accounting processes, pay bills in the ATM by developing transferring funds, making a cash or cheque payment or both. Additionally, the core integration system will increase the productivity of branches by enabling assisted self-service for trickier transactions that allow branch staff to immediately do overrides and approvals at the ATMs using branch-based tablets.

Judy Long, the President and Chief Operating Officer of First Citizens National Bank, said, "As part of our ongoing commitment to providing our customers with an exceptional experience, we are now able to offer sophisticated transactions that were previously only possible over the counter through self-service capabilities at the ATM. By integrating Diebold Nixdorf's Vynamic Transaction Automation, we can give our ATM network a bigger impact on our customers' banking experiences by providing them with advanced self-service options."

Octavio Marquez, the Senior Vice President of Global Banking at Diebold Nixdorf, stated, "The Advisory Services team at Diebold Nixdorf started our close partnership with First Citizens National Bank about ten years ago, and we are happy to be able to grow it. Their fundamental integration strategy promotes branch efficiency, supports creative transactions, and paves the way for future technological investments. Customers who purchase from Vynamic Transaction Automation benefit from a tailored experience and more powerful features."

Rob Lee, the Head of FIS's digital and banking process, said, "We are thrilled that First Citizens National Bank can provide their clients with improved digital experiences thanks to FIS' Code Connect Open APIs. With this technology, our companies will be able to enhance their offerings and operational efficiency while also meeting the rising demands of consumers." The implementation process should be finished across all 26 First Citizens National Bank locations by the end of September 2021.

2. **Digital bank for using best mobile application: a case-based approach Garanti Banco Bilbao Vizcaya Argentaria (BBVA)**
   In the 2020 edition of its Digital Banking Honors, World Finance magazine gave Garanti BBVA two awards. As a result, BBVA's Turkish division won

the award for Best Digital Bank for the fourth year in a row and received recognition for having the Best Mobile Application in the Turkish market. In the banking industry, digitization is assuming more and more diverse forms. Artificial intelligence technology has enabled the development of virtual assistants and chatbots. With the introduction of Ugi in 2016 and Whatsapp and Facebook Messenger bots a few years later, BBVA's Turkish division set a precedent for the nation. In recent years, chatbots have become more and more significant in the digitization process. They are also becoming "smarter," offering quicker answers by replying to consumers' inquiries and demands on various topics, either verbally or in writing. These assistants, which profit from all the advantages of AI technology and have the capacity to process natural language, can meet demands as if they were real customer representatives, whenever and wherever a customer wants, in a world where mobile devices have evolved into the primary channel for digital banking.

Garanti BBVA, a market leader in Turkey with its cutting-edge approach to digital banking and AI applications, believes that digital products, services, and AI will resonate with consumers and help them have a more memorable interaction with banks. Along with Ugi, the first financial smart assistant created with this strategy in Turkey, the bank uses technology to communicate with its clients online using chatbots on Facebook Messenger and WhatsApp. Garanti BBVA recently updated its Facebook Messenger bot, creating a chatbot world with the same knowledge base across all channels. Garanti BBVA already provides 24/7 customer service on more than 200 issues relating to its products and services via its Ugi smart assistant in its mobile app and its WhatsApp bot. Additionally, Ugi and Facebook Messenger bots connect users to customer service agents as necessary, enabling users to conveniently complete transactions (BBVA.com., 2021).

3. **Digital approach: a case-based approach by JP Morgan Chase Bank in the USA**

To advance the four universal pillars of opportunity: jobs and skills, small business expansion, neighbourhood rejuvenation, and financial health, JP Morgan Chase is combining its business and policy experience, resources, and data. As a world leader, it offers enterprises, organizations, and governments strategic advice and solutions, such as capital raising, risk management, and trade finance services. The size and scope of JP Morgan's clientele are considered its biggest advantage. The company works in investment banking with various issuer clients, including businesses, institutions, and governments. It offers thorough strategic guidance, capital raising knowledge, and risk management proficiency. The industry coverage teams can meet the changing needs of clients all over the world because of their in-depth, industry-specific expertise and regional market knowledge. Doing business in a first-class manner has always been the cornerstone of our approach to providing clients. By adopting a comprehensive and forward-looking perspective on our partnerships and looking for ways to assist customers in achieving their most crucial business goals, we work to establish trustworthy, long-lasting relationships.

4. **Embracing technology: a case-based approach by leading multinational financial service provider Zenith Bank Nigeria**

    English-speaking West Africa and Nigeria Zenith Bank Plc is a great supplier of different financial services. The operation is developed as a commercial bank by the Central Bank of Nigeria, which is considered the biggest banking regulator. Leading international financial service provider Zenith Bank is headquartered in Nigeria. It was established in 1990 and has had incredible growth to rank among the top financial institutions in Africa. It is currently the sixth-largest bank in Africa, with more than 500 locations across all 50 states and the Federal Capital Territory, as well as subsidiaries in the United Kingdom, the UAE, Sierra Leone, Ghana, and Gambia.

15.9 Conclusion

The chapter concluded that developing multimedia banking systems requires various technologies essential for achieving financial system expansion. The development of the FinTech sector, defined as the use of advanced information and automation technologies in the financial services sector, has resulted in a change in how technology is used to develop new services and business models. Self-service kiosks, image-enabled ATMs, videoconferencing systems that link experts from around the world to assist clients, and even digital displays to present messages to customers are among the available technological solutions. The conventional approach uses various self-service technologies, with human personnel thrown in occasionally to provide support or handle higher-value transactions. Different perspectives are used to solve problems in the real world, and system development in various nations helps to advance economic growth. The interactions between banks and customers are developing thanks to various multimedia banking technologies. The relevance of the problems created is growing, which is necessary for operating the financial system effectively.

References

Agarwal, S., Qian, W., and Tan, R. (2020). Financial inclusion and financial technology. In *Household Finance* (pp. 307–346). Palgrave Macmillan, Singapore.

Alam, N., Gupta, L., and Zameni, A. (2019). Fintech as disruptors and empowering financial industry. In *Fintech and Islamic Finance* (pp. 37–62). Palgrave Macmillan, Cham.

Bedi, P., Goyal, S. B., Kumar, J., and Choudhary, S. (2022). Smart automobile health monitoring system. In *Multimedia Technologies in the Internet of Things Environment*, vol. 2 (pp. 127–146). Springer, Singapore.

BBVA.com (2021). https://www.bbva.com/en/specials/2021-the-year-bbva-presents-its-long-term-plan-to-grow-and-reward-its-shareholders.

Chen, Z., Mao, Z., Fang, S., and Hu, B. (2022, October). Background layout generation and object knowledge transfer for text-to-image generation. In *Proceedings of the 30th ACM International Conference on Multimedia* (pp. 4327–4335).

Chen, L., and Su, S. (2022). Optimization of the trust propagation on supply chain network based on blockchain plus. *Journal of Intelligent Management Decision*, 1(1), 17–27.

Dagar, D. and Vishwakarma, D. K. (2022). A literature review and perspectives in deepfakes: generation, detection, and applications. *International Journal of Multimedia Information Retrieval*, 11, 1–71. https://www.theuxda.com/blog/tag/ux-architect

Datta, P., Tanwar, S., Panda, S. N., and Rana, A. (2020, June). Security and issues of m-banking: a technical report. In *2020 8th International Conference on Reliability, Infocom Technologies and Optimization (Trends and Future Directions) (ICRITO)* (pp. 1115–1118). IEEE. https://www.bbva.com/en/specials/2021-the-year-bbva-presents-its-long-term-plan-to-grow-and-reward-its-shareholders/

Jhaveri, R. H., Revathi, A., Ramana, K., Raut, R., and Dhanaraj, R. K. (2022). A review on machine learning strategies for real-world engineering applications. *Mobile Information Systems*, 2022, 1–16.

Khan, N. A., Awang, A., and Karim, S. A. B. A. (2022). Security in Internet of Things: a review. *IEEE Access, 3*, 104649–104670.

Mittal, A., Aggarwal, A., and Mittal, R. (2020). Predicting university students' adoption of mobile news applications: the role of perceived hedonic value and news motivation. *International Journal of E-Services and Mobile Applications (IJESMA)*, 12(4), 42–59.

Mittal, A., and Jhamb, D. (2016). Determinants of shopping mall attractiveness: the Indian context. *Procedia Economics and Finance*, 37, 386–390.

Muddumadappa, P. M. B., Anjanappa, S. D. K., and Srikantaswamy, M. (2022). An efficient reconfigurable cryptographic model for dynamic and secure unstructured data sharing in multi-cloud storage server. *Journal of Intelligent Systems and Control*, 1(1), 68–78.

Roztocki, N., Soja, P., and Weistroffer, H. R. (2019). The role of information and communication technologies in socio-economic development: towards a multi-dimensional framework. *Information Technology for Development, 25* (2), 171–183.

Shalender, K. (2021). Building effective social media strategy: case-based learning and recommendations. In *Digital Entertainment* (pp. 233–244). Palgrave Macmillan, Singapore.

Yaacoub, J. P. A., Noura, H. N., Salman, O., and Chehab, A. (2022). Robotics cyber security: vulnerabilities, attacks, countermeasures, and recommendations. *International Journal of Information Security, 21*(1), 115–158.

Chapter 16

Concluding remarks—fintech and technology of today and tomorrow

Simon Grima[1], Kiran Sood[2] and Sharon Seychel[1]

16.1 Introduction

As new players such as fintech and technology companies have entered the financial services industry, customers have access to a wider range of products and services at ever-lower prices due to competition between established financial service providers and unconventional new entrants. Digitisation and the ICT revolution have also allowed financial institutions to adopt new business models that use data collection, storage, and analysis (Muyanja-Ssenyonga Jameaba *et al.*, 2022).

Seven crucial innovations will drive the reimagining of business models over the next ten years while also reshaping the financial sector's competitive environment. The foundation of fintech development is technological advancement and innovation, which will also fuel new, disruptive business models in the financial services industry. Seven important technologies, according to a McKinsey report, will propel fintech development and alter the financial industry's competitive landscape over the coming ten years:

1. Artificial intelligence will drive massive value creation
2. Blockchain will disrupt established financial protocols
3. Cloud computing will liberate financial services players
4. Internet of Things (IoT) will drive a new era of trust in finance
5. Open source, SaaS and serverless will lower barriers to entry
6. No-code and low-code will redefine application development
7. Hyper automation will replace manual work. Hyper automation refers to introducing AI, deep learning, event-driven software and Robotic applications.

These important trends and technologies are entwining and integrating more and more, providing fintech and finance industry innovation with a huge boost. It is now a specialised financial industry. The subsectors that are best at using technical advancements to introduce applications, produce value, and alter the competitive

[1]Insurance and Risk Management, Faculty of Economics, Management & Accountancy, University of Malta, Malta
[2]Chitkara Business School, Chitkara University, Punjab, India

environment. Traditional financial institutions will need to use their significant resources in the future to remain ahead of the growing wave of disruption in the financial industry (Fong *et al.*, 2021).

Thanks to mobile technology's convenience, adaptability, affordability, and security; its quickness and cheap cost; and cross-selling of other financial services, financial inclusion measures have been boosted. Mortgages, insurance, financial planning, and investment management are just a few examples of the financial services available. These services have helped increase educational attainment, financial literacy, and human capital, all of which have been linked to inclusive growth, higher household incomes, and a reduction in poverty and income inequality. A more diverse customer base, new opportunities for collaboration with banking and non-banking businesses, improved ways to leverage customer experience of both existing and new ones, creation of new services, increased capacity and capability to meet an increased array of customer needs, and the ability for banks to reduce costs are all advantages that come from digitisation and Information and Communication Technology (ICT). Additionally, banks have a distinct edge they may utilise to their advantage to harness data analytics tools to deliver new service options that complement the client experience, thanks to aggregation platforms that automatically standardise and normalise financial data. That should be encouraging for improved bank health, which is essential for the stability of the banking industry and the financial system (Mittal and Jhamb, 2016; Mittal *et al.*, 2020). A new set of product offers in the form of crypto assets should diversify asset portfolios, increase the variety of revenue sources, and, therefore, resilience in the event of a slowdown in one or more banks' business lines. Block chain technology (BCT) is also associated with benefits like enhanced cyber security, decentralised authentication, increased operational efficiency, low compliance cost, shorter onboarding rates of new product and service offers, and shorter onboarding rates for new product and service offers. Financial stability benefits from the ability to track assets and transactions in real-time, around the clock, in combination with the immutability of any action that network participants authorise. These features can be added to various product offerings, business processes, and reinvigorating business models (Muyanja-Ssenyonga Jameaba *et al.*, 2022).

However, it is important to recognise that increased digitisation may pose risks to the financial system's sustainability. Since FinTech and TELCOs are using their sizable customer databases to offer savings and lending, peer-to-peer payments, and money transfer services, they are undermining banks' capacity to serve as a channel for the transmission of monetary policy. As a result, there are risks to financial stability that are related to the reduction of interest-earning income sources for banks. While this is going on, potential risks associated with

1. Application Programming Interface (API) includes a rise in partner and counterparty risk.
2. Technology incompatibility and the cascading effects these have on other participants in the financial system.

3. Worries associated with opening up businesses to competitors.
4. Uncertainty regarding the long-term viability of platform-based business models following the organisation's division into smaller, coherent business units necessary for developing APIs and platforms.

BCT-related risks to financial stability are likely to result from the growing susceptibility of BCT to hacking, theft, and data breaches, which raises concerns from critics of the secretive, decentralised distributed record-keeping, anonymous, low-cost, double encryption hyped platform network-based transactions and is increasingly raising the worst fears of financial institutions that are participants of breaching compliance requirements and generating expensive sources of redress (Muyanja-Ssenyonga Jameaba *et al.*, 2022).

16.2   Virtual reality and augmented reality banking

For devoted gamers, virtual reality (VR) and augmented reality (AR) are nothing new, but they might spark a revolution in other areas, particularly banking. The banking sector needs to accept the challenge to illustrate how this type of future banking in the metaverse might function because the promise of VR/power ARs to create an extraordinary user experience is still untapped. They need to expose themselves to the metaverse banking concept, which incorporates tablet, desktop, wearable, virtual reality, and mobile banking (Muddumadappa *et al.*, 2022; Chen and Su, 2022).

No successful business or service exists today in the digital age without having a digital presence. The metaverse will be the next revolutionary disruption. The game industry has already embraced virtual reality and augmented reality. Given its potential, how can banks lead the way in VR and AR banking? In the future, a bank that works to make sure that its users have a simple and seamless experience should be simple to find inside a VR/AR experience.

The forerunners of the new banking in the metaverse will be forward-thinking banks and fintech, who will be the first to discover this and build a blended VR/AR experience for its users.

Some banks and Fintech companies are already testing VR/AR features in their offerings. For instance, most banks currently offer smartphone-based augmented reality budgeting and financial data visualisation. It certainly has a striking appearance, but whether it improves the use and convenience of banking is debatable.

We may anticipate that the situation will drastically change with the broad simplicity. The screen size impacts VR/AR design less than it does on a desktop or mobile device. Although tempting, it is displaying all information at once would not be a good idea because it can lead to cognitive overload and irritate the user. It is also important to remember that simplicity is the primary criterion for quality in VR/AR banking design.

Also, consistency is important. Both augmented reality and virtual reality should be comparable to real-world experience. The uncomfortable effect of a mismatch between the feeling we experience from physical reality through our other senses and the eyes' monitored movement in VR should be lessened by properly structured VR architecture.

One of the biggest issues with VR/AR banking is depth. Banking has been elevated to a whole new level by modern technology. The history of the user experience in banking is being rewritten by ease, speed, delight, and convenience. New Neobanks have quickly arisen, changing the game as conventional banks still struggle to digitise their goods. Making a banking ecosystem that might naturally supply several products as a connected user experience with the potential to grow into a bank-as-a-platform is one of the major problems. The design concept for the ultimate banking super app demonstrates how any financial institution might improve its mobile banking ecosystem using motion video showcasing banking as a Super App design concept. That great app makes the most of the platform's distinctive features to provide an engaging user experience.

A fantastic app is one that users adore and frequently use because it provides such a fluid, cohesive, contextualised, and effective experience. The advantage of super apps is in creating an ecosystem capable of offering several services, as opposed to mono applications, which provide one function most practically and understandably.

WeChat, which was introduced in 2011 by Chinese internet juggernaut ten cents, is the most well-known instance of a mega app. More than a million products and micro applications, including gaming, entertainment, and ticket booking, are available through WeChat. Every month, the app is used by around 800 million people. Examples of other fantastic apps include Grab, Line, and Gojek (Get) (Kharpal *et al.*, 2019).

16.3   Digital revolution in the fintech era

Retailers have traditionally found success with loyalty programs. These programs drive repeat business as customers continue to spend at particular stores to receive incentives in the future by encouraging investment that leads to a pay-off for the consumer. However, recent studies have revealed a change in consumer behaviour that points to problems with the conventional loyalty program. Customers are less interested in point-based programs and discounts and more interested in personalised, emotional experiences that may speak to them directly through technology.

Discounts and loyalty programs based on points still have their uses, but it is obvious that they are not as alluring as they once were. Most consumers have loyalty cards but never use them. However, why are not these schemes still drawing in as many participants? Creating a personalised and smooth shopping experience is the greatest method to achieve consumers who believe that building an emotional connection with the brand is the most crucial component of a loyalty program.

A personalised experience is a key to increasing client loyalty, and to provide that, shops must keep up with the most recent consumer trends and needs. The emergence of technology, particularly mobile phones, has greatly altered how consumers purchase over the past ten years. Smartphones have made it possible for the ordinary user to maintain a constant internet connection, which has led to a significant increase in the importance of digital in all aspects of the buying process, including in-store. More and more customers are using their mobile phones to instantly compare and rate products and shops.

In light of this, it is now more crucial than ever to take into account individual preferences to provide a personalised purchasing experience that encourages repeat business. Consumers yearn for comfort, safety, and familiarity. Retailers may accomplish this in two easy ways: by modernising their digital offerings and by designing a personalised consumer experience.

It is crucial to offer an Omni channel payment service that satisfies customer security and convenience requirements and reaches customers across all touch-points, including mobile. This will provide a wide variety of data from various channels that can be analysed to best target the consumer and promote repeat business through a quick and secure checkout.

This data is also essential to provide a distinctive consumer experience. Points and discounts are always wonderful, but if they can be tailored to the client's needs, they take on a whole new level of allure. Customers want to receive exclusive, experimental offers, and this is now achievable thanks to technology. Artificial intelligence combined with consumer purchasing data can identify what customers want so that these can be sent to them via their mobile phones.

Additionally crucial to simplifying loyalty programs is digitisation. Since it takes up room and there is a danger they will be forgotten and left at home, customers no longer want to carry along hundreds of plastic loyalty cards. Technology must be updated to encourage people to buy with you across all platforms so that customers can enjoy a smooth in-store and online experience.

Push alerts sent through mobile wallets are more effective than emails and 100% more likely to be received by the client while being less expensive than texts. Retailers may then use relocation to send push alerts at convenient and customised times for the user. Customers are more likely to check out an offer or sale immediately if they learn about it while they are already in or about to enter a store. This raises the likelihood of spending money and using the loyalty program.

However, companies must first get customers signed up to drive engagement. The inconvenience of enrolment is one of the problems that retailers have had with loyalty cards. Customers do not want to spend time waiting in line and filling out paperwork at the register, and there's also the problem of line-ups growing and spoiling the experience for other customers.

This is where mobile wallet plug-ins may shine again because they make the sign-up process quick and easy. When using a mobile wallet to pay at a terminal, the option to sign up is present on the device itself. Selecting yes will immediately send a push notification to the customer's phone. This reduces the time-consuming sign-up procedure to only two clicks, and the mobile wallet is then used to collect all the data for the loyalty card. This connects the two and simplifies the procedure for the client.

Shoppers continue to love loyalty programs because there is still a significant desire for incentives, but traditional program engagement is low, and few people use the prizes. Retailers must tailor the program to each customer to resolve this problem. Offers can be provided to customers directly at appropriate times by utilising mobile phones and an Omni channel strategy. By analysing customers' purchasing patterns, businesses can further personalise their offerings. This strategy enhances the purchasing experience and helps forge fidelity by developing an emotional connection to the brand.

16.4   Conclusion

Technology innovation is a superb instrument for advancing society. Banks and other intermediaries will be able to lower their costs and enhance the quality of their services as a result of the adoption of digital technology and more intense use of the vast amount of data now at their disposal. There are enormous potential benefits for customers, businesses, and the entire economy. A less effective player might not be able to endure the increased competition resulting from technology lowering entry barriers in the credit and financial services markets. In ten years, we predict that the structure of the banking and financial markets will be significantly different from what it is today, with non-bank operators likely playing a much larger role.

One of the causes contributing to increased income and wealth inequality in both developed and emerging market economies is the "technical unemployment" that Keynes predicted would occur in 193,016. It also raises the question of how to ensure confidentiality in connection to Big Data and how to use it within the constraints established by the laws and the wishes of our citizens, whose right to privacy must be protected in any event. The boundaries for the ethical and legal use of big data need to be more clearly defined. The worry has been raised by recent developments involving Cambridge Analytica and Facebook.

As of right now, we must carefully consider how to make these developments fully compatible with individual rights, how to balance the protection of our freedom with the rules that govern the operation of contemporary liberal democracy, and how to square the increasing availability of information on each of our private lives about our political beliefs, physical health, or sexual orientation (Panetta, 2018).

References

Chen, L., and Su, S. (2022). Optimization of the trust propagation on supply chain network based on blockchain plus. *Journal of Intelligent Management Decision*, 1(1), 17–27.

Fong, D., Han, F., Liu, L., Qu, J., and Shek, A. (2021). Seven technologies shaping the future of fintech. Available from https://www.mckinsey.com/cn/our-insights/our-insights/seven-technologies-shaping-the-future-of-fintech [Accessed 15 December 2022].

Kharpal, A. (2019). Everything you need to know about WeChat—China's billion-user messaging app. Available from https://www.cnbc.com/2019/02/04/what-is-wechat-china-biggest-messaging-app.html [Accessed 10 December 2022].

Mittal, A., Aggarwal, A., and Mittal, R. (2020). Predicting university students' adoption of mobile news applications: the role of perceived hedonic value and news motivation. *International Journal of E-Services and Mobile Applications (IJESMA)*, 12(4), 42–59.

Mittal, A., and Jhamb, D. (2016). Determinants of shopping mall attractiveness: the Indian context. *Procedia Economics and Finance*, 37, 386–390.

Muddumadappa, P. M. B., Anjanappa, S. D. K., and Srikantaswamy, M. (2022). An efficient reconfigurable cryptographic model for dynamic and secure unstructured data sharing in multi-cloud storage server. *Journal of Intelligent Systems and Control*, 1(1), 68–78.

Muyanja-Ssenyonga, J. (2022) Digitalization, Emerging Technologies, and Financial Stability: Challenges and Opportunities for the Banking Industry. *Qeios ID: CSTTYQ. Preprint.* https://doi.org/10.32388/CSTTYQ.

Panetta, F. (2018). Fintech and banking: today and tomorrow. *Speech of the Deputy Governor of the Bank of Italy, Rome, 12th May.*

Index

academia 254–5

account closure processing 290–2

account payable (AP) 300–1

add-on-services 189

advanced economies (AEs) 46

advanced exhortation stages 143

AIML framework 117

Alexa 3, 162

Amazon 58

Amazon Cash programme 51

Amazon Echo 162

Amazon Web Services (AWS) 49

anomaly detection 215

anti-money laundering (AML) 130, 219, 284–5

Apple 58

application programming interfaces (APIs) 88, 162, 326

ARIMA integration 85

ARIMA model 82, 84

artificial intelligence (AI) 2, 49, 85, 115, 162, 298, 304, 317–18, 325

  economics 122–3

  other financial systems 122–3

  for simulation of markets 122–3

  system lifecycle 119

artificial neural networks (ANNs) 18, 85–7, 155

ASCII language 76

assets under management (AUM) 142

Association of International Certified Professional Accountants (AICPA) 82

attitude toward behavior 38

augmented reality (AR) 6, 300, 327–8

authentication 227–8

authorisation 228

automated feature extraction 18

automated report generation 290

automated telephone banking (ATB) 68

automated teller machine (ATM) 30, 33, 66

automation 305

autoregressive (AR) 82

autoregressive dependent framework 83

availability 214

Averaged One-Reliance Estimators (AODE) 155

Bachelier design 101–2

backpropagation algorithm 155

Banco Bilbao Vizcaya Argentaria (BBVA) 320–1

bandwidth 67

bank guarantee closures 285–6

bank reconciliation process 286–9

bank-centric P2P payment methods 72

banking chatbot business 73

banking sector 255

  ATMs 31–3

CPSIA information can be obtained
at www.ICGtesting.com
Printed in the USA
LVHW051510270623
750891LV00005B/187